COSMIC CONSCIOUSNESS

Cosmic Consciousness

A Study in the Evolution of the Human Mind

By

RICHARD MAURICE BUCKE, M.D.

FORMERLY MEDICAL SUPERINTENDENT OF THE ASYLUM
FOR THE INSANE, LONDON, CANADA

NEW INTRODUCTION BY
GEORGE MOREBY ACKLOM

VINCIT OMNIA VERITAS

NEW YORK
E. P. DUTTON AND COMPANY, INC.
PUBLISHERS

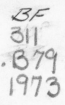
SBN–0–525–08656–0

PRINTED IN THE U.S.A.

MAURICE ANDREWS BUCKE

22 November, 1868 — 8 December, 1899

8 December, 1900

DEAR MAURICE:—

A year ago to-day, in the prime of youth, of health and of strength, in an instant, by a terrible and fatal accident, you were removed forever from this world in which your mother and I still live. Of all young men I have known you were the most pure, the most noble, the most honourable, the most tender-hearted. In the business of life you were industrious, honest, faithful, intelligent and entirely trustworthy. How at the time we felt your loss—how we still feel it—I would not set down even if I could. I desire to speak here of my confident hope, not of my pain. I will say that through the experiences which underlie this volume I have been taught, that in spite of death and the grave, although you are beyond the range of our sight and hearing, notwithstanding that the universe of sense testifies to your absence, you are not dead and not really absent, but alive and well and not far from me this moment. If I have been permitted—no, not to enter, but —through the narrow aperture of a scarcely opened door, to glance one instant into that other divine world, it was surely that I might thereby be enabled to live through the receipt of those lightning-flashed words from Montana which time burns only deeper and deeper into my brain.

Only a little while now and we shall be again together and with us those other noble and well-beloved souls gone before. I am sure I shall meet you and them; that you and I shall talk of a thousand things and of that unforgettable day and of all that followed it; and that we shall clearly see that all were parts of an infinite plan which was wholly wise and good. Do you see and approve as I write these words? It may well be. Do you read from within what I am now thinking and feeling? If you do you know how dear to me you were while you yet lived and what we call life here and how much more dear you have become to me since.

Because of the indissoluble links of birth and death wrought by nature and fate between us; because of my love and because of my grief; above all because of the infinite and inextinguishable confidence there is in my heart,

Dedication from the First Edition

I inscribe to you this book, which, full as it is of imperfections which render it unworthy of your acceptance, has nevertheless sprung from the divine assurance born of the deepest insight of the noblest members of your race. So long! dear boy.

YOUR FATHER

THE MAN AND THE BOOK

Sometimes it happens that out of the continually coming, continually going, tide of books, some single book fails to disappear along with its contemporaries, and because of something which it contains, or something which it is, lives on into another generation—or even further—answering in some way to some real human need.

Cosmic Consciousness is such a book, for it appeared, quietly and unheralded in 1901, the work of a Canadian doctor, of whom few people outside of the intimate circle of Walt Whitman's friends and of the limited world of the alienist had ever heard.

Even today, to the thousands who have read and who value the book, the writer is hardly more than a name—just Richard Maurice Bucke, author of *Cosmic Consciousness.*

Yet Bucke, who died less than a year after the publication of the book, was, during his lifetime, a very definite and very strong personality.

Descended of good sturdy English stock on both sides, his father was a graduate of Trinity College, Cambridge, and a clergyman. His mother, sister to an eminent Q.C., was a granddaughter of Sir Robert Walpole, the famous author and statesman. Bucke was their 7th child, born in 1837, the year before his parents emigrated to Canada and settled down on the remote "Creek Farm," in what is now a suburb of the city of London, Ontario. His father, though he thus became a farmer, was a fine scholar; he knew seven languages, and had brought with him to the farm a library of thousands of volumes.

Young Richard Maurice Bucke had practically no formal schooling. He was taught Latin by his father, and turned loose among the books to educate himself. For the rest, he was a regular farm-boy, knowing and doing all the heavy ceaseless round of hard work which farming called for before the days of the automobile and electricity.

When he was seven years old his mother died, and his father soon married again; but in his seventeenth year, the stepmother also died, and Richard Maurice Bucke decided the time had come for him to set out and see more of the world than he could observe from a farm in the backwoods. He went due south and across the border into the States. For three long years he made his way from place to place, doing odd jobs.

The Man and the Book

Among other things, he was a gardener in Columbus, Ohio, a railroad-hand in Cincinnati, and a deck-hand on a Mississippi steamboat, and he finally hired himself out as a driver in a wagon-train of 26 wagons which was to cross the Plains to the western edge of the Mormon Territory (now part of the State of Nevada).

This was a serious and dangerous undertaking, for at that time there were no permanent white settlements for the last 1200 miles of the journey, and the peacefulness of the Indians was definitely not to be depended on.

The journey to Salt Lake took five months, and there young Bucke drew his accumulated pay for the whole time and decided to go forward with a few others. The adventurers crossed the Rockies by the South Pass, and immediately found their journey a far more exciting and dangerous one, for the roving bands of Indians which they encountered resented the presence of the white men and attacked them on sight. The adventurers had to fight their way from camp to camp, finally being reduced to their very last cartridge. By this time not only their ammunition but their supplies had run out, and Bucke and a companion traveled the last 150 miles on nothing but flour stirred into hot water, until they staggered into a mountain trading-camp and collapsed.

After they had rested there a while, they started off again, crossed the Great American Desert to the Carson River, and finally reached Gold Canyon.

For a year Richard Maurice Bucke settled down as a gold miner in a community of about 100 white men scattered over some 1600 square miles of territory, without laws, without courts, without a church or a school. He met and became friends with the Grosh brothers and their partner Brown, who had discovered the vast deposits of silver known later as the Comstock Lode but were keeping their find dark while they prospected even further for more silver. Disaster overtook them—Brown and one of the Groshes died, and the other brother, Allan, with Bucke set out over the mountains, although it was winter, in an attempt to reach the Coast. It was a terrible experience—Allan Grosh died on the way, and Bucke with both feet frozen was rescued at the last minute by a mining party. The result was that Bucke had to have the whole of one foot and part of the other amputated, and that after a whole winter in bed, he returned to life a young man of 21 so badly maimed that for the 40 years remaining to him he was never free from pain for more than a few hours at a time.

Now of age, he inherited his late mother's small estate and used the

The Man and the Book

money to put himself through McGill Medical School. The five years of desperate adventure he had been through had not interfered with his power of assimilating knowledge, for he not only graduated high on the list, but took the prize for the best thesis. His postgraduate work was done in Europe. The years 1862–63 were spent in London, working with Sir Benjamin Ward Richardson, and visits to France and Germany followed; but in 1864 he returned to Canada and hung out his shingle in Sarnia, Ontario, marrying and settling down to raise a family like any ordinary young professional man.

However, Richard Maurice Bucke was anything but an ordinary professional man. He was a matter-of-fact scientist on one side of his brain, but on the other he was a man of highly developed imaginative faculty and endowed with an enormous memory, especially for poetry—of which he knew volumes by heart. His professional career was a distinguished one. In 1876 he was appointed Superintendent of the newly built Provincial Asylum for the Insane at Hamilton, Ontario, and in 1877 of the London (Ont.) Hospital. He became one of the foremost alienists on this Continent, introducing many reforms in procedure which, though considered dangerously radical at the time, are now a matter of everyday method. In 1882 he became Professor of Mental and Nervous Diseases at Western University (London, Ontario). In 1888 he was elected President of the Psychological Section of the British Medical Association, and in 1890 President of the American Medico-Psychological Association.

So much for the doctor!

But there was the other side of him, which has proved to be of more lasting importance to more people than the very fine and useful work he did in his profession. In 1867, a visitor to his house quoted some verses of Walt Whitman's to him. Their effect on him was extraordinary, instantaneous and permanent. They opened a new door in his mind, and from then to the end of his life he was under the spell of Whitman.

In the spring of 1872 came one of the great moments of his life. In that year Bucke, while on a visit to England, experienced Illumination. Here is the account of the experience, quoted from the *Proceedings and Transactions of the Royal Society of Canada:* *

"He and two friends had spent the evening reading Wordsworth, Shelley, Keats, Browning, and especially Whitman. They parted at midnight, and he

* Series II, Vol. 12, pp. 159-196.

The Man and the Book

had a long drive in a hansom. His mind, deeply under the influence of the ideas, images and emotions called up by the reading and talk of the evening, was calm and peaceful. He was in a state of quiet, almost passive, enjoyment.

"All at once, without warning of any kind, he found himself wrapped around, as it were, by a flame-colored cloud. For an instant he thought of fire—some sudden conflagration in the great city. The next (instant) he knew that the light was within himself.

"Directly after there came upon him a sense of exultation, of immense joyousness, accompanied or immediately followed by an intellectual illumination quite impossible to describe. Into his brain streamed one momentary lightning-flash of the Brahmic Splendor which ever since lightened his life. Upon his heart fell one drop of the Brahmic Bliss, leaving thenceforward for always an after-taste of Heaven."

It is not hard to imagine the effect of this shattering experience on a strong and vivid personality such as Bucke was at the age of 35. It gave him the knowledge and insight which is revealed in *Cosmic Consciousness*, in Part III (pages 61-82), where he describes the conditions which surround such an experience and its effect on the percipient.

With his mental energies extended and refined by this new consciousness he began to ponder more deeply the relation between man's mind and his moral nature, and in 1879 he produced his first book, *Man's Moral Nature* (G. P. Putnam & Sons, New York). This is an examination into the relationship between the great sympathetic nervous system of the body and the moral nature of man—a subject which he had already broached in a paper read by him in 1877 before a meeting of the Association of American Institutions for the Insane, and in another paper on the same subject read the following year before the same Association.

In 1877 Bucke met Walt Whitman for the first time—and this was another crucial experience for him. He has described it himself in the Introduction to his edition of Whitman's *Calamus* (Small Maynard, Boston, 1897) as "a sort of spiritual intoxication" and "the turning-point of my life." *Man's Moral Nature* is dedicated to Whitman.

Horace Traubel has given us an idea of what Whitman thought of Bucke, both as man and doctor (Bucke had treated Whitman professionally, and, as the poet believed, saved his life). "Someone was here the other day and complained that the Doctor was extreme. The sun's extreme, too; and as for me—ain't I extreme?" Again: "It's beautiful to watch him at his work—to see how he can handle difficult people with such an easy manner"; and: "Bucke is a man who enjoys being busy ... is swift of execution, lucid, sure, decisive." And, comparing Bucke with

The Man and the Book

Sir William Osler: "Osler, too, has his points, big points, but, after all, the real man is Doctor Bucke. He is top of the heap."

In 1894 the matter of Illumination and of the Cosmic Consciousness was increasingly in Bucke's mind. In May of that year he read a paper, entitled "Cosmic Consciousness" before the American Medico-Psychological Association at their annual meeting in Philadelphia, and in his presidential address to the British Medical Association in Montreal in August of that same year he developed the idea of this new Consciousness as a mental evolution of mankind, which as it became increasingly common, and eventually general, would lift the whole of human life to a higher plane.

Four years later the book itself, *Cosmic Consciousness,* was published by Messrs. Innes of Philadelphia in a limited edition of 500 copies. Though Bucke outlived his friend and idol Whitman, he did not live long enough to see the success of his own book; for on a night of the winter following—February 19, 1902, to be precise—after coming home with his wife from an evening spent at a friend's house, Bucke stepped out on the veranda before going to bed to have another look at the stars, which, as it happened, that night were exceptionally brilliant in the clear winter sky, slipped on a patch of ice, struck his head violently against a veranda-pillar, and dropped. He was taken up dead.

"The Doctor," as he was affectionately called by so many, was a figure that drew men's eyes as well as their hearts. Upstanding, broad-shouldered, with his long pioneer's beard spreading wide over his chest, he had the prominent nose and deep-set eyes of the man of action, while the eyes themselves sparkled with the light of a vivid and seeking intelligence.

During the formative years when most men are having their originality suppressed and their opinions standardized by school and college routine, Bucke had been at grips with real life; so he became, and remained, something of a heretic. The very last evening of his life he spent discussing the evidence for the Baconian authorship of the Shakespeare plays and poems, a question of which he firmly held to the unorthodox side. He was a brilliant debater when in the vein, his amazing memory enabling him to quote verbatim whole pages of authorities to support his views—it is even said that he could repeat from memory the entire volume of Walt Whitman's *Leaves of Grass*—no mean feat.

Physically and mentally he gave an impression of force and adequateness which made people trust him as well as like him. English by de-

The Man and the Book

scent and birth, Canadian in his upbringing and in his professional life, but knowing from the hard experiences of his wander-years more of the United States than most Americans, he might be said to focus in his own person what is essentially sane and vigorous in the three branches of white civilization which are now being brought so closely together by the current of world events.

Cosmic Consciousness is a book very difficult to classify. It does not fall definitely into any of the regular categories. This is due to the fact that Illumination or Ecstasy, of which it treats, is generally thought to belong to the realm of Religion or of Mysticism, or of Magic and the Occult—or even, by some ultra-materialists, to the domain of insanity. In Christian Mysticism, Illumination is the acknowledged third stage of the mystic's progress, coming after the two preliminary stages of Awakening and Purification.* In both Brahmanism and Buddhism it is the reward of long and rigid self-discipline and effort.

But to Bucke it had nothing whatever to do with mysticism or formal religion, or with conscious preparation and intention. He was a student of the human mind, a psychologist, and he treated Illumination from the standpoint of psychology, as a very rare but definite and recognizable mental condition, of which many well-authenticated instances are on record and available for examination.

He considered, on the evidence, that there have been, in the last three thousand years of human history, at least fourteen undeniable cases of complete and permanent Illumination, and that in addition to these there have been many other instances of partial, temporary or doubtful Illumination, several of which have occurred within the past century.

Noting the increasing frequency of the experience, he deduced that very gradually—and, as it were, sporadically—the human race is in the process of developing a new kind of consciousness, far in advance of the ordinary human self-consciousness, which will eventually lift the race above and beyond all the fears and ignorances, the brutalities and bestialities which beset it today.

Admittedly his argument is based largely on analogy. First he deals with the three distinct stages of consciousness observable in living creatures: the perceptual mind of the lower animals, open only to sense-impressions; the receptual mind of the higher animals, producing simple consciousness; and the conceptual mind of human beings, accompanied

*See *Mysticism*, by Evelyn Underhill, E. P. Dutton & Co., New York, 1912.

by self-consciousness. He shows that the human race has, even in the last few thousand years, added to the original equipment several new kinds of consciousness—the color-sense for instance. The ancient Greeks, Aristotle and Xenophanes, knew only three colors, and there is no word for any color at all in the primitive Indo-European speech. The blazing blue of the oriental sky is not mentioned in Homer or in the Bible, nor in the Rig Veda or the Zend Avesta. But in this present century we know not only the seven primitive colors, but literally thousands of different shades and gradations of them. The sense of fragrance and the musical sense are two other senses which the race in like manner has only recently acquired.

Bucke argued that these new senses must have begun as sporadic, isolated instances of new awareness in a few individuals, and that they spread gradually with the passing of the generations until nearly all civilized races now possess them, though by no means with the same completeness or to the same degree. Even today the Bushmen of Africa and the Aborigines of Australia are entirely without them.

The new, fourth stage of consciousness, which enables man to realize the oneness of the Universe, to sense the presence in it and throughout it of the Creator, to be free of all fears of evil, of disaster or death, to comprehend that Love is the rule and basis of the Cosmos—this is Cosmic Consciousness, which, Bucke prophesied will appear more and more often until it becomes a regular attribute of adult humanity.

Bucke knew very definitely what he was talking about when he described the experience of Illumination, and the temporary entry of the percipient into the Cosmic Consciousness. As already noted, he himself had received at least a temporary Illumination, and it had enriched and enlarged his whole life thereafter in all its aspects. So his descriptions of the conditions of mind which prepare for Illumination, and of its effects on the senses and person of the individual are no mere dry, objective, scientific descriptions. They are glowing with the light of personal experience and warm with the emotion of personal feeling. Throughout the fifty instances of Illumination which he lists and describes, this personal knowledge of the phenomenon and of its effects on the percipient lifts what would have been merely interesting psychological detail into the realm of inspired and inspiring exposition.

Probably no one who reads *Cosmic Consciousness* will agree with its author on all points, for his enthusiasm and his mental energy were such that even in his heresies he was heretical. Yet Ouspensky, the celebrated

The Man and the Book

Russian mathematician and philosopher, who disagreed completely with Bucke on at least one important detail of his belief, valued the book sufficiently to devote nearly a whole chapter of his great work *Tertium Organum* to *Cosmic Consciousness,* quoting whole pages of it in his text.

Professor William James read *Cosmic Consciousness* soon after it first appeared, and wrote to the author:

"I believe that you have brought this kind of consciousness 'home' to the attention of students of human nature in a way so definite and unescapable that it will be impossible henceforward to overlook it or ignore it . . . But my total reaction on your book, my dear Sir, is that it is an addition to psychology of first rate importance, and that you are a benefactor of us all."

This last half-sentence seems to me even more important than Professor James' verdict as a philosopher and psychologist. It explains the continuing life and usefulness of *Cosmic Consciousness,* for I firmly believe that no understanding mind can form a real acquaintance with this book without experiencing a tremendous uplift and stimulation. It is a book of encouragement and promise; it opens a new door in the dark walls of materialism by which we are surrounded to give us a vista of strange and wonderful possibilities, and to admit the sound of lovely harmonies—not far away and elusive, but implicit in ourselves and our race—and to give us back the hope and the wonder which most of us have laid aside, but which we need so desperately for the doubtful days which lie ahead.

GEORGE MOREBY ACKLOM.

New York City
February 25th, 1946.

NOTICE

———

It will be observed that this volume is printed in three types: in the largest is set up that portion of it which was written by the editor, together with certain shorter quotations which will be indicated by inverted commas in the usual manner; extracts from writers having Cosmic Consciousness and from other writers about them will be printed in medium sized type, and it will not be considered necessary to use quotation marks with it, since all matter in this type will be quoted and the writers of it will necessarily be credited each with his own part; the small type will be used for parallel passages and for comment, and with this inverted commas will be used in the ordinary manner.

A LIST OF SOME OF THE WORKS QUOTED AND REFERRED TO IN THIS VOLUME

Reference numbers in brackets in the text point to book in this list and page, except in the cases of the Bible, where they indicate book, chapter and verse, and "Shakespeare's" Sonnets, when they indicate book and sonnet.

1. Anderson, A. A. Twenty-five Years in a Wagon. Chapman & Hall, London, 1888.
2. Arena, The. Boston, Mass., February, 1893.
3. Atlantic Monthly, October, 1896.
4. Balzac, Honoré de. A Memoir of, by K. P. Wormley. Roberts Bros., Boston, 1892.
5. Balzac, Honoré de. Louis Lambert. Roberts Bros., Boston, 1889.
6. Introduction to 5. Same volume but separate pagination. By George Fred. Parsons.
7. Balzac, Honoré de. Seraphita. Roberts Bros., Boston, 1889.
8. Introduction to 7. Same volume but separate pagination. By George Fred. Parsons.
9. Balzac, Honoré de. The Exiles. In same volume with 7.
10. Bible. Compared with the most ancient authorities and revised. University Press, Oxford, 1887.
11. Exodus, in 10.
12. Judges, in 10.
14. Matthew, in 10.
15. Mark, in 10.
16. Luke, in 10.
17. John, in 10.
18. Acts, in 10.
19. Romans, in 10.
20. I Corinthians, in 10.
21. II Corinthians, in 10.
22. Galatians, in 10.
23. Ephesians, in 10.
24. Philippians, in 10.

25. Colossians, in 10.

26. I Thessalonians, in 10.

27. Revelations, in 10.

28. Bormann, Edwin. The Shakespeare Secret. From the German. By H. Brett Wohlleben, London, 1895.

28a. Bucke, Richard Maurice. Man's Moral Nature. G. P. Putnam's Sons, New York, 1879.

29. Burnouf, E. Introduction a l'Histoire du Buddhisme, Indien. Deuzième Edition. Maisonneuve et Cie, Paris, 1852.

30. Burnouf, E. Le Lotus de La Bonne Loi. L'Imprimerie Nationale, Paris, 1852.

30a. Bacon, Roger E. Sa vie ses ouvrages, ses doctrines. Par Emile Charles Hachette, Paris, 1861.

31. Butler, Alban. The Lives of Fathers, Martyrs and Other Principal Saints. D. & J. Sadler, New York, undated, Volume XI.

32. Bacon, Francis, The Works of. Popular Edition by Spedding, Ellis and Heath, in two volumes. Hurd & Houghton, New York, 1878, Part I of Vol. II.

33. Part I of Vol. I of 32.

34. Part II (second pagination) of Vol. I of 32.

35. Part II of Vol. II of 32.

36. Baconiana (American), May, 1892.

37. Baconiana (English), November, 1893.

38. Bucke, Richard Maurice. Walt Whitman. David McKay, Philadelphia, 1883.

39. Behmen, Jacob, Works of, in four volumes. To which is prefixed the life of the author, with figures illustrating his principles, left by Rev. William Law. Printed for M. Richardson, London, 1764-1781.

40. The Life of Jacob Behmen, separate pagination, in Vol. I of 39.

41. Aurora, The Dayspring or Dawning of the Day in the East, separate pagination, in Vol. I of 39.

42. The Three Principles of the Divine Essence, separate pagination, in Vol. I of 39.

43. The Threefold Life of Man, separate pagination, in Vol. II of 39.

44. Forty Questions Concerning the Soul, separate pagination, in Vol. II of 39.

45. The Treatise of the Incarnation, separate pagination, in Vol. II of 39.

46. The Clavis, separate pagination, in Vol. II of 39.

47. Mysterium Magnum, separate pagination, in Vol. III of 39.

48. The Four Tables, separate pagination, in Vol. III of 39.

49. Signatura Rerum, separate pagination, in Vol. IV of 39.

50. The Way to Christ, separate pagination, in Vol. IV of 39.

51. Bucke, R. M. Shakespeare or Bacon? Canadian Magazine, September, 1897. Ontario Publishing Co., Toronto, Ont.

52. Blake, William. Poetical Works. Edited by William Rossetti. George Bell & Sons, London, 1891.

53. Burroughs, John. Notes on Walt Whitman as Poet and Person, second edition. J. S. Redfield, New York, 1871.

54. Browning, Robert, The Poetical Works of, in seventeen volumes. Smith, Elder & Co., London, 1889-1894, Vol. VI.

55. Cyclopedia of Biography. Edited by F. L. Hawks. D. Appleton & Co., New York, 1856.

56. Carpenter, Edward. From Adam's Peak to Elephanta. Swan Sonnenschein & Co., London, 1892.

57. Carpenter, Edward. Civilization: Its Cause and Cure. Swan Sonnenschein & Co., London, 1889.

58. Charles, Emile. Roger Bacon. Sa vie ses ouvrages ses doctrines. Hachette, Paris, 1861.

59. Carlyle, Thomas. Heroes, &c. In Complete Works, in twenty volumes. Estes & Lauriat, Boston, 1885, Vol. I.

60. Century Cyclopedia of Names. Edited by Ben. E. Smith. The Century Co., New York, 1894.

60a. Conservator, May, 1894.

61. Carpenter, Edward. Towards Democracy, third edition. T. Fisher Unwin, London, 1892.

62. Carpenter, Edward. In the Labor Prophet, May, 1894.

63. Carpenter, Edward. Private Letter.

64. Carlyle's Cromwell. Vol. XVII of 59.

65. Comte, Auguste. Catechisme Positiviste. Paris, 1852.

66. Despine, Prosper. Psychologie Naturelle. F. Savy, Paris, 1868.

67. Darwin, Charles. Animals and Plants under Domestication. Orange Judd & Co., New York, 1868, in two volumes, Vol. II.

68. Dante. The New Life. Translated by Charles Eliot Norton. Houghton, Mifflin & Co., Boston and New York, 1892.

69. Dante. Hell. Same translator, publisher and date.

70. Introduction to 69.

71. Dante. Purgatory. Same translator, publisher and date.

72. Dante. Paradise. Same translator, publisher and date.

73. Davis, T. W. Rhys. Buddhism. Society for Promoting Christian Knowledge, London, not dated.

74. Donnelly, Ignatius. The Great Cryptogram. R. S. Peale & Co., Chicago and New York.

75. Dixon, William Hepworth. Personal History of Lord Bacon. John Murray, London, 1861.

76. Ellis, Havelock. The Criminal. Walter Scott, London, 1890.

77. Encyclopedia Britannica, ninth edition. Adam and Charles Black, Edinburgh, 1875-1889.

78. Balzac, in Vol. III of 77.

79. Boehme, in Vol. III of 77.

80. Chronology, in Vol. V of 77.

81. Dante, in Vol. VI of 77.

82. London, in Vol. XIV of 77.

82a. Mohammedanism, in Vol. XVI of 77.

83. Neoplatonism, in Vol. XVII of 77.

84. Paul, in Vol. XVIII of 77.

85. Plotinus, in Vol. XIX of 77.

86. Shakespeare, in Vol. XXI of 77.

87. Schopenhauer, in Vol. XXI of 77.

87a. Swedenborg, in Vol. XXII of 77.

87b. Spinoza, in Vol. XXII of 77.

88. Elam, Charles. A Physician's Problems. Field, Osgood & Co., Boston, 1869.

89. Fiske, John. The Discovery of America, in two volumes. Houghton, Mifflin & Co., Boston, 1892, Vol. II.

90. Fortnightly Review. Leonard Scott Publishing Co., New York, July, 1896.

91. Geiger, Lazarus. Contributions to the History of the Development of the Human Race. Translated by David Asher. Trübner & Co., London, 1880.

92. Galton, Francis. Hereditary Genius. D. Appleton & Co., New York, 1879.

93. Gibbon, Edward. Decline and Fall of the Roman Empire, in six volumes. Crosby, Nichols, Lee & Co., 1860, Vol. VI.

94. Gilchrist, Alexander. Life of William Blake. Macmillan & Co., London and Cambridge, 1863, in two volumes, Vol. I.

95. Vol. II of 94.

96. Hugo, Victor. William Shakespeare. Hachette et Cie, Paris, 1880.

97. Hartman, Franz. The Life and Doctrines of Jacob Boehme. Kegan Paul, Trench, Trübner & Co., London, 1891.

98. Helps, Arthur. Life of Las Casas.

99. Holmes, Nathaniel. The Authorship of Shakespeare. Hurd & Houghton, New York, 1866.

100. Preface to 97, separate pagination.

101. Ireland, W. W. Idiocy and Imbecility.

102. Irving, Washington. Life of Mohammed. Bell & Daldy, London, 1869.

103. In Re Walt Whitman. Edited by his Literary Executors—H. L. Traubel, R. M. Bucke and T. B. Harned. David McKay, Philadelphia, 1893.

104. Finney, Charles G. An Autobiography. Hodder & Stoughton, London, 1892.

105. Jefferies, Richard. The Story of My Heart. Longmans, Green & Co., London, 1883.

106. James, Henry, Jr. French Poets and Novelists. Macmillan & Co., London, 1878.

107. Kennedy, John. Facts and Histories Illustrating the Divine Life. The Religious Tract Society, London, undated.

108. Kidd, Benjamin. Social Evolution. Macmillan & Co., London, 1894.

109. Lillie, Arthur. The Influence of Buddhism on Primitive Christianity. Swan Sonnenschien & Co., London, 1893.

110. Preface to 109, separate pagination.

110a. Lloyd, J. William. Dawn Thought. Mangus Press, Wellesley Hills, Mass., 1900.

111. Longfellow, H. W. Translation of Divine Comedy by Dante Alighieri. George Rutledge & Sons, London, 1867.—The Inferno.

112. Lewis, David. Life of St. John of the Cross, prefixed to 202 infra.

112a. Lelut, F. L'Amulette de Pascal. Bailliere, Paris, 1846.

113. Lyell, Sir Charles. The Geological Evidences of the Antiquity of Man. John Murray, London, 1863.

114. Lecky, W. E. H. History of European Morals. Longmans, Green & Co., London, 1869, Vol. II.

115. Mueller, F. Max. Lectures on the Science of Language, eighth edition, in two volumes. Longmans, Green & Co., London, 1875, Vol. I.

116. Mueller, F. Max. The Science of Thought. Charles Scribner's Sons, New York, 1887, in two volumes, Vol. II.

117. Vol. I of 116.

119. Magee, Thomas. In California, May, 1893.

120. Macaulay, T. B. Critical Historical and Literary Essays, in six volumes. Hurd & Houghton, New York, 1875, Vol. III.

121. Medical Record, New York, May 11, 1895.

122. Medical Record, New York, June 8, 1895.

123. Martensen, Hans Lassen. Jacob Behmen: His Life and Teaching; or, Studies in Theosophy. Translated from the Danish by T. Rhys Evans. Hodder & Stoughton, London, 1885.

124. Morgan, Lewis H. Ancient Society; or, Researches in the Lines of Human Progress from Savagery through Barbarism to Civilization. Henry Holt & Co., New York, 1877.

124a. Notes and fragments. Edited by Dr. R. M. Bucke, 1899.

125. Nineteenth Century, The. New York, August, 1896.

126. Pictet, Adolphe. Les Origines Indo-Européennes. Sandoy et Fritchbacher, Paris, 1877, in three volumes, Vol. II.

127. Plato. Jowett's Translation. Clarendon Press. Oxford, 1875, five volumes, Vol. II.

128. Prescott, William Hickling. Conquest of Mexico. Routledge, Warne & Routledge, 1863, in two volumes, Vol. I.

128a. Peck, Harry Thurston. The Cosmopolitan, July, 1899.

129. Pott, Mrs. Henry. The Promus. By Francis Bacon. Longmans, Green & Co., London, 1883.

130. Pott, Mrs. Henry. Did Francis Bacon Write "Shakespeare?" Robert Banks & Son, London, 1893.

131. Proceedings of the Society for Psychical Research, January, 1894. Kegan Paul, Trench, Trübner & Co., London.

132. Pink, Caleb. The Angel of the Mental Orient. William Reeves, London, 1895.

133. Pollock, Sir Frederick. Spinoza's Life and Philosophy. Duckworth & Co., London, 1899.

133a. Phelps, Elizabeth Stuart. The Story of Jesus Christ. Houghton, Mifflin & Co., Boston, 1897.

134. Romanes, George John. Mental Evolution in Man, Origin of Human Faculty. D. Appleton & Co., New York, 1889.

135. Reference Hand Book of the Medical Sciences. Edited by Albert H. Buck in eight volumes. William Wood & Co., New York, 1885-1889, Vol. II.

136. Renan, Ernest. Etudes d'Histoire Religieuse. Calmann Levy, Paris, 1880.

137. Renan, Ernest. Histoire du Peuple d'Israel, in five volumes. Calmann Levy, Paris, 1889-1894, Vol. I.

138. Vol. II of 137.

139. Rossetti, W. M. Prefatory Memoir of William Blake, in 46 supra.

140. R. P. S. Walk in the Light.

141. Rawley, William D. D. Life of Bacon, in 29.

142. Renan, Ernest. Les Apotres. Michel, Levy Freres, Paris, 1866.

143. Renan, Ernest. Saint Paul. Michel, Levy Freres, Paris, 1869.

144. Ramsay, W. M. St. Paul the Traveler and the Roman Citizen. G. P. Putnam's Sons, New York, 1896.

145. Ruggles, H. J. The Plays of Shakespeare Founded on Literary Form. Houghton, Mifflin & Co., Boston, 1895.

146. Sacred Books of the East. Edited by F. Max Mueller. The Clarendon Press, Oxford, in forty-eight volumes, 1879-1885.

147. Introduction to Vol. I of 146, separate pagination.

148. Khandogya, Upanishad. Translated by F. Max Mueller, in Vol. I of 146.

149. Talavakara, Upanishad. Translated by F. Max Mueller, in Vol. I of 146.

150. Vagasaneyi, Samhita Upanishad. Translated by F. Max Mueller, in Vol. I of 146.

151. Part I of Qur'an. Translated from the Arabic by E. H. Palmer, being Vol. VI of 146.

152. Introduction to Qur'an. By E. H. Palmer, separate pagination, in Vol. VI of 146.

153. Part II of Qur'an. Translated from the Arabic by E. H. Palmer, being Vol. IX of 146.

154. Bhagavadgita. Translated by K. T. Telang, in Vol. VIII of 146.

155. Anugita. Translated by K. T. Telang, in Vol. VIII of 146.

156. Dhammapada. Translated by F. Max Mueller, in Vol. X of 146.

157. Sutta-Nipata. Translated from Pâli by V. Fausboll, in Vol. X of 146.

158. Introduction to 157. By V. Fausboll, in Vol. X of 146, separate pagination.

159. Dhamma-kakka-Ppavattana-Sutta. Translated from Pâli by T. W. Rhys Davids, in Vol. XI of 146.

160. Introduction to 159. By T. W. Rhys Davids, in Vol. XI of 146.

161. Akankheyya-Sutta. Translated from Pâli by T. W. Rhys Davids, in Vol. XI of 146.

162. Introduction to 161. By T. W. Rhys Davids, in Vol. XI of 146.

163. Maha Parinibbana-Sutta. Translated from Pâli by T. Rhys Davids, in Vol. XI of 146.

164. Saddaharina-Pundarika; or, the Lotus of the True Law. Translated by H. Kern, in Vol. XXI of 146.

165. Introduction to 164. By H. Kern, in Vol. XXI of 146.

166. The Texts of Taoism. Translated by James Legge. Vol. XXXIX of 146.

167. Sharpe, William. Introduction to the Songs, Poems and Sonnets of William Shakespeare. Walter Scott, London, 1885.

168. Scott, Walter. Edited by Andrew Lang, in forty-eight volumes. Estes & Lauriat, Boston, 1894. Vol. II of Waverley.

169. Introduction to Vol. XXXVIII of 168.

170. Stead, William Thomas. In Review of Reviews, number not noted, but immediately after Tennyson's death, which took place October 6, 1892.

170a. Spinoza. Ethic. Translated from the Latin by A. H. Stirling, second edition. Macmillan & Co., New York, 1894.

171. Sutherland, Jabez Thomas. The Bible: Its Origin, Growth and Character. G. P. Putnam's Sons, New York, 1893.

172. Salt, H. S. Richard Jefferies: A Study. Swan Sonnenschein & Co., London, 1894.

173. Sharpe, William. The Dual Image. H. A. Copley, London, 1896.

174. Spedding, James. Life and Times of Francis Bacon, in two volumes. Houghton, Osgood & Co., Boston, 1878, Vol. I.

175. Vol. II of 174.

176. Shakespeare's Sonnets and a Lover's Complaint. Reprinted in the Orthography and Punctuation of the original edition of 1609. John Russell Smith, London, 1870.

177. Spedding, James. Evenings with a Reviewer, in two volumes. Houghton, Mifflin & Co., 1882, Vol. I.

178. Vol. II of 177.

179. Symonds, J. A. The Study of Dante. Adam & Charles Black, Edinburgh, 1890.

180. Tyndall, John. Heat Considered as a Mode of Motion. D. Appleton & Co., New York, 1863.

181. Tyndall, John. Fragments of Science. D. Appleton & Co., New York, 1871.

182. Tennyson, Lord Alfred. A Memoir by His Son, in two volumes. Macmillan & Co., London, 1897, Vol. I.

182a. Vol. II of 182.

183. Tennyson, Lord Alfred. Works in ten volumes. Henry T. Thomas, New York, 1893.

184. Vol. III of 183.

185. Vol. IV of 183.

186. Vol. VIII of 183.

187. Tyner, Paul. The Living Christ. Temple Publishing Co., Denver, Col., 1897.

188. Vaughan, Robert Alfred. Hours with the Mystics, sixth edition, in two volumes. Charles Scribner's Sons, New York, 1893, Vol. I.

189. Vol. II of 188.

190. Ward, Lester F. Dynamic Sociology; or, Applied Social Science, in two volumes. D. Appleton & Co., New York, 1883, Vol. I.

191. Whitman, Walt. Leaves of Grass. Brooklyn, N. Y., 1855.

192. Whitman, Walt. Leaves of Grass, author's edition. Camden, N. J., 1876.

193. Whitman, Walt. Leaves of Grass. David McKay, Philadelphia, 1891-1892.

194. Whitman, Walt. Complete Prose Works. David McKay, Philadelphia, 1892.

195. Democratic Vistas, in 194.

196. Pieces in Early Youth, in 194.

197. Wigston, W. F. C. Francis Bacon, Poet, Prophet and Philosopher versus Phantom Captain Shakespeare. Kegan Paul, Trench, Trübner & Co., London, 1891.

198. Wordsworth, William. Poetical Works, seven volumes in three. Hurd & Houghton, Boston, 1877, Vol. II.

199. White, Alexander. Jacob Behmen: An Appreciation. Oliphant, Anderson & Ferrier, Edinburgh and London, 1894.

199a. Walden. By Henry D. Thoreau. Houghton, Osgood & Co., Boston, 1880.

200. Ward, Lester F. Relation of Sociology to Anthropology. The American Anthropologist, July, 1895.

201. Xenophon. The Anabasis and Memorabilia of Socrates. Translated from the Greek by J. S. Watson. Harper & Bros., New York, 1864.

202. Yepes, John, called St. John of the Cross. Life and Works, in two volumes, the former by, and the latter translated from the Spanish by, David Lewis (112 supra). Thomas Baker, London, 1889-1891.

203. Ascent of Mount Carmel, in Vol. I of 202.

204. The Dark Night of the Soul, in Vol. II of 202.

205. A Spiritual Canticle of the Soul and the Bridegroom Christ, in Vol. II of 202.

206. The Living Flame of Love, in Vol. II of 202.

207. Spiritual Maxims, in Vol. II of 202.

208. Poems, in Vol. II of 202.

TABLE OF CONTENTS

Table of Contents

PART V.

Additional—Some of Them Lesser, Imperfect, and Doubtful Instances.

COSMIC CONSCIOUSNESS

COSMIC CONSCIOUSNESS

PART I.

FIRST WORDS.

I.

WHAT is Cosmic Consciousness? The present volume is an attempt to answer this question; but notwithstanding it seems well to make a short prefatory statement in as plain language as possible so as to open the door, as it were, for the more elaborate exposition to be attempted in the body of the work. Cosmic Consciousness, then, is a higher form of consciousness than that possessed by the ordinary man. This last is called Self Consciousness and is that faculty upon which rests all of our life (both subjective and objective) which is not common to us and the higher animals, except that small part of it which is derived from the few individuals who have had the higher consciousness above named. To make the matter clear it must be understood that there are three forms or grades of consciousness. (1) Simple Consciousness, which is possessed by say the upper half of the animal kingdom. By means of this faculty a dog or a horse is just as conscious of the things about him as a man is; he is also conscious of his own limbs and body and he knows that these are a part of himself. (2) Over and above this Simple Consciousness, which is possessed by man as by animals, man has another which is called Self Consciousness. By virtue of this faculty man is not only conscious of trees, rocks, waters, his own limbs and body, but he becomes conscious of himself as a distinct entity apart from all the rest of the universe. It is as good as certain that no animal can realize himself in that way. Further, by means of self consciousness, man (who knows as the animal knows) becomes capable of treating his own mental states as objects of consciousness. The animal is, as it were, immersed in his consciousness as a fish in the sea; he cannot, even in imagination, get outside of it for one moment so as to realize it. But man by virtue of self consciousness can step aside, as it were, from himself and think: "Yes, that thought that I had about that matter is true; I know it is true and I know that I know it is true." The writer has been asked: "How do you know that animals cannot think in the same manner?" The answer is simple and conclusive—it is: There is no evidence that any animal can so think, but if they could we should soon know it. Between two creatures living together, as dogs or horses and men, and each self conscious, it would be the simplest matter in the world to open up communication. Even as it is, diverse as is our psychology, we do, by watching his acts, enter into the dog's mind pretty freely—we see what is going on there—we know that the dog sees and hears, smells and tastes—we know that he has intelligence—adapts means to ends—that he reasons. If he was self conscious we must have learned it long ago. We have not learned it and it is as good as certain that no dog, horse, elephant or ape ever was self conscious. Another thing: on man's self consciousness is built everything in and about us distinctively human. Language is the objective of which self consciousness is the subjective. Self consciousness and language (two in one, for they are two halves of the same thing) are the sine qua non of human social life, of manners, of institutions, of industries of all kinds, of all arts useful and fine. If any animal possessed self consciousness it seems certain that it would upon that master faculty build (as man has done) a superstructure of language; of reasoned out customs, industries, art. But no animal has done this, therefore we infer that no animal has self consciousness.

The possession of self consciousness and language (its other self) by man creates an enormous gap between him and the highest creature possessing simple consciousness merely.

Cosmic Consciousness is a third form which is as far above Self Consciousness as is that above Simple Consciousness. With this form, of course, both simple and self consciousness persist (as simple consciousness persists when self consciousness is acquired), but added to them is the new faculty so often named and to be named in this volume. The prime characteristic of cosmic consciousness is, as its name implies, a consciousness of the cosmos, that is, of the life and order of the universe. What these words mean cannot be touched upon here; it is the business of this volume to throw some light upon them. There are many elements belonging to the cosmic sense besides the central fact just alluded to. Of these a few may be mentioned. Along with the consciousness of the cosmos there occurs an intellectual enlightenment or illumination which alone would place the individual on a new plane of existence—would make him almost a member of a new species. To this is added a state of moral exaltation, an indescribable feeling of elevation, elation, and joyousness, and a quickening of the moral sense, which is fully as striking and more important both to the individual and to the race than is the enhanced intellectual power. With these come, what may be called a sense of immortality, a consciousness of eternal life, not a conviction that he shall have this, but the consciousness that he has it already.

Only a personal experience of it, or a prolonged study of men who have passed into the new life, will enable us to realize what this actually is; but it has seemed to the present writer that to pass in review, even briefly and imperfectly, instances in which the condition in question has existed would be worth while. He expects his work to be useful in two ways: First, in broadening the general view of human life by comprehending in our mental vision this important phase of it, and by enabling us to realize, in some measure, the true status of certain men who, down to the present, are either exalted, by the average self conscious individual, to the rank of gods, or, adopting the other extreme, are adjudged insane. And in the second place he hopes to furnish aid to his fellow men in a far more practical and important sense. The view he takes is that our descendants will sooner or later reach, as a race, the condition of cosmic consciousness, just as, long ago, our ancestors passed from simple to self consciousness. He believes that this step in evolution is even now being made, since it is clear to him both that men with the faculty in question are becoming more and more common and also that as a race we are approaching nearer and nearer to that stage of the self conscious mind from which the transition to the cosmic conscious is effected. He realizes that, granted the necessary heredity, any individual not already beyond the age may enter cosmic consciousness. He knows that intelligent contact with cosmic conscious minds assists self conscious individuals in the ascent to the higher plane. He therefore hopes, by bringing about, or at least facilitating this contact, to aid men and women in making the almost infinitely important step in question.

II.

The immediate future of our race, the writer thinks, is indescribably hopeful. There are at the present moment impending over us three revolutions, the least of which would dwarf the ordinary historic upheaval called by that name into absolute insignificance. They are: (1) The material, economic and social revolution which will depend upon and result from the establishment of aerial navigation. (2) The economic and social revolution which will abolish individual ownership and rid the earth at once of two immense evils—riches and poverty. And (3) The psychical revolution of which there is here question.

Either of the first two would (and will) radically change the conditions of, and greatly uplift, human life; but the third will do more for humanity than both of the former, were their importance multiplied by hundreds or even thousands.

The three operating (as they will) together will literally create a new heaven and a new earth. Old things will be done away and all will become new.

Before aerial navigation national boundaries, tariffs, and perhaps distinctions of language will fade out. Great cities will no longer have reason for being and will melt away. The men who now dwell in cities will inhabit in summer the mountains and the sea shores; building often in airy and beautiful spots, now almost or quite inaccessible, commanding the most extensive and magnificent views. In the winter they will probably dwell in communities of moderate size. As the herding together, as now, in great cities, so the isolation of the worker of the soil will become a thing of the past. Space will be practically annihilated, there will be no crowding together and no enforced solitude.

Before Socialism crushing toil, cruel anxiety, insulting and demoralizing riches, poverty and its ills will become subjects for historical novels.

In contact with the flux of cosmic consciousness all religions known and named to-day will be melted down. The human soul will be revolutionized. Religion will absolutely dominate the race. It will not depend on tradition. It will not be believed and disbelieved. It will not be a part of life, belonging to certain hours, times, occasions. It will not be in sacred books nor in the mouths of priests. It will not dwell in churches and meetings and forms and days. Its life will not be in prayers, hymns nor discourses. It will not depend on special revelations, on the words of gods who came down to teach, nor on any bible or bibles. It will have no mission to save men from their sins or to secure them entrance to heaven. It will not teach a future immortality nor future glories, for immortality and all glory will exist in the here and now. The evidence of immortality will live in every heart as sight in every eye. Doubt of God and of eternal life will be as impossible as is now doubt of existence; the evidence of each will be the same. Religion will govern every minute of every day of all life. Churches, priests, forms, creeds, prayers, all agents, all intermediaries between the individual man and God will be permanently replaced by direct unmistakable intercourse. Sin will no longer exist nor will salvation be desired. Men will not worry about death or a future, about the kingdom of heaven, about what may come with and after the cessation of the life of the present body. Each soul will feel and know itself to be immortal, will feel and know that the entire universe with all its good and with all its beauty is for it and belongs to it forever. The world peopled by men possessing cosmic consciousness will be as far removed from the world of to-day as this is from the world as it was before the advent of self consciousness.

III.

There is a tradition, probably very old, to the effect that the first man was innocent and happy until he ate of the fruit of the tree of the knowledge of good and evil. That having eaten thereof he became aware that he was naked and was ashamed. Further, that then sin was born into the world, the miserable sense whereof replaced man's former feeling of innocency. That then and not till then man began to labor and to cover his body. Stranger than all (so it seems to us), the story runs, that along with this change or immediately following upon it there came into man's mind the remarkable conviction which has never since left it but which has been kept alive by its own inherent vitality and by the teaching of all true seers, prophets and poets that this accursed thing which has bitten man's heel (laming him, hindering his progress and especially making this halting and painful) should eventually be crushed and subjugated by man himself—by the rising up within him of a Saviour—the Christ.

Man's progenitor was a creature (an animal) walking erect but with simple consciousness merely. He was (as are to-day the animals) incapable of sin or of the feeling of sin and equally incapable of shame (at least in the human sense). He had no feeling or knowledge of good and evil. He as yet knew nothing of what we call work and had never labored. From this state he fell (or rose) into self consciousness, his eyes were opened, he knew that he was naked, he felt shame, acquired the sense of sin (became in fact what is called a sinner), and learned to do certain things in order to encompass certain ends—that is, he learned to labor.

For weary eons this condition has lasted—the sense of sin still haunts his pathway—by the sweat of his brow he still eats bread—he is still ashamed. Where is the deliverer, the Saviour? Who or what?

The Saviour of man is Cosmic Consciousness—in Paul's language—the Christ. The cosmic sense (in whatever mind it appears) crushes the serpent's head—destroys sin, shame, the sense

of good and evil as contrasted one with the other, and will annihi-
late labor, though not human activity.

The fact that there came to man along with or immediately
after his acquisition of self consciousness the inchoate premonition of another and higher consciousness which was yet, at that
time, many millenniums in the future is surely most noteworthy
though not necessarily surprising. We have in biology many
analogous facts such as premonition of, and preparation for, by
the individual of states and circumstances of which he has had no
experience and we see the same thing in the maternal instinct in
the very young girl.

The universal scheme is woven in one piece and is permeable
to consciousness or (and especially) to sub-consciousness
throughout and in every direction. The universe is a vast,
grandiose, terrible, multiform yet uniform evolution. The section which especially concerns us is that which extends from
brute to man, from man to demigod, and constitutes the imposing
drama of humanity—its scene the surface of the planet—its time
a million years.

IV.

The purpose of these preliminary remarks is to throw as much
light as possible on the subject of this volume, so as to increase the
pleasure and profit of its perusal. A personal exposition of the
writer's own introduction to the main fact treated of will perhaps
do as much as anything else could to further this end. He will
therefore frankly set down here a very brief outline of his early
mental life and give a short account of his slight experience of
what he calls cosmic consciousness. The reader will readily see
therefrom whence came the ideas and convictions presented in
the following pages.

He was born of good middle class English stock and grew up
almost without education on what was then a backwoods Canadian
farm. As a child he assisted in such labor as lay within his
power: tended cattle, horses, sheep, pigs; brought in firewood,
worked in the hay field, drove oxen and horses, ran errands. His

pleasures were as simple as his labors.   An occasional visit to a neighboring small town, a game of ball, bathing in the creek that ran through his father's farm, the making and sailing of mimic ships, the search for birds' eggs and flowers in the spring, and for wild fruits in the summer and fall, afforded him, with his skates and handsled in the winter, his homely, much loved recreations. While still a young boy he read with keen appreciation Marryat's novels, Scott's poems and novels, and other similar books dealing with outdoor nature and human life.   He never, even as a child, accepted the doctrines of the Christian church; but, as soon as old enough to dwell at all on such themes, conceived that Jesus was a man—great and good no doubt, but a man.   That no one would ever be condemned to everlasting pain.   That if a conscious God existed he was the supreme master and meant well in the end to all; but that, this visible life here being ended, it was doubtful, or more than doubtful, whether conscious identity would be preserved.   The boy (even the child) dwelt on these and similar topics far more than anyone would suppose; but probably not more than many other introspective small fellow mortals.   He was subject at times to a sort of ecstasy of curiosity and hope. As on one special occasion when about ten years old he earnestly longed to die that the secrets of the beyond, if there was any beyond, might be revealed to him; also to agonies of anxiety and terror, as for instance, at about the same age he read Reynold's "Faust," and, being near its end one sunny afternoon, he laid it down utterly unable to continue its perusal, and went out into the sunshine to recover from the horror (after more than fifty years he distinctly recalls it) which had seized him.   The boy's mother died when he was only a few years old, and his father shortly afterwards.   The outward circumstances of his life in some respects became more unhappy than can readily be told.   At sixteen the boy left home to live or die as might happen.   For five years he wandered over North America from the Great Lakes to the Gulf of Mexico and from the Upper Ohio to San Francisco. He worked on farms, on railways, on steamboats, and in the placer diggings of Western Nevada.   Several times he nearly suffered shipwreck by sickness, starvation, freezing, and once on the banks of the Humboldt River, in Utah, fought for his life half a day with the Shoshone Indians. After five years' wandering, at the age of twenty-one, he returned to the country where his childhood had been passed. A moderate sum of money from his dead mother enabled him to spend some years in study, and his mind, after lying so long fallow, absorbed ideas with extraordinary facility. He graduated with high honors four years after his return from the Pacific Coast. Outside of the collegiate course he read with avidity many speculative books, such as the "Origin of Species," Tyndall's "Heat" and "Essays," Buckle's "History," "Essays and Reviews," and much poetry, especially such as seemed to him free and fearless. In this species of literature he soon preferred Shelley, and of his poems, "Adonais" and "Prometheus" were his favorites. His life for some years was one passionate note of interrogation, an unappeasable hunger for enlightenment on the basic problems. Leaving college, he continued his search with the same ardor. Taught himself French that he might read Auguste Comte, Hugo and Renan, and German that he might read Goethe, especially "Faust." At the age of thirty he fell in with "Leaves of Grass," and at once saw that it contained, in greater measure than any book so far found, what he had so long been looking for. He read the "Leaves" eagerly, even passionately, but for several years derived little from them. At last light broke and there was revealed to him (as far perhaps as such things can be revealed) at least some of the meanings. Then occurred that to which the foregoing is preface.

It was in the early spring, at the beginning of his thirty-sixth year. He and two friends had spent the evening reading Wordsworth, Shelley, Keats, Browning, and especially Whitman. They parted at midnight, and he had a long drive in a hansom (it was in an English city). His mind, deeply under the influence of the ideas, images and emotions called up by the reading and talk of the evening, was calm and peaceful. He was in a state of quiet, almost passive enjoyment. All at once, without warning of any kind, he found himself wrapped around as it were by a flame-

colored cloud. For an instant he thought of fire, some sudden
conflagration in the great city; the next, he knew that the light
was within himself. Directly afterwards came upon him a sense
of exultation, of immense joyousness accompanied or immediately
followed by an intellectual illumination quite impossible to describe. Into his brain streamed one momentary lightning-flash of
the Brahmic Splendor which has ever since lightened his life;
upon his heart fell one drop of Brahmic Bliss, leaving thenceforward for always an aftertaste of heaven. Among other things
he did not come to believe, he saw and knew that the Cosmos is not
dead matter but a living Presence, that the soul of man is immortal, that the universe is so built and ordered that without any peradventure all things work together for the good
of each and all, that the foundation principle of the world is what
we call love and that the happiness of every one is in the long run
absolutely certain. He claims that he learned more within the
few seconds during which the illumination lasted than in previous
months or even years of study, and that he learned much that no
study could ever have taught.

The illumination itself continued not more than a few moments, but its effects proved ineffaceable; it was impossible for
him ever to forget what he at that time saw and knew; neither did
he, or could he, ever doubt the truth of what was then presented to
his mind. There was no return, that night or at any other time,
of the experience. He subsequently wrote a book (28a.) in which
he sought to embody the teaching of the illumination. Some who
read it thought very highly of it, but (as was to be expected for
many reasons) it had little circulation.

The supreme occurrence of that night was his real and sole
initiation to the new and higher order of ideas. But it was only
an initiation. He saw the light but had no more idea whence
it came and what it meant than had the first creature that saw the
light of the sun. Years afterwards he met C. P., of whom he had
often heard as having extraordinary spiritual insight. He found
that C. P. had entered the higher life of which he had had a
glimpse and had had large experience of its phenomena. His con-

versation with C. P. threw a flood of light upon the true meaning of what he had himself experienced.

Looking round then upon the world of man, he saw the significance of the subjective light in the case of Paul and in that of Mohammed. The secret of Whitman's transcendent greatness was revealed to him. Certain conversations with J. H. J. and with J. B. helped him not a little. Personal intercourse with Edward Carpenter, T. S. R., C. M. C. and M. C. L. assisted greatly in the broadening and clearing up of his speculations, in the extension and co-ordination of his thought. But much time and labor were still required before the germinal concept could be satisfactorily elaborated and matured, the idea, namely, that there exists a family sprung from, living among, but scarcely forming a part of ordinary humanity, whose members are spread abroad throughout the advanced races of mankind and throughout the last forty centuries of the world's history.

The trait that distinguishes these people from other men is this: Their spiritual eyes have been opened and they have seen. The better known members of this group who, were they collected together, could be accommodated all at one time in a modern drawing-room, have created all the great modern religions, beginning with .Taoism and Buddhism, and speaking generally, have created, through religion and literature, modern civilization. Not that they have contributed any large numerical proportion of the books which have been written, but that they have produced the few books which have inspired the larger number of all that have been written in modern times. These men dominate the last twenty-five, especially the last five, centuries as stars of the first magnitude dominate the midnight sky.

A man is identified as a member of this family by the fact that at a certain age he has passed through a new birth and risen to a higher spiritual plane. The reality of the new birth is demonstrated by the subjective light and other phenomena. The object of the present volume is to teach others what little the writer himself has been able to learn of the spiritual status of this new race.

V.

It remains to say a few words upon the psychological origin of what is called in this book Cosmic Consciousness, which must not be looked upon as being in any sense supernatural or supranormal —as anything more or less than a natural growth.

Although in the birth of Cosmic Consciousness the moral nature plays an important part, it will be better for many reasons to confine our attention at present to the evolution of the intellect. In this evolution there are four distinct steps. The first of them was taken when upon the primary quality of excitability sensation was established. At this point began the acquisition and more or less perfect registration of sense impressions—that is, of percepts.

A percept is of course a sense impression—a sound is heard or an object seen and the impression made is a percept. If we could go back far enough we should find among our ancestors a creature whose whole intellect was made up simply of these percepts. But this creature (whatever name it ought to bear) had in it what may be called an eligibility of growth, and what happened with it was something like this: Individually and from generation to generation it accumulated these percepts, the constant repetition of which, calling for further and further registration, led, in the struggle for existence and, under the law of natural selection, to an accumulation of cells in the central sense ganglia; the multiplication of cells made further registration possible; that, again, made further growth of the ganglia necessary, and so on. At last a condition was reached in which it became possible for our ancestor to combine groups of these percepts into what we to-day call a recept. This process is very similar to that of composite photography. Similar percepts (as of a tree) are registered one over the other until (the nerve center having become competent to the task) they are generalized into, as it were, one percept; but that compound percept is neither more nor less than a recept—a something that has been received.

Now the work of accumulation begins again on a higher plane:

the sensory organs keep steadily at work manufacturing percepts; the receptual centers keep steadily at work manufacturing more and yet more recepts from the old and the new percepts; the capacities of the central ganglia are constantly taxed to do the necessary registration of percepts, the necessary elaboration of these into recepts and the necessary registration of recepts; then as the ganglia by use and selection are improved they constantly manufacture from percepts and from the initial simple recepts, more and more complex, that is, higher and higher recepts.

At last, after many thousands of generations have lived and died, comes a time when the mind of the animal we are considering has reached the highest possible point of purely receptual intelligence; the accumulation of percepts and of recepts has gone on until no greater stores of impressions can be laid up and no further elaboration of these can be accomplished on the plane of receptual intelligence. Then another break is made and the higher recepts are replaced by concepts. The relation of a concept to a recept is somewhat similar to the relation of algebra to arithmetic. A recept is, as I have said, a composite image of hundreds, perhaps thousands, of percepts; it is itself an image abstracted from many images; but a concept is that same composite image—that same recept—named, ticketed, and, as it were, dismissed. A concept is in fact neither more nor less than a *named recept*—the name, that is, the sign (as in algebra), standing henceforth for the thing itself, that is, for the recept.

Now it is as clear as day to any one who will give the least thought to the subject, that the revolution by which concepts are substituted for recepts increases the efficiency of the brain for thought as much as the introduction of machinery increased the capacity of the race for work—or as much as the use of algebra increases the power of the mind in mathematical calculations. To replace a great cumbersome recept by a simple sign was almost like replacing actual goods—as wheat, fabrics and hardware—by entries in the ledger.

But, as hinted above, in order that a recept may be replaced by a concept it must be named, or, in other words, marked with a sign which stands for it—just as a check stands for a piece of baggage or as an entry in a ledger stands for a piece of goods; in other words, the race that is in possession of concepts is also, and necessarily, in possession of language. Further, it should be noted, as the possession of concepts implies the possession of language, so the possession of concepts and language (which are in reality two aspects of the same thing) implies the possession of self consciousness. All this means that there is a moment in the evolution of mind when the receptual intellect, capable of simple consciousness only, becomes almost or quite instantaneously a conceptual intellect in possession of language and self consciousness.

When we say that an individual, whether an adult individual long ago or a child to-day does not matter, came into possession of concepts, of language and of self consciousness in an instant, we, of course, mean that the individual came into possession of self consciousness and of one or a few concepts and of one or a few true words instantaneously and not that he entered into possession of a whole language in that short time. In the history of the individual man the point in question is reached and passed at about the age of three years; in the history of the race it was reached and passed several hundred thousand years ago.

We have now, in our analysis, reached the point where we each individually stand, the point, namely, of the conceptual, self conscious mind. In acquiring this new and higher form of consciousness it must not for a moment be supposed that we have dropped either our receptual intelligence or our old perceptual mind; as a matter of fact we could not live without these any more than could the animal who has no other mind than them. Our intellect, then, to-day is made up of a very complex mixture of percepts, recepts and concepts.

Let us now for a moment consider the concept. This may be considered as a large and complex recept; but larger and more complex than any recept. It is made up of one or more recepts combined with probably several percepts. This extremely complex recept is then marked by a sign; that is, it is named and in virtue of its name it becomes a concept. The concept, after being named or marked, is (as it were) laid away, just as a piece of checked baggage is marked by its check and piled in the baggage-room.

By means of this check we can send the trunk to any part of America without ever seeing it or knowing just where it is at a given moment. So by means of their signs we can build concepts into elaborate calculations, into poems and into systems of philosophy, without knowing half the time anything about the thing represented by the individual concepts that we are using.

And here a remark must be made aside from the main argument. It has been noticed thousands of times that the brain of a thinking man does not exceed in size the brain of a non-thinking wild man in anything like the proportion in which the mind of the thinker exceeds the mind of the savage. The reason is that the brain of a Herbert Spencer has very little more work to do than has the brain of a native Australian, for this reason, that Spencer does all his characteristic mental work by signs or counters which stand for concepts, while the savage does all or nearly all his by means of cumbersome recepts. The savage is in a position comparable to that of the astronomer who makes his calculations by arithmetic, while Spencer is in the position of one who makes them by algebra. The first will fill many great sheets of paper with figures and go through immense labor; the other will make the same calculations on an envelope and with comparatively little mental work.

The next chapter in the story is the accumulation of concepts. This is a double process. From the age, we will say, of three years each one accumulates year by year a larger and larger number, while at the same time the individual concepts are becoming constantly more and more complex. Consider for instance the concept *science* as it exists in the mind of a boy and of a middle aged thinking man; with the former it stood for a few dozen or a few hundred facts; with the latter for many thousands.

Is there to be any limit to this growth of concepts in number and complexity? Whoever will seriously consider that question will see that there must be a limit. No such process could go on to infinity. Should nature attempt such a feat the brain would have to grow until it could no longer be fed and a condition of deadlock be reached which would forbid further progress.

We have seen that the expansion of the perceptual mind had a necessary limit; that its own continued life led it inevitably up to and into the receptual mind. That the receptual mind by its own growth was inevitably led up to and into the conceptual mind. A priori considerations make it certain that a corresponding outlet will be found for the conceptual mind.

But we do not need to depend on abstract reasoning to demonstrate the necessary existence of the supra conceptual mind, since it exists and can be studied with no more difficulty than other natural phenomena. The supra conceptual intellect, the elements of which instead of being concepts are intuitions, is already (in small numbers it is true) an established fact, and the form of consciousness that belongs to that intellect may be called and has been called—Cosmic Consciousness.

Thus we have four distinct stages of intellect, all abundantly illustrated in the animal and human worlds about us—all equally illustrated in the individual growth of the cosmic conscious mind and all four existing together in that mind as the first three exist together in the ordinary human mind. These four stages are, first, the perceptual mind—the mind made up of percepts or sense impressions; second, the mind made up of these and recepts— the so called receptual mind, or in other words the mind of simple consciousness; third, we have the mind made up of percepts, recepts and concepts, called sometimes the conceptual mind or otherwise the self conscious mind—the mind of self consciousness; and, fourth, and last, we have the intuitional mind—the mind whose highest element is not a recept or a concept but an intuition. This is the mind in which sensation, simple consciousness and self consciousness are supplemented and crowned with cosmic consciousness.

But it is necessary to show more clearly still the nature of these four stages and their relation one to the other. The perceptual or sensational stage of intellect is easy enough to understand, so may be passed by in this place with only one remark, namely, that in a mind made up wholly of percepts there is no consciousness of any sort. When, however, the receptual mind comes into existence simple consciousness is born, which means that animals are conscious (as we know they are) of the things they see about them. But the receptual mind is capable of simple consciousness only— that is, the animal is conscious of the object which he sees, but he does not know he is conscious of it; neither is the animal conscious of itself as a distinct entity or personality. In still other words, the animal cannot stand outside of itself and look at itself as any self conscious creature can. This, then, is simple consciousness: to be conscious of the things about one, but not to be conscious of one's self. But when I have reached self consciousness I am not only conscious of what I see, but I know I am conscious of it. Also I am conscious of myself as a separate entity and personality and I can stand apart from myself and contemplate myself, and can analyze and judge the operations of my own mind as I would analyze and judge anything else. This self consciousness is only possible after the formation of concepts and the consequent birth of language. Upon self consciousness is based all distinctively *human* life so far, except what has proceeded from the few cosmic conscious minds of the last three thousand years. Finally the basic fact in cosmic consciousness is implied in its name—that fact is consciousness of the cosmos—this is what is called in the East the "Brahmic Splendor," which is in Dante's phrase capable of transhumanizing a man into a god. Whitman, who has an immense deal to say about it, speaks of it in one place as "ineffable light—light rare, untellable, lighting the very light—beyond all signs, descriptions, languages." This consciousness shows the cosmos to consist not of dead matter governed by unconscious, rigid, and unintending law; it shows it on the contrary as entirely immaterial, entirely spiritual and entirely alive; it shows that death is an absurdity, that everyone and everything has eternal life; it shows that the universe is God and that God is the universe, and that no evil ever did or ever will enter into it; a great deal of this is, of course, from the point of view of self consciousness, absurd;

it is nevertheless undoubtedly true.   Now all this does not mean
that when a man has cosmic consciousness he knows everything
about the universe.   We all know that when at three years of age
we acquired self consciousness we did not at once know all about
ourselves; we know, on the contrary, that after a great many
thousands of years of experience of himself man still to-day knows
comparatively little about himself considered even as a self conscious personality.   So neither does a man know all about the
cosmos merely because he becomes conscious of it.   If it has taken
the race several hundred thousand years to learn a smattering of
the science of humanity since its aquisition of self consciousness,
so it may take it millions of years to acquire a smattering of the
science of God after its acquisition of cosmic consciousness.

As on self consciousness is based the human world as we see it
with all its works and ways, so on cosmic consciousness is based
the higher religions and the higher philosophies and what comes
from them, and on it will be based, when it becomes more general,
a new world of which it would be idle to try to speak to-day.

The philosophy of the birth of cosmic consciousness in the individual is very similar to that of the birth of self consciousness.
The mind becomes overcrowded (as it were) with concepts and
these are constantly becoming larger, more numerous and more
and more complex; some day (the conditions being all favorable)
the fusion, or what might be called the chemical union, of several
of them and of certain moral elements takes place; the result is an
intuition and the establishment of the intuitional mind, or, in
other words, cosmic consciousness.

The scheme by which the mind is built up is uniform from beginning to end: a recept is made of many percepts; a concept of
many or several recepts and percepts, and an intuition is made of
many concepts, recepts and percepts together with other elements
belonging to and drawn from the moral nature.   The cosmic vision or the cosmic intuition, from which what may be called the new
mind takes its name, is thus seen to be simply the complex and union of all prior thought and experience—just as self consciousness
is the complex and union of all thought and experience prior to it

PART II.

EVOLUTION AND DEVOLUTION.

CHAPTER 1.

To Self Consciousness.

IT will be necessary, in the first place, for the reader of this book to have before his mind a tolerably complete idea in outline of mental evolution in all its three branches—sensuous, intellectual and emotional—up to and through the status of self consciousness. Without such a mental image as basis for the new conception this last (that is, cosmic consciousness) to most people would seem extravagant and even absurd. With such necessary foundation the new concept will appear to the intelligent reader what it is: A matter of course—an inevitable sequel to what preceded and led up to it. In attempting to give an idea of this vast evolution of mental phenomena from its beginning in far off geologic ages down to the latest phases reached by our own race anything like an exhaustive treatise could not, of course, be thought of here. The method actually adopted is more or less broken and fragmentary, but enough (it is thought) is given for the present purpose, and those who desire more will have no difficulty in finding it in other treatises, such as the admirable work of Romanes [134]. All the present writer aims at is the exposition of cosmic consciousness and a barely sufficient account of the lower mental phenomena to make that subject fully intelligible; anything further would only burden this book to no good purpose.

The upbuilding or unfolding of the knowable universe presents to our minds a series of gradual ascents each divided from the next by an apparent leap over what seems to be a chasm. For instance, and to begin not at the beginning, but midway: Between the slow and equable development of the inorganic world which prepared it for the reception and support of living creatures and the more rapid growth and branching of vital forms, these having once appeared, there occurred what seems like the hiatus between the inorganic and organic worlds and the leap by which it was over-passed; within which hiatus or chasm has heretofore resided either the substance or shadow of a god whose hand has been deemed necessary to lift and pass on the elements from the lower to the higher plane.

Along the level road of the formation of suns and planets, of earth crust, of rocks and soil, we are carried, by evolutionists, smoothly and safely; but when we reach this perilous pit stretching interminably to right and left across our path, we pause, and even so able and daring a pilot as Lester Ward (190. 300-320) can hardly induce us to attempt the leap with him, so wide and dark frowns the abyss. We feel that nature, who has done all—and much greater things—was competent to cross and did cross the apparent break, although we may not at present be able to place a finger in each one of her footprints. For the moment, however, this stands the first and greatest of the so-called bars to acceptance of the doctrine of absolute continuity in the evolution of the visible world.

Later in the history of creation comes the beginning of Simple Consciousness. Certain individuals in some one leading species in the slowly unfolding life of the planet, some day—for the first time—become conscious; know that there exists a world, a something, without them. Less dwelt upon, as it has been, this step from the unconscious to the conscious might well impress us as being as immense, as miraculous and as divine as that from the inorganic to the organic.

Again, running parallel with the river of time, we perceive a long, equable and gradual ascent stretching from the dawn of Simple Consciousness to its highest excellence in the best pre-human types—the horse, the dog, the elephant and the ape. At this point confronts us another break comparable to those which in order of time preceded it—the hiatus, namely, or the seeming hiatus between Simple and Self Consciousness: the deep chasm or ravine upon one side of which roams the brute while upon the other dwells man. A chasm into which enough books have been thrown to have sufficed (could they have been converted into stones or pig iron) to dam or bridge a great river. And which has only now been made safely passable by the lamented G. J. Romanes, by means of his valuable treatise on the "Origin of Human Faculty" [134].

Only a very short time ago (and even yet by most) this break in the line of ascent (or descent) was supposed to be impassable by ordinary growth. It may be said to be now known to be so passable, but it still stands out and apart from the even path of Cosmic development before our vision as that broad chasm or gap between the brute and the man.

For some hundreds of thousands of years, upon the general plane of Self Consciousness, an ascent, to the human eye gradual, but from the point of view of cosmic evolution rapid, has been made. In a race, large brained, walking erect, gregarious, brutal, but king of all other brutes, man in appearance but not in fact, the so-called alalus homo, was, from the highest Simple Consciousness born the basic human faculty Self Consciousness and its twin, language. From these and what went with these, through suffering, toil and war; through bestiality, savagery, barbarism; through slavery, greed, effort; through conquests infinite, through defeats overwhelming, through struggle unending; through ages of aimless semi-brutal existence; through subsistence on berries and roots; through the use of the casually found stone or stick; through life in deep forest, with nuts and seeds, and on the shores of waters with mollusks, crustaceans, and fish for food; through that greatest, perhaps, of human victories, the domestication and subjugation of fire; through the invention and art of the bow and arrow; through the taming of animals and the breaking of them to labor; through the long learning which led to the cultivation of the soil; through the adobe brick and the building of houses therefrom; through the smelting of metals and the slow births of the arts which rest upon these; through the slow making of alphabets and the evolution of the written word; in short, through thousands of centuries of human life, of human aspiration, of human growth, sprang the world of men and women as it stands before us and within us to-day with all its achievements and possessions [124. 10-13].

Is that all? Is that the end? No. As life arose in a world without life; as Simple Consciousness came into existence where before was mere vitality without perception; as Self Consciousness leaping widewinged from Simple Consciousness soared forth over land and sea, so shall the race of man which has been thus established, continuing its beginningless and endless ascent, make other steps (the next of which it is now in act of climbing) and attain to a yet higher life than any heretofore experienced or even conceived.

And let it be clearly understood that the new step (to explain which this volume is written) is not simply an expansion of self consciousness but as distinct from it as that is from simple consciousness or as is this last from mere vitality without any consciousness at all, or as is the latter from the world of inorganic matter and force which preceded it and from which it proceeded.

CHAPTER 2.

On the Plane of Self Consciousness.

I.

AND in the first place it would be well to get a firm hold of the meaning of the words "self consciousness," upon the definition of which an excellent writer and most competent thinker [200-255] has these remarks: "Self consciousness is often referred to as a distinguishing characteristic of man. Many, however, fail to gain a clear conception of what this faculty is. Dr. Carpenter confounds it with the 'power of reflecting on their own mental states,' while Mr. Darwin associates it with abstraction and other of the derivative faculties. It is certainly something much simpler than introspection, and has an earlier origin than the highly derivative speculative faculties. If it could only be seized and clearly understood, self consciousness would doubtless prove to be the primary and fundamental human attribute. Our language seems to lack the proper word to express it in its simplest form. 'Think' approaches this most nearly, and man is sometimes described as a 'thinking being.' The German language has a better word, viz., besinnen, and the substantive Besonnenheit seems to touch the kernel of the problem. Schopenhauer says: 'The animal lives without any Besonnenheit. It has consciousness, i. e., it knows itself and its weal and woe; also the objects which produce these; but its knowledge remains constantly subjective, never becomes objective: everything that it embraces appears to exist in and of itself, and can therefore never become an object of representation nor a problem for meditation. Its consciousness is thus wholly immanent. The consciousness of the savage man is similarly constituted in that his perceptions of things and of the world remain preponderantly subjective and immanent. He perceives things in the world, but not the world; his own actions and passion, but not himself.' "

Perhaps the simplest definition (and there are scores of them) would be: self consciousness is the faculty by which we *realize*. Or again: without self consciousness a sentient creature can know, but its possession is necessary in order that he may *know that he knows*. The best treatise so far written on this subject is Romanes' book, already several times referred to [134].

The roots of the tree of life being deep sunk in the organic world, its trunk is made up as follows: Beginning at the earth level we have first of all the lowest forms of life unconscious and insensate. These in their turn give birth to forms endowed with sensation and later to forms endowed with Simple Consciousness. From the last, when the right time comes, springs self consciousness and (as already said) in direct ascent from that Cosmic Consciousness. It is only necessary in this place, as clearing the ground for the work to be done, to point out that the doctrine of the unfolding of the human being, regarded from the side of psychology, is strictly in accord with the theory of evolution in general as received and taught to-day by the foremost thinkers.

This tree which we call life and its upper part human life and human mind, has simply grown as grows any other tree, and besides its main stem, as above indicated, it has, as in the case of other trees, thrown off many branches. It will be well to consider some of these. It will be seen that some of them are given off from the lower part of the trunk, as, for instance, contractility, from which great limb, and as a part of it, springs all muscular action from the simple movement of the worm to the marvelously co-ordinated motions made, in the exercise of their art, by a Liszt or a Paderewski. Another of these large lower limbs is the instinct of Self-preservation and (twin with it) the instinct of the continuance of the species—the preservation of the race. Higher up the special senses shoot out from the main trunk and as they grow and divide and again divide they become large and vitally important branches of the great tree. From all these main off-shoots spring smaller arms and from these more delicate twigs.

Thus from the human intellect whose central fact is Self Consciousness, a section of the main trunk of our tree, spring judgment, reason, comparison, imagination, abstraction, reflection, generalization. From the moral or emotional nature, one of the largest and most important of the main limbs, spring love (itself a great branch dividing into many smaller branches), reverence, faith, fear, awe, hope, hate, humor and many more. The great branch called the sense of sight, which in its beginning was a perception of the difference between light and darkness, sent out twigs which we call sense of form, of distance, and later the color sense. The limb named sense of hearing has for branches and twigs the apprehension of loudness, of pitch, of distance, of direction and as a delicate twig just coming into being, the musical sense.

II.

The important fact to notice at present is that, true to the simile of the tree here adopted, the numerous faculties of which (viewed from the side of dynamics) man is composed are all of different ages. Each one of them came into existence in its own time, i. e., when the psychic organism (the tree) was ready to produce it. For instance: Simple Consciousness many millions of years ago; Self Consciousness perhaps three hundred thousand years. General vision is enormously old, but the color sense probably only about a thousand generations. Sensibility to sound many millions of years, while the musical sense is now in the act of appearing. Sexual instinct or passion arose far back in geologic ages—the human moral nature of which human sexual love is a young and vigorous branch does not appear to have been in existence many tens of thousands of years.

III.

To make what has been and what remains to be said more readily and more fully intelligible it will be well to go into some little detail as to the time and mode of becoming and developing of a few faculties as a sample of the divine work that has been going on within us and about us since the dawn of life on this planet. The science of human psychology (in order to illustrate the subject of this volume) should give an account of the human intellect, of the human moral nature, and of the senses. Should give a description of these as they exist to-day, of their origin and evolution and should forecast their future course of either decay or further expansion. Only a very few specimen pages of such a work can be here set forth—and first a hasty glance at the intellect.

The intellect is that part of the mind which knows, as the moral nature is the part that feels. Each particular act of the intellect is instantaneous, whereas the acts (or rather states) of the moral nature are more or less continuous. Language corre-

sponds to the intellect and is therefore capable of expressing it
perfectly and directly; on the other hand, the functions of the
moral nature (belonging, i. e., deriving, as they do, from the great
sympathetic nervous system—while the intellect and speech rest
upon and spring from the Cerebro-Spinal) are not connected
with language and are only capable of indirect and imperfect
expression by its agency. Perhaps music, which certainly has
its roots in the moral nature, is, as at present existing, the beginning of a language which will tally and express emotion as words
tally and express ideas [28a. 106]. Intellectual acts are complex,
and decomposable into many parts; moral states are either absolutely simple (as in the case of love, fear, hate) or nearly so; that
is, are composed of comparatively few elements. All intellectual
acts are alike, or nearly alike, in that regard; moral states have a
very wide range of degree of intensity.

The human intellect is made up principally of concepts, just
as a forest is made up of trees or a city of houses; these concepts
are mental images of things, acts, or relations. The registration
of these we call memory, the comparison of them one with another
reasoning; for the building of these up into more complex images
(as bricks are built into a house) we have in English no good expression; we sometimes call this act imagination (the act of forming a mental copy or likeness)—the Germans have a better name
for it—they call it Vorstellung (the act of placing before),
Anschauungsgabe (the gift of looking upon) and better still
Einbildungskraft (the power of building up). The large intellect is that in which the number of concepts is above the average;
the fine intellect is that in which these are clear cut and well defined; the ready intellect is that in which they are easily and
quickly accessible when wanted, and so on.

The growth of the human intellect is the growth of the concepts, i. e., the multiplication of the more simple and at the same
time the building up of these into others more and more complex.

Although this increase in number and complexity is taking
place constantly in every active mind during at least the first half
of life, from infancy to middle age, and though we each know

that we have concepts now that we had not some time ago, yet probably the wisest of us could not tell from observation made upon his own mind just by what process these new concepts came into existence—where they came from or how they came. But though we cannot perceive this by direct observation either of our own mind or that of another person, still there is another way by which the occult process can be followed and that is by means of language. As said above, language is the exact tally of the intellect: for every concept there is a word or words and for every word there is a concept; neither can exist apart from the other. So Trench says: "You cannot impart to any man more than the words which he understands either now contain or can be made intelligibly to him to contain." Or as Max Mueller expresses it: "Without speech no reason, without reason no speech." Speech and the intellect do not correspond with one another in this way by accident, the relation between them is inevitably involved in the nature of the two things. Or are they two things? Or two sides of one thing? No word can come into being except as the expression of a concept, neither can a new concept be formed without the formation (at the same time) of the new word which is its expression, though this "new word" may be spelled and pronounced as is some old word. But an old word taking on another and a new meaning in reality becomes two words, an old and a new. Intellect and speech fit one another as the hand and the glove, only far more closely; say rather they fit as the skin fits the body, or as the pia mater fits the brain, or as any given species in the organic world is fitted by its environment. As is implied in what has been said, it is to be especially noted that not only does language fit the intellect in the sense of covering it in every part and following all its turnings and windings, but it fits it also in the sense of *not going beyond it*. Words correspond with concepts, and with concepts only, so that we cannot express directly with them either sense impressions or emotions, but are forced always to convey these (if at all) by expressing, not themselves, but the impression they make upon our intellect, i. e., the concepts formed from the contemplation of them by the intellect—in other words, their intellectual image. So that before a sense impression or an emotion can be embodied or conveyed in language a concept has to be formed (supposed more or less truly to represent it), which concept can, of course, be conveyed in words. But as a matter of fact ninety-nine out of every hundred of our sense impressions and emotions have never been represented in the intellect by concepts and therefore remain unexpressed and inexpressible except imperfectly by roundabout description and suggestion. There exists in the lower animals a state of matters which serves well to illustrate this proposition. These have acute sense perceptions and strong emotions, such as fear, rage, sexual passion and maternal love, and yet cannot express them because these have no language of their own, and the animals in question have no system of concepts with corresponding articulate sounds. Granted to us our sense perceptions and our human moral natures and we should be as dumb as are the animals had we not along with these an intellect in which they may be mirrored and by which, by means of language, they can be expressed.

As the correspondence of words and concepts is not casual or temporary but resides in the nature of these and continues during all time and under all circumstances absolutely constant, so changes in one of the factors must correspond with changes in the other. So evolution of intellect must (if it exist) be accompanied by evolution of language. An evolution of language (if it exist) will be evidence of evolution of intellect. What then is here proposed is to study (for a few moments) the growth of the intellect by means of an examination of language, i. e., to study the birth, life and growth of concepts which cannot be seen, by means of words which are their co-relatives and which can be seen.

Sir Charles Lyell, in the "Antiquity of Man" [113], pointed out the parallelism which exists between the origin, growth, decline and death of languages and of species in the organic world. In order to illustrate and at the same time broaden the present argument let us extend the parallel backward to the formation of the worlds and forward to the evolution of words and concepts.

Nebula of Astral System
- Nebula of Solar System
  - System of Jupiter
    - Planet
    - 1st Moon
    - 2d Moon
    - 3d Moon
    - 4th Moon
  - Saturn
  - Uranus
  - Neptune
  - Mars
  - Earth
  - Etc.
- N.
- N.
- N.
- N.

Eohippus (Eocene) Size of Fox — Mesohippus (Early Miocene) — Anchitherium (Miocene) Size of sheep, Miohippus
- Equus Caballus
  - Race Horse
  - Carriage Horse
  - Eng. Dray Horse
  - Eng. Hunter
  - Arabian
  - Shetland Pony
- " Asinus
- " Hemionus
- " Quagga
- " Zebra
- Dauw

?—Aryan
- Latin
  - Italian
    - Venetian
    - Sicilian
    - Calabrian
    - Arcolan
    - Corsican
  - Spanish
  - Portuguese
  - French
  - Wallachian
  - Rhaetian
- Greek
- Sanscrit
- Zend
- Armenian
- Lithuanian
- Old Sclavonic
- Gothic

Expect
- Expecting
- Expectation
- Expected
- Unexpected
- Expectable
- Expectancy
- Expectant
- Expector

- Specimen
- Respect (noun and verb)
- Spectator
- Respite
- Spectacle
- Despise, Despicable
- Respective
- Spite, -ful
- Spectrum
- Speculate, -ation
- Suspect, Suspicious
- Specious, -ly, -ness
- Specific, -ation
- Inspect, -ion, -or
- Speculus
- Species
- Circumspect, -ion
- Spice, Spicy
- Prospect, -ive
- Special, -ly, -ty
- Auspicious, Auspices
- Spicular
- Respectable
- Spy (noun or verb)
- Aspect
- Prospectus
- Specify
- Spectre

Pre-root—Aryan root, Spac
- Latin, Specio, To see, look
- Greek, Skeptomai, I look
  - " Skeptikos, An enquirer
  - " Episkopes, An overseer
- Sanscrit, Pas, To see
  - " Spasa, A spy
  - " Spashta, Manifest
  - " Spas, A guardian
- O. H. G., Spehan, To look, spy
  - " " Speha, A spy

The accompanying table will serve this purpose as well as, or better than, an elaborately reasoned exposition, and will serve at the same time as a summary of the evolution argument which runs through this volume.

A short study of this tabular statement will make plain how orbs, species, languages and words branch, divide and multiply; will make intelligible Max Mueller's estimate that "every thought that has ever passed through the mind of India" may be reduced to one hundred and twenty-one root concepts—that is, to one hundred and twenty-one root words [116. 401]; will make us agree with him that, probably, that number might be still further reduced. If we consider for a moment that this means that the millions of Indo-European words now in use as well as many times the number long since dead and forgotten, nearly all sprang from about one hundred roots and that these in their turn probably from half a dozen, and at the same time remember that reason and speech are one, we shall obtain a glimpse of what the human intellect once was in comparison with what it is to-day; and likewise it becomes apparent at a glance that the evolution not only of species, languages and words is strictly parallel but that the scheme has probably a still wider, perhaps universal, application. As regards the present thesis the conclusion to be drawn from this comparison is that words, and that therefore the constituent elements of the intellect which they represent and which we call concepts, grow by division and branching, as new species branch off from older, and it seems clear that a normal growth is encouraged and an excessive and useless development checked by the same means in the one case as in the other—that is, by natural selection and the struggle for existence.

New concepts, and words expressing them, which correspond with some external reality (whether this is a thing, an act, a state, or a relation), and which are therefore of use to man, since their existence places him in more complete relation with the outer world, on which relation his life and welfare depend, are preserved by the process of natural selection and survival of the fittest. Some again which either do not correspond at all, or only imperfectly, with an objective reality are replaced by others which do correspond or correspond better with the reality which these aimed to express, and so in the struggle for existence fall into disuse and die out.

For it is with words as with every other living thing, thousands are produced for one that lives. Towards whatever object the mind is especially turned it throws out words often with marvelous profusion. When some thousands of years ago, Sanscrit being still a living language and the sun and fire looked upon either as actual gods or at least as especially sacred, fire had (instead of a very few names as now) thirty-five and the sun thirty-seven [115. 437]. But much more remarkable examples are those drawn from Arabic, as, for instance, the eighty names for honey, the two hundred for serpent, the five hundred for lion, the one thousand for sword, and the five thousand seven hundred and forty-four words all relating to the camel, these being subjects upon which the Arab mind is strongly and persistently bent [115. 438]. So again Max Mueller tells us: "We can hardly form an idea of the boundless resources of dialects. When literary languages have stereotyped one general term their dialects will supply fifty, though each with its special shade of meaning. If new combinations of thoughts are evolved in the progress of society, dialects will readily supply the required names from the store of their so-called superfluous words. There are not only local and provincial but also class dialects. There is a dialect of shepherds, of sportsmen, of soldiers, of farmers. I suppose there are few persons here present who could tell the exact meaning of a horse's poll, crest, withers, dock, hamstring, cannon, pastern, coronet, arm, jowl and muzzle. Where the literary language speaks of the young of all sorts of animals, farmers, shepherds and sportsmen would be ashamed to use so general a term. The idiom of nomads, as Grimm says, contain an abundant wealth of manifold expressions for sword and weapons, and for the different stages in the life of cattle. In a more highly cultivated language these expressions become burthensome and superfluous. But in a peasant's mouth the bearing, calving, falling and killing

of almost every animal has its own peculiar term, as the sports-
man delights in calling the gait and members of game by different
names.   Thus Dame Juliana Berners, lady prioress of the nun-
nery of Sopwell, in the fifteenth century, the reputed author of
the 'Book of St. Albans,' informs us that we must not use names
of multitudes promiscuously, but we are to say: A congregcyon of
people, a hoost of men, a felyshyppynge of women, and a bevy of
ladyes, we must speak of a herde of hartys, swannys, cranys, or
wrennys, a sege of herons, or bytourys, a muster of peacockys, a
watche of nyghtyngalys, a flyghte of doves, a claterynge of
choughes, a pryde of lyons, a slewthe of beerys, a gagle of geys, a
skulke of foxes, a sculle of frerys, a pontyfycalate of prelates, a
bomynable syght of monkes, a dronkenshyp of cobblers, and so of
other human and brute assemblages.   In like manner in dividing
game for the table the animals were not carved, but a dere was
broken, a gose reryd, a chekyn frusshed, a cony unlacyd, a crane
dysplayed, a curlewe unjointyd, a quayle wynggyd, a swanne lyfte,
a lambe sholderyd, a heron dysmembryd, a pecocke dysfygured, a
samon chynyd, a hadoke sydyd, a sole loynyd, and a breme
splayed" [115. 70].

These instances will serve to show how the human intellect
feels along the face of the outer world presented to it, attempting
a lodgment in each cranny it finds, however slight and precarious
may be the hold that it gets.   For the mind of man from age to
age ceaselessly seeks to master the facts of the outer world; its
growth indeed consists in tallying or covering these as ivy spreads
over, tallies and covers the stones of a wall; the twig that secures
a hold strengthens and puts out other twigs; that which does not
secure a hold after a time ceases to grow and eventually dies.

The main thing to notice for our present purpose is that just
as in the case of the child learning to talk, the race began also with
a few, or, as Geiger [91. 29] says, with a single word.   That is to
say, man began to think with very few or with a single concept
(of course, at that time, and before, he had a large stock of percepts and of recepts [134. 193], otherwise he could have done
little with his one or few concepts).   From these few or that one

the enormous number of concepts and words that have since come into existence have proceeded; nor will the evolution of the entire human intellect from a single initial concept seem incredible or even very marvelous, to those who bear in mind that the whole complex human body, with all its tissues, organs and parts, is built up of hundreds of millions of cells, each one of which, however much it may differ in structure and function from those belonging to other organs and tissues than its own, is yet lineally descended from the one single primordial cell in which each one of us (and only a few years ago) had his origin.

As we reach back into the past, therefore, we find language, and with it the human intellect, drawing into a point, and we know that within a measurable distance from where we stand to-day they must have both had their beginning. The date of that beginning has been approximately fixed by many writers and from many indications, and we cannot be far astray in placing it (provisionally) about three hundred thousand years anterior to our own times.

IV.

Much more modern than the birth of the intellect was that of the color sense. We have the authority of Max Mueller [117. 299] for the statement that: "It is well known that the distinction of color is of late date; that Xenophanes knew of three colors of the rainbow only—purple, red and yellow; that even Aristotle spoke of the tricolored rainbow; and that Democritus knew of no more than four colors—black, white, red and yellow."

Geiger [91. 48] points out that it can be proved by examination of language that as late in the life of the race as the time of the primitive Aryans, perhaps not more than fifteen or twenty thousand years ago, man was only conscious of, only perceived, one color. That is to say, he did not distinguish any difference in tint between the blue sky, the green trees and grass, the brown or gray earth, and the golden and purple clouds of sunrise and sunset. So Pictet [126] finds no names of colors in primitive Indo-

European speech. And Max Mueller [116:616] finds no Sanscrit root whose meaning has any reference to color.

At a later period, but still before the time of the oldest literary
compositions now extant, the color sense was so far developed
beyond this primitive condition that red and black were recognized as distinct. Still later, at the time when the bulk of the Rig
Veda was composed, red, yellow and black were recognized as
three separate shades, but these three included all color that man
at that age was capable of appreciating. Still later white was
added to the list and then green; but throughout the Rig Veda,
the Zend Avesta, the Homeric poems and the Bible the color of
the sky is not once mentioned, therefore, apparently, was not recognized. For the omission can hardly be attributed to accident;
the ten thousand lines of the Rig Veda are largely occupied with
descriptions of the sky; and all its features—sun, moon, stars,
clouds, lightning, sunrise and sunset—are mentioned hundreds of
times. So also the Zend Avesta, to the writers of which light and
fire, both terrestrial and heavenly, are sacred objects, could hardly
have omitted by chance all mention of the blue sky. In the Bible
the sky and heaven are mentioned more than four hundred and
thirty times, and still no mention is made of the color of the
former. In no part of the world is the blue of the sky more intense than in Greece and Asia Minor, where the Homeric poems
were composed. Is it possible to conceive that a poet (or the
poets) who saw this as we see it now could write the forty-eight
long books of the Iliad and Odyssey and never once either mention
or refer to it? But were it possible to believe that all the poets
of the Rig Veda, Zend Avesta, Iliad, Odyssey and Bible could
have omitted the mention of the blue color of the sky by mere accident, etymology would step in and assure us that four thousand
years ago, or, perhaps, three, blue was unknown, for at that time
the subsequent names for blue were all merged in the names for
black.

The English word *blue* and the German *blau* descend from a
word that meant *black*. The Chinese *hi-u-an*, which now means
sky-blue, formerly meant black. The word *nil,* which now in

Persian and Arabic means blue, is derived from the name *Nile,* that is, the *black river,* of which same word the Latin *Niger* is a form.

It does not seem possible that at the time when men recognized only two colors, which they called red and black, these appeared to them as red and black appear to us—though just what the sensations were which they so named cannot of course be now ascertained. Under the name *red* it seems they included with that color white, yellow and all intermediate tints; while under the name *black* they seem to have included all shades of blue and green. As the sensations red and black came into existence by the division of an original unital color sensation, so in process of time these divided. First red divided into red-yellow, then that red into red-white. Black divided into black-green, then black again into black-blue, and during the last twenty-five hundred years these six (or rather these four—red, yellow, green, blue) have split up into the enormous number of shades of color which are now recognized and named. The annexed diagram shows at a glance the order in which the spectrum colors became visible to man.

It can be shown in an entirely independent manner that if the color sense did come into existence as here supposed the successive order in which the colors are said (following ancient documents and etymology) to have been recognized by man is actually the order in which they must have been so recognized and the scientific facts now about to be adduced must be admitted to be remarkably confirmatory of the above conclusions, while being drawn from sources entirely separate and distinct.

The solar or other light rays that excite vision are named red, orange, yellow, green, blue, indigo, violet. These rays differ the one from the other in the length and amplitude of the waves which compose them, and both the length and amplitude of the waves diminish in the order in which the names have just been given. But the force or energy of a light wave—that is to say, its power of exciting vision, is proportional to the square of its amplitude [180. 272, and especially 181. 136]. According to this law the energy—the power of exciting vision—of the red rays is several thousand times as great as the energy of the violet, and there is a regular and rapid decrease of energy as we pass down the spectrum from red to violet. It is plain that if there has been such a thing as a growing perfection in the sense of vision in virtue of which, from being insensible to color the eye became gradually sensible of it, red would necessarily be the first color perceived, then yellow, then green, and so on to violet; and this is exactly what both ancient literature and etymology tell us took place.

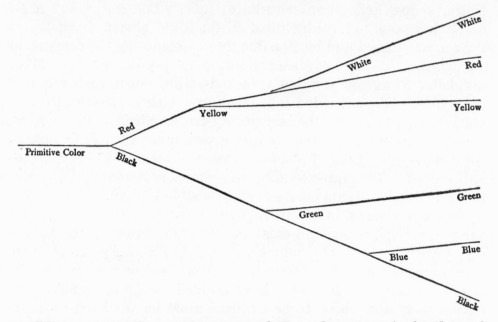

The comparative modernness of the color sense is further attested by the large number of persons in all countries who are what is called color-blind—that is, persons who are at the present day entirely or partially without color sense. "Wilson's assertion that probably one in five and twenty is color-blind long remained doubted because not proved in reference to sufficiently large numbers. Till we had comparison methods, and principally Hohngren's, no satisfactory data could be obtained. His in proper hands so quickly decides a case that tests have already been made in thousands of persons. Based on at least two hundred thousand examinations is the result that four per cent. of males are color blind in greater or less degree, and one-fourth of one per cent. of females." [135. 242.] This would make one case of color-blindness to every forty-seven persons.

The degree of universality of the color sense in a race is, of course, an important fact in estimating its degree of evolution as compared with other races. In this connection the following facts are of interest [122. 716]: "In Japan among 1,200 soldiers 1.58 per cent. were red-blind, and 0.833 per cent. green-blind. Among 373 boys 1 per cent. were red-blind; among 270 girls 0.4 per cent. Among 596 men examined by Dr. Berry, of Kyoto, 5.45 per cent. showed defective color sense. Among the Japanese, as a whole, the percentage of color-blindness is less than in Europeans or Americans. Among 796 Chinese examined in various places no cases of color-blindness were found, but there was a tendency often seen to mix green and blue. This peculiarity was brought out with much greater emphasis by Dr. Fielde, of Swatow, China, who examined 1,200 Chinese of both sexes, using Thompson's wool tests. Among the 600 men were 19 who were color-blind, and among 600 women only 1. The percentage of color-blindness among Chinamen is, then, about 3 per cent., and does not vary greatly from that of Europeans."

In color-blindness the general vision is not affected; the individual distinguishes light and shade, form and distance, as well as do other persons. This also goes to show that the color sense is more superficial, less fundamental, and probably therefore acquired later than the other powers that belong to the function of sight. For a person could not lose one of the more fundamental elements of vision (the sense of visual form, for instance) and retain the other sight faculties unimpaired.

Color-blindness is in fact an instance of what is called atavism, or relapse to a condition which was normal in the ancestry of the individual, but which does not properly belong to the species at the time in which he lives. The frequency of this relapse (estimated, as we have seen, to occur in one person out of every forty-seven) indicates that the color sense is comparatively modern; for atavism is more frequent in inverse proportion to the length

of time that has elapsed since the organ or function lost or im-
properly taken on (as the case may be) has (in the one case) normally existed in the race or (in the other) been discarded in the
process of evolution. The rationale of this law (which will be
again referred to) is obvious: it depends upon the simple fact
that the longer any organ or function has been in existence in a
race the more certainly will it be inherited. The existence of
color-blindness, then, in so large a percentage of the population
shows that the color sense is a modern faculty. The relative visi-
bility of the different colored light rays makes it certain that if
the color sense was acquired it would undoubtedly have been so
in the order in which philologists claim it actually was acquired,
and the concurrence of these two sets of facts, the one drawn from
natural philosophy and the other from etymology, together with
the fact of color-blindness, is so striking that it seems impossible
to refuse assent to the conclusions reached.

V.

Another recently acquired faculty is the sense of fragrance.
It is not mentioned in the Vedic hymns and only once in the Zend
Avesta. Geiger [91. 58] tells us that the custom of offering in-
cense with the sacrifice is not yet met with in the Rig Veda, though
it is found in the more recent Yadshurveda. Among the Biblical
books the sense of the fragrance of flowers first makes its appearance in the "Song of Songs." According to the description in
Genesis there were in Paradise all kinds of trees "that were pleasant to the sight and good for food," no mention being made of
pleasant odors. The Apochryphal book of Henoch (of the first
century B. C., or even later), extant in Ethiopian, likewise describes Paradise, but does not omit to extol the delightful fragrance of the Tree of Knowledge, as well as other trees, in the
Garden of Eden.

Besides this evidence it is said to be capable of proof from language that no such sense as that of fragrance existed in the early
times of the Indo-Europeans. And it is also worth mentioning

in this connection that no animal (although many of these so greatly surpass us in recognition by scent) possesses, so far as we know or can discover, any sense of fragrance, and that children do not acquire it until they are several years old—not, indeed, for several years after they have acquired, more or less perfectly, the sense of color; thus corresponding in their mental development (as pointed out above) with the evolution of the general human mind, for the color sense probably came into existence in the race many thousand years before the sense of fragrance.

VI.

Instincts which are both human and animal, as the sexual and maternal, undoubtedly came down to man through long lines of descent and have been in possession of himself and his ancestors for millions of years; but the human moral nature, though it is rooted in and has grown from these, is of comparatively recent origin. It not only does not go back behind the birth of self consciousness, but it is certainly very much more recent than this.

Man, that is, Self Consciousness, as has been said, must have come into being some three hundred thousand years ago when the first Alalus Homo uttered the first true word. In the individual to-day *man* is born when the child becomes self conscious—at the average age of, say, three years. Among the Indo-European races not more than about one individual (so-called idiot) in a thousand grows to maturity without attaining to Self Consciousness. Self Consciousness having appeared in an individual, is only lost in great and rare crises—as in the delirium of fever and in some forms of insanity, notably mania; on the other hand the human moral nature does not appear in the individual (on the average) until, say, half-way between three years old and maturity. Instead of one or two in a thousand, several times the same number in a hundred are born, grow up and die without a moral nature. Instead of being lost in great and rare crises it is constantly being temporarily lost. All these indications go to prove that the human moral nature is a much more recent birth of time than is the human intellect, and that if we suppose the latter to be three hundred thousand years old we cannot suppose the former to be anything like that age.

VII.

Primeval man, from whom we are all descended, has still upon the earth in these later days, two representatives—first, the savage; second, the child.   It would be true to say that the child is a savage and the savage a child, and through the mental state represented by these two, not only each individual member of the race, but the race itself as a whole, has passed.   For, as in his intra-uterine evolution the individual man retraces and summarizes in a few brief months the evolution of the human race, physically considered, from the initial unicellular form in which individual life began through all intervening phases between that and the human form, resuming in each day the slow evolution of millions of years, so likewise does the individual man in his mental development from birth to maturity retrace and summarize the evolution of the psychical life of the race; and as the individual physical man begins at the very bottom of the scale as a unicellular monad, so does the psychical man begin on the bottom round of the ladder of mind, and in his ascent of a few dozen months passes through the successive phases each of which occupied in its accomplishment by the race thousands of years.   The characteristics of the mind of the savage and of the child will give us, when found, the characteristics of the primeval human mind from which has descended the average modern mind that we know, as well as the exceptional minds of the great men of history of the present day.

The chief differences between the primeval, the infantile and the savage mind on the one hand and the civilized mind on the other, is that the first (called for the sake of brevity the lower mind) is wanting in personal force, courage, or faith, and also in sympathy, or affection; and that it is more easily excited to terror or anger than is the second or civilized mind.   There are of course other differences than these between the lower mind and the higher—differences in intellect, and even in sense perceptions; but these, though great in themselves, have not the supreme significance of the basic, fundamental, moral differences just mentioned. The lower mind then lacks faith, lacks courage, lacks personal force, lacks sympathy, lacks affection—that is (to sum up), it lacks peace, content, happiness. It is prone to the fear of things known, and still more to vague terror of things unknown; it is prone to anger, rage, hatred—that is (to again sum up), to unrest, discontent, unhappiness. On the other hand, the higher mind (as compared with the lower) possesses faith, courage, personal force, sympathy, affection; that is, it possesses (relatively) happiness; is less prone to fear of things known and unknown and to anger and hatred—that is, to unhappiness.

The statement thus broadly made does not seem at first sight to mean very much, but in fact it means almost everything; it contains the key to our past, our present and our future, for it is the condition of the moral nature (thus briefly adverted to) that decides for each one of us, from moment to moment, and for the race at large, from age to age, what sort of a place this world in which we live shall appear to be—what sort of a place it is indeed for each one of us. For it is not our eyes and ears, nor even our intellects, that report the world to us; but it is our moral nature that settles at last the significance of what exists about us.

The members of the human race began by fearing much and disliking much, by loving or admiring little and by trusting still less. It is safe to say that those earliest men of the river drift, and the cave men, their successors, saw little beauty in the outer world in which they lived, though perhaps their eyes, in most other respects, were fully as keen as ours. It is certain that their family affections (as in the case of the lowest savages of to-day) were, to say the least, rudimentary, and that all men outside their immediate family were either feared or disliked, or both. When the race emerged from the cloud-covered past into the light of what may be called inferential history, the view men took of the government of the universe, of the character of the beings and forces by which this government was carried on, of the position in which man stood to the governing powers, of his prospects in this life and after it, were (as in the case of the lower races of to-day) gloomy in an extreme degree. Since that time neither the world nor the government of the world have changed, but the gradual alteration in the moral nature of man has made it in his eyes a different place. The bleak and forbidding mountains, the awe-inspiring sea, the gloomy forests, the dark and fearful night, all the aspects of nature which in that old time were charged with dread, have in the place of it become clothed with a new and strange beauty. The whole human race and all living things have put on (in our eyes) a charm and sacredness which in the old times they were far from possessing. The governing powers of the universe (obedient to the same beneficent influence) have been gradually converted from demons into beings and forces less and less inimical, more and more friendly, to man; so that in all respects each age has interpreted the universe for itself, and has more or less discredited the interpretations of previous ages.

Which is the correct interpretation? What mind, of all the vast diversity of the past and present, in all this long series, pictures to itself most correctly the outer world? Let us see. Let us consider for a moment our spiritual genealogy, and dwell on its meaning. Our immediate ancestors were Christians. The spiritual progenitor of Christianity was Judaism. Judaism, having its beginning in that group of tribes collectively called Terachite or Hebrew—Ibrim, those of the other side (i. e., of the Euphrates)—descended from the mythical Ab-orham or Abraham [137-91f]; these tribes being themselves a twig of the great Semitic branch of the Caucasian race stock, sprang directly from Chaldean polytheism. Chaldean polytheism again in its turn was a development in direct descent of the Sun and Nature worship of the primitive undivided Caucasian family. The Sun and Nature worship again no doubt had its root in, and drew its life from, initial Fetishism, or the direct worship of individual earthly objects. In this long descent (although we apply different names to different parts of the continuous series, as if there were lines of demarcation between these different parts) there has been no break, and in all the thousands of years never such a thing as a new departure. In these spiritual matters the maxim "Natura non facit saltum" holds as firmly as it does in physics and geology. The whole affair is a simple matter of growth strictly analogous to the unfolding of the branch from the bud, or of the plant from its seed. As has been well said: "La religion étant un des produits vivants de l'humanité doit vivre, c'est-a-dire, changer avec elle" [136: 45]. And on last analysis it will be found that under the vast diversity of external appearance, from Fetishism to Christianity—underlying the infinite variety of formulas, creeds and dogmas resumed under these five heads—the essential element upon which all else depends, which underlies all and is the soul of all, is the attitude of the moral nature. And all changes in the intellectual form and outer aspect of religion are as obedient to the gradual change taking place in this as are the movements of the hands and wheels of the watch to the expansive force of its mainspring. The external world stands fast, but the spirit of man continually grows, and as it does so its own vast Brocken shadow (thrown out by the moral nature but shaped by the intellect), which it projects on the midst of the infinite unknown, necessarily (like a dissolving view) changes and changes, following the alterations in the substance (that is, the soul of man) which gives life and reality to the shadowy phantom which plain folk call their creed, and which metaphysicians call the philosophy of the absolute.

But in thus interpreting, from age to age, the unknown universe in which we live, it is to be observed that we are (on the whole) constantly giving a better and better report of it. We attribute to our gods (as the ages pass) better and better characters, and we constantly expect at their hands better and better treatment, both in the present life and after death. That means (of course) that the quantity of trust or faith which we possess is steadily increasing and encroaching upon its opposite, fear, which is as constantly lessening. So equally it may be said of charity, sympathy, or affection, that the constant increase of that faculty is steadily changing to us the aspect of the visible world, just as the growth of faith is altering the image we form for ourselves of that greater world which is invisible. Nor is there any indication that this double process has come to an end or that it is likely to come to an end.

VIII.

The length of time during which the race has been possessed of any given faculty may be more or less accurately estimated from various indications. In cases in which the birth of the faculty took place in comparatively recent times—within, for instance, the last twenty-five or thirty thousand years—philology (as we have seen) may assist materially in determining the approximate date of its appearance. But for comparatively old faculties, such as the human intellect or simple consciousness, this means necessarily entirely fails us. We fall back, then, upon the following tests:

1. The age at which the faculty appears in the individual man at the present time.
2. The more or less universality of the faculty in the adult members of the race to-day.
3. The readiness, or the reverse, with which the faculty is lost —as in sickness.
4. The relative frequency with which the faculty makes its appearance in dreams.

1. Of each of our mental faculties it may be predicated that it has its own normal or average age for appearing in the individual; as, for instance, memory and simple consciousness appear within a few days after birth; curiosity ten weeks after; use of tools twelve months after; shame, remorse, and a sense of the ludicrous —all of them about fifteen months after birth. Now it is to be noted that in every instance the time of appearance of a faculty in an infant corresponds with the stage at which the same faculty

appears (as far as can be at present ascertained) in the ascending animal scale, just as in the case of later appearing faculties, their age of appearing in the individual corresponds with their period of appearance in the race; for instance, memory and simple consciousness occur in animals as primitive as the echinodermata, while the use of tools is not met with below monkeys; and shame and remorse and a sense of the ludicrous are almost if not entirely confined (among animals) to the anthropoid ape and the dog. So of purely human faculties, self consciousness, which appears in the individual at the average age of about three years, made its appearance in the race certainly more than a thousand centuries ago, while the musical sense, which does not appear in the individual before adolescence or puberty, cannot (to judge by the records) have existed in the race more than a very few thousand years.

2. The longer a race has been in possession of a given faculty the more universal will that faculty be in the race. This proposition scarcely needs proof. Every new faculty must occur first of all in one individual, and as other individuals attain to the status of that one they too will acquire it, until, after perhaps many thousand years, the whole race, having attained to that status, the faculty will have become universal.

3. The longer a race has been in possession of a given faculty the more firmly is that faculty fixed in each individual of the race who possesses it. In other words: the more recent is any given faculty the more easily is it lost. Authority for this proposition (which indeed it scarcely needs) will be quoted where it is stated in another connection. It is almost, if not quite, a self-evident proposition.

4. A study of dreaming seems to reveal the fact that in sleep such mind as we have differs from our waking mind, especially by being more primitive; that, in fact, it would be almost strictly true to say that in dreams we pass backward into a prehuman mental life; that the intellectual faculties which we possess in dreams are, especially, recepts as distinguished from our waking concepts; while in the moral realm they are equally those facul-

ties, such as remorse, shame, surprise, along with the older and more basic sense functions, which belonged to us before we reached the human plane, and that the more modern mental faculties, such as color sense, musical sense, self consciousness, the human moral nature, have no existence in this condition, or if any of them do occur it is only as a rare exception.

Let us now compare one with the other a few of the faculties which have been already mentioned in the light of the rules laid down. To do this will give us, more clearly than perhaps anything else could, a definite notion of the growth of mind by the successive addition of new functions. For this purpose let us take (as a few examples and to stand for all) simple consciousness, shame, self consciousness, color sense, the human moral nature, the musical sense, cosmic consciousness.

Simple consciousness makes its appearance in the human infant within a few days after birth; it is absolutely universal in the human race; it dates far back before the earliest mammals; it is lost only in deep sleep and coma; it is present in all dreams.

Shame, remorse and a sense of the ludicrous are all said to be born in the human infant at about the age of fifteen months; they are all prehuman faculties and are all found in the dog and in apes, and they undoubtedly existed in our prehuman ancestors; they are all almost universal in the race, being absent only in very low idiots; they are all three common in dreams.

Self consciousness makes its appearance in the child at the average age of three years; it is not present in any species but the human; it is, in fact, that faculty, the possession of which by an individual constitutes him a man. It is not universal in our race, being absent in all true idiots; that is, it is permanently absent in about one in each thousand human beings in Europe and America.*

---

* As regards the absence of self consciousness in idiots the examination of the inmates of a large idiot asylum revealed the fact that the faculty was absent in fully ninety per cent. The patients examined were nearly all over ten years of age. Of course a few of them might attain to self consciousness later on. Dictionaries and works on idiocy [101] define an idiot as ''a human being destitute of the ordinary mental powers''; but it would seem that ''a human being in whom, the usual age being past, in consequence of atavism, self consciousness has not been developed,'' would be more accurate and better. While the defini-

There must, however, be many members of low races, such as the Bushmen of South Africa * and native Australians, who never attain to this faculty. In our ancestry self consciousness dates back to the first true man. Thousands of years must have elapsed between its first appearance and its universality, just as thousands of years are now passing between the first cases of cosmic consciousness and *its* universality. A race, we are told, unclothed, walking erect,† gregarious, without a true language, to a limited extent tool-using, destitute of marriage, government, or any insti-

---

tion of imbecile would be: "A human being, who, though self conscious, is, in consequence of atavism, to a large extent destitute of the ordinary mental powers."

* For the mental status of Bushmen see Anderson [1-9, 216, 217, 218, 227, 228, 232, 291], who gives the facts from actual observation without speculation or theory; he is a close observer and evidently a faithful reporter. See also some remarkable pages by Olive Schreiner [90-2, 4] in which she describes these same Bushmen (as does Anderson) from personal observation. Along with much else she states, for instance, that: "These small people had no fixed social organization; wandering about in hordes or as solitary individuals, without any settled habitation, they slept at night under the rocks or in wild-dog holes, or they made themselves a curious little wall of loose bushes, raised up on the side from which the wind blew, and strangely like an animal's lair; and this they left again when the morning broke. They had no flocks or herds and lived on the wild game, or when that failed them, ate snakes, scorpions, insects or offal, or visited the flocks of the Hottentots. They wore no clothing of any kind, and their weapons were bows and arrows, the strings of the bows being made from the sinews of wild animals, and the arrows tipped with sharpened bones or flint stones, poisoned with the juice of a bulb or dipped in the body of a poisonous caterpillar: and these formed their only property. They had no marriage ceremony and no permanent sex relations, any man or woman cohabiting during pleasure; maternal feeling was at its lowest ebb, mothers readily forsaking their young or disposing of them for a trifle; and paternal feeling was non-existent. Their language is said by those who have closely studied it to be so imperfect that the clear expression of even the very simplest ideas is difficult. They have no word for wife, for marriage, for nation: and their minds appear to be in the same simple condition as their language. The complex mental operations necessary for the maintenance of life under civilized conditions they have apparently no power of performing; no member of the race has in any known instance been taught to read or write, nor to grasp religious conceptions clearly, though great efforts have been made to instruct them." It seems impossible to believe that as a race these creatures are self conscious.

† *Walking erect.* If the view here taken of mental, and human, evolution should be accepted it would throw some light on our remote past. One corollary from it would be that our ancestors walked erect for hundreds of thousands of years before they became self conscious—that is, before they became men and began to speak. The age at which infants begin to walk is (mentally) the age of the dog and the ape. From fifteen or eighteen months to three years of age the child passes through the mental strata which lie between these animals and self consciousness. During that time the child's receptual intelligence becomes more and more perfect, the recepts themselves become more and more complex, nearer and nearer to concepts, until these last are actually formed and self consciousness is established. It would seem that something like a half million of years of evolution must have elapsed between the status of the highest anthropoid apes and that of man. Perhaps this may be a comforting reflection to those people who do not like the idea of having descended from some Simian form.

tution; animal, but in virtue of its relatively high moral nature (making it gregarious) and its highly developed receptual intelligence, king of animals, developed self consciousness, and by that fact became man. It is impossible to say how long ago it was when this event occurred, but it could not have been less than several hundred thousand years. This faculty is lost much more easily than is simple consciousness. We lose it in coma and also often in the delirium of fever; in certain forms of insanity, as in mania, it is often lost for weeks and months at a time; lastly, it is never present in dreams.

The color sense has been already considered. It remains to say a few words from the present point of view. It comes into existence gradually in the individual—at three or four years there may be a trace of it. At eight years of age it was found by Jeffries [135-242] still absent in a large percentage of children. Twenty to thirty per cent. of schoolboys are said to be color-blind, while only four per cent. of adult males are so. Dr. Favre, of Lyons [135-243] reported in 1874 to the French Congress for the Advancement of Science, at Lille, "some observations that seemed to him to prove that congenital color-blindness was curable" [135-242], but it does not seem to have occurred to him that the color sense, being invariably absent in very young children, and making its appearance at a variable age, as the child advances toward maturity, color blindness would necessarily appear to the teacher, watching the development of the child and exercising its sense of sight upon colors, to be "cured." We have seen above that the color sense in the race cannot be many tens of thousands of years old.

Color sense is absent in one human being out of every forty-seven. It is seldom present in dreams, and when it does occur, that is, when any color is seen in a dream, it is generally that color which for good reasons was first perceived by man, namely, red.

The following occurrence illustrates (in a striking manner) the usual absence of the color sense during the partial consciousness which occurs in sleep. A man whose hair is white dreamed that he was looking in a glass and saw plainly that his hair was not only much thicker than he knew it to be in fact, but instead of being white, as he also knew it to be, it was black. Now he well remembered in his dream that his hair had never been black. It had, in fact, been a light brown. He wondered (it is worth mentioning here that wonder or surprise is a prehuman faculty, and is common in dreams) in his dream that his hair should be black, remembering distinctly that it had never been so. The important thing to note about the dream under consideration is that, though it was clear to the dreamer's mind that his hair had never been black, yet he did not remember that it had been brown. For some reason there was a difficulty in calling up before consciousness any color. The same man dreamed that he had wounded with a knife an enemy who had attacked him; the bleeding was profuse but the blood was *white;* he knew in his dream that it should not be white, but no image of its true color or of any color presented itself.

The human moral nature includes many faculties, such as conscience, the abstract sense of right and wrong, sexual love as distinguished from sexual desire or instinct, parental and filial love as distinguished from the corresponding instincts (man has both these instincts in common with the brutes as well as the higher feelings), love of our fellow men as such, love of the beautiful, awe, reverence, sense of duty or responsibility, sympathy, compassion, faith. No human nature is complete without these and others; it is therefore a very complex function; but for the purpose of the present argument it must be treated as if it were a simple sense. Now at what age does this human moral nature appear in individual man? It is never present in quite young children. It is often still absent at puberty and even at adolescence. It is a late acquired faculty. It would probably not be far wrong to say that the average age for its appearance in the individual is somewhere about fifteen years. It would seem clear from a study of history that our human moral nature cannot be more than some ten or twelve thousand years old. For a careful consideration of the records that have come down to us from the early Romans, Hellenes, Hebrews, Egyptians, Assyrians and Babylonians would indicate unmistakably that as we go back into the past this faculty tapers down toward the vanishing point, and if it continues so to taper as we ascend the ages all of what we distinctively call our human moral nature would certainly have disappeared by the time we had got back the number of centuries mentioned—ten or twelve thousand years.

In what proportion of the men and women of civilized countries does the human moral nature fail to appear? There are so many men and women who have a partial moral nature, so many who, having little or none, wear (as well as may be) the outer semblance of one; the judging of men and women in this regard is so difficult—the problem is so veiled and so complicated—that it is impossible to give more than an opinion. But let any one who is curious read a few such books as those by Despine [66] and Ellis [76]—then view the men and women among whom he lives by the light thus supplied, and he will be forced to the conclusion that the proportion of the adults who have little or no, or an undeveloped, moral nature is far greater than of those who have little or no, or an undeveloped, color sense. We probably should not be far wrong if we said that at least forty men and women out of every thousand in America and Europe are in the position indicated.

Then how many races of men are there still living upon the earth none or very few of the members of which have what could be called from the point of view of our civilization a human moral nature? Again, while self consciousness is lost, not of course always, but frequently, in insanity and fever, the moral nature is, we must all admit, subject to much more frequent lapses and absences and with far less cause.

Self consciousness appeared in the race, as we have seen, about three hundred thousand years ago. The above considerations would point to a very much later date for the appearance of the moral nature. And do not all records and historic indications, so far as they go, support this inference?

Finally, the musical sense (a faculty which is now in act of being born) does not appear in the individual before adolescence.

PSYCHOGENESIS OF MAN—ILLUSTRATED BY A FEW FACULTIES

Name of Faculty	Approximate Average Age of Appearance in Man	Absent in what proportion of Adult Members of Race at Present Time	Time of Appearance of Faculty in Race	How far back does Faculty Reach into Prehuman forms?	With what Degree of Facility is the Faculty Lost in Man?
Memory	Few days after birth	None	Prehuman	To the Echinodermata	Only lost in deep sleep and coma; present in dreams
Simple Consciousness	Few days after birth	None	Prehuman	To the Echinodermata	Only lost in deep sleep and coma; present in dreams
Curiosity	Ten weeks	None	Prehuman	Insects and spiders	Only lost in deep sleep and coma; present in dreams
Use of Tools	Twelve months	None	Prehuman	Monkeys	Present in dreams
Shame	Fifteen months	None	Prehuman	Anthropoid apes and dogs	Present in dreams
Remorse	Fifteen months	None	Prehuman	Anthropoid apes and dogs	Present in dreams
Sense of Ludicrous	Fifteen months	None	Prehuman	Anthropoid apes and dogs	Present in dreams
Self Consciousness	Three years	In 1 in 1,000	300,000 years ago	Peculiar to man	Lost in coma, delirium, often in mania; never present in dreams
Color Sense	Four years	In 1 in 47	30,000 or 40,000 years ago	Not in man's progenitors	Seldom present in dreams
Sense of Fragrance	Five years	?	?	Not in man's progenitors	Not present in dreams
Human Moral Nature	Fifteen years	In 1 in 20 or 25	10,000 years ago	Peculiar to man	Unstable—easily and constantly lost; not present in dreams
Musical Sense	Eighteen years	In more than half	Less than 5,000 years ago	Not in man's progenitors	Only occasionally present; hardly ever present in dreams, even in case of musicians
Cosmic Consciousness	Thirty-five years	In all but one in many millions	Just dawning now	Peculiar to man	Only present few seconds to few hours in any case; then passes away of itself

It does not exist in more than half the members of our race. It has existed less (perhaps considerably less) than five thousand years. It is never, or almost never, present in dreams, even in the case of professional musicians. While self consciousness in insanity is lost, as said, occasionally, the musical sense in that condition might be said to be invariably lost—at least after an experience of twenty-five years, with about five thousand cases of lunacy, the writer cannot recall a case where the musical sense was retained, the person being insane.

The accompanying summary, in tabular form, of the main facts concerning the evolution of the faculties mentioned and some others, will make, it is believed, the whole subject more intelligible than any long exposition thereof. The figures in the table and text are not given as being exact, but for the sake of conveying a clear idea which it is thought will be correct enough for the present purpose.

To sum up: as ontogeny is nothing else but philogeny in petto —that is, as the evolution of the individual is necessarily the evolution of the race in an abridged form, simply because it cannot in the nature of things be anything else—cannot follow any other lines, there being no other lines for it to follow—it is plain that organs and faculties (speaking broadly and generally) *must* appear in the individual in the same order in which they appeared in the race, and the one being known, the other may with confidence be assumed.

When a new faculty appears in a race it will be found, in the very beginning, in one individual of that race; later it will be found in a few individuals; after a further time in a larger percentage of the members of the race; still later in half the members; and so on, until, after thousands of generations, an individual who misses having the faculty is regarded as a monstrosity. Note, too—and this is important—when the new faculty appears, especially if it be in the direct line of the ascent of the race, as in the case of Simple, Self, or Cosmic, Consciousness, it *must* appear first *in a member, then in members, of the race who have reached full maturity.* For an immature individual (other things being equal) cannot over-pass or go beyond a mature individual of the same race.

Thus, as the eons pass, has the great trunk of the tree of life grown taller and from time to time shot forth twigs which have grown to branches, and these again to noble limbs, which in their turn have put out twigs and branches, many of them of great size and in number uncountable. We know that the tree has not ceased to grow, that even now, as always, it is putting forth new buds, and that the old shoots, twigs and branches are most of them increasing in size and strength. Shall the growth stop to-day? It does not seem likely. It seems more likely that other limbs and branches undreamed of to-day shall spring from the tree, and that the main trunk which from mere life grew into sensitive life, simple consciousness and self consciousness shall yet pass into still higher forms of life and consciousness.

CHAPTER 3.

Devolution.

As in the evolution of an individual tree some branches flourish while others fail; as in a forest some trees grow tall and stretch out wide branches while others are stunted and die out; as in the onward and upward progress of any species some individuals are in advance of the main body while others lag behind; so in the forward march of the collective human mind across the centuries some individual minds are in the van of the great army, while in the rear of the column stagger and fall vast numbers of defective specimens.

In any race the stability of any faculty is in proportion to the age of the faculty in the race. That is, a comparatively new faculty is more subject to lapse, absence, aberration, to what is called disease, and is more liable to be lost, than an older faculty. To many this proposition will seem a truism. If an organ or faculty has been inherited in a race for, say, a million generations, it seems, a priori, certain that it is more likely to be inherited by a given individual of that race than is an organ or faculty which originated, say, three generations back. A case in point is what is called genius. Genius consists in the possession of a new faculty or new faculties, or in an increased development of an old faculty or old faculties. This being the case, it seems to Galton [92] necessary to write a good sized volume to prove that it is hereditary. So far was that from being an obvious fact that even yet the heredity of genius is far from being universally accepted. But no one ever wrote a book to prove that either sight, hearing, or self consciousness is hereditary, because every one (even the most ignorant) knows without any argument that they are so. On the point in question Darwin says, speaking of horses: "The want of uniformity in the parts which, at the time, are undergoing selection chiefly depends on the strength of the principle of reversion" [67: 288]. That is, parts or organs which are undergoing change by means of selection are liable to lose what has been gained by reverting to the initial condition. And again he says: "It is a general belief among breeders that characters of all kinds become fixed by long continued inheritance" [67: 289]. In another place he speaks of the "fluctuating and, as far as we can judge, never ending variability of our domestic productions, the plasticity of their whole organization" [67: 485], and he attributes this instability to the recent changes these have undergone under the influence of the artificial selection to which they have been subjected. And in still another place Darwin speaks of "the extreme variability of our domesticated animals and cultivated plants."

But it is scarcely necessary to carry this argument further. Any one who is willing to give the matter a thought will admit that the shorter time an organ or faculty has been possessed by a race the more unstable must it be in the race, and, consequently, in the individual; the more liable will it be to be dropped; the more liable to be defective; the more liable to vary; the more liable to be or to become imperfect—as we say, diseased. And that, per contra, the longer time an organ or faculty has existed in any race, the more certain it is to be inherited and the more certain it is to assume a definite, typical character—that is, the more certain it is to be normal, the more certain it is to agree with the norm or type of the said organ or faculty.   In other words, the less likely it is to be imperfect—what we call defective or diseased.   This being allowed, it will readily be granted: 1st, That the race whose evolution is the most rapid will (other things being equal) have the most breakdowns; and, 2d, That in any given race those functions whose evolution is the most rapid will be the most subject to breakdowns.

If these principles be applied to the domesticated animals (which have, most of them, within the last few hundred generations, been much differentiated by artificial selection), they will explain what has often been looked upon as anomalous—namely, the much greater liability to disease and early death of these as compared with their wild prototypes.   For that domestic animals *are* more liable to disease and premature death than wild, is admitted on all hands.   The same principle will explain also how it is that the more highly bred an animal is—that is, the more widely it has been differentiated in late generations from a previous type —the more liable will it be to disease and premature death.

Taking now these general rules home to ourselves—to the human race—we find them to mean that those organs and functions which have been the latest acquired will be most often defective, absent, abnormal, diseased.   But it is notorious that in civilized man, especially in the Aryan race, the functions which have undergone most change in the last few thousand years are those called mental—that great group of functions (sensuous, intellectual, moral) which depend upon, spring from, the two great nervous systems—the cerebro-spinal and the great sympathetic. This great group of functions has grown, expanded, put forth new shoots and twigs, and is still in the act of producing new faculties, at a rate immeasurably greater than any other part of the human organism.   If this is so then within this great congeries of faculties it is inevitable that we should meet with constant lapses, omissions, defects, breakdowns.

Clinical observation teaches day by day that the above reasoning is solidly grounded. It presents lapses of all degrees and in unlimited varieties; lapses in sense function, such as color-blindness and music deafness; lapses in the moral nature, of the whole or a part; in the intellect, of one or several faculties; or lapses, more or less complete, of the whole intellect, as in imbecility and idiocy. But over and above all these lapses, and as a necessary accompaniment of them, we have that inevitable breaking down of function, once established in the individual, which we call insanity, as distinguished from the various forms and degrees of idiocy. For it is easy to see that if a function or faculty belonging to any given species is liable for any general cause to be dropped in a certain proportion of the individuals of that species, it must be also liable to become diseased—that is, to break down—in cases where it is not dropped. For if the faculty in question is by no means always developed in the individual—if it quite frequently fails to appear—that must mean that in many other cases in which it does appear it will not be fully and solidly formed. We cannot imagine a jump from the total non-appearance of a given function in certain members of a species to the absolute perfection and solidity of the same function in the rest of the members. We know that species do not grow that way. We know that in a race in which we have some men seven feet high and others only four that we shall find, if we look, men of all statures between these extremes. We know that in all cases extremes presented by the race are bridged (from one to the other) by full sets of intermediary specimens. One man can lift a thousand pounds, another can lift only a hundred; but between these are men the limit of whose strength fills up the whole gap between the hundred and the thousand pounds. One man dies of old age at forty years, another at one hundred and thirty years, and every year and month between forty years and one hundred and thirty years is the limit of some man's possible life. The same law that holds for the limit of faculties holds also for the solidity and permanence of faculties. We know that in some men the intellectual functions are so unstable that as soon as they are established they crumble down—crushed (as it were) by their own weight—like a badly built house, the walls of which are not strong enough to sustain the roof. Such are extreme cases of so-called developmental insanity—cases in which the mind falls into ruins as soon as it comes into existence or even before it is fully formed; cases of insanity of puberty and adolescence, in which nature is barely able to form or half form a normal mind and totally unable to sustain it, the mind, consequently, running down at once back into chaos. The hopelessness of this class of cases (as regards recovery) is well understood by all alienists, and it is not difficult to see why such insanities should and must be practically incurable, since their very existence denotes the absence of the elements necessary to form and maintain a normal human mind in the subjects in question.

In the realm of insanity, properly so called—that is, excluding the idiocies—these cases occupy the extreme position at one end of the scale, while those persons who only become maniacal or melancholic under the most powerful exciting causes, such as child-birth and old age, occupy the other end. That is, we have a class in whom the mind, without a touch, crumbles into ruin as soon as formed or even before it is fully formed. Then we have another class in which the balance of the mental faculties is only overturned by the rudest shocks, and then only temporarily, since the cases to which I refer recover in a few weeks or months if placed under favorable conditions. But between these extremes the whole wide intermediate space is filled with an infinite variety of phases of insanity, exhibiting every possible condition of mental stability and instability between the two extremes noticed. But throughout the whole range of mental alienation this law holds, namely: that the latest evolved of the mental functions, whether intellectual or moral, suffer first and suffer most, while the earliest evolved of the mental and moral functions suffer (if at all) the latest and the least.

If the mind be likened to a growing tree, then it can be said that the lesser onsets of insanity shrivel its leaves—paralyze, or partially paralyze, their functions for a time, the leaves standing for the later formed and more fragile emotions and concepts, and especially for the later formed combinations of these; that deeper attacks kill the leaves and damage the finer twigs; that still more profound disturbances kill the finer twigs and injure the larger; and so on, until, in the most profound and deep-rooted insanities, as in the developmental dementias, the tree is left a bare, ghastly trunk, without leaves or twigs and almost without branches.

And in all this process of destruction the older formed faculties, such as perception and memory, desire for food and drink, shrinking from injury, and the more basic sense functions, endure the longest; while, as has been said, the latest evolved functions crumble down first, then the next latest, and so on.

A fact that well illustrates the contention that insanity is essentially the breaking down of mental faculties which are unstable chiefly because they are recent, and that it rests therefore upon an evolution which is modern and still in progress, is the comparative absence of insanity among negroes.

It has been said that the large percentage of insanity in America and Europe depends directly upon the rapid evolution in late millenniums of the mind of the Aryan people. Very few would claim that the negro mind is advancing at anything like the same rate. As a consequence of these different rates of progression we have in the Aryan people of America a much higher percentage of insanity than is found in the negro race.

When the United States census of 1880 was taken it was found that among forty-three millions of white people there were eighty-six thousand insane—exactly one in five hundred—while among six and three-quarter million negroes only a little more than six thousand were insane, which is a proportion of only about one to eleven hundred. Doubtless if we had statistics of other backward and stationary peoples a similar state of matters would be found—all such facts as we have leading to the conclusion that among savages and semi-savages there exists comparatively little insanity.

In conclusion the results arrived at in this chapter may be summed up as follows:

1. The stability of a faculty in the individual depends upon its age in the race. The older the faculty the more stable it is, and the less old the less stable.

2. The race whose evolution is most rapid will be the most subject to breakdown.

3. Those functions in any given race whose evolutions are the most rapid will be the most subject to breakdown.

4. In the more progressive families of the Aryan race the mental faculties have for some millenniums last past developed with great rapidity.

5. In this race the large number of mental breakdowns, commonly called insanity, are due to the rapid and recent evolution of those faculties in that race.

PART III.

FROM SELF TO COSMIC CONSCIOUSNESS.

I.

As the faculties referred to in the last division of this volume, and many more, came into existence in the race, each in its own time, when the race was ready for it, let us assume, as we must, that growth, evolution, development, or whatever we choose to call it, has (as thus exemplified) always gone on, is going on now, and (as far as we can tell) will always go on. If we are right in such an assumption new faculties will from time to time arise in the mind as, in the past, new faculties have arisen. This being granted, let us assume that what in this book is called Cosmic Consciousness is such a nascent, such a werdende, faculty. And now let us see what we know about this new sense, state, faculty, or whatever it may be called. And, first, it may be noted that the new sense does not appear by chance in this man or that. It is necessary for its appearance that an exalted human personality should exist and supply the pre-conditions for its birth. In the great cases especially is there an exceptional development of some or all of the ordinary human faculties. Note particularly, since that case is unmistakably known to us, the singular perfection of the intellectual and moral faculties and of the special senses in Walt Whitman [103: 57-71]. It is probable that an approximation to this evolutionary excellence is necessary in all cases. Then certainly in some, probably in all, cases the person has an exceptional physique—exceptional beauty of build and carriage, exceptionally handsome features, exceptional health, exceptional sweetness of temper, exceptional magnetism.

II.

The faculty itself has many names, but they have not been understood or recognized. It will be well to give some of them here. They will be better understood as we advance. Either Gautama himself, or some one of his early disciples, called it "Nirvâna" because of the "extinction" of certain lower mental faculties (such as the sense of sin, fear of death, desire of wealth, etc., etc.) which is directly incident upon its birth. This subjugation of the old personality along with the birth of the new is, in fact, almost equivalent to the annihilation of the old and the creation of a new self. The word Nirvâna is defined as "the state to which the Buddhist saint is to aspire as the highest aim and highest good." Jesus called the new condition "the Kingdom of God" or the "Kingdom of Heaven," because of the peace and happiness which belong to it and which are perhaps its most characteristic features. Paul called it "Christ." He speaks of himself as "a man in Christ," of "them that are in Christ." He also calls it "the Spirit" and "the Spirit of God." After Paul had entered Cosmic Consciousness he knew that Jesus had possessed the cosmic sense and that he was living (as it were) the life of Jesus—that another individuality, another self, lived in him. This second self he called Christ (the divinely sent deliverer), identifying it not so much with the man Jesus, as with the deliverer which was to be sent and which had been sent in his person, who was both Jesus (the ordinary self conscious man) and Messiah (the herald and exemplar of the new, higher race). The duplex personality of men having cosmic consciousness will appear many times as we proceed and will be seen to be a constant and prominent phenomenon. Mohammed called the cosmic sense "Gabriel," and seems to have looked upon it as a distinctly separate person who lived in him and spoke to him. Dante called it "Beatrice" ("Making Happy"), a name almost or quite equivalent to "Kingdom of Heaven." Balzac called the new man a "specialist" and the new condition "Specialism." Whitman called cosmic con-

sciousness "My Soul," but spoke of it as if it were another person;
for instance:

> O soul repressless, I with thee and thou with me. . . .
> We too take ship O soul. . . .
> With laugh and many a kiss . . .
> O soul thou pleasest me, I thee.

Bacon (in the Sonnets) has treated the cosmic sense so emphatically as a distinct person that the world for three hundred years has taken him at his word and has agreed that the "person" in question (whatever his name may have been) was a young friend of the poet's!

To illustrate the objectification of this purely subjective phenomenon (though it must be remembered that to the person with cosmic consciousness the terms objective and subjective lose their old meaning—and "objects gross" and the "unseen soul" become "one"), it will not be amiss to quote a passage [173: 5] from a poet who, though he is a case of cosmic consciousness, is not included in the present volume for the reason that the present writer has not been able to obtain the details necessary for that purpose.

> So mused a traveler on the earthly plane
> Being in himself a type of all mankind.
> For aspirations dim at first possessed
> Him only, rising vaguely in his dreams,
> Till in ripe years his early musings changed
> To inspiration and the light of soul.
> Then vision came, and in the light he saw
> What he had hoped now openly revealed;
> And much besides—the inmost soul of things,
> And "beauty" as the crown of life itself,
> Ineffable, transcending mortal form;
> For robed in light, no longer fantasy,
> Before his gaze the true "ideal" stood,
> Sublimely fair, beyond conception, clothed
> In beauty and divinest symmetry.
> Yet pined he not like him of Latmos when
> In dreaming ecstasy, upon the hills
> Beneath the moon, he saw his love unveiled;
> For well he knew the crowning of his life
> Was in that vision and would be fulfilled.

Nay, was fulfilled, for henceforth by his side
A radiant being stood, his guiding light
And polar star, that as a magnet held
Him in the hold of ever-during love!
But how describe this being henceforth his?
What words can tell what words transcend, but say
That she was fair beyond all human thought?
For who could paint those features and that form
So exquisitely moulded that no art
Could reach them, or convey in any mode
The smile upon those rosy lips or catch
And give the full expression of those eyes,
So wonderful, half veiled beneath the sweep
Of soft and curving lashes, that enhanced
Beyond describing the effect that flowed
From out the liquid depths of those full orbs,
The founts of love, so full of smouldering fire
And passion, yet so tender and so chaste?
Her every movement, too, so perfect, seemed
Like nature heightened by unconscious art,
And all her bearing gentleness itself;
For not that majesty that overawes—
That high, imperious consciousness of worth,
That makes the lowly shrink abashed—was hers,
But in its stead was all the winning grace
And sweetness that immortal Love could add
To beautify its shrine and make thereof
A fitting habitation for itself:
For bending forward with that wondrous look,
So inexpressible, she seemed to say:
"Thou art mine own, mine equal and my spouse,
My complement, without whom I were nought;
So in mine eyes thou art more fair than I,
For in thee only is my life fulfilled."
Then added, in harmonious voice, aloud:
"Thou long hast thought upon life's mystery,
Its vast, eternally recurring rounds
Of rest and rebirth and activity,
And sought therein the passage of the soul
From light to dark, from dark to light again.
Come then with me, and we will see in part
The latter in its human phase unveiled."
So saying, with her presence she endowed
Him with new senses, faculties and powers,
That far surpassed the limits of the old.

III.

It has already been incidentally mentioned that a race entering upon the possession of a new faculty, especially if this be in the line of the direct ascent of the race, as is certainly the case with cosmic consciousness, the new faculty will necessarily be acquired at first not only by the best specimens of the race but also when these are at their best—that is, at full maturity and before the decline incident to age has set in. What, now, are the facts in this regard as to the coming of the cosmic sense?

They may be summarized in a few words as follows: Of thirty-four cases, in which illumination was instantaneous and the period at which it occurred was with some degree of certainty known, the age at which the person passed into cosmic consciousness was in one instance twenty-four years; in three, thirty years; in two, thirty-one years; in two, thirty-one and a half years; in three, thirty-two years; in one, thirty-three years; in two, thirty-four years; in eight, thirty-five years; in two, thirty-six years; in two, thirty-seven years; in two, thirty-eight years; in three, thirty-nine years; in one, forty years; in one, forty-nine years, and, in one, fifty-four years.

Evidence will be given as the cases are treated individually, and the age of each person at illumination will be given below in a tabular statement, along with other facts.

IV.

Cosmic Consciousness, then, appears in individuals mostly of the male sex, who are otherwise highly developed—men of good intellect, of high moral qualities, of superior physique. It appears at about that time of life when the organism is at its high watermark of efficiency, at the age of thirty to forty years. It must have been that the immediate precursor of Cosmic Consciousness—Self Consciousness—also appeared at first in mid-life, here and there, in isolated cases, in the most advanced specimens of the race, becoming more and more nearly universal (as the race grew up to it), manifesting itself at an earlier and earlier age, until (as we see) it declares itself now in every fairly constituted individual, at about the age of three years.

Analogy, then, would lead us to believe that the step in promotion which is the subject of this volume also awaits the whole race —that a time will come when to be without the faculty in question will be a mark of inferiority parallel to the absence at present of the moral nature. The presumption seems to be that the new sense will become more and more common and show itself earlier in life, until after many generations it will appear in each normal individual at the age of puberty or even earlier; then go on becoming still more universal, and appearing at a still earlier age, until, after many thousands of generations, it shows itself immediately after infancy in nearly every member of the race.

V.

It must be clearly understood that all cases of Cosmic Consciousness are not on the same plane. Or, if we speak of Simple Consciousness, Self Consciousness and Cosmic Consciousness as each occupying a plane, then, as the range of Self Consciousness on *its plane* (where one man may be an Aristotle, a Cæsar, a Newton, or a Comte, while his neighbor on the next street may be intellectually and morally, to all appearance, little if at all above the animal in his stable) is far greater than the range of Simple Consciousness *in any given species* on its plane, so we must suppose that the range of Cosmic Consciousness (given millions of cases, as on the other planes) is greater than that of Self Consciousness, and it probably is in fact very much greater both in kind and degree: that is to say, given a world peopled with men having Cosmic Consciousness, they would vary both in the way of greater and less intellectual ability, and greater and less moral and spiritual elevation, and also in the way of variety of character, more than would the inhabitants of a planet on the plane of Self Consciousness. Within the plane of Cosmic Consciousness one man shall be a god while another shall not be, to casual observation, lifted so very much above ordinary humanity, however much his inward life may be exalted, strengthened and purified by the new sense.   But, as the Self Conscious man (however degraded) is in fact almost infinitely above the animal with merely simple consciousness, so any man permanently endowed with the Cosmic Sense would be almost infinitely higher and nobler than any man who is Self Conscious merely.   And not only so, but the man who has had the Cosmic Sense for even a few moments only will probably never again descend to the spiritual level of the merely self conscious man, but twenty, thirty or forty years afterwards he will still feel within him the purifying, strengthening and exalting effect of that divine illumination, and many of those about him will recognize that his spiritual stature is above that of the average man.

VI.

The hypothesis adopted by the present writer requires that cases of cosmic consciousness should become more numerous from age to age, and not only so but that they should become more perfect, more pronounced.   What are the facts?   Putting aside minor cases, such as must have appeared and been forgotten by hundreds in the last few millenniums, of those given above at least thirteen are so great that they can never fade from human memory—namely: Gautama, Jesus, Paul, Plotinus, Mohammed, Dante, Las Casas, John Yepes, Francis Bacon, Jacob Behmen, William Blake, Balzac, Walt Whitman.

From Gautama to Dante we count eighteen hundred years, within which period we have five cases.   Again from Dante to the present day we count six hundred years, in which we have eight cases.   That is to say, while in the earlier period there was one case to every three hundred and sixty years, in the later there was a case to each seventy-five years.   In other words, cosmic consciousness has been 4.8 times more frequent during the latter period than it was during the former.   And before the time of Gautama?   There were probably no, or few and imperfectly developed, cases.

We know that at present there are many of what may be called lesser cases, but the number of these cannot be compared with the number of similar cases in the past, for the reason that the latter are lost. It must also be remembered that the thirteen "great cases" given above are only perhaps a small fraction of cases just as great which have occurred since the time of Gautama, for probably only a small proportion of the "great cases" undertake and carry through work which ensures them remembrance. How easily might the memory even of Jesus have been obliterated from the minds of his contemporaries and followers almost before it was born. Many to-day think that, all else granted, if he had not been immediately followed by Paul, his work and name would have expired together almost with the generation that heard him speak.

So true is this that so able a man as Auguste Comte considers St. Paul "le vrai fondateur du Catholicisme" (which in this connection is synonymous with "Christianisme") [65: 356], gives him the eighth month in the "Calendrier Positiviste" [65: 332], and does not even award a day to Jesus, so little part did this latter seem to him to have played in the evolution of religion and of the race.

And even of those who write, the work and memory must have often died and been lost. Of one of the greatest of these it may be said that had the great fire occurred only a few years earlier it might possibly have destroyed every copy of the 1623 folio and deprived the world forever of the "Shakespeare" drama. Either the spoken or written work of these men can only, in the nature of things, be appreciated by a select few of their contemporaries and is in almost every case exceedingly liable to be forgotten. That this is as true to-day as in the day of Gautama no one can doubt who has closely followed the career of Walt Whitman. Even in his case the written word would almost certainly have been lost if he had died (as he easily might) from accident or disease during the war, even although at that time three editions of the "Leaves" had been printed. He himself did not consider his message secure from extinction even almost down to the time of his death, although he had labored unremittingly for thirty-five years at the planting of it.

Then as to the relative greatness of ancient and modern cases. The judgment of the world at large must necessarily be against the latter, because the time required to arrive at an appreciation of them has not elapsed. And what is reason and so-called common sense worth in such a question as this, anyway?

As Victor Hugo says of Les Genies: "Choisir entre ces hommes, preferer l'un a l'autre, indiquer du doigt le premier parmi ces premiers, cela ne se peut" [96: 72-3]. What living man, indeed, is able to say, time enough having surely gone by, who was the greater, Gautama or Jesus? And if we cannot decide between these two, still less can we between either of them and, for instance, Whitman.

Many believe to-day that the last named was the greatest spiritual force yet produced by the race—which would mean that he is the greatest case of cosmic consciousness to date. But the balance of opinion would be, of course, thousands to one averse to this contention.

VII.

While its true nature has been (and necessarily so) entirely unapprehended, the *fact* of cosmic consciousness has been long recognized both in the Eastern and Western Worlds, and the great majority of civilized men and women in all countries to-day bow down before teachers who possessed the cosmic sense, and not only so but because they possessed the cosmic sense. And not only does the world at large look up with reverence to these men, but perhaps it would be nothing more than the simple truth to say that all uninspired teachers derive the lessons which they transmit directly or indirectly from the few who have been illumined.

VIII.

It seems that in every, or nearly every, man who enters into cosmic consciousness apprehension is at first more or less excited, the person doubting whether the new sense may not be a symptom or form of insanity. Mohammed was greatly alarmed. I think it is clear that Paul was, and others to be mentioned further on were similarly affected.

The first thing each person asks himself upon experiencing the new sense is: Does what I see and feel represent reality or am I suffering from a delusion? The fact that the new experience seems even more real than the old teachings of simple and self consciousness does not at first fully reassure him, because he probably knows that delusions, when present, possess the mind just as firmly as do actual facts.

True or not true, each person who has the experience in question eventually, perforce, believes in its teachings, accepting them as absolutely as any other teachings whatsoever. This, however, would not prove them true, since the same might be said of the delusions of the insane.

How, then, shall we know that this is a new sense, revealing fact, and not a form of insanity, plunging its subject into delusion? In the first place, the tendencies of the condition in question are entirely unlike, even opposite to, those of mental alienation, these last being distinctly amoral or even immoral, while the former are moral in a very high degree. In the second place, while in all forms of insanity self-restraint—inhibition—is greatly reduced, sometimes even abolished, in cosmic consciousness it is enormously increased. The absolute proof of this last statement can be found in the lives of the men here cited as examples. In the third place (whatever the scoffers of religion may say) it is certain that modern civilization (speaking broadly) rests (as already said) very largely on the teachings of the new sense. The *masters* are taught by it and the rest of the world by them through their books, followers and disciples, so that if what is here called cosmic consciousness is a form of insanity, we are confronted by the terrible fact (were it not an absurdity) that our civilization, including all our highest religions, rests on delusion. But (in the fourth place), far from granting, or for a moment entertaining, such an awful alternative, it can be maintained that we have the same evidence of the objective reality which corresponds to this faculty that we have of the reality which tallies any other sense or faculty whatever. Sight, for instance: You know that the tree standing there, across the field, half a mile away, is real and not an hallucination, because all other persons having the sense of sight to whom you have spoken about it also see it, while if it were an hallucination it would be visible to no one but yourself. By the same method of reasoning do we establish the reality of the objective universe tallying cosmic consciousness. Each person who has the faculty is made aware by it of essentially the same fact or facts. If three men looked at the tree and were asked half an hour afterwards to draw or describe it the three drafts or descriptions would not tally in detail, but in general outline would correspond. Just in the same way do the reports of those who have had cosmic consciousness correspond in all essentials, though in detail they doubtless more or less diverge (but these divergences are fully as much in our misunderstanding of the reports as in the reports themselves). So there is no instance of a person who has been illumined denying or disputing the teaching of another who has passed through the same experience. Paul, however little disposed by his prepossessions to accept them, as soon as he attained to the cosmic sense saw that the teachings of Jesus were true. Mohammed accepted Jesus as not only the greatest of the prophets, but as standing on a plane distinctly above that upon which stood Adam, Noah, Moses and the rest. He says: "And we sent Noah and Abraham and placed in their seed prophecy and the book; and some of them are guided, though many of them are workers of abomination! Then we followed up their footsteps with our apostles; and we followed them up with Jesus the son of Mary; and we gave him the gospel; and we placed in the hearts of those who followed him kindness and compassion" [153: 269]. And Palmer testifies: "Mohammed regards our Lord with particular veneration, and even goes so far as to call him the 'Spirit' and 'Word' of God, the 'Messiah'" [152: 51]. Walt Whitman accepts the teachings of Buddha, Jesus, Paul, Mohammed, especially of Jesus, of whom he knew the most. As he says: "Accepting the gospels, accepting him that was crucified, knowing assuredly that he is divine" [193: 69]. And if, as Whitman once wished: "The great masters might return and study me" [193: 20], nothing is more certain than that they would each and all accept him as "a brother of the radiant summit." So all the men known to the present writer who have been (in greater or less degree) illumined, agree in all essentials with one another, and with all past teachers who have been so. Also, it seems that all men, free from prejudice, who know something of more than one religion, recognize, as does Sir Edwin Arnold, that the great faiths are "Sisters," or, as Arthur Lillie says, that "Buddha and Christ taught much the same doctrine" [110: 8].

IX.

As has been either said or implied already, in order that a man may enter into Cosmic Consciousness he must belong (so to speak) to the top layer of the world of Self Consciousness. Not that he need have an extraordinary intellect (this faculty is rated, usually far above its real value and does not seem nearly so important, from this point of view, as do some others) though he must not be deficient in this respect, either. He must have a good physique, good health, but above all he must have an exalted moral nature, strong sympathies, a warm heart, courage, strong and earnest religious feeling. All these being granted, and the man having reached the age necessary to bring him to the top of the self conscious mental stratum, some day he enters Cosmic Consciousness. What is his experience? Details must be given with diffidence, as they are only known to the writer in a few cases, and doubtless the phenomena are varied and diverse. What is said here, however, may be depended on as far as it goes. It is true of certain cases, and certainly touches upon the full truth in certain other cases, so that it may be looked upon as being provisionally correct.

a. The person, suddenly, without warning, has a sense of being immersed in a flame, or rose-colored cloud, or perhaps rather **a** sense that the mind is itself filled with such a cloud of haze.

b. At the same instant he is, as it were, bathed in an emotion of joy, assurance, triumph, "salvation." The last word is not strictly correct if taken in its ordinary sense, for the feeling, when fully developed, is not that a particular act of salvation is effected, but that no special "salvation" is needed, the scheme upon which the world is built being itself sufficient. It is this ecstasy, far beyond any that belongs to the merely self conscious life, with which the *poets,* as such, especially occupy themselves: As Gautama, in his discourses, preserved in the "Suttas"; Jesus in the "Parables"; Paul in the "Epistles"; Dante at the end of the "Purgatorio" and beginning of "Paradiso"; "Shakespeare" in the "Sonnets"; Balzac in "Seraphita"; Whitman in the "Leaves"; Edward Carpenter in "Towards Democracy"; leaving to the *singers* the pleasures and pains, loves and hates, joys and sorrows, peace and war, life and death, of self conscious man; though the *poets* may treat of these, too, but from the new point of view, as expressed in the "Leaves": "I will never again mention love or death inside a house" [193: 75]—that is, from the old point of view, with the old connotations.

c. Simultaneously or instantly following the above sense and emotional experiences there comes to the person an intellectual illumination quite impossible to describe. Like a flash there is presented to his consciousness a clear conception (a vision) in outline of the meaning and drift of the universe. He does not come to believe merely; but he sees and knows that the cosmos, which to the self conscious mind seems made up of dead matter, is in fact far otherwise—is in very truth a living presence. He sees that instead of men being, as it were, patches of life scattered through an infinite sea of non-living substance, they are in reality specks of relative death in an infinite ocean of life. He sees that the life which is in man is eternal, as all life is eternal; that the soul of man is as immortal as God is; that the universe is so built and ordered that without any peradventure all things work together for the good of each and all; that the foundation principle of the world is what we call love, and that the happiness of every individual is in the long run absolutely certain. The person who passes through this experience will learn in the few minutes, or even moments, of its continuance more than in months or years of study, and he will learn much that no study ever taught or can teach. Especially does he obtain such a conception of THE WHOLE, or at least of an immense WHOLE, as dwarfs all conception, imagination or speculation, springing from and belonging to ordinary self consciousness, such a conception as makes the old attempts to mentally grasp the universe and its meaning petty and even ridiculous.

This awakening of the intellect has been well described by a writer upon Jacob Behmen in these words: "The mysteries of which he discoursed were not reported to him, he BEHELD them. He saw the root of all mysteries, the UNGRUND or URGRUND, whence issue all contrasts and discordant principles, hardness and softness, severity and mildness, sweet and bitter, love and sorrow, heaven and hell. These he SAW in their origin; these he attempted to describe in their issue and to reconcile in their eternal results. He saw into the being of God; whence the birth or going forth of the divine manifestation. Nature lay unveiled to him— he was at home in the heart of things. His own book, which he himself was (so Whitman: 'This is no book; who touches this touches a man') [193: 382], the microcosm of man, with his three-fold life, was patent to his vision" [79: 852].

d. Along with moral elevation and intellectual illumination comes what must be called, for want of a better term, a sense of immortality. This is not an intellectual conviction, such as comes with the solution of a problem, nor is it an experience such as learning something unknown before. It is far more simple and elementary, and could better be compared to that certainty of distinct individuality, possessed by each one, which comes with and belongs to self consciousness.

e. With illumination the fear of death which haunts so many men and women at times all their lives falls off like an old cloak— not, however, as a result of reasoning—it simply vanishes.

f. The same may be said of the sense of sin. It is not that the person escapes from sin; but he no longer sees that there is any sin in the world from which to escape.

g. The instantaneousness of the illumination is one of its most striking features. It can be compared with nothing so well as with a dazzling flash of lightning in a dark night, bringing the landscape which had been hidden into clear view.

h. The previous character of the man who enters the new life is an important element in the case.

i. So is the age at which illumination occurs. Should we hear of a case of cosmic consciousness occurring at twenty, for instance, we should at first doubt the truth of the account, and if forced to believe it we should expect the man (if he lived) to prove himself, in some way, a veritable spiritual giant.

j. The added charm to the personality of the person who attains to cosmic consciousness is always, it is believed, a feature in the case.

k. There seems to the writer to be sufficient evidence that, with cosmic consciousness, while it is actually present, and lasting (gradually passing away) a short time thereafter, a change takes place in the appearance of the subject of illumination. This change is similar to that caused in a person's appearance by great joy, but at times (that is, in pronounced cases) it seems to be much more marked than that. In these great cases in which illumination is intense the change in question is also intense and may amount to a veritable "transfiguration." Dante says that he was "transhumanized into a God." There seems to be a strong probability that could he have been seen at that moment he would have exhibited what could only have been called "transfiguration." In subsequent chapters of this book several cases will be given in which the change in question, more or less strongly marked, occurred.

X.

The passage from self to cosmic consciousness, considered from the point of view of the intellect, seems to be a phenomenon strictly parallel to the passage from simple to self consciousness.

As in the latter, so in the former, there are two chief elements:

a. Added consciousness;

b. Added faculty.

a. When an organism which possesses simple consciousness only, attains to self consciousness, it becomes aware for the first time that it is a separate creature, or *self* existing in a world which is apart from it. That is, the oncoming of the new faculty instructs it without any new experience or process of learning.

b. It, at the same time, acquires enormously increased powers of accumulating knowledge and of initiating action.

So when a person who was self conscious only, enters into cosmic consciousness—

a. He knows without learning (from the mere fact of illumination) certain things, as, for instance: (1) that the universe is not a dead machine but a living presence; (2) that in its essence and tendency it is infinitely good; (3) that individual existence is continuous beyond what is called death. At the same time:

b. He takes on enormously greater capacity both for learning and initiating.

XI.

The parallel holds also from the point of view of the moral nature. For the animal that has simple consciousness merely cannot possibly know anything of the pure delight in simply living that is possessed (at least part of the time) by every healthy, well-constituted young or middle-aged man or woman. "Cannot possibly," for this feeling depends on self consciousness and without that can have no existence. The horse or dog enjoys life while experiencing an agreeable sensation or when stimulated by an agreeable activity (really the same thing), but cannot realize that everyday calm in the enjoyment of life, independent of the senses, and of outward things, which belongs to the moral nature (the basic fact, indeed, of the *positive* side of this), starting, as may be truly said, from the central well-spring of the life of the organism (the sense of bien-etre—"well-being") that belongs to man as man and is in truth one of his most valued heritages. This constitutes a plain or plateau, in the region of the moral nature, upon which the sentient creature steps when passing, or as it passes, from simple to self consciousness.

Corresponding with this moral ascent and with those steps, above noted, taken by the intellect from simple to self, and from self to cosmic consciousness, is the moral ascent that belongs to the passage from self to cosmic consciousness. This can only be realized, therefore only described, by those who have passed through the experience. What do they say about it? Well, read what Gautama and the illuminati of the Buddhists tell us of Nirvâna; namely, that it is the "highest happiness" [156:9]. Says the unknown, but unquestionably illumined writer, in the Mahabbharata: "The devotee, whose happiness is within himself, and whose light [of knowledge] also is within himself, becoming one with the Brahman, obtains the Brahmic bliss" [154:66]. Note the dicta of Jesus on the value of the "Kingdom of Heaven," to purchase which a man sells all that he has; remember the worth that Paul ascribes to "Christ," and how he was caught up into the third heaven; reflect on Dante's "transhumanization" from a man "into a God," and on the name he gives the cosmic sense: Beatrice —"Making Happy." Here, too, is his distinct statement of the joy that belongs to it: "That which I was seeing seemed to me a smile of the universe, for my inebriation was entering through the hearing and through the sight. O joy! O ineffable gladness! O life entire of love and of peace! O riches secure without longing!" [72:173]. See what Behmen says on the same subject: "Earthly language is entirely insufficient to describe what there is of joy, happiness, and loveliness contained in the inner wonders of God. Even if the eternal Virgin pictures them to our minds, man's constitution is too cold and dark to be able to express even a spark of it in his language" [97:85]. Observe Elukhanam's oft-repeated exclamation: "Sandosiam, Sandosiam Eppotham" —"Joy, always joy." And again Edward Carpenter's "All sorrow finished," "The deep, deep ocean of joy within," "Being filled with joy," "singing joy unending." Above all, bear in mind the testimony of Walt Whitman—testimony unvarying, though given in ever varying language, and upon almost every page of the Leaves, covering forty years of life: "I am satisfied—I see, dance, laugh, sing." "Wandering, amazed at my own lightness and glee." "O the joy of my spirit—it is uncaged—it darts like lightning." "I float this carol with joy, with joy to thee, O death." And that forecast of the future taken from his own heart—that future "when through these states walk a hundred millions of superb persons"—that is, persons possessed of the cosmic sense. And finally: "The ocean filled with joy—the atmosphere all joy! Joy, joy, in freedom, worship, love! Joy in the ecstasy of life: Enough to merely be! Enough to breathe! Joy, Joy! All over joy" [193: 358]!

XII.

"Well," some one will say, " if these people see and know and feel so much, why don't they come out with it in plain language and give the world the benefit of it?" This is what "speech" said to Whitman: "Walt, you contain enough, why don't you let it out, then?" [193: 50]. But he tells us:

> "When I undertake to tell the best I find I cannot,
>   My tongue is ineffectual on its pivots,
>   My breath will not be obedient to its organs,
>   I become a dumb man" [193: 179].

So Paul, when he was "caught up into paradise," heard "unspeakable words." And Dante was not able to recount the things he saw in heaven. "My vision," he says, "was greater than *our speech,* which yields to such a sight" [72: 212]. And so of the rest. The fact of the matter is not difficult to understand; it is that speech (as fully explained above) is the tally of the self conscious intellect, can express that and nothing but that, does not tally and cannot express the Cosmic Sense—or, if at all, only in so far as this may be translated into terms of the self conscious intellect.

XIII.

It will be well to state here (partly in recapitulation) for the benefit of the reader of the next two parts, briefly and explicitly, the marks of the Cosmic Sense.   They are:

a. The subjective light.

b. The moral elevation.

c. The intellectual illumination.

d. The sense of immortality.

e. The loss of the fear of death.

f. The loss of the sense of sin.

g. The suddenness, instantaneousness, of the awakening.

h. The previous character of the man—intellectual, moral and physical.

i. The age of illumination.

j. The added charm to the personality so that men and women are always (?) strongly attracted to the person.

k. The transfiguration of the subject of the change as seen by others when the cosmic sense is actually present.

XIV.

It must not be supposed that because a man has cosmic consciousness he is therefore omniscient or infallible.   The greatest of these men are in a sense in the position, though on a higher plane, of children who have just become self conscious.   These men have just reached a new phase of consciousness—have not yet had time or opportunity to exploit or master this.   True, they have reached a higher mental level; but on that level there can and will be comparative wisdom and comparative foolishness, just as there is on the level of simple or of self consciousness.   As a man with self consciousness may sink in morals and intelligence below the higher animal with simple consciousness merely, so we may suppose a man with cosmic consciousness may (in certain circumstances) be little if at all above another who spends his life on the plane of self consciousness. And it must be still more evident that, however godlike the faculty may be, those who first acquire it, living in diverse ages and countries, passing the years of their self conscious life in different surroundings, brought up to view life and the interests of life from totally different points of view, must necessarily interpret somewhat differently those things which they see in the new world which they enter. The marvel is that they all see the new world for what it is as clearly as they do. The main point is that these men and this new consciousness must not be condemned because neither the men nor the new consciousness are absolute. That could not be. For should man (passing upward from plane to plane) reach an intellectual and moral position as far above that of our best men to-day as are those above the average mollusk, he would be as far from infallibility and as far from absolute goodness or absolute knowledge as he is at present. He would have the same aspiration to achieve a higher mental position that he has to-day, and there would be as much room over his head for growth and amelioration as ever there was.

XV.

As summary and introductory anticipation of the cases that are to follow, a tabular statement of those considered as probably genuine is here given. A few words upon this may be of interest. Upon glancing over it the first thing to strike the reader will be the immense preponderance of men over women among those who have had the new faculty. The second will be the, at first sight, curious fact (to be referred to again later) that in nearly all the cases in which the time of year is known illumination occurred between early spring and late summer, half of all the cases occurring in or about May and June. The third will be (and this fact is interesting from the point of view of physiology) that there appears to be a general correspondence between the age at illumination and the length of life of the individual. Thus the average age at illumination of Socrates, Mohammed, Las Casas and J. B. was 39 years, and the average age at death was 74½ years (though

No.	Name	Date of Birth	Age at Illumination	Sex	Time of Year of Illumination	Age at Death
1	Moses	1650?		M		Old
2	Gideon	1350?		M		
3	Isaiah	770?		M		
4	Li R	604?		M		Old
5	Gautama	560?	35	M		80
6	Socrates	469?	39?	M	Summer	71?
7	Jesus	4	35	M	January?	38?
8	Paul	0	35	M		67?
9	Plotinus	204		M		66?
10	Mohammed	570	39	M	May?	62
11	Roger Bacon	1214		M		80?
12	Dante	1265	35	M	Spring	56
13	Las Casas	1474	40	M	June	92
14	John Yepes	1542	36	M	Early Summer	49
15	Francis Bacon	1561	30?	M		66
16	Behmen	1575	35	M		49
17	Pascal	1623	31½	M	November	39
18	Spinoza	1632		M		45
19	Mde. Guyon	1648	33	W	July	69
20	Swedenborg	1688	54	M		84
21	Gardiner	1688	32	M	July	58
22	Blake	1759	31	M		68
23	Balzac	1799	32	M		51
24	J. B. B.	1817	38	M		
25	Whitman	1819	34	M	June	73
26	J. B.	1821	38	M		73
27	C. P.	1822	37	M		
28	H. B.	1823		M		
29	R. R.	1830	30	M	Early Summer	69
30	E. T.	1830	30	M		
31	R. P.	1835		M		
32	J. H. J.	1837	34	M	Late Spring	
33	R. M. B.	1837	35	M	Spring	
34	T. S. R.	1840	32	M		
35	W. H. W.	1842	35	M		
36	Carpenter	1844	36	M	Spring	
37	C. M. C.	1844	49	W	September	
38	M. C. L.	1853	37	M	February	
39	J. W. W.	1853	31	M	January	
40	J. William Lloyd	1857	39	M	January	
41	P. T.	1860	35	M	May	
42	C. Y. E.	1864	31½	W	September	
43	A. J. S.	1871	24	W		

one of them was executed while still hale and strong.   In the case
of Bacon, Pascal, Blake and Gardiner, the average age at illumination was 31 years, and at death only $55\frac{1}{4}$ years, being thus (on
the average) 8 years younger at illumination and $9\frac{1}{4}$ years
younger at death; while Gautama, Paul, Dante, Behmen, Yepes
and Whitman, who all entered cosmic consciousness at the mean
age of 34 to 36, had an average life duration of 62 years, one of
them, Paul, having been executed at 67.   We might expect this
correspondence, for, as illumination takes place at full maturity,
this would of course (in a general way) correspond with the life
limit of the person.

PART IV.

INSTANCES OF COSMIC CONSCIOUSNESS.

CHAPTER 1.

Gautama the Buddha.

IT is not, of course, intended to write biographies here of the men given in this volume as cases of Cosmic Consciousness, nor, equally of course, can more than the faintest hint be given of their teaching. The facts quoted from their lives and the passages from their words are simply intended to establish and illustrate the fact that these men were illumined in the sense in which that word is used in this book.

I.

Siddhartha Gautama was born of wealthy parents (his father being rather a great landowner than a king, as he is sometimes stated to have been), between the years 562 and 552 B. C. It seems sufficiently certain that he was a case of Cosmic Consciousness, although, on account of the remoteness of his era, details of proof may be somewhat lacking. He was married very young. Ten years afterwards his only son, Rahula, was born. Shortly after Rahula's birth, Gautama, being then in his twenty-ninth year, suddenly abandoned his home to devote himself entirely to the study of religion and philosophy. He seems to have been a very earnest-minded man who, realizing keenly the miseries of the human race, desired above all things to do something to abolish, or at least lessen, them. The orthodox manner of attaining to holiness in Gautama's age and land was through fasting and penance, and for six years he practiced extreme self-mortification. He gained extraordinary fame, for which he cared nothing, but did not gain the mental peace nor the secret of human happiness, for which he strove. Seeing that that course was vain and led to nothing, he abandoned asceticism and shortly afterwards, at about the age of thirty-five, attained illumination under the celebrated Bo tree.

II.

For our present purpose it is important to fix the age of the oncoming of the Cosmic Sense in this, as in other cases, as precisely as possible. A very recent and probably good authority [60] gives it as thirty-six. Ernest de Bunsen in his work "The Angel Messiah" says that Buddha, like Christ, "commenced preaching at thirty years of age. He certainly must have preached at Vaisali, for five young men became his disciples there and exhorted him to go on with his teachings. He was twenty-nine when he left that place; therefore he might well have preached at thirty. He did not turn the wheel of the law (became illumined) until after a six years' meditation under the tree of knowledge" [109: 44].

III.

Now as to the result of his illumination. What did he say about it? And what change did it effect in the man? The Dhamma-Kakka-Ppavattana-Sutta [159] is accepted by all Buddhists as a summary of the words in which the great Indian thinker and reformer for the first time successfully promulgated his new ideas [160: 140]. In it over and over again Gautama declares that the "noble truths" taught therein were not "among the doctrines handed down," but that "there arose within him the eye to perceive them, the knowledge of their nature, the understanding of their cause, the wisdom that lights the true path, the light that expels darkness." He could not well more definitely state that he did not derive his authority to teach from the merely Self Conscious, but from the Cosmic Conscious, mind—that is, from illumination or inspiration. Compare with this what Behmen says of himself in the same connection: "I am not collecting my knowledge from letters and books, but I have it within my own Self; because heaven and earth with all their inhabitants, and moreover God himself, is in man" [97: 39].

IV.

In the Maha Vagga [162: 208] it is said that "during the first watch of the night following on Gautama's victory over the evil one (the night following upon his attainment of Cosmic Consciousness) he fixed his mind upon the *chain of causation;* during the second watch he did the same, and during the third watch he did the same." This tradition exists among both northern and southern Buddhists, has come down from the time before the separation of these churches, and is therefore probably genuine and from Gautama himself. But it embodies in clear and concise language one of the most fundamental phenomena belonging to the oncoming of the Cosmic Sense: most probably "the revelation of exceeding greatness" of which Paul speaks; the vision of the "eternal wheels" of Dante; "the knowledge that passes all the argument of the earth" of Whitman; the "inner illumination by which we can ultimately see things as they are, beholding all creation—the animals, the angels, the plants, the figures of our friends, and all the ranks and races of human kind—in their true being and order," of Edward Carpenter.

V.

Again in the Akankheyya-Sutta [161: 210-18] is set forth the spiritual characteristics which belong to those who possess the Cosmic Sense. No one, not having it, could have written the description which, doubtless proceeds, as claimed, directly from

Gautama. Neither could any later possessor of the faculty set forth more clearly in the same number of words the distinctive marks which belong to it. For instance, it is said there that the attainment of Arhatship (supernatural insight—Nirvâna—illumination—Cosmic Consciousness) "will cause a man to become":

Gautama's Words.

Beloved, popular, respected among his fellows, victorious over discontent * and lust; over spiritual danger and dismay; will bestow upon him the ecstasy of contemplation; † will enable him to reach with his body, and remain in, those stages of deliverance which are incorporeal and pass beyond phenomena; ‡ cause him to become an inheritor of the highest heavens; § make him being one to become multiple, being multiple to become one; ‖ will endow him with clear and heavenly ear, surpassing that of men; enable him to comprehend by his own heart the hearts of other beings, and of other men, to understand all minds, the passionate, the calm, the angry, the peaceable, the deluded, the wise, the concentrated, the ever-varying, the lofty, the narrow, the sublime, the mean, the steadfast, the wavering, the free and the enslaved; give him the power to call to mind his various temporary states in days gone by; such as one birth, two births, three, four, five, ten, twenty, thirty, forty, fifty, a hundred, a thousand or a hundred thousand births; his births in many an eon of renovation; in many an eon of both destruction and renovation; to call to mind his temporary states in days gone by in all their modes and in all their details; * to see with pure and heavenly vision surpassing that of men, beings as they pass from one state of existence and take form in others; beings base or noble, goodlooking or ill-favored, happy or miserable; to know and realize emancipation of heart and emancipation of mind.

Parallel Passages.

* "Were mankind murderous or jealous upon you my brother, my sister? I am sorry for you, they are not murderous or jealous upon me, all has been gentle with me, I keep no account with lamentation (what have I to do with lamentation?)" [193 : 71]. "The holy breath kills lust, passion and hate" [M. C. L. infra].

† "Yet O my soul supreme! Knowest thou the joys of pensive thought? Joys of the free and lonesome heart, the tender, gloomy heart?" [193 : 147].

‡ "Tomb-leaves, body-leaves growing up above me, above death" [193 : 96].

§ "Heirs of God, and joint heirs with Christ" [19 : 8-17].

‖ "The other I am" [193 : 32]. "Thou teachest how to make one twain" [176 : 39].

Is this not a perfect description of a large and important part of what the Cosmic Sense did, for instance, for Dante, "Shakespeare," Balzac, Whitman?

* "I pass death with the dying and birth with the new washed babe." "No doubt I have died myself ten thousand times before" [193 : 34-37].

Compare "Faces" [193 : 353] where this "heavenly vision" is seen in action.

The final and supreme test.

VI.

A few other passages alluding to the cosmic sense and having more or less close parallels in the writings of more modern illuminati may be given in further illustration, but it is almost needless to say that whoever desires light on this subject should read for himself—not once, but over and over again—the words left us by these lords of thought. Here is a passage from "The Book of the Great Decease." Gautama is teaching his disciples; he speaks as follows:

So long as the brethren shall not engage in, or be fond of, or be connected with business—so long as the brethren shall not be in the habit of, or be fond of, or be partakers in idle talk—so long as the brethren shall not be addicted to, or be fond of, or indulge in slothfulness—so long as the brethren shall not frequent, or be fond of, or indulge in society—so long as the brethren shall neither have nor fall under the influence of sinful desires—so long as the brethren shall not become the friends, companions or intimates of sinners—so long as the brethren shall not come to a stop on their way (to Nirvâna) because they have attained to any lesser thing (as riches or power)—so long may the brethren be expected not to decline, but to prosper [163:7 et seq.].

It is needless to quote parallel passages from Jesus, they are so numerous and will occur to everyone. But it is worth noting that Paul uses almost the same language, referring to the same figure which is in the mind of the Buddhist writer, when he says (comparing Nirvâna, the Cosmic Sense and the things belonging to it to the prize of a race): "one thing I do, forgetting the things (the lesser things of the Buddhist text) which are behind, and stretching forward to the things which are before, I press on toward the goal unto the prize" [24:3:13]. Compare also "The Song of the Open Road," in which the same thought is elaborately worked out [193:120]. Then as to the admonition against "business" and the "lesser things," such as wealth, consider the lives of Gautama, Jesus, Paul, Whitman and E. C., most of whom either were or might easily have been "well off," but either turned their backs upon their wealth (as Gautama or E. C.) or simply declined

to have any (as Jesus and Whitman).   In commentary upon this
fact read these words of Whitman:

Beyond the independence of a little sum laid aside for burial money, and of
a few clapboards around and shingles overhead on a lot of American soil owned
and the easy dollars that supply the year's plain clothing and meals, the melancholy prudence of the abandonment of such a great being as a man is to the
toss and pallor of years of money making with all their scorching days and icy
nights . . . is the great fraud upon modern civilization [191:10].

VII.

The following lines are quoted as a plain allusion to the Cosmic Sense—the whole Upanishad should be read:

There lived once Svetaketu Aru-
neya (the grandson of Aruna).   To
him his father (Uddâlaka, the son of
Aruna) said: "Svetaketu, go to school;
for there is none belonging to our race,
darling, who, not having studied (the
Veda), is, as it were, a Brahmana by
birth only."

"That seeing they may see and not perceive; and hearing they may hear and not
understand" [15 : 4. 12]: "I do not doubt
interiors have their interiors, and exteriors
have their exteriors, and that the eyesight
has another eyesight, and the hearing another hearing, and the voice another voice"
[193 : 342].

Having begun his apprenticeship with a teacher when he was twelve years
of age, Svetaketu returned to his father when he was twenty-four, having studied
all the Vedas, conceited, considering himself well read and stern.

His father said to him: "Svetaketu, as you are so conceited, considering
yourself so well read, and so stern, my dear, have you ever asked for that instruction by which we hear what cannot be heard, by which we perceive what
cannot be perceived, by which we know what cannot be known" [148:92]?

VIII.

In the same connection read this verse:

The teacher replies: It is the ear of the ear, the mind of the mind, the
speech of speech, the breath of breath, and the eye of the eye [149:147].

Just one more passage:

That one (the self), though never stirring, is swifter than thought. The
senses never reached it, it walked before them. Though standing still, it over-

takes the others who are running. The moving spirit bestows powers upon it. It stirs and it stirs not. It is far and likewise near. It is inside of all this and it is outside of all this.

"The sense is a sense that one *is* those objects and things and persons that one perceives, and the whole universe" [62].

And he who beholds all beings in the self and the self in all beings, he never turns away from it. When to a man who understands, the self has become all things, what sorrow, what trouble can there be to him who once beheld that unity [150:311]?

IX.

The specific reasons for believing that Gautama was a case of Cosmic Consciousness are:

a. The initial character of his mind, which seems to have been ardent, earnest and aspiring; such, indeed, as usually (always?) precedes the oncoming of the Cosmic Sense.

b. The definiteness and suddenness of the change in the man from unceasing aspiration and endeavor to achievement and peace. "A religious life is well taught by me" (says Gautama). "An instantaneous, an immediate life" [157:104]. And, again, Gautama is said to teach "the instantaneous, the immediate, the destruction of desire, freedom from distress, whose likeness is nowhere" [157:211].

c. The age at which illumination is said to have been attained —the typical age for the oncoming of the Cosmic Sense—thirty-five years.

d. The general teaching of the "Suttas," said to have come from Gautama, which teachings undoubtedly spring from a mind possessed of Cosmic Consciousness.

e. The intellectual illumination—"supernatural insight" [157:78]—ascribed, and justly ascribed, to Gautama and proved by the above teachings—if these proceed from him.

f. The moral elevation attained by Gautama which nothing but the possession of Cosmic Consciousness will account for.

g. Gautama seems to have had the sense of eternal life which belongs to Cosmic Consciousness. The Mahavagga is supposed to give with considerable accuracy his actual teaching in such matters [158:11] and [162:208]. In it we find these words: "The man who has no desire, who knowingly is free from doubt, and has attained the depth of immortality, him I call a Brahmana" [157:114]. It is important to note that the test is not a belief or assurance (however strong) in a future eternal life. The man, in order to be a Brahmana (to have attained Nirvâna—Cosmic Consciousness), must *already have acquired* eternal life.

h. The personal magnetism exerted directly by him upon his contemporaries, and through his words upon his disciples in all ages since.

i. There is a tradition of the characteristic change in appearance known as "transfiguration." When he came down "from the mountain Mienmo a staircase of glittering diamonds, seen by all, helped his descent. His appearance was blinding" [109:63]. Allowing for Oriental exaggeration, a germ of truth may be contained in this tradition.

X.

If, now, Gautama had Cosmic Consciousness, and if, as seems almost certain, it has appeared among his followers generation after generation from his time until now, then it must have a name in the copious literature of the Buddhists. There is, in fact, a word used by these people as to the exact value of which Western students have always been more or less in doubt, but if to that word we assign this meaning all difficulty seems to be ended and the passages in which that word occurs are seen to have a clear and simple signification. The word referred to is *Nirvâna.*

Kinza M. Hirai says [2:263]: "Nirvâna is interpreted by Western nations as the actual annihilation of human desire or passion; but this is a mistake. Nirvâna is nothing else than universal reason."

It may be doubted whether Mr. Hirai by "universal reason" means "Cosmic Consciousness," but his intention in using the expression is the same. If he realizes or shall ever realize what

Cosmic Consciousness is it is certain that he will say that Nirvâna is a name for it.

XI.

In further illustration of this point read (as follows) part of a chapter on Nirvâna by an excellent authority [73:110]—Rhys Davids:

One might fill pages with the awestruck and ecstatic praise which is lavished in Buddhist writings on this condition of mind, the Fruit of the Fourth Path, the state of an Arahat, of a man made perfect according to the Buddhist faith. But all that could be said can be included in one pregnant phrase—*this is Nirvâna.*

There is no suffering for him who has finished his journey, and abandoned grief, who has freed himself on all sides, and thrown off all fetters. The gods even envy him whose senses like horses well broken in by the driver, have been subdued, who is free from pride, and free from appetites. Such a one who does his duty is tolerant like the earth,* like Indra's bolt; he is like a lake without mud; no new births are in store for him. His thought is quiet, quiet are his word and deed when he has obtained freedom by true knowledge [131:27].

* "Who in his spirit in any emergency neither hastens nor avoids death" [193:291].

"The earth neither lags nor hastens, does not withhold, is generous enough, the truths of the earth continually wait, they are not so concealed either, they are calm, subtle, untransmissible by print" [193:176].

† Karma—one's action or acts considered as determining his lot after death and in a following existence.

They who by steadfast mind have become exempt from evil desire, and well trained in the teachings of Gautama; they, having obtained the Fruit of the Fourth Path, and immersed themselves in that Ambrosia, have received without price and are in the enjoyment of Nirvâna. Their old Karma † is exhausted, no new Karma is being produced; their hearts are free from the longing after a future life;* the cause of their existence being destroyed, and no new yearning springing up within them, they the wise are extinguished like this lamp (Ratana Sutta). That mendicant conducts himself well who has conquered (sin) by means of holiness, from whose eyes the veil of error has been removed, who is well trained in religion; and who, free from yearning, and skilled in the knowledge, has attained unto Nirvâna (Sammaparibbājanīya Sutta). What, then, is Nirvâna, which

* A man who has acquired the Cosmic Sense does not desire eternal life—he has it.

* Nir, "out," vana "blowing," from root va, "blow," with suffix ana. That Nirvâna

means simply blowing out—extinction; * it being quite clear from what has gone before, that this cannot be the extinction of a soul? *It is the extinction of that sinful, grasping condition of mind and heart which would otherwise, according to the great mystery of Karma, be the cause of renewed individual existence.* [Italics belong to text quoted.]

cannot mean extinction in the sense of death is clear from the following passage: "And erelong he attained to that supreme goal of Nirvâna—the higher life—for the sake of which men go out from all and every household gain and comfort to become homeless wanderers, yea that supreme goal did he by himself, and while yet in this visible world, bring himself to the knowledge of and continue to realize and to see face to face" [163 : 110].

That extinction is to be brought about by, and runs parallel with, the growth of the opposite condition of mind and heart; and it is complete when that opposite condition is reached. Nirvâna is therefore the same thing as a sinless, calm state of mind; and if translated at all may best, perhaps, be rendered "holiness"—holiness, that is, in the Buddhist sense—*perfect peace, goodness and wisdom.*

To attempt translations of such pregnant terms is, however, always dangerous, as the new word—part of a new language which is the outcome of a different tone of thought—while it may denote the same or nearly the same idea, usually calls up together with it very different ones. This is the case here; our word holiness would often suggest the idea of love to, and awe in the felt presence of, a personal creator—ideas inconsistent with Buddhist holiness. On the other hand. Nirvâna implies the ideas of intellectual energy,* and of the cessation of individual existence; † of

* Would need to, if it means Cosmic Consciousness.

† Not so much cessation as the swallowing up of individual in universal existence.

which the former is not essential to, and the latter is quite unconnected with our idea of holiness.

Holiness and Nirvâna, in other words, may represent states of mind not greatly different; but these are due to different causes and end in different results; and, in using the words, it is impossible to confine one's thought to the thing expressed, so as not also to think of its origin and its effect.

It is better, therefore, to retain the word Nirvâna as the name of the Buddhist summum bonum, which is a blissful holy state, a moral condition, a modification of personal character;* and we should allow the word to remind us, as it did the early Buddhists, both of the Path which leads to the extinction of sin,† and also of the break of the transfer of Karma, which the extinction of sin will bring about.

* A modification of the man's personality.

† The loss of the sense of sin is one of the most striking characteristics of the state of Cosmic Consciousness.

That this must be the effect of Nirvâna is plain; for that state of mind which in Nirvâna is extinct (upādāna klesa, trishna) is precisely that which will, according to the great mystery of Buddhism, lead at death to the formation of a new individual, to whom the Karma of the dissolved or dead one will be transferred. That new individual would consist of certain bodily and mental qualities or tendencies, enumerated, as already explained in the five Skandhas or aggregates. A comprehensive name of all five is *upādi*, a word derived (in allusion to the name of their cause, upādāna) from upāda, to grasp, either with the hand or the mind.* Now when a Buddhist has become an Arahat, when he has reached Nirvâna, the Fruit of the Fourth Path, he has extinguished upādāna and klesa,† but he is still alive; the upādi, the skandhas, his body with all its powers—that is to say, the fruit of his former sin—remain. These, however, are impermanent, they will soon pass away,‡ there will then be nothing left to bring about the rise of a new set of skandhas, of a new individual; and the Arahat will be no longer alive or existent in any sense at all, he will have reached Parinibbāna, complete extinction, or Nir-upāna-sesa-Nibbāna dhātu, extinction so complete that the upādi, the five skandhas, survive no longer—that is, in one word, death.

The life of man, to use a constantly recurring Buddhist simile or parable, is like the flame of an Indian lamp, a metal or earthenware saucer in which a cotton wick is laid in oil. One life is derived from another, as one flame is lit at another; it is not the same flame, but without the other it would not have been. As flame cannot exist without oil, so life, individual existence, depends on the cleaving to law and earthly things, the sin of the heart. If there is no oil in the lamp it will go out, though not until the oil which the wick has drawn up is exhausted; and then no new flame can be lighted there. And so the parts and powers of the sinless man will be dissolved, and no new being will be born to sorrow. The wise will pass away, will go out like the flame of a lamp, and their Karma will be individualized no longer.

Stars long ago extinct may be still visible to us by the light they emitted

---

* In other words, desire (no matter of what)—desire in the abstract—is the basis of sin, of Karma, and is the thing that must be got rid of. But desire is inseparable from the self conscious state and only ceases with the oncoming of the Cosmic Sense.

† i.e., desire and sin.

‡ We have here the same point of view as that taken by Paul—the worthlessness, the essential sinfulness, of the flesh. To the Buddhist Nirvâna (the Cosmic Sense) is all in all; as to Paul, Christ (the Cosmic Sense) is all in all. The body is nothing or less than nothing. It is against this most natural view (for the glory of the Cosmic Sense is well calculated to throw into deep shade all the rest of life) that Whitman from first to last set himself. He saw with the eye of a true seer—with the eye of absolute sobriety and common sense—that the self conscious life was as great in its way as was that of the new sense—let that be as divine as it would; saw that nothing ever was or could be greater than simple seeing, hearing, feeling, tasting, knowing—and on that he took his stand. "The other I am," he says (the old self) "must not be abased to you" (the new sense) "and you must not be abased to the other."

Whitman has, and will always have, the eternal glory of being the first man who was so great that even the Cosmic Sense could not master him.

before they ceased to burn; but the rapidly vanishing effect of a no longer active cause will soon cease to strike upon our senses; and where the light was will be darkness. So the living, moving body of the perfect man is visible still, though its cause has ceased to act; but it will soon decay, and die and pass away; and, as no new body will be formed, where life was will be nothing.

Death, utter death, with no new life to follow, is then the result of, but is not, Nirvâna. The Buddhist heaven is not death, and it is not on death, but on a virtuous life here and now, that the Pitakas lavish those terms of ecstatic description which they apply to Nirvâna, as the Fruit of the Fourth Path of Arahatship.

> The man who has entered into Nirvâna (the Cosmic Sense) *has* eternal life—any death that can then happen is the death of something no longer wanted.
> For the words ''virtuous life'' read ''life with the Cosmic Sense.''

Thus Professor Max Mueller, who was the first to point out the fact, says (Buddhaghosha's Parables): "If we look in the Dhamma-pada, at every passage where Nirvâna is mentioned there is not one which would require that its meaning should be annihilation, while most, if not all, would become perfectly unintelligible if we assigned to the word Nirvâna that signification. The same thing may be said of such other parts of the Pitakas as are accessible to us in published texts. Thus the commentator on the Jātaka quotes some verses from the Buddhavansa, or history of the Buddhas, which is one of the books of the second Pitaka. In those verses we have (inter alia) an argument based on the logical assumption that if a positive exists, its negative must also exist; if there is heat, there must be cold; and so on. In one of these pairs we find existence opposed, not to Nirvâna, but to non-existence; whilst in another the three fires (of lust, hatred and delusion) are opposed to Nirvâna (Fausboll Jātaka texts). It follows, I think, that to the mind of the composer of the Buddhavansa, Nirvâna meant not the extinction, the negation of being, but the extinction, the absence, of the three fires of passion." *

So little is known of the books of the northern Buddhist Canon, that it is difficult to discover their doctrine on any controverted point; but so far as it is possible to judge, they confirm that use of the word Nirvâna which we find in the Pitakas. In the Lalita Vistara the word occurs in a few passages, in none of which is the sense of annihilation necessary, and in all of which I take Nirvâna to mean the same as the Pâli Nibbāna.†

> * And this, a life of joy and exalted intelligence, free from desire, is life with Cosmic Consciousness.
>
> † Gautama says: "I went to Benares, where I preached the law to the five Solitaries. From that moment the wheel of my law has been moving, and the name of Nirvâna made its appearance in the world" [164 : 56]. This refers to the date of Gautama's illumination, and seems to plainly show that ''Nirvâna'' is a name of Cosmic Consciousness. Elsewhere in the same book we are told of ''men who walk in the knowledge of the law *after the attaining of*

Nirvâna'' [164 : 125]. And again: ''Nirvâna is a consequence of understanding that all things are equal'' [164 : 129]. Once more: ''There is no real Nirvâna without all-knowingness (Cosmic Consciousness); try to reach this'' [164 : 140]. Also, Gautama speaks of himself as having explained in this world the perfect law, of having conducted to Nirvâna innumerable persons [30 : 179]. If he explained the perfect law and conducted to Nirvâna while still living he must certainly have reached Nirvâna himself *during his life.* Gautama also addresses himself to men who have reached Nirvâna. How could he do so if Nirvâna was annihilation? The words of Burnouf's translation are: ''Je m'adresse á tous ces Çravakas, aux hommes qui sont parvenus á l'etat de Pratyêkabuddha, á ceux qui ont éte établis par moi dans le Nirvâna, á ceux qui sont entièrement délivrés de la succession incessante des douleurs'' [30 : 22]. So, too, Sariputra, thanking and praising Gautama, says: ''To-day I have reached Nirvâna''—''Aujour d'hui ô Bhagavat, j'ai acquis le Nirvâna.'' Nirvâna, therefore, is certainly something which a man may acquire and still go on living.

The Tibetan rendering of the word is a long phrase, meaning, according to Burnouf,* ''the state of him who is delivered from sorrow,'' or ''the state in which one finds one's self when one is so delivered.'' This is confirmed by Mr. Beal's comprehensive and valuable work on Chinese Buddhism, where the Chinese version of the Sanskrit Parinirvâna Sutra has the following: ''Nirvâna is just so. In the midst of sorrow there is no Nirvâna and in Nirvâna there is no sorrow.''

* Burnouf's words are: ''L'idée d'affranchissement est la seule que les interpretes tibétains aient vue dans le mot de Nirvâna car c'est la seule qu'ils ont traduite. Dans les versions qu'ils donnent des textes sanscrits du Népâl, le terme de *Nirvâna* est rendu par les mots mya-ngan-las-hdah-ba, qui signifient litteralment 'l'etat de celui qui est affranchi de la douleur,' ou 'l'etat dans lequel on se trouve quand on est ainsi affranchi' '' [29 : 17].

The early Sanskrit texts of the northern Buddhists, like the Pâli texts of the Pitakas, all seem to look upon Nirvâna as a moral condition, to be reached here, in the world, and in this life.

XII.

Finally, in order to show that as the word is used by those who know its meaning best it can hardly mean death and may well mean what is here called cosmic consciousness, read the following passages culled from the Dhamma-pada, one of the oldest and most sacred of the Buddhist scriptural books. Every passage in this book in which the word Nirvâna occurs is here given and with them parallel passages from other analogous writings:

Earnestness is the path of immortality (Nirvâna), thoughtlessness the path of death. Those who are in earnest do not die, those who are thoughtless are as if dead already [156:9]. These wise people, meditative, steady,

It has been many times pointed out in this volume that earnestness of mind is a sine qua non to the attainment of cosmic consciousness. The verses here quoted bring out strongly this point.

always possessed of strong powers, attain to Nirvâna, the highest happiness [156:9]. A Bhikshu (mendicant) who delights in reflection, who looks with fear on thoughtlessness, cannot fall away (from his perfect state)—he is close upon Nirvâna [156:11]. ''One is the road that leads to wealth, another the road that leads to Nirvâna;" if the Bhikshu, the disciple of Buddha, has learnt this, he will not yearn for honor, he will strive after separation from the world [156:22].

Men who have no riches, who live on recognized food, who have perceived void and unconditioned freedom (Nirvâna), their path is difficult to understand, like that of birds in the air [156:27]. He whose appetites are stilled, who is not absorbed in enjoyment, who has perceived void and unconditioned freedom (Nirvâna), his path is difficult to understand, like that of birds in the air [156:28]. Some people are born again; evil-doers go to

After Confucius had seen Li R he said to his disciples: "I know birds can fly, fish swim and animals run, but the runner may be snared, the swimmer hooked and the flyer shot with the arrow. But there is the dragon; I cannot tell how he mounts on the wind through the clouds and rises to heaven. To-day I have seen Laotsze and can only compare him to the dragon." We might say the same in our own way of nearly any of the persons mentioned in this book as having the cosmic sense.

hell; righteous people go to heaven; those who are free from all worldly desires attain Nirvâna [156:35]. If, like a shattered metal plate (gong), thou utter not, then thou hast reached Nirvâna; contention is not known to thee [156:37]. The Awakened call patience the highest penance, long-suffering the highest Nirvâna; for he is not an anchorite (pravragita) who strikes others, he is not an ascetic (stramana) who insults others [156:50].

Hunger is the worst of diseases, the body the greatest of pains; if one knows this truly, that is Nirvâna, the highest happiness [156:54]. Health

The true place of the body and of the appetites in life can only be perceived by one having cosmic consciousness.

is the greatest of gifts; contentedness the best riches; trust is the best of relationships; Nirvâna the highest happiness [156:55]. He in whom a desire for the Ineffable (Nirvâna) has sprung up, who is satisfied in his mind, and whose thoughts are not bewildered by love, he is called ûrdhvamsrotas (carried upward by the stream) [156:57]. The sages who injure nobody, and who always control their body, they will go to the unchangeable place (Nirvâna), where, if they have gone, they will suffer no more [156:58]. Those who are ever watchful, who study day and night, and who strive after Nirvâna, their passions will come to an end [156:58]. Cut out the love of self, like an autumn lotus, with thy hand! Cherish the road of peace. Nirvâna has been shown by Sugata (Buddha) [156:69]. A wise and good man who knows the meaning of this, should quickly clear the way that leads to Nirvâna [156:69]. For with these animals does no man reach the untrodden country (Nirvâna), where a tamed man goes on a tamed animal—viz., on his own well tamed self [156:77]. He who having got rid of the forest (of lust) (i.e., after having reached Nirvâna), gives himself over to forest-life (i.e., to lust), and who, when removed from the forest (i.e., from lust), runs to the forest (i.e., to lust), look at that man! though free, he runs into bondage [156:81]. The Bhikshu who acts with kindness, who is calm in the doctrine of Buddha, will reach the quiet place (Nirvâna), cessation of natural desires, and happiness [156:86]. O Bhikshu, empty this boat! if emptied, it will go quickly; having cut off passion and hatred, thou wilt go to Nirvâna [156:86]. Without knowledge there is no meditation, without meditation there is no knowledge: he who has knowledge and meditation is near unto Nirvâna [156:87]. As soon as he has considered the origin and destruction of the elements (khandha) of the body, he finds happiness and joy which belong to those who know the immortal (Nirvâna) [156:87]. The Bhikshu, full of delight, who is calm in the doctrine of Buddha, will reach the quiet place (Nirvâna), cessation of natural desires and happiness [156:88].

XIII.

Gautama, then, was a case of Cosmic Consciousness, and the central doctrine in his system, Nirvâna, was the doctrine of the Cosmic Sense. The whole of Buddhism is simply this: There is a mental state so happy, so glorious, that all the rest of life is worthless compared to it, a pearl of great price to buy which a wise man willingly sells all that he has; this state can be achieved. The object of all Buddhist literature is to convey some idea of this state and to guide aspirants into this glorious country, which is literally the Kingdom of God.

CHAPTER 2.

Jesus the Christ.

BALZAC says [5:143] that Jesus was a Specialist—that is, that he had Cosmic Consciousness. As Balzac was himself undoubtedly illumined, he would be high, if not absolute, authority upon the point. Paul, as soon as his own eyes were opened, recognized Jesus as belonging to a superior spiritual order—that is, as having the Cosmic Sense. But let us not take any one's word, but try and see for ourselves what reasons there are for including this man in the list of those having Cosmic Consciousness.

I.

Jesus was born B. C. 4 [80], and would be, according to this authority, thirty-four or thirty-five years old when he began to teach, so would have been at least thirty-three at the time of illumination—supposing him a case.

Other writers make him older. Sutherland [171:140] says: "The death of Jesus occurred in the year 35." This would make him thirty-nine at his death, thirty-six or thirty-eight when he began to teach (the former, if he taught three years, as John says; the latter, if he taught only one year, as the synoptics tell us), and, say, thirty-five or thirty-six at illumination.*

All goes to show that at about the age specified a marked change took place in him; that whereas up to a certain age he was

---

* The *Review of Reviews* for January, 1897, sums up the evidence bearing on the point as follows:

"One of the most eminent of living authorities on the life of Christ, Dr. Cunningham Geikie, writes in the *Homiletic Review* on the various attempts to fix the exact date of the birth of the Messiah.

"It is clear that the received chronology of the Abbot Dyonisius the Dwarf, which dates from the first half of the sixth century, must have begun several years too late in fixing the birth of Christ as having taken place in the 754th year of Rome, since it is known that Herod died in 750, and Jesus must have been born while Herod was still reigning. Dr. Geikie points out other fundamental errors in the calculations of the Abbot Dyonisius.

"Dyonisius had based his calculations on the mention by St. Luke that John the Baptist, who was a little older than Jesus, began his public work in the fifteenth year of Tiberius, and that Jesus was 'about thirty years old' when he began to teach (Luke iii : 1-23). This fifteenth year of Tiberius would be perhaps 782 or 783, and thirty deducted from this would give 752 or 753, to the latter of which Dionysius added a year, on the supposition that Luke's expression, 'about thirty years,' required him to add a year. But the vague 'about' was a weak ground on which to go, and, besides, the reign of Tiberius may be reckoned from his association in the government with Augustus, and thus from 765 instead of from 767. The texts I have quoted from St. Luke cannot, therefore, be used to fix either the birthday or the month of the birth, or even the year. This is seen, indeed, in the varying opinions on all these points in the early church, and from the fact that the 25th of December has been accepted as the birth day only since the fourth century, when it spread from Rome, as that which was to be thus honored."

THE MOST REASONABLE CONCLUSION.

"The nearest approach to a sound conclusion is, in fact, supplied by the statement that Herod was alive for some time after Christ was born. The infant Redeemer must have been six weeks old when presented in the temple, and the visit of the Magi fell we do not know how much later. That the massacre of all the children at Bethlehem from two years old and under presupposes that the Magi must have come to Jerusalem a long time after the birth of the expected King, for there would have been no sense in killing children two years old if Christ had been born only a few weeks or even months before. That there was a massacre, as told in the Gospel, is confirmed by a reference to it in a Satire of Macrobius (Sat. ii, 4), so that the crime is historically true and the higher criticism which treated it as a fable is convicted of error. But if Christ was born two years before Herod's death— and He may have been born even earlier—this would make the great event fall in the year 748, or six years before our era."

If we accept the conclusions of this writer, Jesus was about thirty-five years of age at illumination.

very much as others, he all at once ascended to a spiritual level quite over the heads of ordinary men. Those who knew him at home, as a boy and a young man, could not understand his superiority. "Is not this the carpenter's son" [14: 13: 55]? they ask. Or as elsewhere reported: "Is not this the carpenter the son of Mary? . . . and they were offended at him" [15: 6: 3]. This marked spiritual ascent occurring suddenly at this age is in itself almost diagnostic of the oncoming of the cosmic sense.

The earliest written and probably most authentic account of the illumination of Jesus runs as follows: "And straightway coming up out of the water, he saw the heavens rent asunder, and the Spirit as a dove descending upon him: and a voice came out of the heavens saying **Thou art my beloved Son, in thee I am well pleased.** And straightway the Spirit driveth him forth into the wilderness" [15: 1: 10-12]. There is a tradition that the illumination of Jesus took place the 6th or 10th of January [133a: 63].

The fact that Jesus went to John to be baptized shows that his mind was directed to religion and makes it probable that he had (before illumination) the earnest temperament out of which, when at all, the Cosmic Sense springs. It is not necessary to suppose that illumination took place immediately upon the baptism or that there was any special connection between these two things. The impulse that drove Jesus to solitude after his illumination is usual, if not universal. Paul felt it and obeyed it; so did Whitman.

The expression: "He saw the heavens rent asunder," describes well enough the oncoming of the Cosmic Sense, which is (as has been said) instantaneous, sudden, and much as if a veil were with one sharp jerk torn from the eyes of the mind, letting the sight pierce through.

So, describing this same oncoming of Cosmic Consciousness, John Yepes says (he has been inquiring whether, in this seemingly miraculous occurrence, it is God or the human soul which acts), and he concludes: "It is the soul that is moved and awakened; it is as if God drew back some of the many veils and coverings that are before it, so that it might see what he is" [206: 502].

So, too, the sense of the words, "𝔗𝔥𝔬𝔲 𝔞𝔯𝔱 𝔪𝔶 𝔟𝔢𝔩𝔬𝔳𝔢𝔡 𝔖𝔬𝔫," agrees perfectly with the message conveyed in all the cases. The "I know that the spirit of God is the brother of my own" of Whitman; and Dante's words: "O love that governest the heavens, who with thy light didst lift me," being strictly parallel expressions. The (apparently) objective voice, too, is a common phenomenon; it was heard by Paul, also by Mohammed.

Another important element in the case is the so-called "Temptation." The theory here accepted is that Jesus, at the age of thirty-three, or even thirty-five, was simply an intelligent, very earnest-minded mechanic, with an excellent heredity and an exceptional physique. That he was in no way distinguishable, in no way different, save in his eligibility for spiritual expansion, which was hidden in the depths of his nature even from himself, and which may equally exist in any of them, from hundreds of young mechanics in every city and town of Christendom to-day. Suddenly, instantaneously, the change came, and this young man felt and knew within himself the seemingly illimitable spiritual force through the exercise of which almost anything might be accomplished. How was it to be used? To gain what end? Power? Wealth? Fame? Or what [14: 4: 1-10]?

Jesus quickly decided, as these men all decide, that the power must be used for the benefit of the race. Why should he, why should they all, decide in this sense?

Because the moral elevation, which is a part of Cosmic Consciousness, will not permit any other decision. Were it not so, were the intellectual illumination *not* accompanied by moral exaltation, these men would undoubtedly be in effect so many demons who would end by destroying the world. This temptation is necessarily common to all the cases, though they do not all speak of it. The essence of it is the appeal of the old self conscious self to the new power to assist it in accomplishing *its* old desires. The devil, therefore, is the self conscious self. The devil (Mâra) appeared to Gautama as well as to Jesus [157: 69] and urged him not to launch out on a new path, but to keep to the old religious practices, to live quietly and comfortably. "What dost thou want

with exertion?'' he said to him.   Mâra did not seek to allure Gautama with offers of wealth and power, for these he had already
possessed, and even the self conscious Gautama knew their futil-
ity.   As already intimated, every man who enters Cosmic Consciousness necessarily passes through the same temptation.   As
all the rest, Bacon was tempted, and, as doubtless many others
have fallen, he, in a sense, fell.   He felt in himself such enormous
capacity that he imagined he could absorb the wealth of both the
Cosmic Sense and Self Consciousness—both heaven and earth.
Later he bitterly repented his greed.   He acknowledges the gift
(from God) of the divine faculty—''the gracious talent''—which
he says he ''neither hoarded up unused, nor did he employ it to
the best advantage, as he should have done, but misspent it in
things for which (he) was least fit'' [175: 469].

The superiority of Jesus to ordinary men consisted (among
other things) in
Intellectual acuteness,
Moral elevation,
An all-embracing optimism,
A sense (or *the* sense) of immortality.
The mental superiority thus characterized is again almost
certainly confined to those who have passed into Cosmic Con-
sciousness, and therefore, if granted, would settle the question.

The accounts given in the synoptic gospels of the transfiguration of Jesus can only be explained (if accepted) by supposing
that he was seen while in the condition of Cosmic Consciousness,
the change in appearance (striking enough in itself) being probably exaggerated (as it would almost certainly be) in the narration.   Here are the accounts as given: ''And he was transfigured
before them: and his face did shine as the sun, and his garments
became white as the light'' [14: 17: 2].   ''And he was transfigured
before them: and his garments became glistening, exceeding
white; so as no fuller on earth can whiten them'' [15: 9: 2-3].   It
is singular that this observer should confine his observations to
the *garments* of Jesus.   Again: ''As he was praying the fashion
of his countenance was altered and his raiment became white and

dazzling" [16:9:29]. It is believed that there is no known human condition, except that of Cosmic Consciousness, which would justify the above words. The change in the "raiment" of Jesus spoken of must be understood as reflected from his face and person.

In the Gospel according to the Hebrews occurs the following passage: "Just now my mother, the Holy Spirit, took me by one of my hairs and bore me upon the great mountain of Tabor" [109:63]. Baur and Hilgenfield, it seems, hold that this is the original of the transfiguration narrative; but if it is, it does not necessarily weaken the testimony of Mark and Luke.

There are people living to-day (the writer knows one of them) who have seen what is described (and well described) in the above words of the gospels.

Here there are several strong reasons for believing that Jesus had the Cosmic Sense. A further reason is (if further is needed) that Jesus stands spiritually at or near the summit of the human race, and if there is such a faculty as Cosmic Consciousness, as described in this volume, he must have possessed it, otherwise he could not occupy such a position.

II.

It is most unfortunate that the world possesses no words that we can be sure this extraordinary man uttered. What a priceless possession would be a volume, howsoever small, actually written by himself! We have, however, so many sayings which are attributed to him, and apparently on such good authority, that we may be pretty certain that many of them convey with sufficient accuracy the sense of what he actually said.

If, now, Jesus had Cosmic Consciousness, he must have referred to it over and over again in his teaching, just as all other such men have done. If he did so, it should be easy for any one who knows about the Cosmic Sense to detect the references, while for those who do not know there is such a thing these would necessarily be otherwise interpreted.

It is not necessary to attribute a *misinterpretation,* since the words of Jesus (as those of Dante, "Shakespeare" and Whitman) would carry, and doubtless would be uttered with the intention of carrying, more than one meaning.

At the same time, as Jesus did not write, and as his words were carried down by tradition (for some short time at least), and as these words (according to the present supposition) were imperfectly understood by those who passed them on, they would inevitably be altered. In some passages they certainly were, and in many others they probably were. Phrases, the meaning of which is only partially apprehended, cannot be carried down verbally intact unless they have already become sacred, as was the case with the Vedas. The incomplete meaning attributed to them would inevitably suggest and lead to more or less important changes to match it.

If, then, Jesus had the Cosmic Sense, and referred to it more or less often in his teaching, the passages in which he so referred to it would probably some, if not all, of them be more or less altered. But there is a long series of passages coming ostensibly directly from him and running especially through the synoptic gospels, which passages, even in their present form, seem to refer unmistakably to the faculty now in question. And if some of them do not so clearly as others, it may be that such divergence can be fairly accounted for as above. The passages in question are those treating of what Jesus sometimes called "the Kingdom of Heaven" and sometimes "the Kingdom of God."

III.

The following quotations embrace all the more important and significant passages in which either expression is used in the gospels when the words in question are reported as coming from the lips of Jesus:

Blessed are the poor in spirit for theirs is the kingdom of heaven * [14:5:3].

* A proud man is hardly likely to acquire the Cosmic Sense.

Blessed are they that have been persecuted for righteousness sake for theirs is the kingdom of heaven † [14:5:10].

Whoever therefore shall break one of these least commandments and shall teach men so shall be called least in the kingdom of heaven; ‡ but whosoever shall do and teach them he shall be called great in the *kingdom of heaven.* For I say unto you that except your righteousness shall exceed the righteousness of the scribes and Pharisees, ye shall in no wise enter into the kingdom of heaven [14:5:19-20].

But seek ye first his kingdom § (the kingdom of God) and his righteousness, and all these things shall be added unto you [14:6:33].

Not everyone that saith unto me Lord, Lord, shall enter into the kingdom of heaven,‖ but he that doeth the will of my Father which is in heaven [14:7:21].

And I say unto you that many shall come from the east and the west and shall sit down with Abraham and Isaac and Jacob in the kingdom of heaven; ¶ but the sons of the kingdom shall be cast forth into the outer darkness; there shall be weeping and the gnashing of teeth [14:8:11-12].

Verily I say unto you, among them that are born of women there hath not arisen a greater than John the Baptist; yet he that is but little in the kingdom of heaven is greater than he. And from the days of John the Baptist until now the kingdom of heaven suffereth violence and men of violence take it by force [14:11:11-12].

But if I by the spirit of God cast out devils, then is the kingdom of God * come unto you [14:12-28].

Unto you is given to know the mysteries of the kingdom of heaven,† but to them it is not given [14: 13:11].

† Persecution would hardly lead to Cosmic Consciousness, but the latter almost inevitably leads to the former.

‡ A man leading an ill life and encouraging others to do the same, would be called "least," as a conscientious good man would be called "great" from the point of view of the Cosmic Sense. But no man could ever enter into Cosmic Consciousness because he had kept any commandments, no matter how strictly. Unless a man's spiritual life pass the orthodoxies and conventions he shall in no case enter into Cosmic Consciousness.

§ Let a man have the Cosmic Sense and he will not be likely to worry about worldly goods. He will probably have all he wants, be his possessions ever so little.

‖ No man shall attain to the Cosmic Sense by prayer, but, if at all, by heredity and by a high and pure life.

¶ It is not exclusively for the Jews, but equally for the Gentiles.

Among the merely self conscious (among "those who are born of women"—distinguishing between those who are not and those who are "born anew") there are none greater than John. But the least of those who have the Cosmic Sense is greater than he. From the days of John the kingdom of heaven had suffered violence (misinterpretation, etc.) in the person of Jesus.

* His spiritual ascendancy was evidence that he had entered Cosmic Consciousness (the kingdom of heaven).

† Through their personal intimacy with Jesus they saw and realized the preterhuman loftiness of his mind. They saw, in him, the kingdom of heaven—the higher life.

The kingdom of heaven ‡ is likened unto a man that sowed good seed in his field; but while men slept his enemy came and sowed tares also among the wheat, and went away [14:13:24]. The kingdom of heaven is like unto a grain of mustard seed which a man took and sowed in his field; which indeed is less than all seeds; but when it is grown, it is greater than the herbs, and becometh a tree, so that the birds of the heaven come and lodge in the branches thereof [14:13:31-2].

‡ The antagonism between the Cosmic Sense and the merely self conscious mind and the final inevitable subjection of the latter to the former. A perfect image of the initial apparent insignificancy of the Cosmic Sense as it exists in one or a few obscure individuals, and of its ultimate overwhelming preponderance in view both of the universal influence of the teaching of these (say Gautama, Jesus, Paul and Mohammed), and more especially in view of the inevitable universality of the Cosmic Sense in the future.

The kingdom of heaven § is like unto leaven, which a woman took and hid in three measures of meal, till it was all leavened [14:13:33].

§ If possible a still more exact simile—the Cosmic Sense leavens the individual, and is to-day leavening the world.

The kingdom of heaven ‖ is like unto a treasure hidden in the field; which a man found and hid; and in his joy he goeth and selleth all that he hath and buyeth that field [14:13:44].

‖ Men who have the Cosmic Sense give up everything for it—this whole volume is proof of it.

The kingdom of heaven ¶ is like unto a man that is a merchant seeking goodly pearls; and having found one pearl of great price he went and sold all he had and bought it.

¶ The same statement in other language.

Again, the kingdom of heaven ** is like unto a net that was cast into the sea and gathered of every kind; which when it was filled they drew up on the beach and they sat down and gathered the good into vessels but the bad they cast away [14:13:45-47].

** Corresponds with the simile of the wheat and tares.

I will give unto thee the keys of the kingdom of heaven;* and whatsoever thou shalt bind on earth shall be bound in heaven and whatsoever thou shalt loose on earth shall be loosed in heaven [14:16:19].

* The Cosmic Sense is the final arbiter of good and ill. Jesus seems to have looked forward to the establishment of a school or sect the members of which should possess the Cosmic Sense.

In that hour came the desciples unto Jesus, saying: Who, then, is greatest in the kingdom of heaven? And he called to him a little child and said: Verily I say unto you: except ye turn and become as little children ye shall in no wise enter into the kingdom of heaven [14:18:1].

"This face," says Whitman, "of a healthy, honest boy is the programme of all good" [193 : 355].

Therefore is the kingdom of heaven likened unto a certain king which

The Cosmic Sense is like a king raised far above the common self conscious mind. It

would make a reckoning with his servants. And when he had begun to
reckon one was brought unto him
which owed him ten thousand talents.
But for as much as he had not wherewith to pay, his Lord commanded him
to be sold and his wife and children
and all that he had and payment to be

has absolute charity with the latter, which
constantly wars with itself, but in the end
the cosmic conscious mind will utterly wipe
from off the earth and replace the merely
self conscious mind.

Meanwhile, men on the self conscious plane
are greatly wanting in patience and mercy.

made. The servant, therefore, fell down and worshipped him, saying, Lord
have patience with me and I will pay thee all. And the Lord of that servant
being moved with compassion, released him, and forgave him the debt. But
that servant went out and found one of his fellow servants which owed him a
hundred pence, and he laid hold on him and took him by the throat, saying:
Pay what thou owest. So his fellow servant fell down and besought him saying: Have patience with me and I will pay thee. And he would not; but
went and cast him into prison until he should pay that which was due. So
when his fellow servants saw what was done they were exceeding sorry and
came and told unto their Lord all that was done. Then his Lord called him
unto him and saith unto him: Thou wicked servant, I forgave thee all that
debt because thou besoughtest me: Shouldst not thou also have had mercy
on thy fellow servant even as I had mercy on thee? And his Lord was
wroth and delivered him to the tormentors till he should pay all that was due
[14:18:23-34].

*It is easier for a camel to go
through a needle's eye than for a rich
man to enter into the kingdom of God
[14:19:24].

* The writer has found no instance of a
man absorbed in money making entering into
Cosmic Consciousness. The whole spirit of
the former is antagonistic to the latter.

The kingdom of heaven † is like
unto a man that is a householder, which
went out early in the morning to hire
laborers into his vineyard. And when
he had agreed with the laborers for a

† The Cosmic Sense is not given for work
done or according to merit, as this can be
estimated by the self conscious mind. Why
should Jesus, Yepes and Behmen be chosen,
and Goethe, Newton and Aristotle left?

penny a day he sent them into his vineyard. And he went out about the third
hour and saw others standing in the market-place idle; and to them he said:
Go ye also into the vineyard and whatsoever is right I will give you. And they
went their way. And again he went out about the sixth and the ninth hour
and did likewise. And about the eleventh hour he went out and found others
standing: And he saith unto them: Why stand ye here all the day idle?
They say unto him: Because no man hath hired us.

He saith unto them: Go ye also into the vineyard. And when even was
come the lord of the vineyard saith unto his steward: Call the laborers and
give them their hire, beginning from the last unto the first. And when they
came that were hired about the eleventh hour, they received every man a penny.

And when the first came, they supposed they would receive more; and they
likewise received every man a penny. And when they received it, they murmured against the householder, saying: These last have spent but one hour,

and thou hast made them equal unto us, which have borne the burden of the day and the scorching heat. But he answered and said to one of them: Friend, I do thee no wrong: didst thou not agree with me for a penny? Take up that which is thine, and go thy way: it is my will to give unto this last even as unto thee. Is it not lawful for me to do what I will with mine own? or is thine eye evil, because I am good? So the last shall be first and the first last [14: 20: 1-15].

A man had two sons; and he came to the first and said: Son, go work to-day in the vineyard. And he answered and said: I will not; but afterwards he repented himself and went. And he came to the second, and said likewise. And he answered and said: I go, sir, and went not. Whether of the twain did the will of his father? They say the first. Jesus saith unto them: Verily I say unto you that the publicans and the harlots go into the kingdom of God before you [14: 21: 28-31].

By their answer the chief priests and elders condemned themselves, for they said: "I go, sir," and went not, while the publicans and harlots professed nothing, but, as shown elsewhere in the gospel, sometimes had excellent hearts. They may be easily nearer Cosmic Consciousness than the self-righteous upper class. Where, indeed, is a case of a self-righteous man becoming il-lumined?

The kingdom of God* shall be taken away from you and shall be given to a nation bringing forth the fruits thereof [14: 21: 43].

* The Cosmic Sense comes especially to those people who have the highest moral nature.

And Jesus answered and spake again in parables unto them, saying: the kingdom of heaven † is likened unto a certain king which made a marriage feast for his son, and sent forth his servant to call them that were bidden to the marriage feast: and they would not come. Again he sent forth other servants, saying: Tell them that are bidden: Behold, I have made ready my dinner; my oxen and my fatlings are killed, and all things are ready: Come to the marriage feast. But they made light of it, and went their ways, one to his own farm, another to his merchandise; and the rest laid hold on his servants and entreated them shame-fully, and killed them. But the king

† The king is God, the marriage feast is Cosmic Consciousness, those who are bidden are those who have been given the best oppor-tunities for spiritual advancement—plenty, leisure, etc.—but instead of using these for the purpose designed (spiritual growth) they became absorbed in them alone. Then God sent his prophets to persuade them that they were making a mistake, but they would not listen, and even misused the prophets. So when the well-off and the educated and the religious would not come the invitation was extended to all. But rich or poor, learned or ignorant, religious or outcast, whoever comes, must have on a wedding gar-ment—the mind must be clothed in humility, sincerity, reverence, candor and fearlessness. *Could* a man secure access to the feast with-out these it is easily imaginable that he would be torn to pieces.

was wroth; and he sent his armies and destroyed those murderers, and burned their city. Then saith he to his servants: The wedding is ready, but they that were bidden were not worthy. Go ye therefore into the partings of the highways, and as many as ye shall find bid to the marriage feast. And those servants went out into the highways and gathered together all as many as they found both bad and good: And the wedding was filled with guests. But when the king came in to behold the guests he saw there a man who had not on a wedding garment, and he said unto him: Friend, how camest thou in thither not having a wedding garment? And he was speechless. Then the king said to the servants: Bind him hand and foot and cast him out into the outer darkness; there shall be the weeping and gnashing of teeth. For many are called but few chosen [14:22:1-14].

But woe unto you scribes and Pharisees, hypocrites! Because ye shut the kingdom of heaven * against men: For ye enter not in yourselves, neither suffer ye them that are entering in to enter [14:23:13].

*The formal, soulless religion of the scribes and Pharisees (and the same is true of much of the Christianity of to-day) was antagonistic to the growth of the spirit to Cosmic Consciousness. Neither would they allow (in as far as they could prevent) of any spiritual life and growth outside the narrow limits laid down by their "law."

Then shall the kingdom of heaven † be likened unto ten virgins, which took their lamps and went forth to meet the bridegroom. And five of them were foolish and five were wise. For the foolish, when they took their lamps, took no oil with them; but the wise took oil in their vessels with their lamps. Now, while the bridegroom

† The Cosmic Sense does not come to the careless but to the earnest, who diligently use all means of spiritual advancement. The virgins *all* slumbered; *none* of them knew that "the bridegroom" was coming, but some had taken the necessary means—the others had not.

tarried, they all slumbered and slept. But at midnight there is a cry: Behold the bridegroom! Come ye forth to meet him. Then all those virgins arose and trimmed their lamps. And the foolish said unto the wise: Give us of your oil; for our lamps are going out. But the wise answered, saying: Peradventure there will not be enough for us and you: Go ye rather to them that sell and buy for yourselves. And while they went away to buy the bridegroom came; and they that were ready went in with him to the marriage feast: And the door was shut. Afterwards came also the other virgins, saying: Lord, lord, open to us. But he answered and said: Verily I say unto you, I know you not. Watch, therefore, ye know not the day nor the hour [14:25:1-12].

For it [the kingdom of God *] is as when a man, going into another country, called his own servants, and delivered unto them his goods. And unto one he gave five talents, to another two, to another one; to each according to his several ability; and he went on his journey. Straightway he that received the five talents went and traded with them, and made other five talents. In like manner he also that received the two gained other two. But he that received the one went away and digged in the earth, and hid his lord's money.

* Man is endowed with Self Consciousness, and must make the most possible of it before he can rise above it. Or in other words, and to convert the proposition into a truism, man must reach the top of the mental stratum called Self Consciousness before he can pass into the superimposed stratum called Cosmic Consciousness. Jesus, in the parable, says: God has given to each man the self conscious faculties in varying measure, whether he (any given individual) shall pass beyond Self Consciousness into the kingdom of heaven (Cosmic Consciousness) depends not so much upon the measure of these faculties as upon the use made of them. That there is much truth in this proposition

Now after a long time the lord of those servants cometh, and maketh a reckoning with them. And he that received the five talents came and brought other five talents, saying: Lord, thou deliveredst unto me five talents: lo, I have gained other five talents. His lord said unto him: Well done, good and faithful servant: thou hast been faithful over a few things, I will set thee over many things: enter thou into the joy of thy lord. And he also that received the two talents came and said: Lord, thou deliveredst unto me two talents; lo, I have gained other two talents. His lord said unto him: Well done, good and faithful servant: thou hast been faithful over a few things, I will set thee over many things: enter thou into the joy of thy lord. And he also that had received the one talent came and said: Lord, I knew thee that thou art a hard man, reaping where thou didst not sow, and gathering where thou didst not scatter: And I was afraid, and went away and hid thy talent in the earth; lo, thou hast thine own. But his lord answered and said unto him: Thou wicked and slothful servant, thou knewest that I reap where I sowed not, and gather where I did not scatter; thou oughtest therefore to have put my money to the bankers, and at my coming I should have received mine own with interest. Take ye away therefore the talent from him, and give it unto him that hath the ten talents. For unto every one that hath shall be given, and he shall have abundance: but from him that hath not, even that which he hath shall be taken away. And cast ye out the unprofitable servant into the outer darkness: there shall be weeping and gnashing of teeth [14: 25: 14-30].

And he said: So is the kingdom of God * as if a man should cast seed upon the earth, and should sleep and rise night and day, and the seed should spring up and grow he knoweth not how [15: 4: 26-7].

And he said unto them: Verily I say unto you there be some here of them that stand by which shall in no wise taste of death until they see the kingdom of God † come with power [15: 9: 1].

And if thine eye cause thee to stumble, cast it out: It is good for thee to enter into the kingdom of God ‡ with one eye, rather than having two eyes to be cast into hell; where their worm dieth not, and the fire is not quenched. For every one shall be salted with fire [15: 9: 47].

is certain. If, on the other hand, the cultivation of these faculties is neglected the man remains hopelessly on the self conscious plane; *there* has been, is and always will be weeping and gnashing of teeth.

* The seed (a life of aspiration) *must* be sown. We do not know what is to grow from it—days and nights pass and at some instant—in bed, walking, driving, "the guest that has waited long" appears. See above same parable from Matthew.

† There be some here present who shall enter into Cosmic Consciousness. To a man with Cosmic Consciousness it seems so simple and certain that others will enter it. "I bestow upon any man or woman (says Whitman) the entrance to all the gifts of the universe" [193 : 216].

‡ Allow nothing to stand in the way of spiritual advancement. Anything is better than to remain in the merely self conscious state, which is full of miseries.

The law and the prophets were until John: from that time the gospel of the kingdom of God § is preached and every man entereth violently into it [16:16:16].

And being asked by the Pharisees when the kingdom of God ‖ cometh he answered them and said: The kingdom of God cometh not with observation; neither shall they say, Lo, here! or there, for lo, the kingdom of God is within you [16:17:20-1].

He said unto them, Verily I say unto you: There is no man that hath left house, or wife or brethren, or parents, or children, for the kingdom of God's ¶ sake, who shall not receive manifold more in this time, and in the world to come eternal life [16:18:29-30].

Jesus answered and said unto him: Verily, verily I say unto thee, except a man be born anew he cannot see the Kingdom of God.** Nicodemus saith unto Him: How can a man be born when he is old?   Can he enter a second time into his mother's womb and be born?   Jesus answered: Verily, verily I say unto thee, except a man be born of water and the spirit, he cannot enter into the kingdom of God [17:3:3-5].

§ Tries to enter violently or awkwardly into it. Tries to get in while still only self conscious. How true is this to-day!

‖ It is not outside but inside. It is a part (a faculty) of the mind itself.

¶ Men with Cosmic Consciousness have generally been of this opinion, have often parted from their relations, and have either not married or have broken the tie—cf. Buddha, Jesus, Paul, Balzac (until the very end of his life), Whitman, Carpenter.

** This passage does not seem to need comment. It is, as it stands, as clear as words can be. The oncoming of the Cosmic Sense is a new birth into a new life.

Looked at from the present point of view, the objects of the teachings of Jesus, as of Gautama, were two: (*a*) To tell men what he had learned upon entering into Cosmic Consciousness, which things he saw it was of the very greatest importance that they should know; and (*b*) to lead men up into or at least towards Cosmic Consciousness, or, in his words, into the kingdom of God.

SUMMARY

We have in this case:

a. Some evidence of the characteristic suddenness that belongs to the oncoming of the new sense.

b. No definite record of subjective light, though it is impossible to say what the words "Heaven rent asunder," "Spirit as a dove descending," and "A voice out of the heavens" really mean. As the experience was subjective, Jesus must have told some one of it, and perhaps it passed through several minds before the words we have were written down, no one (not even Jesus) having any idea as to the meaning of the experience.

c. Presumably we have intellectual illumination.

d. Moral elevation well marked, though unfortunately we know nothing for certain of the personality of Jesus before the time of his illumination, when, as above stated, he was about thirty-three or thirty-five years of age.

e. We have the sense of immortality and the extinction of the sense of sin and of the fear of death.

f. Finally, the characteristic change of appearance which accompanies the presence of the Cosmic Sense and spoken of by the synoptics as Jesus' "transfiguration."

CHAPTER 3.

Paul.

THAT the great apostle had the Cosmic Sense seems as clear and certain as that Cæsar was a great general.

He was, in fact, "great" and an "apostle" because he had it, and for no other reason whatever.

I.

In his case meet all the elements both of probability and proof. As shown by his enthusiasm for the religion in which he was brought up, he had the earnest temperament which seems always to form the matrix in which the new life is brought forward to its birth. He was at the time of his (supposed) illumination probably about the age at which the Cosmic Sense usually shows itself. Sutherland (171:137) has the following bearing on this point: He says that Paul:

Could not have been very much younger than Jesus. He was of an ardent and impetuous nature, and not long after the crucifixion (perhaps within two years) began to be conspicuous as a persecutor of the little companies of believers in Christ that were gathered not only in Jerusalem but in many other places. The same zeal which made him afterward such an efficient missionary of Christianity now caused him to carry his persecutions of the hated sect of the "Nazarenes" beyond Jerusalem to the cities and villages of Judea, and finally even beyond the bounds of Palestine. It was while he was on his way to the city of Damascus, a little way outside of Palestine on the northeast, bent on extirpating the new heresy there, that the remarkable event occurred which changed his whole life.

If, now, Paul was, say, four or five years younger than Jesus, his illumination took place at the same age as that of his great predecessor.

One word more on this last point. It is a little singular that neither the apostle himself nor his historian, Luke, who was deeply interested in all that related to his personality, have let fall a single expression from which the date of Paul's birth can be positively and definitely deduced. Speaking of his life before his illumination, however, Paul says [18: 22: 4]: "I persecuted this way unto the death, binding and delivering into prison both men and women." A very young man, unless born into some place of authority, could hardly have occupied the position thus described. The leaders of the chief party of the Jews would scarcely employ a very young man as Paul was employed. Paul's "conversion" possibly took place in the year 33 [144: 45-6]. Supposing he was born shortly before the year 1, then when Philippians was written —that is, A. D. 61 [144: 357-8]—he would be between sixty and sixty-five years of age, which would agree very well with certain expressions in that epistle which would hardly have been uttered by a much younger man. For instance: "I am in a strait betwixt the two, having the desire to depart and be with Christ; for it is very far better: yet to abide in the flesh is more needful for your sake" [24: 1: 23-4]. When writing these words it does not appear that he was sick, neither was he in any danger from the result of his trial, which was then going on [144: 357-8]. The near prospect of death must have been due to his age at the time. But if he was, say, sixty-five in A. D. 61, then he would be thirty-seven at the time of his illumination. He might not have been as old as that, but could hardly have been much younger.

The chronology of the early church is very obscure. Renan [142: 163] gives the date of Paul's birth 10 or 12 A. D., that of the stoning of Stephen 37, that of Paul's "conversion" 38. Paul, then, would have been between twenty-six and twenty-eight on the occurrence of that event; also he would have been no more than forty-nine to fifty-one when the above passage in Philippians was written. But this, for reasons given, seems exceedingly unlikely. Weighing all probabilities (for we have nothing else) it seems likely that Paul was about four years younger than Jesus and that his illumination took place about the same length of time after that of his great predecessor.

II.

We have three separate accounts of the oncoming of his new life, two of them ostensibly and probably in his own words, and each of the three containing the essential elements of the fact of illumination as positively known in other cases. Again we have elsewhere [21: 12: 1-7] a description, certainly given by himself, of certain subjective experiences which would alone be strong, if not convincing, evidence of the fact of illumination; for it is safe to say that the words there set down could hardly have been written unless the writer of them had actually experienced the passage from self to Cosmic Consciousness. Then over and above all these evidences there exists a body of writings by this man which over and over again demonstrates the existence in the writer of the faculty in question. His conduct immediately following illumination is also characteristic. Taking the usual course, he retires for some time into more or less complete solitude; whether to the Hauran, as Renan supposes, or to the Sinaitic peninsula, as Holsten thinks, does not matter [84: 417]. As regards his illumination itself—his "conversion," the oncoming of Cosmic Consciousness in his case—we are told [18: 9: 3-9] that:

As he journeyed it came to pass that he drew nigh unto Damascus: and suddenly there shone round about him a light out of heaven: and he fell upon the earth and heard a voice saying unto him, **Saul, Saul, why persecutest thou me?** And he said, Who art thou, Lord? And he said, **I am Jesus whom thou persecutest: but rise and enter into the city, and it shall be told thee what thou must do.** And the men that journeyed with him stood speechless, hearing the voice, but beholding no man. And Saul arose from the earth; and when his eyes were opened, he saw nothing; and they led him by the hand into Damascus. And he was three days without sight, and did neither eat nor drink.

The second account runs as follows [18:22:6-11]:

And it came to pass, that as I made my journey, and drew nigh unto Damascus, about noon, suddenly there shone from heaven a great light round about me. And I fell unto the ground, and heard a voice saying unto me, **Saul, Saul, why persecutest thou me?** And I answered, Who art thou, Lord? And he said unto me, **I am Jesus of Nazareth, whom thou persecutest:** And they that were with me beheld indeed the light, but they heard not the voice of him that spake to me. And I said, What shall I do, Lord? And the Lord said unto me, **Arise, and go into Damascus. And there it shall be told thee of all things which are appointed for thee to do.** And when I could not see for the glory of that light, being led by the hand of them that were with me, I came into Damascus.

And the third account [18:26:12-18] is as follows:

As I journeyed to Damascus with the authority and commission of the chief priests, at midday, O king, I saw on the way a light from heaven, above the brightness of the sun, shining round about me and them that journeyed with me. And when we were all fallen to the earth I heard a voice saying unto me in the Hebrew language, **Saul, Saul, why persecutest thou me? It is hard for thee to kick against the goad.** And I said, Who art thou, Lord! And the Lord said, **I am Jesus whom thou persecutest. But arise and stand upon thy feet; for to this end have I appeared unto thee, to appoint thee a minister and a witness both of the things wherein thou hast seen me, and of things wherein I will appear unto thee; delivering thee from the people and from the Gentiles, unto whom I send thee, to open their eyes, that they may turn from darkness to light, and from the power of Satan unto God.**

These three narratives, which agree well enough one with another, their slight discrepancies being of little or no consequence, give the usual sensuous phenomena that nearly always accompany the oncoming of the new sense.

Next comes a recital of even, if possible, still greater importance [21:12:1-7]. It conveys, in few words, an account of Paul's moral elevation and intellectual illumination during and following his "conversion." He says:

I must needs glory, though it is not expedient; but I will come to visions and revelations of the Lord. I know a man in Christ,* fourteen years ago (whether in the body I know not or whether out of the body I know not; God knoweth) such a one caught up even to the third heaven. And I know such a man (whether in the body or apart from the body I know not; God knoweth) how that he was caught up into paradise and heard *unspeakable words*,† which it is not lawful for a man to utter. On behalf of such a one will I glory; but on mine own behalf I will not glory, save in my weaknesses. For if I should desire to glory I shall not be foolish; for I shall speak the truth; but I forbear, lest any man should account of me above that which he seeth me to be, or heareth from me. And by reason of the exceeding greatness of the revelations—wherefore that I should not be exalted overmuch there was given to me a thorn in the flesh, a messenger of Satan to buffet me.

* "Christ" is Paul's name for Cosmic Consciousness.

† *Unspeakable words,* so Whitman: "When I undertake to tell the best I find I cannot, my tongue is ineffectual on its pivots; my breath will not be obedient to its organs; I become a dumb man" [193:179].

III.

To complete the case it only remains to transcribe certain utterances of Paul's from the point of view of the Cosmic Sense; which utterances, did they stand alone, would prove that the man from whom they proceeded possessed it, since without it they could not have been made.

For this we say unto you by the word of the Lord, that we that are alive, that are left unto the coming of the Lord, shall in no wise precede them that are fallen asleep. For the Lord himself shall descend from heaven, with a shout, with the voice of the archangel, and with the trump of God; and the dead in Christ shall rise first: Then we that are alive, that are left, shall together with them be caught up in the clouds, to meet the Lord in the air; and so shall we ever be with the Lord. Wherefore comfort one another with these words [26:4:15-18].

The usual assurances of immortality that belong to Cosmic Consciousness.

For I make known to you, brethren, as touching the gospel which was preached by me, that it is not after man. For neither did I receive it from man, nor was I taught it, but it came to me through revelation of Jesus Christ [22:1:11-12].

As regards his "Gospel," Paul was instructed by the Cosmic Sense only.

But when it was the good pleasure of God, who separated me, even from my mother's womb, and called me through His grace to reveal His Son in me, that I might preach him among the gentiles; immediately I conferred not with flesh and blood; neither went I up to Jerusalem to them which were apostles before me; but I went away into Arabia; and again I returned unto Damascus [22:1:15-17].

He knew, however, enough about Jesus and his teachings to be able to recognize (when it came to him) that the teachings of the Cosmic Sense were practically identical with the teachings of Jesus.

Christ redeemed us from the curse of the law [22:3:13]. But before faith came, we were kept inward under the law, shut up unto the faith which should afterwards be revealed. So that the law has been our tutor to bring us unto Christ that we might be justified by faith; but now that faith is come we are no longer under a tutor. For ye are all sons of God through faith in Christ Jesus. For as many of you as were baptised into Christ did put on Christ [22:3:23-27].

Christ is the Cosmic Sense conceived as a distinct entity or individuality. That *does* redeem any to whom it comes from the "curse of the law"—i.e., from the shame and fear and hate that belong to the self conscious life. Paul seems to suppose a baptism *into* Cosmic Consciousness (Christ). Doubtless there *is* such a baptism; but where is the priesthood which is able to administer it?

With freedom did Christ set us free [22:5:1].

The "freedom" of the Cosmic Sense is supreme. It absolves a man from his former self and makes future slavery impossible.

For ye, brethren, were called for freedom [22:5:13].

Paul loves and values freedom as keenly as does the modern American Walt Whitman. They both knew (what, alas! so few have known) what true freedom is.

The fruit of the spirit is love, joy, peace, long suffering, kindness, goodness, faithfulness, meekness, temperance: against such as these there is no law. And they that are of Christ Jesus have crucified the flesh with the passions and the lusts thereof [22:5:22-24].

For "The Spirit" and "Christ Jesus" read Cosmic Consciousness. Cf. M. C. L. infra. "The holy breath kills lust, etc.," and Bhagavadgita: "Even the taste for objects of sense departs from him who has seen the supreme."

Neither is circumcision anything, nor uncircumcision, but a new creature [22:6:15].

Called by Balzac: "The second existence" [5 : 100].

We speak wisdom among the perfect: yet a wisdom not of this world, nor of the rulers of this world, which are coming to nought; but we speak God's wisdom in a mystery, even the wisdom that hath been hidden, which God foreordained before the worlds unto our glory: which none of the rulers of this world knoweth [20: 2: 6-8].

The spirit searcheth all things, yea, the deep things of God. For who among men knoweth the things of a man, save the spirit of the man which is in him? Even so the things of God none knoweth, save the spirit of God. But we received, not the spirit of the world, but the spirit which is of God; that we might know the things that are freely given to us by God. Which things also we speak, not in words which man's wisdom teacheth, but which the spirit teacheth; comparing spiritual things with spiritual. Now the natural man receiveth not the things of the spirit of God: For they are foolishness unto him; and he cannot know them, because they are spiritually judged. But he that is spiritual judgeth all things, and he himself is judged of no man. For who hath known the mind of the Lord, that he should instruct him? But we have the mind of Christ.* And I, brethren, could not speak unto you as unto spiritual, but as unto carnal, as unto babes in Christ. I fed you with milk, not with meat; for ye were not yet able to bear it; nay, not even now are ye able; for ye are yet carnal [20: 2: 10-16 and 3: 1-3].

If any man thinketh that he is wise among you in this world, let him become a fool, that he may become wise. For the wisdom of this world is foolishness with God [20: 3: 18-19].

If we sowed unto you spiritual things, is it a great matter if we shall reap your carnal things [20: 9: 11]? and a breakfast as I journey through the states. Why should I be ashamed to own such gifts? Why to advertise for them? For I myself am not one who bestows nothing upon man and woman, for I bestow upon any man or woman the entrance to all the gifts of the universe.

For if I preach the gospel, I have nothing to glory of; for necessity is laid upon me [20: 9: 16].

He speaks from the standpoint of the Cosmic Sense, which was to come when the time was ripe and has come now to him.

Paul is informed, not by the human (the self conscious) mind, but by the spirit of God (Cosmic Consciousness), and no man merely self conscious can judge him any more than an animal (having simple consciousness merely) can judge a (self conscious) man.

* The merely self conscious man cannot be made to understand the things seen by the Cosmic Sense. These things, if presented, appear foolish to him. But he that has the Cosmic Sense (being, of course, also self conscious) is able to judge "all things"— i.e., the things of both regions. Paul could not therefore speak to the Corinthians as he would have liked to have done, they not having Cosmic Consciousness,

Paul says the wisdom of self consciousness is not wisdom to those who have the Cosmic Sense, and the wisdom of the latter is foolishness to the merely self conscious.

Compare Whitman's poem, "To Rich Givers" [193 : 216]: "What you give me I cheerfully accept, a little sustenance, a hut and garden, a little money as I rendezvous with my poems, a traveler's lodging

This seems to be the experience of all persons who have had the Cosmic Sense either in greater or less degree. So Blake says: "I have written this poem ('Jerusalem') without premeditation *and even against my will.''* So also Behmen ''became impressed with the necessity of writing down what he saw,'' though writing was far from easy with him.

If I speak with the tongues of men and of angels, but have not love, I am become sounding brass, or a clanging cymbal. And if I have the gift of prophecy, and know all mysteries and all knowledge; and if I have all faith, so as to remove mountains, but have not love, I am nothing. And if I bestow all my goods to feed the poor, and if I give my body to be burned, but have not love, it profiteth me nothing.

A splendid exposition of the morality that belongs to the Cosmic Sense. The same spirit may be traced in every case—but see especially [193 : 273]: ''Give me the pay I have served for, give me to sing the song of the great idea, take all the rest, I have loved the earth, sun, animals, I have despised riches, I have given alms to every one that asked, stood up for the stupid and crazy, devoted my income and labor to others.''

Love suffereth long, and is kind; love envieth not; love vaunteth not itself, is not puffed up, does not behave itself unseemly, seeketh not its own, is not provoked, taketh not account of evil; rejoiceth not in unrighteousness, but rejoiceth with the truth; beareth all things, believeth all things, hopeth all things, endureth all things. Love never faileth; but whether there be prophecies, they shall be done away; whether there be tongues, they shall cease; whether there be knowledge, it shall be done away. For we know in part and we prophesy in part; but when that which is perfect is come, that which is in part shall be done away. When I was a child, I spake as a child, I felt as a child, I thought as a child; now that I am become a man, I have put away childish things. For now we see in a mirror, darkly; but then face to face: now I know in part; but then shall I know even as also I have been known. But now abideth faith, hope, love, these three; and the greatest of these is love [20 : 13 : 1-13].

For as in Adam all die, so also in Christ shall all be made alive. But each in his own order, Christ the first fruits; then they that are Christ's, at his coming. Then cometh the end when he shall deliver up the kingdom to God, even the Father; when he shall have abolished all rule and all authority and power [20 : 15 : 22-25].

Behold, I tell you a mystery: We shall not all sleep, but we shall all be changed, in a moment, in the twinkling of an eye, at the last trump. For the trumpet shall sound, and the dead shall be raised incorruptible, and we shall be changed. For this corruptible must put on incorruption, and this mortal must put on immortality, but when this corruptible shall have put on incorruption and this mortal shall have put on

A comparison between the self conscious and the Cosmic Conscious states. Self Consciousness, he says, the Adamic state, is a condition of death. With ''Christ'' begins true life, which shall spread and become universal; that is the end of the old order. After that there shall be no more ''rule,'' ''authority'' or ''power''; all shall be free and equal. ''The angel borne upon the blast saith not 'Ye dead arise,' he saith 'Arise, ye living' '' [5 : 145].

Expresses the sense of immortality which belongs to Cosmic Consciousness. Compare [193 : 77]: ''There is that in me—I do not know what it is—but I know that it is in me. Wrenched and sweaty—calm and cool then my body becomes, I sleep, I sleep long. I do not know it—it is without name—it is a word unsaid—it is not in any dictionary, utterance, symbol. Something it swings on more than the earth I swing on, to it the creation is the friend whose embracing awakes me. Perhaps I might tell more. Outlines! I plead for my brothers and sis-.

immortality, then shall come to pass the saying that is written, Death is swallowed up in victory [20:15:51-55].

But though our outward man is decaying, yet our inward man is renewed day by day. For our light affliction, which is for the moment, worketh for us more and more exceedingly an eternal weight of glory; while we look not at the things which are seen, but at the things which are not seen: for the things which are seen are temporal: but the things which are not seen are eternal. For we know that if the earthly house of our tabernacle be dissolved we have a building from God, a house not made with hands, eternal, in the heavens. For verily in this we groan, longing to be clothed upon with our habitation which is from heaven; if so be that being clothed we shall not be found naked. For indeed we that are in this tabernacle do groan, being burdened; not for that we would be unclothed, but that we would be clothed upon, that what is mortal may be swallowed up of life [21:4:16-18 and 5:1:5].

If any man is in Christ he is a new creature; the old things are passed away; behold, they are become new [21:5:17].

ters. Do you see, O my brothers and sisters? It is not chaos or death, it is form, union, plan—it is eternal life—it is happiness.''

The writer contrasts the self with the Cosmic Conscious life. His consciousness of eternal life is made plain.

No expression could be more clear cut, more perfect. The man who enters Cosmic Consciousness is really a new creature, and all his surroundings ''become new''—take on a new face and meaning. You get around to the other side of things, as it were; they are the same, but also entirely different. ''Things are not dismissed from the places they held before. The earth is just as positive and direct as it was before. But the soul is also real; it too is positive and direct; no reasoning, no proof, has established it, undeniable growth has established it'' [193 : 180].

There is therefore now no condemnation to them that are in Christ Jesus. For the law of the Spirit of life in Christ Jesus made me free from the law of sin and of death. For what the law could not do, in that it was weak through the flesh, God, sending His own Son in the likeness of sinful flesh and

In Cosmic Consciousness there is absolutely no sense of sin nor of death, the person feels that this last is merely an incident in continuous life. The merely self conscious man cannot, by the keeping of the ''law'' or in any other way, destroy either sin or the sense of sin, but, ''Christ''—i.e., the Cosmic Sense, can and does accomplish both.

as offering for sin, condemned sin in the flesh; that the ordinance of the law might be fulfilled in us, who walk not after flesh but after the Spirit. For they that are after the flesh do mind the things of the flesh; but they that are after the Spirit the things of the Spirit. For the mind of the flesh is death; but the mind of the Spirit is life and peace; because the mind of the flesh is enmity against God [19:8:1-7].

The Spirit himself beareth witness with our spirit that we are children of God; and if children then heirs; heirs of God, and joint heirs of Christ [19:8:16-17].

All men who have Cosmic Consciousness are on the same spiritual level in the same sense that all who are self conscious are men—belong to the same species.

For I reckon that the sufferings of this present time are not worthy to be compared with the glory which shall be revealed to usward. For the earnest expectation of the creation waiteth for the revealing of the sons of God. For the creation was subjected to vanity, not of its own will, but by reason of him who subjected it, in hope that the creation itself also shall be delivered from the bondage of corruption into the liberty of the glory of the children of God. For we know that the whole creation groaneth and travaileth in pain together until now. And not only so, but ourselves also, which have the first fruits of the spirit, even we ourselves groan within ourselves, waiting for our adoption, to wit, the redemption of our body [19:8:18-24].

Paul speaks of the glory and joy of the Cosmic Conscious life just dawning upon the world compared with the self conscious state theretofore universal. "Vistas of glory," says Whitman, "incessant and branching." "Joy, always joy," says Elukhanam. "Joy beginning but without ending," says E. C. "When you have once," says Seraphita [that is, Balzac] "felt the delights of the divine intoxication (illumination) then all is yours" [7 : 182]. Compare also the following extracts from Behmen, in which he in like manner with Paul contrasts the Self with the Cosmic Conscious life: "The external world or the external life is not a valley of suffering for those who enjoy it, but only for those who know of a higher life. The animal enjoys animal life; the intellect the intellectual realm; but he who has entered into regeneration recognises his terrestrial existence as a burden and prison. With this recognition he takes upon himself the cross of Christ" [97 : 325].

"The holy and heavenly man, hidden in the monstrous (external) man, is as much in heaven as God, and heaven is in him, and the heart or light of God is begotten and born in him. Thus is God in him and he in God. God is nearer to him than his bestial body" [97 : 326].

And we know that to them that love God all things work together for good [19:8:28]. For I am persuaded that neither death, nor life, nor angels, nor principalities, nor things present, nor things to come, nor powers, nor height, nor depth, nor any other creature, shall be able to separate us from the love of God [19:8:38-39]. I know and am persuaded in the Lord Jesus, that nothing is unclean of itself; save that to him who accounteth anything to be unclean, to him it is unclean [19:14:14].

An expression of the optimism which belongs to Cosmic Consciousness. Compare Whitman; "Omnes! Omnes! Let others ignore what they may, I make the poem of evil also, I commemorate that part also, I am myself just as much evil as good, and my nation is, and I say there is in fact no evil" [193 : 22].

To sum up: We have in this case:

a. The characteristic suddenness that belongs to the oncoming of the New Sense. The new birth takes place at a given place and moment.

b. We have the subjective light clearly, very strongly, manifested.

c. We have intellectual illumination of the most pronounced character.

d. We have very strongly marked moral exaltation.

e. We have the conviction, the *sense* of immortality, the extinction of the sense of sin and the extinction of the fear of death.

CHAPTER 4.

Plotinus.

PLOTINUS was born A. D. 204 and died 274.

Plotinus held that in order to perfect knowledge the subject and object must be united—that the intelligent agent and the thing understood . . . must not be in separation * [55 : 716].

* "When to a man who understands, the Self has become all things" [150 : 312].

He held that in order to perfect knowledge the subject and object must be united † [85 : 716].

† "Objects gross and the unseen soul are one" [193 : 173]. "The perception seems to be one in which all the senses unite into one sense. In which *you become* the object" [63].

Here follows a letter:

Plotinus to Flaccus [188 : 78-81].

I applaud your devotion to philosophy: I rejoice to hear that your soul has set sail, like the returning Ulysses, for its native land—that glorious, that only real country—the world of unseen truth. To follow philosophy the senator Rogatianus, one of the noblest of my disciples, gave up the other day all but the whole of his patrimony, set free his slaves and surrendered all the honors of his station.

Tidings have reached us that Valerian has been defeated, and is now in the hands of Sapor. The threats of Franks and Allemanni, of Goths and Persians, are alike terrible by turns to our degenerate Rome. In days like these, crowded with incessant calamities, the inducements to a life of contemplation are more than ever strong. Even my quiet existence seems now to grow somewhat sensible of the advance of years. Age alone I am unable to debar from my retirement. I am weary already of this prison-house, the body, and calmly await the day when the divine nature within me shall be set free from matter.

The sense of continued life. "And as for you, death, and you bitter lung of mortality, it is idle to try to alarm me" [193 : 77].

The Egyptian priests used to tell us that a single touch with the wing of their holy bird could charm the crocodile into torpor; it is not thus speedily, my dear friend, that the pinions of your soul will have power to still the untamed body. The creature will yield only to watchful, strenuous constancy of habit. Purify your soul from all undue hope and fear about earthly things, mortify the body, deny self—affections as well as appetites—and the inner eye will begin to exercise its clear and solemn vision.

You ask me to tell you how we know, and what is our criterion of certainty. To write is always irksome to me. But for the continual solicitations of Porphyry I should not have left a line to survive me. For your own sake and for your father's my reluctance shall be overcome.

External objects present us only with appearances. Concerning them, therefore, we may be said to possess opinion rather than knowledge. The distinctions in the actual world of appearance are of import only to ordinary and practical men. Our question lies with the ideal reality that exists behind appearance. How does the mind perceive these ideas? Are they without us, and is the reason, like sensation, occupied with objects external to itself? What certainty would we then have—what assurance that our perception was infallible? The object perceived would be a something different from the mind perceiving it. We should have then an image instead of reality. It would be monstrous to believe for a moment that the mind was unable to perceive ideal truth exactly as it is, and that we had not certainty and real knowledge concerning the world of intelligence. It follows, therefore, that this region of truth is not to be investigated as a thing external to us, and so only imperfectly known. It is within us. Here the objects we contemplate and that which contemplates are identical—both are thought. The subject cannot surely know an object different from itself. The world of ideas lies within our intelligence. Truth, therefore, is not the agreement of our apprehension of an external object with the object itself. It is the agreement of the mind with itself. Consciousness, therefore, is the sole basis of certainty. The mind is its own witness. Reason sees in itself that which is above itself as its source; and again, that which is below itself as still itself once more.

Knowledge has three degrees—opinion, science, illumination. The means or instrument of the first is sense; of the second dialectic; of the third intuition. To the last I subordinate reason. It is absolute knowledge founded on the identity of the mind knowing with the object known.

"The world of ideas divides itself into three spheres—that of instinct; that of abstractions; that of specialism" [5 : 141]. Compare Bacon: "The first creature of God in the work of the days was the light of the sense, the last the light of reason, and His Sabbath work ever since is the illumination of His Spirit" [35 : 82]. Plotinus, Bacon and Balzac all teach (and every one who has had experience will agree with them) that there is as great an interval between Cosmic Consciousness and Self Consciousness as exists between the latter and Simple Consciousness.

There is a raying out of all orders of existence, an external emanation from the ineffable One. There is again a returning impulse, drawing all upwards and inwards towards the centre from whence all came. Love, as Plato in the "Banquet" beautifully says, is child of poverty and plenty. In the amorous quest of the soul after the good lies the painful sense of fall and deprivation.

But that love is blessing, is salvation, is our guardian genius; without it the centrifugal law would overpower us, and sweep our souls out far from their source toward the cold extremities of the material and the manifold. The wise man recognizes the idea of the good within him. This he develops by withdrawal into the holy place of his own soul. He who does not understand how the soul contains the beautiful within itself, seeks to realize beauty without by laborious production. His aim should rather be to concentrate and simplify, and so to expand his being; instead of going out into the manifold, to forsake it for the One, and so to float upwards towards the divine fount of being whose stream flows within him.

You ask, how can we know the Infinite? I answer, not by reason. It is the office of reason to distinguish and define. The Infinite, therefore, cannot be ranked among its objects. You can only apprehend the Infinite by a faculty superior to reason, by entering into a state in which you are your finite self no longer—in which the divine essence is communicated to you. This is ecstasy [Cosmic Consciousness]. It is the liberation of your mind from its finite consciousness. Like only can apprehend like; when you thus cease to be finite, you become one with the Infinite. In the reduction of your soul to its simplest self, its divine essence, you realize this union—this identity.

But this sublime condition is not of permanent duration. It is only now and then that we can enjoy this elevation (mercifully made possible for us) above the limits of the body and the world. I myself have realized it but three times as yet, and Porphyry hitherto not once. All that tends to purify and elevate the mind will assist you in this attainment, and facilitate the approach and the recurrence of these happy intervals. There are, then, different roads by which this end may be reached.

Plotinus (as he tells us) had had three periods of illumination at the time of writing this letter to Flaccus—that is, by the time he was fifty-six years old. We are told by Porphyry that between the age of fifty-nine and sixty-four (that is, during the six years of their intercourse) that he had four periods, making at least seven altogether. It will be noticed that what Plotinus says as to what aids in the passage to Cosmic Consciousness is precisely what is taught by all those who have attained—by Gautama, Jesus, Paul and the rest.

The love of beauty which exalts the poet; that devotion to the One and that ascent of science which makes the ambition of the philosopher, and that love and those prayers by which some devout and ardent soul tends in its moral purity towards perfection. These are the great highways conducting to that height above the actual and the particular, where we stand in the immediate presence of the Infinite, who shines out as from the deeps of the soul.

The following passage [83: 336] may be taken as a fair summing up of Plotinus' philosophy as this was understood by the Neoplatonists:

The human souls which have descended into corporeality are those which have allowed themselves to be ensnared by sensuality and overpowered by lust.

They now seek to cut themselves loose from their true being; and, striving after independence, they assume a false existence. They must turn back from this; and, since they have not lost their freedom, a conversion is still possible.

Here, then, we enter upon the practical philosophy. Along the same road by which it descended, the soul must retrace its steps back to the supreme Good. It must first of all return to itself. This is accomplished by the practice of virtue, which aims at likeness to God, and leads up to God. In the ethics of Plotinus all the older schemes of virtue are taken over, and arranged in a graduated series. The lowest stage is that of the civil virtues, then follow the purifying, and last of all the divine virtues. The civil virtues merely adorn the life, without elevating the soul. That is the office of the purifying virtues, by which the soul is freed from sensuality, and led back to itself, and thence to the *nous*. By means of ascetic observances the man becomes once more a spiritual and enduring being, free from all sin. But there is still a higher attainment; it is not enough to be sinless, one must become "God." This is reached through contemplation of the primeval Being, the One; or, in other words, through an ecstatic approach to it. Thought cannot attain to this, for thought reaches only to the *nous,* and is itself a kind of motion. Thought is a mere preliminary to communion with God. It is only in a state of perfect passivity and repose that the soul can recognize and touch the primeval Being. Hence in order to this highest attainment the soul must pass through a spiritual curriculum. Beginning with the contemplation of corporeal things in their multiplicity and harmony, it then retires upon itself and withdraws into the depths of its own being, rising thence to the *nous,* the world of ideas. But even there it does not find the Highest, the One; it still hears a voice saying, "Not we have made ourselves." The last stage is reached when, in the highest tension and concentration, beholding in silence and utter forgetfulness of all things, it is able as it were to lose itself. Then it may see God, the fountain of life, the source of being, the origin of all good, the root of the soul. In that moment it enjoys the highest indescribable bliss; it is as it were swallowed up of divinity, bathed in the light of eternity.

SUMMARY.

The writer has been able to learn but little of the outer life of Plotinus. Details of his illumination beyond what he tells us in the letter above quoted are equally wanting. But his own mention of the three "happy intervals," what he says of "this sublime condition" and the character of his philosophy makes it certain that he was a genuine case of Cosmic Consciousness. Unfortunately his age at the time of first illumination is unknown. Plotinus, however, having been born 204, having commenced the study of philosophy in the year 232, at the age of twenty-eight, and having written the above letter in 260, when fifty-six years of age (it was in that year that Valerian was taken prisoner by Sapor), would probably have been between thirty and forty at the time of his first illumination.

Chapter 5.

Mohammed.

Born 570; died 632.

This case, both in detail and ensemble, is marvellously complete. The contempt entertained towards this man by Christians is as creditable to them as is the corresponding contempt entertained towards Jesus by Mussulmans creditable to these. Mohammed was born in the tribe of Koreish, in August, in the year 570. His inheritance was five camels and a slave girl. His father died before his birth and his mother when he was six years old. As a boy and youth he earned his living tending sheep and goats.

Later he was a camel driver. At the age of twenty-five he married Cadijah, who was forty. The union was an eminently happy one. He was an honest, upright man, irreproachable in his domestic relations and universally esteemed by his fellow-citizens, who bestowed upon him the sobriquet of El Amin—"the trusty." "Mohammed was a man of middle height but a commanding presence; rather thin, but with broad shoulders and a wide chest; a massive head, a frank, oval face, with a clear complexion, restless black eyes, long, heavy eyelashes, a prominent, aquiline nose, white teeth and a full, thick beard. . . . He was a man of highly nervous organization, thoughtful, restless, inclined to melancholy and possessing an extreme sensibility, being unable to endure the slightest unpleasant odor or the least physical pain. . . . He was simple in his habits, kind and courteous in his demeanor and agreeable in conversation" [152: 19-20].

It seems that Mohammed had been, as a young and middle-

aged man, before his experience on Mount Hara, serious, devout,
earnest and deeply religious. It also seems (as already stated)
that this mental constitution is an essential prerequisite to the
attainment of Cosmic Consciousness. He clearly saw that the
religion of his countrymen was far from being in a satisfactory
condition, and it appeared to him that the time for reform or a
new departure had arrived.

We are told that he gradually absented himself from society and sought
the solitude of a cavern on Mount Hara (about three leagues north of Mecca),
where, in emulation of the Christian anchorites of the desert, he would remain
days and nights together engaged in prayer and meditation. . . . He became
subject to visions, ecstasies and trances. . . . At length, it is said, what had
hitherto been shadowed out in dreams was made apparent and distinct by an
angelic apparition and a divine annunciation.

It was in the fortieth year of his age when this famous revelation took
place. Accounts are given of it by Moslem writers, as if received from his own
lips, and it is alluded to in certain passages of the Koran. He was passing,
as was his wont, the month of Ramadan in the cavern of Mount Hara, endeavoring by fasting, prayer and solitary meditation to elevate his thoughts to
the contemplation of divine truth.

It was on the night called by Arabs Al Kader, or The Divine Decree; a night
in which, according to the Koran, angels descend to earth and Gabriel brings
down the decrees of God. During that night there is peace on earth, and a
holy quiet reigns over all nature until the rising of the morn.

As Mohammed, in the silent watches of the night, lay wrapped in his mantle,
he heard a voice calling upon him. Uncovering his head, a flood of light
broke upon him of such intolerable splendor that he swooned. On regaining
his senses he beheld an angel in a human form, which, approaching from a
distance, displayed a silken cloth covered with written characters. "𝕽𝖊𝖆𝖉!"
said the angel. "I know not how to read!" replied Mohammed. "𝕽𝖊𝖆𝖉!"
repeated the angel, "𝖎𝖓 𝖙𝖍𝖊 𝖓𝖆𝖒𝖊 𝖔𝖋 𝖙𝖍𝖊 𝕷𝖔𝖗𝖉, 𝖜𝖍𝖔 𝖍𝖆𝖘 𝖈𝖗𝖊𝖆𝖙𝖊𝖉 𝖆𝖑𝖑 𝖙𝖍𝖎𝖓𝖌𝖘; 𝖜𝖍𝖔
𝖈𝖗𝖊𝖆𝖙𝖊𝖉 𝖒𝖆𝖓 𝖋𝖗𝖔𝖒 𝖆 𝖈𝖑𝖔𝖙 𝖔𝖋 𝖇𝖑𝖔𝖔𝖉. 𝕽𝖊𝖆𝖉, 𝖎𝖓 𝖙𝖍𝖊 𝖓𝖆𝖒𝖊 𝖔𝖋 𝖙𝖍𝖊 𝕸𝖔𝖘𝖙 𝕳𝖎𝖌𝖍, 𝖜𝖍𝖔
𝖙𝖆𝖚𝖌𝖍𝖙 𝖒𝖆𝖓 𝖙𝖍𝖊 𝖚𝖘𝖊 𝖔𝖋 𝖙𝖍𝖊 𝖕𝖊𝖓; 𝖜𝖍𝖔 𝖘𝖍𝖊𝖉𝖘 𝖔𝖓 𝖍𝖎𝖘 𝖘𝖔𝖚𝖑 𝖙𝖍𝖊 𝖗𝖆𝖞 𝖔𝖋 𝖐𝖓𝖔𝖜𝖑𝖊𝖉𝖌𝖊 𝖆𝖓𝖉
𝖙𝖊𝖆𝖈𝖍𝖊𝖘 𝖍𝖎𝖒 𝖜𝖍𝖆𝖙 𝖇𝖊𝖋𝖔𝖗𝖊 𝖍𝖊 𝖐𝖓𝖊𝖜 𝖓𝖔𝖙."

Upon this Mohammed instantly felt his understanding illumined with celestial light and read what was written on the cloth, which contained the decree
of God, as afterwards promulgated in the Koran. When he had finished the
perusal the heavenly messenger announced: "𝕺𝖍, 𝕸𝖔𝖍𝖆𝖒𝖒𝖊𝖉, 𝖔𝖋 𝖆 𝖛𝖊𝖗𝖎𝖙𝖞 𝖙𝖍𝖔𝖚
𝖆𝖗𝖙 𝖙𝖍𝖊 𝖕𝖗𝖔𝖕𝖍𝖊𝖙 𝖔𝖋 𝕲𝖔𝖉! 𝕬𝖓𝖉 𝕴 𝖆𝖒 𝖍𝖎𝖘 𝕬𝖓𝖌𝖊𝖑 𝕲𝖆𝖇𝖗𝖎𝖊𝖑!"

Mohammed, we are told, came trembling and agitated to Cadijah in the
morning, not knowing whether what he had heard and seen was indeed true,
and that he was a prophet decreed to effect that reform so long the object of

his meditations; or whether it might not be a mere vision, a delusion of the senses, or worse than all, the apparition of an evil spirit [102:32-3].

Illumination in Mohammed's case took place in or about the month of April. It occurred in the Arabic month Ramadan (82a:553). Now in the first year after the Hegira this month fell in our December. But the Mohammedan year is ten days shorter than the time actually taken by the revolution of the earth in its orbit. It is plain, therefore, that any given Mohammedan date would recur ten days earlier year by year. Now the Hegira was twelve years after Mohammed's illumination. That is to say, if the month Ramadan corresponded with December just after the Hegira it would have corresponded with April at the time of the prophet's illumination. That illumination, therefore, would have taken place in April.

If Mohammed was a case of Cosmic Consciousness this fact ought to appear clearly in the writings which he left to the world. Does it? As a matter of fact these are not easily understood in an English translation and from the modern, western, point of view. Note, for instance, the remarks of one reader who might be supposed competent to appreciate such a work as the Qur'an. Carlyle says of it [59:295]: "It is as toilsome reading as ever I undertook. A wearisome, confused jumble, crude, incondite, endless iterations, longwindedness, entanglement, insupportable stupidity in short," and so on at some length.

In spite of all this, however, even if multiplied a thousand times, the greatness, power, spirituality of the book must be considered established by the results it has produced in the world. No effect can be greater than its cause, and the effect in this case (the spiritual elevation of many millions of men for many generations) must be admitted to have been enormous. Moreover, it seems to the writer that, in spite of the undoubted difficulty above referred to, almost any candid reader may perceive for himself, upon its perusal, that the book has great qualities, even though he may not be able to fully grasp them.

But there is another reason why we do not find just what we want for our present purpose in the Qur'an. It is written entirely from the point of view of the Cosmic Sense; as its author would say, it is all dictated by Gabriel.   There are no passages in which the self conscious tells us about the cosmic conscious Mohammed—such passages as occur with great frequency in the writings of Yepes, Whitman and others—passages written from the point of view of the "Shakespeare" Sonnets.   Nevertheless, there are here and there sentences in the Qur'an that almost certainly refer to the experience in question, as, for instance, the following:

Verily, in the creation of the heavens and the earth, and the alternation of night and day, and in the ship that runneth in the sea with that which profits man, and in what water God sends down from heaven and quickens therewith the earth after its death, and spreads abroad therein all kinds of cattle, and in the shifting of the winds, and in the clouds that are pressed into service betwixt heaven and earth, are signs to people who can understand [151: 22].

Mohammed is seeking to point out the (to him) certainty of an infinitely good God and eternal life. He uses here very much the same language as does Whitman in the same connection: "I hear you whispering there O stars of heaven, O suns, O grass of graves, O perpetual transfers and promotions, if you do not say anything how can I say anything" [193 : 77]?

And when we said to thee, "Verily, thy Lord encompasses men!" and we made the vision which we showed thee only a cause of sedition unto men, and the cursed tree as well; for we will frighten them, but it will only increase them in great rebellion [153: 7].

"The vision"—evidently the cosmic vision.

They will ask thee of the spirit. Say, "The spirit comes at the bidding of my Lord, and ye are given but a little knowledge thereof." If we had wished we would have taken away that with which we have inspired thee: then thou wouldst have found no guardian against us, unless by a mercy from thy Lord; verily, his grace towards thee is great [153: 10]!

He speaks of "the spirit" who visits him—"Gabriel," the Cosmic Sense—and uses almost the same words as Jesus: "The wind bloweth where it listeth, and thou hearest the voice thereof, but knowest not whence it cometh and whither it goeth: *so is every one that is born of the Spirit*" [17 : 3 : 8].

We do not descend save at the bidding of thy Lord: His is what is before us, and what is behind us, and what is between those; for thy Lord is never forgetful—the Lord of the heavens and the earth, and of what is between the two; then serve Him and persevere in His service [153: 31-2].

"We do not descend." Palmer's note to these words is: "Among various conjectures the one most usually accepted by the Mohammedan commentators is, that these are the words of the angel Gabriel in answer to Mohammed's complaint of long intervals elapsing between the periods of revelation. Compare, in chapter on Bacon, infra Sonnet xxxiii, and comment thereon.

Verily, the hour is coming, I almost make it appear, that every soul may be recompensed for its efforts [153:35].

an individual having the faculty can bestow it almost at will. "I bestow," says Whitman, "upon any man or woman the entrance to all the gifts of the universe." There is a sense, of course, in which both these propositions are true: (1) The new faculty is becoming universal and (2) these men, having the faculty, do bestow it upon such others as coming into contact with them are eligible.

The words, "I almost make it appear," would seem to refer to the feeling almost or quite universal with those having cosmic consciousness that universal endowment with this faculty is near, is imminent, and that

This life of the world is nothing but a sport and a play; but, verily, the abode of the next world—that is, life. If they did but know! [153:124.]

The distinction between the self and cosmic conscious lives.

He who wishes for the tilth of the next world, we will increase for him the tilth; and he who desires the tilth of this world, we will give him thereof; but in the next he shall have no portion [153:207].

A rich man, from the mere fact of being such, is unlikely to enter cosmic consciousness. If he does he probably abandons his wealth, as did Gautama and E. C. If, however, a man (not having it) very earnestly desires wealth, or (having it) sets his heart upon it, such shall certainly in Cosmic Consciousness "have no portion."

The life of this world is but a play and a sport; but if you believe and fear God, he will give you your hire [153:232].

Insignificance of the self conscious as compared with the cosmic conscious life.

And every soul shall come—with it a driver and a witness! Thou wert heedless of this, and we withdrew thy veil from thee, and to-day is thine eyesight keen! [153:243.]

"Withdrew thy veil"—reference to the illumination of Mohammed. He "saw the heavens rent asunder" [15:1:10].

And paradise shall be brought near to the pious—not far off [153:243].

This is what ye are promised, to every one who turns frequently (to God) and keeps His commandments, who fears the merciful in secret and brings a repentant heart. Enter into it in peace; this is the day of eternity! [153:244.]

"The kingdom of God is nigh at hand" [16:21:31]. "The kingdom of God is *within you*" [16:17:21].

Illumination—the Cosmic Sense—the Brahmic bliss—the kingdom of God—is rightly called here "the day of eternity," since the entrance to it is the entrance to immortality —eternity.

And listen for the day when the crier shall cry from a near place—the day when they shall hear the shout in truth—that is, the day of coming forth [153:244].

The suddenness and unexpectedness of the oncoming of Cosmic Consciousness is noted in the writings of nearly all of those who have experienced illumination. "That day —the day of deliverance—shall come to you in what place you know not; it shall come, but you know not the time. In the pulpit

while you are preaching the sermon, behold! suddenly the ties and the bands shall drop off; in the prison One shall come, and you shall go free forever. In the field, with the plough and chain-harrow; by the side of your horse in the stall; in the midst of fashionable life; in making and receiving morning calls; in your drawing-room—even there, who knows? It shall duly, at the appointed hour, come [61 : 231].

Know that the life of this world is but a sport, and a play, and an adornment, and something to boast of amongst yourselves; and the multiplying of children is like a rain-growth, its vegetation pleases the misbelievers; then they wither away, and thou mayest see them become yellow; then they become but grit [153 : 268].

Insignificance of the merely self conscious life.

Verily, we set it down on the Night of Power! And what shall make thee know what the Night of Power is? The Night of Power is better than a thousand months! The angels and the spirits descend therein, by the permission of their Lord with every bidding [153 : 337].

"It," the Qur'an, "the Night of Power" (the night of Mohammed's illumination), "is better than a thousand months!" So Böhme, referring to his illumination, says [40 : 15]: "The gate was opened to me that in *one-quarter of an hour* I saw and knew more than if I had been many years together at an university."

In this case we have authentically reported (as it seems) all the fundamental elements required to constitute a case of Cosmic Consciousness:

a. The subjective light.

b. The moral elevation.

c. The intellectual illumination.

d. The sense of immortality.

e. The definiteness, suddenness and unexpectedness of the on-coming of the new state.

f. The previous mental and physical character of the man.

g. The age of illumination, in his fortieth year, later than the average, but while he was still in his prime.

h. The added charm to his personality, so that he was able to gain and hold devoted followers.

CHAPTER 6.

Dante.

BORN 1265; Died 1321.

Balzac [9 : 241 and 263] clearly intimates his conviction that Dante was a "Specialist," which is his name for a man who has

Cosmic Consciousness. Balzac probably knew Dante very thoroughly, and could not be mistaken on this point, he being himself a "Specialist"; for as a musician knows of another man whether or not he is a musician, as a poet knows of another man whether or not he is a poet, as a painter knows of another man whether or not he is a painter, as a man with the sense of sight living in a country inhabited with men nearly all of whom are blind must know who among his acquaintances can see and who cannot, so to-day, and all days, a man who has the Cosmic Sense will know of any given man with whom he is acquainted, either personally or by his works, whether or not he also has it. We could therefore accept with confidence Balzac's word that Dante had the Cosmic Sense, but let us not do so—let us try to see for ourselves.

I.

Dante's outward life and personality are as good as lost to us of the nineteenth century. It seems clear, however, and the character of his writings would indicate the same thing, that, as Boccaccio says [81: 809], even as a young man he was:

Taken by the sweetness of knowing the truth of the things concealed in heaven, and finding no other pleasure dearer to him in life, he left all other worldly care and gave himself to this alone, and, that no part of philosophy might remain unseen by him, he plunged with acute intellect into the deepest recesses of theology, and so far succeeded in his design that, caring nothing for heat or cold, or watchings, or fastings, or any other bodily discomforts, by assiduous study he came to know of the divine essence and of the other separate intelligences all that the human intellect can comprehend.

And Leonardo Bruni says of him that:

By study of philosophy, of theology, astrology, arithmetic and geometry, by reading of history, by the turning over many curious books, watching and sweating in his studies, he acquired the science which he was to adorn and explain in his verses.

All which means that Dante was of a thoughtful, studious, earnest nature, and we may interpret this fact to mean either that in his case such a life led up to a high poetic genius *within the limits of self consciousness,* or that it led up (as claimed here) to Cosmic Consciousness.   In any case, Dante's youth seems to have been such as we often find in men who attain illumination.

II.

Now, as to the outward man, Boccaccio says [111:200]:

Our poet was of middle height, and after reaching mature years he went somewhat stooping; his gait was grave and sedate; always clothed in the most becoming garments, his dress was suited to the ripeness of his years; his face was long, his nose aquiline, his eyes rather large than small, his jaw heavy and his under lip prominent; his complexion was dark, and his hair and beard thick, black and crisp, and his countenance was always sad and thoughtful. . . . His manners, whether in public or at home, were wonderfully composed and restrained, and in all his ways he was more courteous and civil than any one else.

Again Charles E. Norton [111:204] says of an undoubtedly authentic death-mask of the poet:

The face is one of the most pathetic upon which human eyes ever looked, for it exhibits in its expression the conflict between the strong nature of the man and the hard dealings of fortune—between the idea of his life and its practical experience.   Strength is the most striking attribute of the countenance, displayed alike in the broad forehead, the masculine nose, the firm lips, the heavy jaw and wide chin; and this strength, resulting from the main forms of the features, is enforced by the strength of the lines of expression.   The look is grave and stern almost to grimness; there is a scornful lift to the eyebrows, and a contraction of the forehead as from painful thought; but obscured under this look, yet not lost, are the marks of tenderness, refinement and self-mastery, which, in combination with more obvious characteristics, give to the countenance of the dead poet an ineffable dignity and melancholy.   There is neither weakness nor failure here.   It is the image of the strong fortress, of a strong soul "buttressed on conscience and impregnable will," battered by the blows of enemies without and within, bearing upon its walls the dints of many a siege, but standing firm and unshaken against all attacks until the warfare was at an end.

III.

As to the quality of Dante's mind and of his work, it will be well to quote here, briefly, perhaps as high an authority as has lived in recent times. He says:

The Dantesque account of Hell, Purgatory and Paradise is not an arbitrary or fantastic dream, but the vivid and substantial embodiment of a profound philosophy * [179:104].

*This is of course necessarily true of every book that springs from, is dictated by, the Cosmic Sense.

Meanwhile, leaving antiquarians to elucidate the pedigree of Dante's ideas, we may observe that from his earliest boyhood he was familiar with dreams and visions, and that he hints himself, at the end of the "Vita Nuova," that the vision of the "Comedy" came to him as a revelation, while he was pondering on the thought of death and upon the memory of Beatrice * [179:109].

*The writer, while knowing nothing about Cosmic Consciousness, adopts, as it were perforce, the same theory of Dante and his work as that propounded here.

The object of the whole work (he writes to Can Grande) is to make those who live in this life leave their state of misery and to lead them to a state of happiness † [179:110].

† The main object in life in the case of every (?) man having the Cosmic Sense is to bestow it upon the race, and each feels in himself some power to so bestow it.

IV.

In the "Divine Comedy" (a book strictly parallel to the "Comédie Humaine," or the "Leaves of Grass," in the sense that it is a picture of the world from the point of view of the writer), Dante tells, first, in the "Inferno," of human life as seen among ill-doers, the "sinful," the "wicked." Then, in the "Purgatorio"—"that second realm where the human spirit is purified and becomes worthy to ascend to heaven" [71:1]—he speaks of human life as seen in those who are struggling towards the light —who are trying to lead good lives but are so far overburdened by hereditary flaws, faults committed, bad habits formed, unfortunate surroundings and other adverse circumstances. These are the better people—short of illumination. But in the "Paradiso" Dante treats of the new world of the Cosmic Sense—of the kingdom of God—Nirvâna.

Beatrice—"Making Happy"—is the Cosmic Sense (which, in fact, alone, makes happy). The name may have been suggested by a beautiful girl (so named). If so, the coincidence is curious.

That the meaning is as here said, seems clear from a hundred passages. Take one. Virgil says to Dante: "So much as reason seeth here can I tell thee; beyond that [beyond reason, the self conscious mind] awaits still for Beatrice" [71: 114]. What *is* beyond reason—the self conscious mind—but Cosmic Consciousness?

Dante wanders through the self conscious world ("Inferno" and "Purgatorio") guided by Virgil (chosen as a splendid example and type of the self conscious mind, and also probably because he had really been one of Dante's principal guides before his illumination). But Virgil was not a case of Cosmic Consciousness, and of course he cannot enter into Paradise. Beatrice (the Cosmic Sense) leads Dante into that realm and is his guide there.

Dante's "Vita Nuova," written at the end of the thirteenth century, was first published in 1309, when he was forty-four years of age. At the very end of it he seems to speak of the oncoming of Cosmic Consciousness.

The "Divine Comedy" was finished in 1321, the time of the action being strictly confined to the end of March and the beginning of April, 1300 [81: 815] at which time Dante was thirty-five years old. It seems almost certain that this was the date of his illumination. It would be at the typical age and in the typical season, and there seems nothing against the supposition. It is a reasonable presumption that the earlier book, "Vita Nuova," was being written up to the early spring of 1300; that when illumination took place it was closed to give place to a greater work then to be begun; that the latter book, the "Divine Comedy," was actually begun at that date.

V.

The "Vita Nuova" [68] closes as follows:

After this sonnet a wonderful vision appeared to me, in which I saw things which made me resolve to speak no more of this blessed one (Beatrice) until I could more worthily treat of her. And, to attain to this, I study to the utmost of my power, as she truly knows. So that, if it shall please Him through whom all things live, that my life be prolonged for some years, I hope to say of her what was never said of any woman.

VI.

We will now follow Dante's experience as closely as possible in his own words, using always, as we have done above, the translation of Charles Elliot Norton. And we take first from the "Purgatorio" passages descriptive of Dante's approach to the divine land. When Dante is about to enter Cosmic Consciousness Virgil says of him:

Expect no more or word or sign from me. Free, upright and sane in thine own free will, and it would be wrong not to act according to its pleasure; wherefore thee over thyself I crown and mitre [71: 176].

There are two points here well worthy of being noted: (1) When the Cosmic Sense comes the rules and standards belonging to self consciousness are suspended. "Confronted, turned back, laid away" [193 : 153], is Whitman's expression. No man with the Cosmic Sense will take direction (in the affairs of the soul) from any other man or any so-called God. In his own heart he holds the highest accessible standard, and to that he will and must adhere; that only can he obey. (2) The other is the duplication of the individual: "Thee over thyself." Compare with these words "The other I am," of Whitman: " 'Tis thee (myself) that for myself I praise," of "Shakespeare" [176 : 62]; "If any man is in Christ he is a new creature," of Paul; "Except a man be born anew," of Jesus. A new individual must be born within the old one, and, being so born, will live its own distinct life.

Virgil withdraws. The self conscious mind abdicates its sovereignty in presence of the greater authority. Dante comes into immediate relation with Beatrice—Cosmic Consciousness.

A lady appeared to me robed with the color of living flame. I turned me to the left with the confidence with which the little child runs to his mother when he is frightened, or when he is troubled, to say to Virgil: "Less than a drachm of blood remains in me that does not tremble, I recognize the signals of the ancient flame;" but Virgil had left us deprived of himself [71: 191].

The Cosmic Sense robed with the subjective light. At the threshold of the new sense Virgil (the type here of human faculty short of it) leaves Dante. Not that simple and self consciousness leave us when we enter Cosmic Consciousness, *but they do cease to guide us*—"the eyesight has another eyesight, the hearing another hearing, and the voice another voice" [193 : 342].

And as my face stretched upward my eyes saw Beatrice. Beneath her veil and beyond the stream she seemed to me more to surpass her ancient self than she surpassed the others here when she was here [71: 198].

The new world is still ve.led and far off, but even so its glory far transcends anything in the old world of mere self consciousness.

When I was near the blessed shore the beautiful lady [nature?] opened her arms, clasped my head and plunged me in where it behooved that I should swallow the water [71: 199].

"The drinking of the waters of Lethe, which obliterate the memory of sin."—Norton's note. There is no sense of sin in Cosmic Consciousness.

Oh, splendor of living light eternal! who hath become so pallid under the shadow of Parnassus, or hath so drunk at its cistern that he would not seem to have his mind encumbered, trying to represent thee as thou didst appear there, where in harmony the heaven overshadows thee when in the open air thou didst thyself disclose [71: 201]?

The best prepared poet (on the level of self consciousness) by study and practice could not portray the new world, when it freely (in the open air) discloses itself. "No shuttered room or school can commune with me," says the Cosmic Sense by the tongue of Whitman [193 : 75].

Beatrice (the Cosmic Sense) says to Dante:

Thou shalt be with me without end a citizen of that Rome whereof Christ is a Roman [71: 206].

Dante enters into equality with Jesus. Compare Whitman's "To him who was crucified" [193 : 298].

Again Beatrice says to him:

From fear and from shame I wish that thou henceforth divest thyself [71: 211].

Compare Balzac's "Jesus was a Specialist," and Paul's "Heirs of God and joint heirs with Christ." Neither fear nor shame can exist along with the Cosmic Sense.

VII.

So much for the approach to the Cosmic Sense. Let us see next what Dante says of it after having entered into it.

The glory of Him who moves everything penetrates through the universe and shines in one part more and in another less. In the heaven that receives most of its light I have been, and have seen things which he who descends from there above neither knows how nor is able to recount [72: 1].

So Paul heard "unspeakable words," and Whitman when he "tried to tell the best" of that which he had seen became dumb.

On a sudden day seemed to be added to day as if he who is able had adorned the heaven with another sun [72: 4].

"As in a swoon, one instant, another sun, ineffable, full dazzles me" [192 : 207].

This is, of course, the subjective light seen by Mohammed, Paul and others at the moment of entrance into the Cosmic Sense.

Beatrice was standing with her eyes wholly fixed on the eternal wheels, and on her I fixed my eyes from there above removed. Looking at her, I inwardly became such as Glaucus * became on tasting of the herb which made him consort in the sea of the other gods. Transhumanizing cannot be signified in words; therefore, let the example † suffice for him to whom grace reserves experience. If I were only what of me thou didst last create,‡ O love that governest the heavens, thou knowest, who with thy light didst lift me.

When the revolution which thou, being desired, makest eternal § made me attent unto itself with the harmony which thou attunest and modulatest, so much of the heaven then seemed to me enkindled by the flame of the sun, that rain or river never made so broad a lake [72:4].

* Glaucus—the steersman of the ship Argo —who was changed into a god.

† Of Glaucus.

‡ If I continued to be a mere man.

§ The desire for God leads a man from self to Cosmic Consciousness, and that revolution, when effected, is eternal.

When Dante awoke into the Cosmic Sense, into the new Cosmos, the first thing to strike him (as it is and must be the first thing to strike every one who so awakes) was the vision of the "Eternal Wheels"—the "Chain of Causation"—the universal order—a vision infinitely beyond expression by human words. His new self—Beatrice—had its eyes fixed on this, the Cosmic unfolding. Gazing thereupon the Cosmic vision and the Cosmic rapture transhumanized him into a god. It is this vision of the universal order coming instantaneously, lighting the world as lightning illumines the landscape, but, unlike lightning, remaining, that has led the present writer to adopt the name "Cosmic Consciousness"—a Consciousness of the Cosmos. Compare with Dante's Gautama's experience as given in the Maha Vegga [163 : 208]: "During the first watch of the night he fixed his mind upon the chain of causation; during the second watch he did the same; during the third he did the same." And, as already shown, this is among the very earliest and most reliable accounts of the illumination of the Buddha.

After illumination Dante wrote the "Divine Comedy." In it (as a whole) must be sought the expression, such as Dante could give, of the Cosmic vision. It is, therefore, a parallel statement with the Qur'an, the Upanishads, Suttas, the Pauline Epistles, the words of Jesus, the "Comédie Humaine," the "Leaves of Grass," the "Shakespeare" drama and "Sonnets," the works of Behmen, and "Towards Democracy."

To sum up, we have in this case:

a. The characteristic suddenness that belongs to the oncoming of the Cosmic Sense.

b. Illumination occurs at the typical age and time of year.

c. The subjective light is a strongly marked feature.

d. Intellectual illumination.

e. Moral elevation.

f. The sense of immortality.

g. The extinction of the sense of sin and of shame and of fear of death.

CHAPTER 7.

Bartolomé Las Casas.

BORN 1474; died 1566.

"One of the most remarkable men of the sixteenth century" [128: 206]. "Las Casas was the brightest star of this small constellation [the early Spanish-Americans]. With the eye of a seer he saw, and, in the words of a prophet, he foretold the judgment that would fall on Spain for the horrors perpetrated on the wretched aborigines" [119: 706].

"Bartolomé de las Casas was born in Seville in 1474. His family, one of the noblest in Spain, was of French origin, descended from the Viscounts of Limoges. They were already in Spain before the thirteenth century, and played a distinguished part in the conquest of Seville from the Moors by Ferdinand III of Castile, in 1252. From that time forward members of the family were to be found in positions of trust, and among their marked traits of character were invincible courage and spotless integrity. By birth and training Bartolomé was an aristocrat to the very tips of his fingers" [89: 437].

Las Casas went to Hispaniola and settled on an estate in that island in 1502.

Little is known of his first occupation there, except that he seems to have been more or less concerned in money-making, like all the other settlers. About 1510 he was ordained as a priest. He fulfilled three or four vocations, being an eager man of business, a laborious and accurate historian, a great reformer, a great philanthropist and a vigorous ecclesiastic [98: 2].

He was eloquent, acute, truthful, bold, self-sacrificing, pious [98: 3].

His was one of the lives that are beyond biography, and require a history to be written in order to illustrate them. His career affords, perhaps, a solitary instance of a man who, being neither a conqueror, a discoverer nor an inventor, has, by the pure force of benevolence, become so notable a figure that large portions of history cannot be written, or at least cannot be understood, without the narrative of his deeds and efforts being made one of the principal threads upon which the history is strung. In early American history Las Casas is, undoubtedly, the principal figure. He has been justly called "the Great Apostle of the Indies" [98:289].

He was a person of such immense ability and strength of character that in whatever age of the world he had lived he would undoubtedly have been one of its foremost men. As a man of business he had rare executive power. He was a great diplomatist and an eloquent preacher, a man of titanic energy, ardent but self-controlled, of unconquerable tenacity, warm-hearted and tender, calm in his judgments, shrewdly humorous, absolutely fearless and absolutely true. He made many and bitter enemies, and some of them were unscrupulous enough; but I believe no one has ever accused him of any worse sin than extreme fervor of temperament. His wrath would rise to a white heat and indeed there was occasion enough for it. He was also very apt to call a spade a spade, and to proclaim unpleasant truths with pungent emphasis [89:439].

By the year 1510 the slavery of the Indians, under the names repartimentos and encomiendas, had become deplorably cruel. An Indian's life was counted of no value. It was cheaper to work an Indian to death and get another than to take care of him, and accordingly the slaves were worked to death without mercy. From time to time they rose in rebellion, then they were "slaughtered by the hundreds, burned alive, impaled on sharp stakes, torn to pieces by bloodhounds" [89:443].

Las Casas was by natural endowment a many-sided man, who looked at human affairs from various points of view. Under other circumstances he need not necessarily have developed into a philanthropist, though any career into which he might have been drawn could not have failed to be honorable and noble. At first he seems to have been what one might call worldly-minded. But the most interesting thing about him we shall find to be his steady intellectual and spiritual development; from year to year he rose to higher and higher planes of thought and feeling. He was at first a slave-owner, like the rest, and had seen no harm in it. But from the first his kindly, sympathetic nature asserted itself, and his treatment of his slaves was such that they loved him. He was a man of striking and easily distinguishable aspect, and the Indians in general, who fled from the sight of a white man, came soon to recognize him as a friend who could always be trusted [89:448].

About 1512-13 Velasquez conquered Cuba, reducing the natives to slavery. Las Casas presently followed him into the island, and received from him a half interest in a large village of Indians. He entered into possession as a mere matter of course, and settled down in the island.

We come now to the definite fact which, if it can be relied upon
as having happened as told, proves (along with the facts of his
life) that Las Casas was a case of Cosmic Consciousness. Not
only so, but it would seem—from his supreme physical and mental
vigor, prolonged to a great age, from his splendid moral nature,
from his intellect, said to be proved by his writings to be first-class,
from his personal magnetism and from his high spiritual endowments—that this man stands among the supreme examples of
those who have been endowed with this splendid faculty.

It was the duty of Las Casas to say mass, and now and then to preach, and
in thinking of his sermon for Pentecost, 1514, he opened his Bible, and his eyes
alighted upon these verses, in the thirty-fourth chapter of Ecclesiasticus:
"The Most High is not pleased with the offerings of the wicked; neither is
he pacified for sin by the multitude of sacrifices.
"The bread of the needy is their life; he that defraudeth him thereof is a
man of blood.
"He that taketh away his neighbor's living slayeth him; and he that defraudeth the laborer of his hire is a shedder of blood."
As he read these words a light from heaven seemed to shine upon Las
Casas. The scales fell from his eyes. He saw that the system of slavery was
wrong in principle [89:450].

At this time Las Casas was forty years of age. Fiske goes on
to tell how for fifty-two more years he lived one of the most active,
beautiful and beneficent of lives, dying at last "in Madrid, after a
few days' illness, at the age of ninety-two. In all this long and
arduous life—except for a moment, perhaps, on the crushing news
of the destruction of his colony upon the Pearl Coast—we find
no record of work interrupted by sickness, and to the very last
his sight was not dim nor his natural force abated" [89:481].
Fiske concludes:

In contemplating such a life as that of Las Casas all words of eulogy seem
weak and frivolous. The historian can only bow in reverent awe before a figure
which is in some respects the most beautiful and sublime in the annals of Christianity since the apostolic age. When now and then in the course of the centuries God's providence brings such a life into this world, the memory of it
must be cherished by mankind as one of its most precious and sacred possessions. For the thoughts, the words, the deeds of such a man, there is no death.
The sphere of their influence goes on widening forever. They bud, they blossom, they bear fruit, from age to age [89:482].

As Las Casas wrote, evidence more or less decisive on the point here raised should be found under his own hand. But most of his compositions were short and were occupied with special and current topics; the work in which (if at all) he may have touched upon the supposed event in his personal history is his "Historia General de las Indias," and this, unfortunately, has never been printed.

At his death he left it to the convent of San Gregorio, at Valladolid, with directions that it should not be printed for forty years, nor be seen during that time by any layman or member of the fraternity. . . . The Royal Academy of History revised the first volume some years since with a view to the publication of the whole work; but the indiscreet and imaginative style of the composition, according to Navarrete, and the consideration that its most important facts were already known through other channels, induced that body to abandon the design. With deference to their judgment, it seems to me a mistake. Las Casas, with every deduction, is one of the great writers of the nation—great from the important truths which he discerned when none else could see them, and with the courage with which he proclaimed them to the world. They are scattered over his history as well as his other writings. They are not, however, the passages transcribed by Herrara [128:212].

It is a fair inference, from the above remarks, that the writings of Las Casas have the qualities usually found in those which proceed from Cosmic Consciousness, such as boldness, originality, unconventionality, keen insight, sympathy, courage. And over and above these it is quite possible that were they examined they would be found to contain proof, by direct statement, that their author possessed the Cosmic Sense.

To sum up: Las Casas was presumably possessed of Cosmic Consciousness, because:

a. Of his unusual health and strength; for this great faculty commonly occurs in exceptional physical organizations.

b. Of his "striking aspect" and of the affection felt for him by the Indians and others.

c. Of his mental growth after the age at which the intellectual and moral stature is usually complete.

d. Of the sudden and immense change that took place in him

at the age of forty, when he was past the period of moral evolution within the compass of the ordinary, self conscious man.

e. Because of the intellectual, but especially of the moral, stature attained by him—higher (it may be safely said) than is ever attained within the limits of mere self consciousness.

f. And because of (if it can be depended upon, and it seems so likely that it is easy to believe it) the subjective light said to have been experienced by him about Pentecost, 1514. If this could be shown to be of the same character as the light that shone within Paul, Mohammed and others, then it would be certain that Las Casas possessed the Cosmic Sense. Even as the case stands there is little doubt of it. It must not be forgotten that the (supposed) subjective light was the immediate forerunner of Las Casas' spiritual new birth, nor that this latter occurred at the characteristic time of year—while he was thinking of his sermon for Pentecost—therefore towards the end of May or early in June.

CHAPTER 8.

John Yepes (Called St. John of the Cross).

BORN 1542; died 1591.

John Yepes was born at Fontibere, near Avila, in old Castile, on the twenty-fourth of June, 1542. His father died when he was a child, and his mother was left poor. He studied at the College of Jesuits. At twenty-one years of age he took the religious habit among the Carmelite Friars at Medina. His religious zeal continually increased. When he arrived at Salamanca, in order to commence his higher studies, the austerities which he practiced were excessive. At twenty-five years of age he was promoted to the priesthood. At the age of about thirty, or perhaps between that age and thirty-three, he passed through a period of "interior trouble of mind, scruples and a disrelish of spiritual exercises; . . . the devils assaulted him with violent temptations; . . . the most terrible of all these pains was that of scrupulosity and interior desolation, in which he seemed to see hell open, ready to swallow him up" [31:552].

After some time certain rays of light, comfort and divine sweetness scattered these mists and translated the soul of the servant of God into a paradise of interior delights and heavenly sweetness [31:552].

He had another period of depression, followed by still more perfect illumination and happiness.

A certain brightness darted from his countenance on many occasions—especially when he came from the altar or from prayer. It is said that a heavenly light at times shone from his countenance [31:554].

He enjoyed the happiness characteristic of the Cosmic Conscious state. Butler quotes him as saying: "The soul of one who serves God always swims in joy, always keeps a holiday, is always in her palace of jubilation, ever singing with fresh ardor and fresh pleasure a new song of joy and love" [31:557].

Two hours before he died he repeated aloud the Miserere psalm with his brethren; then he desired one to read him part of the book of Canticles, appearing himself in transports of joy. He at length cried out: *"Glory be to God!"* pressed the crucifix on his breast, and, after some time, said: *"Lord, into thy hands I commend my soul,"* with which words he calmly died, fourteenth of December, 1591, at the age of forty-nine [31:558].

For originating, or adhering to, some monastic forms he was, in 1578, imprisoned for some months, and it was during this time, at the age of thirty-six, that he entered Cosmic Consciousness.

On the fifteenth of August, 1578, he had been eight months in prison. On the twenty-fourth of June the same year he was thirty-six years of age.

Illumination occurred when he was in prison and apparently (but the record is not clear on this point) a very few months before the fifteenth of August. All available evidence considered, it seems about certain that illumination took place in spring or early summer, and that Yepes was within a month or two (before or after) of his thirty-sixth birthday at the time [112:108].

It was in the same year, after illumination [112:141], that he began to write.

The phenomenon of the subjective light seems to have manifested itself with unusual intensity in this case.

Others are said to have seen it. Also it is said to have lighted him about the monastery. These latter statements doubtless rest upon exaggeration or confusion such as is found in the description of the same phenomenon in Paul's case. It is curious, too, that in the case of John Yepes, partial blindness, lasting some days, followed, and was evidently in some way connected with the subjective light.

In the case of Paul the blindness was more marked and lasted longer. It would seem that the centric disturbance which must coexist with the subjective light may be so great as to leave the optic centre, for a time, incapable of reacting under its ordinary stimulus. It seems clear that both in the case of Paul and in that of Yepes the change that gave rise to the blindness was centric. One of Yepes' biographers describes the phenomenon of the light itself and its effects upon his eyes in the following words:

His cell became filled with light seen by the bodily eye. One night the friar who kept him went as usual to see that his prisoner was safe, and witnessed the heavenly light with which the cell was flooded. He did not stop to consider it, but hurried to the prior, thinking that some one in the house had keys to open the doors of the prison. The prior, with two religious went at once to the prison, but on his entering the room through which the prison was approached the light vanished. The prior, however, entered the cell, and, finding it dark, opened the lantern with which he had provided himself, and asked the prisoner who had given him light. St. John answered him, and said that no one in the house had done so, that no one could do it and that there was neither candle nor lamp in the cell. The prior made no reply and went away, thinking that the gaoler had made a mistake.

St. John, at a later time, told one of his brethren that the heavenly light, which God so mercifully sent him, lasted the night through, and that it filled his soul with joy and made the night pass away as if it were but a moment. When his imprisonment was drawing to its close he heard our Lord say to him, as it were out of the soft light that was around him, "John, I am here; be not afraid; I will set thee free" [112: 108].

A few moments later, while making his escape from the prison of the monastery, it is said that he had a repetition of the experience as follows:

He saw a wonderful light, out of which came a voice, "Follow me." He followed, and the light moved before him towards the wall which was on the bank, and then, he knew not how, he found himself on the summit of it without effort or fatigue. He descended into the street, and then the light vanished. So brilliant was it, that for two or three days afterwards, so he confessed at a later time, his eyes were weak, as if he had been looking at the sun in its strength [112:116].

After illumination, and upon the solicitation of persons about him who saw that he had, as Emerson says, "a new experience," he wrote several books, the object of which was to convey to others a knowledge of the new life that had come to him, and, if possible, to convey something of that new life itself. The following extracts are chosen because they exhibit with some clearness the mental status and attitude of the man John Yepes after illumination, and so contribute toward a picture of Cosmic Consciousness:

It is clearly necessary for the soul, aiming at its own supernatural transformation, to be in darkness and far removed from all that relates to its natural condition, the sensual and rational parts. The supernatural is that which transcends nature, and, therefore, that which is natural remains below. Inasmuch as this union and transformation are not cognizable by sense or any human power, the soul must be completely and voluntarily empty of all that can enter into it, of every affection and inclination, so far as it concerns itself [203:71].

On this road, therefore, to abandon one's own way is to enter on the true way, or, to speak more correctly, to pass onwards to the goal; and to forsake one's own way is to enter on that which has none, namely, God. For the soul that attains to this state has no ways or methods of its own, neither does it nor can it lean upon anything of the kind. I mean ways of understanding, perceiving, or feeling, though it has *all ways at the same time*, as one who possessing nothing, yet possesseth everything. For the soul courageously resolved on passing, interiorly and exteriorly, beyond the limits of its own nature, enters illimitably within the supernatural, which has no measure,

This is the doctrine of the suppression and effacement of thought, and the subjection of desire taught by Hindu illuminati from the time of Buddha until to-day—a doctrine undoubtedly resting on actual experience [154 : 68 and 56 : 164 et seq.].

N.B.—The author of the Bhagavatgita is not given in this volume as a case of Cosmic Consciousness for the reason that nothing is known of his personality. The Divine Lay, itself, however, carries on its face the proof that he was so—in it Krishna is the Cosmic Sense, and the speeches of Krishna the utterances of Cosmic Consciousness.

Method of attainment of Cosmic Consciousness and general description of it.

All ways at the same time: Carpenter tries to express this experience as follows: "What is the exact nature of this mood—of this illuminant splendor? All I can say is, there seems to be a vision possible to man as from some more universal standpoint, free from the obscurity and localism which especially connect themselves with the passing clouds of desire, fear and all ordinary thought and emotion—in that sense another

but contains all measure imminently within itself. To arrive there is to depart hence, going away, out of oneself, as far as possible from this vile state to that which is the highest of all. Therefore, rising above all that may be known and understood, temporally and spiritually, the soul must earnestly desire to reach that which in this life cannot be known, and which the heart cannot conceive; and, leaving behind all actual and possible taste and feeling of sense and spirit, must desire earnestly to arrive at that which transcends all sense and all feeling. In order that the soul may be free and unembarrassed for this end it must in no wise attach itself—as I shall presently explain when I treat of this point—to anything it may receive in the sense or spirit, but esteem such as of much less importance. For the more importance the soul attributes to what it understands, feels and imagines, and the greater the estimation it holds it in, whether it be spiritual or not, the more it detracts from the supreme good, and the greater will be its delay in attaining to it. On the other hand, the less that it esteems all that it may have in comparison with the supreme good, the more does it magnify and esteem the supreme good, and consequently the greater the progress towards it. In this way the soul draws nearer and nearer to the divine union, in darkness, by the way of faith, which, though it be also obscure, yet sends forth a marvellous light. Certainly, if the soul will [if it persists in wishing and striving to] see, it thereby becomes instantly more blind as to God, than he who should attempt to gaze upon the sun shining in its strength. On this road, therefore, to have our own faculties in darkness is to see the light [203: 74-5].

and separate faculty; and as vision always means a sense of light, so here is a sense of inward light, unconnected of course with the mortal eye, but bringing to the eye of the mind the impression that it *sees* and by means of a medium which washes, as it were, the *interior* surfaces of all objects and things and persons—how can I express it?—and yet this is most defective, for the sense is a sense that one *is* those objects and things and persons that one perceives (and the whole universe)—a sense in which sight and touch and hearing are all fused in identity'' [62].

The more the soul strives to become blind and annihilated as to all interior and exterior things, the more it will be filled with faith and love and hope. But this love at times is neither comprehended nor felt, because it does not

So Balzac says that self consciousness, while glorious for what it has done, is at the same time baneful, because it precludes man from entering the Cosmic Conscious life, which leads to the infinite—which alone can explain God [5 : 142].

establish itself in the senses with tenderness, but in the soul with fortitude, with greater courage and resolution than before; though it sometimes overflows into the senses, and shows itself tender and gentle. In order, then, to attain to this love, joy and delight which visions effect, it is necessary that the soul should have fortitude and be fortified, so as to abide willingly in emptiness and darkness, and to lay the foundation of its love and delight on what it neither sees nor feels, on what it cannot see nor feel—namely, on God incomprehensible and supreme. Our way to Him is therefore, of necessity, in self denial [203:202].

Though it be true, as I have said, that God is always in every soul, bestowing upon it and preserving to it,

The distinction between the self conscious life even at its best and the life of Cosmic Consciousness.

by His presence, its natural being, yet for all this He does not always communicate the supernatural life. For this is given only by love and grace, to which all souls do not attain, and those who do, do not in the same degree, for some rise to higher degrees of love than others. That soul, therefore, has greater communion with God which is most advanced in love—that is, whose will is most conformable to the will of God. And that soul which has reached perfect conformity and resemblance is perfectly united with, and supernaturally transformed in, God. For which cause, therefore, as I have already explained, the more the soul cleaves to created things, relying on its own strength, by habit and inclination, the less is it disposed for this union, because it does not completely resign itself into the hands of God, that He may transform it supernaturally [203: 78].

At other times, also, the divine light strikes the soul with such force that the darkness is unfelt and the light unheeded; the soul seems unconscious of all it knows, and is therefore lost, as it were, in forgetfulness, knowing not where it is nor what has happened to it, unaware of the lapse of time.

"Louis had a well-defined attack of catalepsy. He remained standing for fifty-nine hours motionless, his eyes fixed, without speaking or eating, etc." [5 : 127]. This experience of Lambert's (Balzac's) belongs to the period of illumination as in the case of Yepes.

It may and does occur that many hours pass while it is in this state of forgetfulness; all seems but a moment when it again returns to itself [203 : 127].

It is probable that a similar experience in the same circumstances is common though not universal.

Yepes' thought is that God is always existent in the human soul, but (in general) in a passive or sleeping state, or at least outside consciousness. The soul that knows that God is in it is blessed, but the soul in which God wakes is that which is supremely blessed. This waking of God in the soul is what is called in the present volume "Cosmic Consciousness."

O how blessed is that soul which is ever conscious of God reposing and resting within it. . . . He is there, as it were, asleep in the embraces of the soul and the soul is in general conscious of His presence and in general delights exceedingly in it. If He were always awake in the soul the communications

Yepes says: God is always in man, and very commonly the soul is aware of His (passive) presence. It is as if He slept in the soul. If He wakes up only once in a man's whole life the experience of that instant affects the whole of life. If the experience of that instant should be indefinitely prolonged what soul could bear it?

of knowledge and love would be unceasing, and that would be a state of glory. If He awakes but once, merely opening his eyes, and affects the soul so profoundly, what would become of it if He were continually awake within it [206:506]?

One of the characteristics of the Cosmic Sense many times touched, and to be touched, upon is the identification of the person with the universe and everything in the universe. When Gautama or Plotinus expresses this fact it is called "Mysticism." When Whitman gives it voice it is "Yankee bluster." What shall we call it when a simple, humble-minded Spanish monk of the sixteenth century says of it in such plain language as the following?

The heavens are mine, the earth is mine, and the nations are mine! mine are the just, and the sinners are mine; mine are the angels and the Mother of God; all things are mine, God himself is mine and for me, because Christ is mine and all for me. What dost thou then ask for, what dost thou seek for, O my soul? All is thine—all is for thee. Do not take less nor rest with the crumbs which fall from the table of thy father. Go forth and exult in thy glory, hide thyself in it, and rejoice, and thou shalt obtain all the desires of thy heart [206:607].

So Whitman tells us: "As if one fit to own things could not at pleasure enter upon all and incorporate them into himself or herself" [193:214]. And again: "What do you suppose I would intimate to you in a hundred ways but that man or woman is as good as God? And that there is no God any more divine than yourself" [193:299].

Visions of incorporeal substances, as of angels and of souls, are neither frequent nor natural in this earthly life, and still less so is the vision of the divine essence, which is peculiar to the blessed, unless it be communicated transiently by a dispensation of God, or by conservation of our natural life and condition, and the abstraction of the spirit; as was perhaps the case of St. Paul when he heard the unutterable secrets in the third heaven. "Whether in the body," saith he, "I know not, or out of the body, I know not; God knoweth." It is clear from the words of the apostle that he was carried out of himself, by the act of God, as to his natural existence [203:198-9].

The Cosmic vision compared in a few common sense words with more ordinary "visions" of, for instance, angels and spirits, in which Yepes seems to have little faith.

Knowledge of pure truth requires, for its proper explanation, that God should hold the hand and wield the pen of the writer. Keep in mind, my dear reader, that these matters are beyond all words. But as my purpose is not to discuss them but to teach and direct the soul through them to the divine union, it will be enough if I speak of them

"Beyond all words." This is the universal experience.

concisely within certain limits, so far as my subject requires it. This kind of vision is not the same with the intellectual visions of bodily things. It consists in comprehending or seeing with the understanding the truths of God, or of things or concerning things which are, have been, or will be. It is most like to the spirit of prophecy, as I shall perhaps hereafter explain. This kind of knowledge is twofold: one relates to the Creator, the other to creatures. And though both kinds are most full of sweetness, the delight produced by that which relates to God is not to be compared with aught beside; and there are neither words nor language to describe it, for it is the knowledge of God himself and his delights [203:205].

An attempt to indicate the radical difference between the knowledge which belongs to the self conscious mind and the consciousness of truth proper to the Cosmic Conscious mind. To indicate also the joy of Cosmic Consciousness and the impossibility of expressing in the only language we have (the language of self consciousness) either what is seen or what is felt in the Cosmic Conscious state. "When I undertake," says Whitman, "to tell the best I find I cannot, my tongue is ineffectual on its pivots, my breath will not be obedient to its organs, I become a dumb man" [193 : 179].

In so far as this becomes pure contemplation, the soul sees clearly that it cannot describe it otherwise than in general terms which the abundance of delight and happiness forces from it. And though at times, when this knowledge is vouchsafed to the soul, words are uttered, yet the soul knows full well that it has in nowise expressed what it felt, because it is conscious that there are no words of adequate signification [203:206].

This divine knowledge concerning God never relates to particular things, because it is conversant with the Highest, and therefore cannot be explained unless when it is extended to some truth less than God, which is capable of being described; but this general knowledge is ineffable. It is only a soul in union with God that is capable of this profound loving knowledge, for it is itself that union. This knowledge consists in a certain contact of the soul with the Divinity, and it is God Himself who is then felt and tasted, though not manifestly and distinctly, as it will be in glory. But this touch of knowledge and sweetness is so strong and so profound that it penetrates into the inmost substance of the soul, and the devil cannot interfere with it, nor produce anything like it—because there is nothing else comparable with it—nor infuse any sweetness or delight which shall at all resemble it. This knowledge savors, in some measure, of the divine essence and of everlasting life, and the devil has no power to simulate anything so great [203:207].

Compare Behmen: "Spiritual knowledge cannot be communicated from one intellect to another, but must be sought for in the spirit of God" [97 : 56].

And Whitman's dicta: "Wisdom is of the soul; cannot be passed from one having it to another not having it" [193 : 123].

Such is the sweetness of deep delight of these touches of God, that one of them is more than a recompense for all the sufferings of this life, however great their number [203:208].

"For I reckon that the sufferings of this present time are not worthy to be compared with the glory that shall be revealed to usward" [19 : 8 : 18].

These images, thus imprinted on the soul, produce *whenever they are adverted to*, the divine effects of love, sweetness, and light, sometimes more, sometimes less, for that is the end for which they are impressed. He with whom God thus deals receives a great

Whenever they are adverted to: Compare Bacon:
''So am I as the rich, whose blessed key
Can bring him to his sweet up-locked treasure,
The which he will not every hour survey,
For blunting the fine point of seldom pleasure.
[176 : 52].

gift, for he has a mine of blessings within himself. The images which produce such effects as these are vividly grounded in the spiritual memory [203: 275].

The way of proficients, which is also called the illuminative way, or the way of infused contemplation, wherein God himself teaches and refreshes the

He tells of the passage from self consciousness to Cosmic Consciousness and what it is like to be in the latter condition.

soul without meditation or any active efforts that itself may deliberately make [203: 55-6]. I went forth out of myself, out of my low conceptions and lukewarm love, out of my scanty and poor sense of God, without being hindered by the flesh or the devil. I went forth out of the scanty works and ways of my own to those of God; that is, my understanding went forth out of itself, and from human became divine. My will went forth out of itself, becoming divine; for now united with the divine love, it loves no more with its former scanty powers and circumscribed capacity, but with the energy and pureness of the divine spirit [203: 67].

Now this is nothing else but the supernatural light giving light to the understanding, so that the human un-

As Dante says, this is being ''transhumanized into a God'' [72 : 4].

derstanding becomes divine, made one with the divine. In the same way divine love inflames the will so that it becomes nothing less than divine, loving in a divine way, united and made one with the divine will and the divine love. The memory is affected in like manner; all the desires and affections also are changed divinely according to God. Thus the soul will be of heaven, heavenly, divine rather than human [204: 111].

It was a happy lot for the soul when God in this night put all its household to sleep—that is, all the powers, passions, affections, and desires of the sensual and spiritual soul, that

Further allusions to the necessary subjugation or even obliteration of the old self conscious mind before the cosmic conscious mind can emerge.

it may attain to the spiritual union of the perfect love of God ''unobserved'' —that is, unhindered, by them, because they were all asleep and mortified in that night. O how happy must the soul then be when it can escape from the house of its sensuality! None can understand it, I think, except that soul which has experienced it [204: 113]. It is, therefore, plain that no distinct object whatever that pleases the will can be God; and for that reason, if it is to be united with Him, it must empty itself, cast away every disorderly affection of the desire, every satisfaction it may distinctly have, high and low, temporal and spiritual, so that, purified and cleansed from all unruly satisfactions, joys and desires, it may be wholly occupied, with all its affections, in loving God [204:534].

This abyss of wisdom now so exalts and elevates the soul—orderly disposing it for the science of love—that it makes it not only understand how mean are all created things in relation to the supreme wisdom and divine knowledge, but also how low, defective, and, in a certain sense, improper, are all the words and phrases by which in this life we discuss divine things and how utterly impossible by any natural means, however profoundly and learnedly we may speak, to understand and see them as they are, except in the light of mystical theology. And so the soul in the light thereof, discerning this truth, namely, that it cannot reach it, and still less explain it by the terms of ordinary speech, justly calls it secret [204:126].

The spirit is now so strong, and has so subdued the flesh, and makes so little of it, that it is as regardless of it as a tree is of one of its leaves. It seeks not for consolation or sweetness either in God or elsewhere, neither does it pray for God's gifts through any motive of self interest, or its own satisfaction. For all it cares for now is

> Yepes resembles Buddha and Paul in despising and contemning the old self conscious life. Jesus and Whitman reached a higher level—they saw that all life is good, all divine.

how it shall please God and serve Him in some measure in return for His goodness and for the graces it has received, and this at any and every cost [204:134].

But if we speak of that light of glory which in this, the soul's embrace, God sometimes produces within it, and which is a certain spiritual communion wherein He causes it to behold and enjoy at the same time the abyss of delight and riches which He has laid up within it, there is no language to express any degree of it. As the sun when it shines upon the sea illumes its great depths and reveals the pearls and gold and precious stones therein, so the divine sun of the bridegroom, turning towards the bride, reveals in a way the riches of her soul, so that even the angels behold her with amazement [205:292].

I have said that God is pleased with nothing but love. He has need of nothing, and so if He is pleased with anything it is with the growth of the soul; and as there is no way in which the soul can grow but in becoming in

> "What do you suppose," says Whitman, "I would intimate to you in a hundred ways but that man or woman is as good as God and that there is no God any more divine than yourself" [193:299].

a manner equal to Him, for this reason only is He pleased with our love. It is the property of love to place him who loves on an equality with the object of his love. Hence the soul, because of its perfect love, is called the bride of the Son of God, which signifies equality with Him [205:333].

Before the soul succeeded in effecting this gift and a surrender of itself, and of all that belongs to it, to the Beloved, it was entangled in many unprofitable occupations, by which it sought to please itself and others, and

> Antecedent self conscious state. Compare Whitman: "Trippers and askers surround me, people I meet, the effect upon me of my early life or the ward and city I live in, or the nation, the latest dates, discoveries, inventions, societies, authors old and new, my

it may be said that its occupations at this time were as many as its habits of imperfection [205 : 236].

dinner, dress, associates, looks, compliments, dues, the real or fancied indifference of some man or woman I love, the sickness of one of my folks or of myself, or ill doing, or loss or lack of money, or depressions or exalta-tions, battles, the horrors of fratricidal war, the fever of doubtful news, the fitful events; these come to me days and nights and go from me again, but they are not the *Me* my-self'' [193 : 31-2].

It is not without some unwilling-ness that I enter at the request of others upon the explanation of the four stanzas, because they relate to matters

Expressions by which he tries to suggest mental states that cannot be represented by language.

so interior and spiritual as to baffle the powers of language [206 : 407]. All I say falls far short of that which passes in this intimate union of the soul with God. That love still more perfect and complete in the same state of trans-formation [206 : 408].

I entered, but I knew not where, and there I stood not knowing, all science transcending.

I knew not where I entered, for when I stood within, not knowing where I was, I heard great things. What I heard I will not tell; I was there as one who knew not, all science transcending.

In this short poem John Yepes has tried to state the essential facts of the entrance into the Cosmic Conscious state. He says he entered it, but (having so done) he did not know where he was. He heard great things, but will not (cannot?) relate what. He found (in that state) perfect peace and knowledge.

Of peace and devotion the knowl-edge was perfect, in solitude profound; the right way was clear, but so secret was it, that I stood babbling, all science transcending.

I stood enraptured in ecstasy, be-side myself, and in my every sense no sense remained. My spirit was en-dowed with understanding, under-standing nought, all science transcend-ing.

The higher I ascended the less I understood. It is the dark cloud illu-mining the night. Therefore he who understands knows nothing, ever all science transcending.

''Swiftly arose and spread around me the *peace* and *knowledge* that pass all the argu-ments of the earth'' [193 : 32].

The right way (the right course of ac-tion), too, was clear (Whitman says the new sense ''held his feet'' [193 : 32]. Yepes, like Whitman and all the rest, became filled with joy. He then goes on to describe Nir-vâna, even to the use of the word ''anni-hilation.''

Finally he pronounces the word which all the illuminati utter each in his own way. He says this profound wisdom consists in a *sense of the essence of God.* It is the Cos-mic Sense—a sense, intuition, or conscious-ness of the Cosmos. The birth of the faculty which alone can comprehend God. It is that new birth through which only can a man see the kingdom of God.

He who really ascends so high an-nihilates himself, and all his previous knowledge seems ever less and less; his knowledge so increases that he knoweth nothing, all science transcending.

This knowing that knows nothing is so potent in its might that the prudent in their reasoning never can defeat it; for their wisdom never reaches to the understanding that understandeth nothing, all science transcending.

This sovereign wisdom is of an excellence so high that no faculty nor science can ever unto it attain. He who shall overcome himself by the knowledge which knows nothing will always rise, all science transcending.

And if you would listen, this sovereign wisdom doth consist in a sense profound of the essence of God: it is an act of His compassion, to leave us, nought understanding, all science transcending [208: 624-5].

SUMMARY

a. In the case of John Yepes the subjective light seems to have been present and even unusually intense, although there may be some confusion in the report of it.

b. Moral elevation was strongly marked.

c. Intellectual illumination well but not perhaps as strikingly as in some other cases.

d. His sense of immortality is so perfect that it does not occur to him to discuss it as a separate question or as a question at all. He has simply become God, a God, or a part of God, and he would no more think of discussing his immortality than he would think of discussing that of God.

e. Of course he lost (if he ever had it) all fear of death. Death is simply nothing to him. It is a matter that does not concern him in the least.

f. The instantaneousness of the change from self consciousness to Cosmic Consciousness in his prison in the spring or early summer of the year 1578, when he was thirty-six years old, seems to be clear from Lewis' narrative.

g. The change in the appearance of the person illumined—called in the gospels "transfiguration"—seems to have been well marked.

CHAPTER 9.

Francis Bacon.

BORN 1561; died 1626.

Nothing approaching to an exhaustive study of this case can be attempted here. The mere flanges of the subject have filled a moderate-sized library, while the core of the matter has hardly been touched upon.

I.

Without more ado or any beating about the bush it may as well be frankly stated at once that the view of the present editor is:

a. That Francis Bacon wrote the "Shakespeare" plays and poems.

b. That he entered into Cosmic Consciousness at about the age of thirty, or perhaps a year earlier, as his intellectual and moral development was very precocious.

c. That he began writing the "Sonnets" immediately after his illumination. The "Sonnets," as considered here, are the first one hundred and twenty-six, which distinctly constitute a poem in and by themselves and deal with the subject here considered.

d. That the earlier of these one hundred and twenty-six "Sonnets" are addressed to the Cosmic Sense, and the later to it and its offspring, the plays.

e. That in the "Sonnets" the following individualities may be recognized: (*a*) the Cosmic Sense; (*b*) the Bacon of the Cosmic Sense, and of the plays and "Sonnets"; (*c*) the special offspring of the Cosmic Sense—the plays; (*d*) the ostensible Bacon of the court, politics, prose writings, business, etc., and possibly others.

II.

It is not absolutely denied that the first one hundred and twenty-six "Sonnets" can be read as if addressed to a young male friend (although in the case of several this might be, it seems to the writer, successfully disputed), but it is clear that so read they lack meaning and dignity—that, in fact, looked at from this point of view, they are entirely unworthy of the man (whoever he was) who wrote "Lear" and "Macbeth." And it may be claimed that an almost (or quite) constant characteristic of the writings of the class of men dealt with in this volume is exactly this double meaning corresponding with the duplex personality of the writer. Of this double, often triple, meaning the works of Dante and Whitman supply perhaps the best examples.

T. S. Baynes [86:764] says that these speculations "cannot be regarded as successful"; but let us, for the sake of argument, suppose that there really was such a young man, such a dark woman [Mary Fitton, 167:30 et seq. or another], that would prove absolutely nothing. These people might have had a real existence and might have been spoken to and spoken of as the superficial meaning of the "Sonnets," just as the ocean is spoken to and of in the superficial meaning of "With Husky Haughty Lips" [193:392]. Or take for another example the "Prayer of Columbus" [193:323]. Columbus might have made just such a prayer, and there is no reason why Whitman should not have put such a prayer into his mouth; but nothing is more certain than that the words in question are addressed to the All Powerful by Whitman himself. But why select instances? There is perhaps not a line in the "Leaves" which has one meaning only. Then who to-day does not understand that in the "Divine Comedy" Dante used the theological terms current in his day to veil and express far deeper and loftier thoughts than had theretofore ever been annexed to them? Attach the current signification to the terms used and his verses had one meaning, but ascribe to these terms his *intention* and they have another vastly wider and deeper. So his last and best translator, who undoubtedly knew him profoundly, says that "a far deeper-lying and more-prevailing source of imperfect comprehension of the poem than any verbal difficulty exists in the double or triple meaning that runs through it" [70:16]. Or is "Seraphita" a sort of fairy tale having for central figure an idealized hysterico-maniacal Norwegian girl?

III.

That a man having Cosmic Consciousness is, in fact, at least a dual person is abundantly shown and illustrated in the present volume. and "Shakespeare," the author of the plays and "Sonnets," is really another (while the same) self of the Bacon who wrote the prose works, spoke in Parliament, lived before the world as jurist, courtier and citizen. Just as "Seraphita" (Seraphitus), while being Balzac, is totally distinct from the ostensible Balzac who was seen in Parisian drawing rooms. Just as the Whitman of the "Leaves" is wholly distinct (yet the same) from the Whitman who rode on omnibusses and ferries, "lived the same life with the rest," and died in Camden, March 26, 1892. Just as "Gabriel," while being Mohammed, is at the same time another and distinct personality.

This identity (at the same time) and disparateness is the true solution (it is believed) of the Bacon-Shakespeare controversy.

IV.

It is perhaps impossible for the merely self conscious man to form any conception of what this oncoming of Cosmic Consciousness must be to those who experience it. The man is lifted out of his old self and lives rather in heaven than upon the old earth— more correctly the old earth becomes heaven. One of the prime necessities of this period is solitude. Why? Probably because the person is so occupied with, so enraptured by, his new world (his new self), that he simply cannot bear to be called back to the old world (the old self). So Balzac would (at this period of his life) shut himself up—hide himself—for weeks and months at a stretch. So Paul conferred not with flesh and blood, "neither went up to Jerusalem" [22: 1-17], but "away into Arabia," and seems to have lived very much to himself for some time. Solitude (although naturally he was so eminently sociable) became, under the same circumstances, a necessity to Whitman, and in the early part of his Cosmic Conscious life he would frequently spend days, weeks and even months at a stretch in the sparsely peopled or uninhabited districts of Long Island—especially along the sea-shore.

Immediately upon the illumination of Jesus (if we can depend upon the account given in Matthew and Mark) he was "led up of the spirit into the wilderness," and remained in solitude for a certain time. And it is probable that sufficient research would reveal action of this kind as universal in pronounced cases. Be this as it may, Spedding [174: 49] says that: "From April, 1590, until the latter part of 1591 [nearly two years] I find no other composition of Bacon's [than a letter of five pages!] nor any important piece of news concerning him." While (referring to the very same period in his life) Bacon says, writing to Burghley late in 1591 or early in 1592, when he was thirty-one years old, and, according to the hypothesis, one to two years after his illumination: "I do not fear that action shall impair it [his health], because I account my ordinary course of study and meditation to be more painful [more laborious] than most parts of action are" [174: 56].

Then again it seems that, especially during these two years, 1590 and 1591, Bacon frequently, to use his own words, "fled into the shade" at Twickenham and "enjoyed the blessings of contemplation in that sweet solitariness which collecteth the mind as shutting the eyes doth the sight" [129: 71]. So "there are times noted by Mr. Spedding when Bacon wrote with closed doors, and when the subject of his studies is doubtful; and there is one long vacation of which the same careful biographer remarks that he cannot tell what work the indefatigable student produced during those months, for that he knows of none whose date corresponds with the period" [129: 71-2]. And doubtless Mrs. Pott is in the right when she suggests that it was during such periods and probably during 1590-91 that many of the early plays were written [129: 71].

V.

Thus we have the frame into which to set the picture: Bacon's mind is exceedingly precocious and he enters Cosmic Consciousness, let us suppose, early in 1590, at or shortly after the age of twenty-nine; he had probably written several plays before that, a few of which may have been thought worthy of inclusion in the

1623 folio. In the spring of 1590 (in his thirtieth year) he acquires the Cosmic Sense. For the next two years (1590-91) he is much secluded and produces a number of plays, while, as a sort of running commentary upon his mental experiences and his work, he wrote the earlier "Sonnets," the rest being written one or two at a time as occasion called them forth, between this period and the date of their publication—1609.

It would be proper in this place to give some account of Bacon's personality were it not that the subject is too large for the limits of this volume. The question which concerns us here is, of course: were his intellect and moral nature (especially the latter) such as belong to persons having Cosmic Consciousness? Upon the answers to the last half of this question a doubt (fostered chiefly by Pope and Macaulay) has arisen. The point cannot be argued here. All that can be said is that the present writer believes that Bacon was as great morally as he was intellectually; and he believes that whoever will take the pains to seriously consider the standard works on the subject written by able and impartial men (such as Dixon's "Personal History" [75], Spedding's "Life and Times" [174], Spedding's "Evenings with a Reviewer" [177], and especially the "Life," by Rawley, who knew Bacon well) will inevitably come to the same conclusion. Rawley says of him: "He was free from malice; he was no revenger of injuries; he was no defamer of any man; but would always say the best that could be said of any person, even an enemy" [141:52]. And after many years' study of the subject Spedding sums up as follows:

The evidence which everybody had to judge from led me to suppose him a very different person from what he was commonly taken for. That idea led me to seek for further evidence, and all the further evidence which I discovered confirmed the impression. I do not find fault with people for not knowing what advice Bacon gave the king about calling a parliament and dealing with it; but I say that the tenor of the advice, being now produced, shows that they were very bad guessers; that the inference they drew as to Bacon's character from the very abundant evidence which they had before them was strangely inaccurate; as far from the truth as if one should hold up Flavius as an example of a bad steward, because the economy was bad of the house in which he served. I take these newly discovered pieces as tests. If I had been wrong, they would have convicted me; if Macaulay had been right, they would have confirmed him [178:189].

And then, at the end of his book, after all the facts of Bacon's life that have come down to us had been reviewed and considered he goes on:

For myself at least, much as one must grieve over such a fall of such a man, and so forlorn a close of such a life, I have always felt that had he not fallen, or had he fallen upon a fortune less desolate in its outward conditions, I should never have known how good and how great a man he really was—hardly, perhaps, how great and how invincible a thing intrinsic goodness is. Turning from the world without to the world which was within him, I know nothing more inspiring, more affecting, more sublime, than the undaunted energy, the hopefulness, trustfulness, clearness, patience, and composure, with which his spirit sustained itself under that most depressing fortune. The heart of Job himself was not so sorely tried, nor did it pass the trial better. Through the many volumes which he produced during these five years, I find no idle repining, no vain complaint of others, no weak justification of himself; no trace of a disgusted, a despairing or a faltering mind [178:407].

Compare with this estimate of Bacon's mental attitude under the depressing circumstances of his last years the undying and inexhaustible cheer of Walt Whitman, Jacob Behmen, and William Blake in like case.

VI.

Here (while speaking of the personal traits of this man) will be as good an opportunity as any to quote a few passages which seem to glance at some certain quality in Bacon's mind such as this master faculty of which there is question in this book. For instance, Rawley [141:47], as a result of personal observation, says of him: "I have been induced to think that if there were a beam of knowledge derived from God upon any man in these modern times, it was upon him. For though he was a great reader of books, yet he had not his knowledge from books, but from some grounds and notions from within himself; which, notwithstanding, he vented with great caution and circumspection." In other words, Rawley thinks that Bacon was inspired, and says that he was exceedingly careful in publishing the truths or ideas derived from that source. And this is exactly what is claimed by the present editor as one reason for the concealed authorship of the plays and sonnets.

Note again these words of Bacon's, taken from his essay "Of Truth" [35:82]: "The first creature of God, in the works of the days, was the light of the sense; the last was the light of reason; and his Sabbath work ever since is the illumination of his spirit." In other words: In the evolution of the human mind simple consciousness was first produced; then self consciousness; and lastly, there is being produced to-day Cosmic Consciousness. Bacon proceeds: "First he breathed light upon the face of the matter of chaos [and produced life, simple consciousness]; then he breathed light into the face of man [and produced self consciousness]; and still he breatheth and inspireth light into the face of his chosen" [endowing them with Cosmic Consciousness]. Compare: "It has been said, great are the senses, greater than the senses is the mind [simple consciousness], greater than the mind is the understanding [self consciousness]. What is greater than the understanding is that [Cosmic Consciousness]. Thus knowing that which is higher than the understanding and restraining yourself by yourself [note the inevitable reduplication of the individual], destroy the unmanageable enemy in the shape of desire" [154: 57]. And again: "It is not by reasoning that the law is to be found, it is beyond the pale of reasoning" [164: 39].

It is worthy of notice that Bacon seems to have recognized an interval between the light of reason and the illumination of the spirit as great as the interval between the light of sense and that of reason. That is, he recognized as great an interval between Cosmic and Self Consciousness as exists between the latter and simple consciousness—just as is claimed by the present writer. But within the field of self consciousness where could he find such an interval as this between reason and anything above reason?

Again in his great prayer [175: 469] Bacon says:

I am a debtor to Thee for the gracious talent of Thy gifts and graces, which I have neither put into a napkin, nor put it (as I ought) to exchangers, where it might have made best profit; but misspent it in things for which I was least fit; so as I may truly say, my soul hath been a stranger in the course of my pilgrimage.

The talent in question is the Cosmic Sense. He did not let it lie idle, but he did not make as much use of it as he might and ought to have done. He should have lived his life for it (as Gautama, Jesus and Paul did) whereas he tried to live (did live) two lives and misspent a large part of his life "in things for which he was least fit"—law, politics, etc.; so it may be truly said his soul (the Bacon of the Cosmic Sense) was a stranger in the life of the ostensible (the self conscious) Bacon.

The Cosmic Sense produced the plays. If Bacon had openly lived his whole life for the Cosmic Sense what other perhaps greater works might he not have produced? And instead of his almost hidden, misunderstood life, we might have had another of those open, exalted lives, each one of which is a source of endless inspiration to the race which is slowly toiling up from what we see around us to that divine goal.

To close this part of the subject, glance at two other short extracts. The first from the "Plan of the Work," the second from the "Novum Organum." Bacon says:

If we labor in thy works with the sweat of our brows thou wilt make us partakers of thy vision and thy Sabbath. Humbly we pray that this mind

This passage seems plainly to allude to a higher spiritual life, which may be attained to in this life, and of which it may be supposed the writer had had experience.

may be steadfast in us, and that through these our hands, and the hands of others to whom thou shalt give the same spirit, thou wilt vouchsafe to endow the human family with new mercies [34:54].

And again:

I may say then of myself that which one said in jest (since it marks the distinction so truly): "It cannot be that we should think alike, when one

If the "liquor strained from countless grapes" is not the Cosmic Sense it does not seem very clear what it is.

drinks water and the other drinks wine." Now, other men, as well in ancient as in modern times, have in the matter of sciences drunk a crude liquor like water, either flowing spontaneously from the understanding, or drawn up by logic, as by wheels from a well. Whereas I pledge mankind in a liquor strained from countless grapes, from grapes ripe and fully seasoned, collected in clusters, and gathered, and then squeezed in the press, and finally purified and clarified in the vat. And therefore it is no wonder if they and I do not think alike [34:155].

VII.

This, of course, is not the place for a discussion of the author-ship of the plays, but since it is here taken as certain that they are to be credited to Bacon, it will be right to give a few of the principal reasons for the adoption of that view. The testimony of the writer himself on the point will be produced when certain of the "Sonnets" fall under consideration. Exclusive of these passages in the "Sonnets" the "reasons" in question may be summed up as follows:

a. The large number of new words in the plays, estimated at five hundred, mostly from the Latin, and the much larger number of old words used in a new sense, estimated at five thousand, make it clear that these were written not merely by a genius but by a learned man—a man who read Latin so continuously as that he came almost to think in that language. Then the similarity of Bacon's style to that of the plays, and above all the striking identity of the vocabulary in the prose works and plays, so marvelous that 98.5 per cent. of "Shakespeare's" words are also Bacon's [37: 133], the use of the same metaphors and similes, of the same antitheta, etc. [37: 136], makes it nearly certain (especially when it is borne in mind that that vocabulary, those metaphors, similes and antitheta are largely new) that the same mind produced both sets of books—the "Shakespearean" and Baconian.

b. Not only are there great numbers of new words and old words with new meanings, metaphors, similes, etc., common to the "Shakespeare" plays and to the Baconian prose, but the large number of phrases and turns of expression which are also found in both cannot possibly be attributed to accident. See these given by the hundred by Donnelly [74], by Wigston [197], by Holmes [99] and others.

c. Bacon and "Shakespeare" read the same books, and not only so, but the favorite books of the one were the favorite books of the other.

d. They write on the same subjects. The philosophy of the

"De Augmentis," the "Novum Organum" and other prose works is constantly being reproduced in the plays; while Bacon's essays and the plays treat throughout the same subjects (human life and human passions) *and always from the same point of view* [197: 25 et seq.]

e. On all sorts of subjects, large and small, their point of view is the same—they never express irreconcilable opinions.

f. They were (if two) the two greatest men living in the world at that time. For thirty years they lived in what we to-day should consider a small city of one hundred and sixty thousand inhabitants [82: 820]. And it does not appear that they ever met, and there is no evidence that either of them ever knew of the existence of the other. The lesser man of the (supposed) two—Bacon—left behind him abundant evidence of the literary activity of his life in the form of manuscripts, letters to and from friends, etc. The greater "Shakespeare"—left none; not a manuscript, not a letter.

g. The localities of the plays are all such as are known to have been known to Bacon either by residence, visiting or reading—largely the two former. With these localities the writer frequently evinces an intimate familiarity. The one especial locality which must have been minutely known to William Shakespeare—Stratford and its neighborhood—is not introduced.

h. There exists a distinct parallelism between the successive plays (their incidents, scenes, etc.) and the occurrences of Bacon's life (his position, circumstances, residences, etc.), while there seems none between them and "Shakespeare's" life, so far as this is known to us [130].

i. The relation existing between "Shakespeare's" "Richard III" and his "Henry the VIII" on the one hand and Bacon's prose history of Henry the VII on the other makes it about certain that the same man wrote the three works [197: 1-24].

j. It is sometimes said that Bacon was a scientist, a philosopher, a courtier, a lawyer, a man of affairs, but not a great wit or poet, such as might have written the plays. But, in the first place, and putting aside the plays, Bacon *was* both a wit and a poet. Macaulay does not exaggerate when he writes that, as shown in his prose works: "The poetical faculty was powerful in Bacon's mind, but not, like his wit, so powerful as occasionally to usurp the place of his reason and to tyrannize over the whole man." "No imagination," he adds, "was ever at once so strong and so thoroughly subjugated" [120: 487].

k. The "Promus" argument would alone seem, to an impartial mind, pretty conclusive of the Baconian authorship of the plays. If this collection [129] was not made to aid in the production of these, will some one kindly tell us with what end Bacon undertook and prosecuted the labor of its compilation? Those who have still doubts upon the subject would do well to read Bacon's openly acknowledged writings. Then, in the second place, it is claimed here that Bacon was really two men (the self conscious Bacon and the Cosmic Conscious Bacon); that the man seen by Bacon's contemporaries and in the prose works was the former, while the concealed man who produced the plays and "Sonnets" was the latter. The Cosmic Conscious Bacon had (of course) the use of all the learning and of all the faculties of the self conscious Bacon, and along with these the vast spiritual insight and powers which go with possession of Cosmic Consciousness.

l. About April 18th, 1621, after his fall, Bacon composed a prayer which Addison quoted as resembling the devotions of an angel rather than those of a man [175: 467]. No truer or higher poetry is found in the plays or "Sonnets" than is found in it. No man with a soul in his body can read it and doubt its absolute candor and honesty. In it he says: "I have (though in a despised weed) procured the good of all men." No one has ever explained what this "good of all men," which Bacon had procured and which went about in a despised dress, might be. Is there anything else it could be except the plays? "The good of all men" is such an immense phrase that the object referred to must necessarily be enormous. What other such object could there have been in Bacon's mind at the time? Well, his philosophical works —the "De Augmentis" and the "Novum Organum" and the rest? Yes, it would doubtless be true of them. But the object spoken of, was in a despised dress.   Were they?   Quite the contrary.   They were in a genuine, high-class, philosophic garb as to form and style—more, they were in the best Latin that could, for love or money, be procured for them.

m. Bornmann [28] and Ruggles [145], in two fascinating volumes and from somewhat different points of view, have ably pointed out (as indeed had been done several times before but not so systematically) how persistently the thought of Bacon and that of "Shakespeare" run in the same channel; how the science and philosophy of the first are constantly worked into the poetry of the second, becoming its very life blood and soul, and how the method laid down and followed by the one is never lost sight of by the other.   Indeed, if nothing had ever been written on the subject except these two books (and they do not touch the main, stock arguments) they would go far along to a demonstration of the proposition that the man who wrote the "Tempest," "Lear" and "Merchant of Venice" wrote also the "De Augmentis" and the "Silva Silvarium."

n. Finally, consider the anagram discovered by Dr. Platt, at that time of New Jersey, in "Love's Labor's Lost" [51: 376]: "Beginning at the commencement of the fifth act, we meet one after another the following: Satis quod sufficit (that which suffices is enough).   Novi hominen tanquam te (I know the man as well as I know you).   Ne intelligis domine (do you understand me, sir)?   Laus Deo, bene, intelligo (praise God, I understand well).   Videsne quis venit (do you see who comes)?   Video et gaudeo (I see and rejoice).   Quare (wherefore)?   Then, a few lines further on, the word Honorificabilitudinitatibus is (as it were) flung into the text.   Immediately afterwards one says: 'Are you not lettered?'   The answer is: 'Yes, he teaches boys the hornbook.'   'What is a b spelt backward, with the horn on his head?'   The answer to that, of course, is 'Ba, with a horn added.' Now, 'Ba' with a horn added is Bacornu, which is not, but suggests, and was probably meant to suggest, Bacon.   But whence is derived the a b which is to be spelt backward?   In the middle of the long word we find these letters in that order—a b.   Begin, now, at the b and spell backward as you are told. You get bacifironoh. From these letters it is not hard to pick out Fr. Bacon. Now take the other half of the word spelt forward— ilitudinitatibus. It is not hard to pick out from it ludi (the plays), tuiti (protected or guarded), nati (produced). These words, with those we had before, give us: Ludi tuiti Fr. Bacono nati. The remaining letters are hiiibs, which are easily read as hi sibi. Now put the words together in grammatical order and you have: Hi ludi, tuiti sibi, Fr. Bacono nati (these plays entrusted to themselves proceeded from Fr. Bacon). It is a perfect anagram. Each letter is used once and once only. The form of the long word is Latin and it is read in Latin. The sense of the infolded words corresponds with the sense, so far as it has any [compare honorificare, honorifico; see Century Dictionary], of the infolding word. The infolded Latin is grammatical. The intention is fully declared and plain. There is no flaw.

"But where, now, does the long word come from, and can a connection be traced between it and the actual man, Francis Bacon? To answer this, turn back to the Northumberland House MS. mentioned above. That MS. belonged to Bacon, and could never have been seen by the actor, Shakespeare. On the outer leaf is written the word: Honorificabilitudino. This also is an anagram. It infolds the words: Initio hi ludi Fr. Bacono (in the beginning these plays from Fr. Bacon). It seems to have been a first thought. The Latin words do not form a complete sentence; they suggest a meaning, but do not actually contain one. The anagram in this form was not considered satisfactory, and was amended into the form found in 'Love's Labor's Lost.'

"Thus we have before us the making of the word by Bacon. The sense of the word and its history correspond. The case seems to be complete."

o. But arguments such as above, though cogent and indeed of themselves sufficient if frankly considered, are no longer necessary to establish, although they may be allowed to suggest, the Baconian authorship of the plays and poems, since the writer within the last two years has discovered that these are all or nearly all signed by Francis Bacon, by means of a cipher invented by himself and kept to himself for forty odd years. The evidence upon which this statement rests, if not already published by the time this volume is issued, will very soon thereafter be given to the world.

VIII.

But the present volume has nothing to do with the Bacon-Shakespeare question except incidentally, by the way, and perforce. *Somebody* wrote the plays and "Sonnets," and that person, whoever he might be, had, it is believed, Cosmic Consciousness. And just as there is found in nearly all these cases two classes of writing—that, namely, which flows from the Cosmic Sense and that which, springing up in the self conscious mind, treats directly of the Cosmic Sense as an (to it) objective reality —so these two classes of writing are found here: (1) The plays, treating of the world of men and flowing directly from the Cosmic Sense, and (2) the "Sonnets," treating (from the point of view of the self conscious man) in a subtle, hidden manner, as is usual and indeed inevitable, of the Cosmic Sense itself.

It remains (all that can be done here) to give as many of the "Sonnets" as there is space for, accompanied by the necessary explanatory remarks.

IX.

The first seventeen "Sonnets" urge the Cosmic Sense to produce. The theory is that they were written, as they stand, earliest, and that they were the first writings of their author after illumination. If it be thought singular that a man should so write, then compare this with an undoubted case of precisely the same thing as is here supposed. The 1855 edition of "Leaves of Grass" was written by Whitman immediately after illumination. On the third page of the "Leaves" (the preface was written afterwards) stand these words, addressed to the Cosmic Sense:

"Loose the stop from your throat—not words, not music or rhyme I want; not custom or lecture, not even the best, only the lull I like, the hum of your valved voice." In the case of Whitman, as in the case of Buddha and Jesus, the special urge of the Cosmic Sense was towards an exalted life. In the case of Bacon, as in that of Balzac, it was especially towards literary expression. In accordance with this distinction, Whitman writes, in a long life, two small volumes; Bacon, in a shorter life, ten or twenty times as much. Whitman's invocation occupies three lines; Bacon's, two hundred lines.

Sonnet I.

From fairest creatures we desire increase,
That thereby beauty's rose might never die,
But as the riper should by time decease,
His tender heir might bear his memory:
But thou contracted to thine own bright eyes,
Feed'st thy light's flame with self-substantial fuel,
Making a famine where abundance lies,
Thyself thy foe, to thy sweet self too cruel.
Thou that art now the world's fresh ornament,
And only * herald to the gaudy spring,
Within thy own bud buriest thy content,
And, tender churl, mak'st waste in niggarding.
  Pity the world, or else this glutton be,
    To eat the world's due, by the grave and thee.

* Only—i.e., incomparable herald of the gaudy spring. In forty-three cases of Cosmic Consciousness the time of year of first illumination is known with more or less certainty in twenty, and in fifteen of these it took place in the first half of the year—January to June. Did perhaps Bacon's illumination take place in the spring? And is that the meaning of the line?

The fairest of all things is what Plotinus calls "this sublime condition," and of which Dante said: "Oh splendor of living light eternal! Who hath become so pallid under the shadow of Parnassus, or hath so drunk at its cistern, that he would not seem to have his mind encumbered, trying to represent thee as thou didst appear there where in harmony the heaven overshadows thee when in the open air thou didst thyself disclose" [71 : 201].

Sonnet II.

When forty winters shall besiege thy brow,
And dig deep trenches in thy beauty's field,
Thy youth's proud livery, so gazed on now,
Will be a tattered weed, of small worth held:
Then being ask'd where all thy beauty lies,
Where all the treasure of thy lusty days,—
To say, within thine own deep sunken eyes,
Were an all-eating shame and thriftless praise.
How much more praise deserv'd thy beauty's use,
If thou could'st answer—"This fair child of mine

When the Cosmic Sense would be forty years old Bacon would be seventy.

Shall sum my count, and make my old excuse,—''
Proving his beauty by succession thine!
  This were to be new made when thou art old,
  And see thy blood warm when thou feel'st it cold.

SONNET III.

Look in thy glass, and tell the face thou viewest,
Now is the time that face should form another;
Whose fresh repair if not thou renewest,
Thou dost beguile the world, unbless some mother.*
For where is she so fair † whose unear'd womb
Disdains the tillage of thy husbandry?
Or who is he so fond will be the tomb
Of his self-love, to stop posterity?
Thou art thy mother's glass,‡ and she in thee
Calls back the lovely April of her prime:
So thou through windows of thine age shalt see,
Despite of wrinkles, this thy golden time.
  But if thou live, remembered not to be,
  Die single, and thine image dies with thee.

* Unbless some mother: deprive some art of the offspring it might (should) have had from the generative influence of the ''lovely boy''—the Cosmic Sense.

† *Where is she so fair?* What art is there so fair, etc.

‡ *Thou art thy mother's glass*—that is, nature's mirror. ''Hold the mirror up to nature'' (Hamlet). In the Cosmic Sense all nature, including the human heart, is reflected. In this connection consider (besides the ''Shakespeare'' plays) the ''Comédie Humaine'' of Balzac; the ''Divine Comedy'' of Dante; the ''Leaves of Grass'' of Whitman.

SONNET XV.

When I consider everything that grows
Holds in perfection but a little moment,
That this huge stage presenteth nought but shows,
Whereon the stars in secret influence comment;
When I perceive that men as plants increase,
Cheered and check'd even by the selfsame sky,
Vaunt in their youthful sap, at height decrease,
And wear their brave state out of memory;
Then the conceit of this inconstant stay
Sets you most rich in youth before my sight,
Where wasteful Time debateth with Decay,
To change your day of youth to sullied night;
  And, all in war with Time, for love of you,
  As he takes from you, I engraft you new.

All things, after a momentary period of maturity, fade and lapse. The Cosmic Sense itself is subject to the same universal law. In order that it may not die absolutely with the death of its possessor he (the self conscious Bacon) engrafts it anew in the ''Sonnets.''

SONNET XVI.

But wherefore do not you a mightier way
Make war upon this bloody tyrant, Time?
And fortify yourself in your decay
With means more blessed than my barren rhyme?

He (the self conscious Bacon) will (he says) engraft the Cosmic Sense in the ''Sonnets.'' But (he says to the Cosmic Sense) why do not you

Now stand you on the top of happy hours;
And many maiden gardens, yet unset,
With virtuous wish would bear your living flowers,
Much liker than your painted counterfeit:
So should the lines of life that life repair,
Which this, Time's pencil, or my pupil pen,
Neither in inward worth, or outward fair,
Can make you live yourself in eyes of men.
    To give away yourself keeps yourself still;
    And you must live drawn by your own sweet skill.

(yourself) adopt a mightier way to ensure your earthly immortality? You are now in your young prime, and many maiden gardens (art, poetry, the drama, etc.) would be glad to bear your children—your living flowers. And these would be much more like you than would a description of you made from without (as in the case of the "Sonnets"). For the "Sonnets" are a description of the Cosmic Sense from

the point of view of self consciousness, whereas the really desirable thing was that the Cosmic Sense should itself speak. "Only the lull I like," says Whitman, "the hum of your valved voice." If you would put yourself out, Bacon says to the Cosmic Sense, you would make yourself immortal. You would "keep yourself still."

Sonnet XVII.

Who will believe my verse in time to come,
If it were fill'd with your most high deserts?
Though yet, Heaven knows, it is but as a tomb
Which hides your life, and shows not half your parts.
If I could write the beauty of your eyes,
And in fresh numbers number all your graces,
The age to come would say, "this poet lies;
Such heavenly touches ne'er touch'd earthly faces."
So should my papers, yellow'd with their age,
Be scorn'd, like old men of less truth than tongue;
And your true rights be term'd a poet's rage,
And stretched metre of an antique song:
    But were some child of yours alive that time,
    You should live twice—in it, and in my rhyme.

Let me say what I may (as in the "Sonnets") about you, no one could realize from my words what you really are. Let me tell how you appear to me and it will be said I have exaggerated, lied. But produce—leave behind you children like yourself—worthy of yourself—as they must be—then you cannot be denied. You will live, unmistakably, twice: (1) In your own offspring, whose divinity none will be able to question, and (2) In my description of you, in the "Sonnets," which description will be seen, from a comparison with your own offspring, to be truthful.

Sonnet XVIII.

Shall I compare thee to a summer's day?
Thou art more lovely and more temperate:
Rough winds do shake the darling buds of May,
And summer's lease hath all too short a date:
Sometime too hot the eye of heaven shines,
And often in his gold complexion dimm'd;
And every fair from fair sometimes declines,
By chance, or nature's changing course, untrimm'd;
But thy eternal summer shall not fade,
Nor lose possession of that fair thou owest;

The first part of the sonnet is a eulogy of the Cosmic Sense. It would seem that at the time this sonnet was composed Bacon had settled in his own mind how the Cosmic Sense was to express itself, and some of the work seems to have been done—that is, some of the plays written. He speaks of the Cosmic Sense as having grown to time in eternal lines.

Nor shall Death brag thou wander'st in his shade,
When in eternal lines to time thou growest:
So long as men can breathe, or eyes can see,
So long lives this, and this gives life to thee.

Sonnet XXXIII.

Full many a glorious morning have I seen
Flatter the mountain-tops with sovereign eye,
Kissing with golden face the meadows green,
Gilding pale streams with heavenly alchemy;
Anon permit the basest clouds to ride
With ugly rack on his celestial face,
And from the forlorn world his visage hide,
Stealing unseen to west with this disgrace:
Even so my son one early morn did shine
With all triumphant splendor on my brow;
But, out alack! he was but one hour mine,
The region cloud hath mask'd him from me now.
  Yet him for this my love no whit disdaineth;
  Suns of the world may stain, when heaven's sun
    staineth.

Sonnet XXXIII refers to the intermittent character of illumination, which holds true in all cases of Cosmic Consciousness, in which there is more than one flash of the divine radiance. It treats of the cheerlessness and barrenness of the intervals as compared with those periods when the Cosmic Sense is actually present. So Behmen, referring to the intermittent character of his illumination, says [40 : 16]: "The sun shone on me a good while but not constantly, for the sun hid itself, and then I knew not nor well understood my own labor" (*his own writings*). Note the use of the same figure by both writers. So also Yepes tells us: "When these visions occur, it is as if a door were opened into a most marvellous light, whereby the soul sees, as men do when the lightning flashes in a dark night. The lightning makes surrounding objects visible for an instant, and then leaves them in darkness, though the forms of them remain in the fancy. But in the case of the soul the vision is much more perfect; for those things it saw in spirit in that light are so impressed upon it, that whenever God enlightens it again, it beholds them as distinctly as it did at first, precisely as in a mirror, in which we see objects reflected whenever we look upon it. These visions once granted to the soul never afterward leave it altogether; for the forms remain, though they become somewhat indistinct in the course of time. The effects of these visions in the soul are quietness, enlightenment, joy-like glory, sweetness, pureness, love, humility, inclination or elevation of the mind to God, sometimes more, sometimes less, sometimes more of one, sometimes more of another, according to the disposition of the soul and the will of God" [203 : 200-1]. With the last words of Yepes compare Paul: "The fruit of the spirit [Christ, the Cosmic Sense] is love, joy, peace, long suffering, kindness, goodness, faithfulness, meekness, temperance" [22 : 5 : 22].

Sonnet XXXVI.

Let me confess that we two must be twain,
Although our undivided loves are one:
So shall those blots that do with me remain,
Without thy help, by me be borne alone.
In our two loves there is but one respect,
Though in our lives a separate spite,
Which though it alter not love's sole effect,
Yet doth it steal sweet hours from love's delight.

It is reasonable to suppose that this sonnet represents a later date than those above quoted. It is fair to imagine, therefore, that when it was written quite a body of the plays was in existence. For some years Bacon has been leading a dual life: on the one hand the life of a lawyer,

I may not evermore acknowledge thee,
Lest my bewailed guilt should do thee shame;
Nor thou with public kindness honor me,
Unless thou take that honor from thy name:
  But do not so; I love thee in such sort
  As, thou being mine, mine is thy good report.

courtier, politician—his self conscious life: on the other the life of the seer, poet—the life lit by that "light rare, untellable, lighting the very light"—the "light that never was on land or sea"—the life, in a word, of Cosmic Consciousness. He had kept these two lives entirely apart. None or few (Anthony, perhaps, and Mathews) knew that he was living any other life than the first. It had for many strong reasons, and feelings stronger than reasons, become with him a settled policy that the two lives were to be kept apart. The frank duality of this and some other of the "Sonnets" will be almost or quite incomprehensible to many as applied to two parts of the same person or two personalities in the same individual. But we know that (supposing the interpretation here adopted to be correct) the language of the "Sonnets" is not more extreme in this respect than is language in other of these cases in which there can be no doubt as to its meaning. Thus Whitman writes: "With laugh and many a kiss O soul thou pleasest me, I thee" [193 : 321]. And again: "I, turning, call to thee O soul, thou actual me [ib.].

    The writer of the sonnet says, or seems to say, that should he acknowledge his other self, the Cosmic Sense, and its offspring, the plays, any good that could do him (the self conscious person) would be taken from this higher self, and that he will not consent to.

Sonnet XXXIX

O, how thy worth with manners may I sing,
When thou art all the better part of me?
What can mine own praise to mine own self bring?
And what is't but mine own, when I praise thee?
Even for this let us divided live,
And our dear love lose name of single one,
That by this separation I may give
That due to thee which thou deserv't alone.
O absence, what a torment wouldst thou prove,
Were it not thy sour leisure gave sweet leave
To entertain the time with thoughts of love,—
Which time and thoughts so sweetly doth deceive,—
  And that thou teachest how to make one twain,
  By praising him here, who doth hence remain!

The meaning of this sonnet seems unmistakable. It scarcely needs a commentary. The author says that the Cosmic Sense is the best part of him (as, of course, it was), and being part of himself, it is scarcely mannerly in him to praise it. But (he says) for this very reason let us live as two. His absence from the Cosmic Sense is, of course, the time he is occupied with law, politics, business, worldly affairs—all that time, in fact, between the periods of illumination, when his time and mind were not occupied with the things of the Cosmic Sense.

That absence is made happy by the knowledge that at any time he can turn to thoughts of the Cosmic Sense and of the things belonging to it. The most striking expression in this sonnet is: "Thou [the Cosmic Sense] teachest how to make one twain." This is, as pointed out many times in this volume, a prime characteristic of the cases in question. "The attainment of Arahatship" (Cosmic Consciousness), says Gautama, will cause a man, "being one, to become multiform" [161 : 214]. "I live," says Paul, "yet no longer I but Christ [the Cosmic Sense] liveth in me" [22 : 2 : 20]. And again: "If any man be in Christ [if any man live the life of the Cosmic Sense] he is a new creature" [21 : 5 : 17]; and Paul says that the man Jesus "made both [that is, (1) the Cosmic Sense—Christ, and (2) the self conscious man—Jesus] one," . . . "that he might create of the twain one new man" [23 : 2 : 14-15], and in many other places he bears testimony to his own dual personality. Mohammed called the Cosmic Sense "Gabriel"; the Koran was dictated by him (or it): the ostensible Mohammed was a second individuality. Balzac, speaking of Louis

Lambert (i.e., himself), after giving his life down to the period of illumination, says: "The events I have still to relate form the *second existence* of this creature destined to be exceptional in all things" [5 : 100]. He then goes on to describe the oncoming of the Cosmic Conscious condition, and, in the aphorisms, Cosmic Consciousness itself. Whitman constantly refers to the Cosmic Sense as his soul, and calls the every day, visible, Walt Whitman, "The other I am" [193 : 32], and so on.

Sonnet LII

So am I as the rich, whose blessed key
Can bring him to his sweet up-locked treasure,
The which he will not every hour survey,
For blunting the fine point of seldom pleasure.
Therefore are feasts so solemn and so rare,
Since, seldom coming, in the long year set,
Like stones of worth they thinly placed are,
Or captain jewels in the carkanet.
So is the time that keeps you, as my chest,
Or as the wardrobe which the robe doth hide,
To make some special instant special blest,
By new unfolding his imprison'd pride.
   Blessed are you whose worthiness gives scope,
   Being had to triumph, being lack'd to hope.

Compare Plotinus: "This sublime condition is not of permanent duration. It is only now and then that we can enjoy the elevation (mercifully made possible for us) above the limits of the body and the world. I myself have realized it but three times as yet" [188 : 81]. Bacon's periods of illumination were probably longer and more frequent than those of Plotinus. Neither Plotinus nor Bacon, apparently, could control the periods of lumination. It seems likely hat Jesus refers to this apparently causeless and arbi-

trary coming and going of the divine light when he said [17 : 3 : 8]: "The wind bloweth where it listeth and thou hearest the voice thereof, but knowest not whence it cometh and whither it goeth; *so is every one that is born of the spirit.*"

Sonnet LIII.

What is your substance, whereof are you made,
That millions of strange shadows on you tend?
Since every one hath, every one, one shade,
And you, but one, can every shadow lend.
Describe Adonis, and the counterfeit
Is poorly imitated after you;
On Helen's cheek all art of beauty set,
And you in Grecian tires are painted new:
Speak of the spring, and foison of the year;
The one doth shadow of your beauty show,
The other as your bounty doth appear;
And you in every blessed shape we know.
   In all external grace you have some part,
   But you like none, none you, for constant heart.

A description, from one point of view, of Cosmic Consciousness. Compare with it a description by Gautama from the same point of view. He says: "Arahatship [Cosmic Consciousness] enables a man to comprehend by his own heart the hearts of other beings and of other men, to understand all minds, the passionate, the calm, the angry, the peaceable, the deluded, the wise, the concentrated, the ever varying, the lofty, the narrow, the sublime, the mean, the steadfast, the wavering, the free, and the enslaved" [161 : 215]. That

is, it reveals all character, as is so well exemplified in the "Shakespeare" drama. Compare Dante's world-wide vision; Balzac's insight into the structure and operation of the infinite human heart; Whitman's "I am of old and of young, of the foolish as much as the wise, regardless of others, ever regardful of others, maternal as well as paternal, a child as well as a man," etc. [193 : 42], and the almost universal knowledge of man and his environment which his writings, especially the "Leaves," indicate.

Sonnet LV.

Not marble, nor the gilded monuments
Of princes, shall outlive this powerful rhyme;
But you shall shine more bright in these contents
Than unswept stone, besmear'd with sluttish time.
When wasteful war shall statues overturn,
And broils root out the work of masonry,
Nor Mars his sword nor war's quick fire shall burn
The living record of your memory.
'Gainst death and all oblivious enmity
Shall you pace forth; your praise shall still find room,
Even in the eyes of all posterity
That wear this world out to the ending doom.
　　So, till the judgment that yourself arise,
　　You live in this, and dwell in lovers' eyes.

By "this powerful rhyme," in which the Cosmic Sense shall endure and shine in the far future, is probably not intended the "Sonnets" but the plays or some particular play, such as "Romeo and Juliet" (written 1596, printed 1597 and 1599). Until the judgment brought to birth by the elevation of human taste by the plays themselves, you (Cosmic Consciousness) shall live in this play and delight the eyes and hearts of lovers.

Sonnet LIX.

If there be nothing new, but that which is
Hath been before, how are our brains beguil'd,
Which, laboring for invention, bears amiss
The second burden of a former child!
O that record could with a backward look,
Even of five hundred courses of the sun,
Show me your image in some antique book,
Since mind at first in character was done!
That I might see what the old world could say
To this composed wonder of your frame;
Whether we are mended, or whether better they,
Or whether revolution be the same.
　　O, sure I am, the wits of former days
　　To subjects worse have given admiring praise.

The writer asks: "Is this illumination of which I am conscious a new phenomenon or did it exist in the old world? I wish," he says, "I could find it or a description of it in literature. If it has existed it ought to be found in the records of the human mind, and if I could find such records I could judge whether the human mind was advancing, retreating, or standing still." He seems to reach the conclusion that few or none of the great writers of the past experienced it. Bacon was exceedingly familiar with the Bible, and therefore with the gospels and the Pauline epistles, but his reverence for these writings would probably prevent his comparing his experience to that of the sacred writers. It does not seem that he knew much of Dante; and the Buddhistic literature, in which it is fully treated, was an absolutely sealed book to Englishmen of his time. It would never have occurred to him to examine the Koran and the life of Mohammed, if, indeed, they were accessible to him. Bacon was thus probably entirely cut off from any knowledge of other cases than his own.

Sonnet LXII.

Sin of self-love possesseth all mine eye,
And all my soul, and all my every part;
And for this sin there is no remedy,
It is so grounded inward in my heart.
Methinks no face so gracious is as mine,

In this sonnet the duality of the person writing is brought out very strongly—no doubt purposely. When he dwells on his Cosmic Conscious self he is, as it were, lost in admira-

No shape so true, no truth of such account;
And for myself my own worth do define,
As I all other in all worth surmount.
But when my glass shows me myself indeed,
Beated and chopp'd with tann'd antiquity,
Mine own self-love quite contrary I read;
Self so self-loving were iniquity.
   'Tis thee (myself) that for myself I praise,
    Painting my age with beauty of thy days.

tion of himself. When he turns to the physical and self conscious self he is inclined, on the contrary, to despise himself. He is at the same time very much and very little of an egotist. Those who knew the man Walt Whitman know that this same seeming contradiction, resting on the same foundation, existed most markedly in him. Whitman's admiration for the Cosmic Conscious Whitman and his works (the "Leaves") was just such as pictured in this sonnet, while he was absolutely devoid of egotism in the ordinary way of the self conscious individual. It is believed that the above remarks would remain true if applied to Paul, Mohammed or Balzac. Reduced to last analysis, the matter seems to stand about as follows: The Cosmic Conscious self, from all points of view, appears superb, divine. From the point of view of the Cosmic Conscious self, the body and the self conscious self appear equally divine. But from the point of view of the ordinary self consciousness, and so compared with the Cosmic Conscious self, the self conscious self and the body seem insignificant and even, as well shown in Paul's case, contemptible.

SONNET LXX.

That thou art blam'd shall not be thy defect,
For slander's mark was ever yet the fair;
The ornament of beauty is suspect,
A crow that flies in heaven's sweetest air.
So thou be good, slander doth but approve
Thy worth the greater, being woo'd of time;
For canker vice the sweetest buds doth love,
And thou present'st a pure unstained prime.
Thou hast pass'd by the ambush of young days,
Either not assail'd, or victor being charg'd;
Yet this thy praise cannot be so thy praise,
To tie up envy, evermore enlarg'd:
   If some suspect of ill mask'd not thy show,
    Then thou alone kingdoms of hearts shouldst owe.

Bacon says: That a Cosmic Sense (as seen in its offspring, the plays) should be blamed (as for license in language, contempt of received rules, etc.) shall be no proof of defect. Great original work, such as the "Shakespeare" drama, is never appreciated at first, is, in fact, always the object of grave suspicion and often of absolute condemnation. If, he says, the Cosmic Sense is really the divine thing it seems to be, evil speaking of it and its offspring only proves it the more divine, as showing it is over the heads and above the judgment of ordinary men. If it was not for this inevitable blindness all eyes and hearts would recognize and bow down before its supremacy.

SONNET LXXVIII.

So oft have I invok'd thee for my Muse,
And found such fair assistance in my verse,
As every alien pen hath got my use,
And under thee their poesy disperse.
Thine eyes, that taught the dumb on high to sing,
And heavy ignorance aloft to fly,
Have added feathers to the learned's wing,

At the time this sonnet was written many of the plays were composed, published, and doubtless imitated. The writer speaks of himself as "ignorant" because he has had no training or practice in verse writing. The Cosmic Sense had immediately upon its appear-

And given grace a double majesty.
Yet be most proud of that which I compile,
Whose influence is thine, and born of thee:
In others' works thou dost but mend the style,
And arts with thy sweet graces graced be;
  But thou art all my art, and dost advance
  As high as learning my rude ignorance.

ance "taught the hitherto dumb" man "on high to sing." Becoming illumined at about the age of thirty, he not only began without any apprenticeship to write poetry, but to write a new and higher poetry than had hitherto been written in English. And he says that the divine light shining through his compositions (the plays) has been (to some extent, at all events) absorbed and utilized by the verse writers of the day; has added feathers to their wings, and given a double majesty to the grace of their lines. So Lang says of Scott that he "was being driven from post to pillar by his imitators, whom he had taught, like Captain Boabdil, to write nearly as well as himself" [169 : 9]. But he says to the Cosmic Sense, be most proud of what I produce, for the merits of that come not all from study, cleverness or practice, but entirely from yourself.

Compare with the above statement the cases of Jesus, Paul, Mohammed, Balzac and Walt Whitman, who either had no practice or training, or (as in the case of Balzac) derived little or no benefit therefrom, but who in middle life, began immediately upon illumination, either to speak or to write undying words.

SONNET LXXXVI.

Was it the proud full sail of his great verse,
Bound for the prize of all-too-precious you,
That did my ripe thoughts in my brain inherse,
Making their tomb the womb wherein they grew?
Was it his spirit, by spirits taught to write
Above a mortal pitch, that struck me dead?
No, neither he, nor his compeers by night
Giving him aid, my verse astonished.
He, nor that affable familiar ghost
Which nightly gulls him with intelligence,
As victors, of my silence cannot boast;
I was not sick of any fear from thence:
  But when your countenance fill'd up his line
  Then lack'd I matter; that enfeebled mine.

In this sonnet reduplication of the individual, Bacon-Shakespeare, is carried to the farthest pitch. We are forcibly reminded (once more) of Gautama's words in this connection, viz., that Cosmic Consciousness (or Arahatship, as he calls it), "will make a man, being one, to become multiform"—not merely two, but multiform. Few or no sonnets (it would seem) have been written for some time by the "other I am." But the Cosmic Conscious personality had been producing rapidly. Several or many plays had been written within a brief period. The Cosmic Conscious Bacon had been taught by the Cosmic Sense to write "above a mortal pitch." It was not that, however, which struck dumb the self conscious Bacon. But it was the fact that the Cosmic Conscious individual had absorbed (for the time at least) into himself all the forces of the complex organism. As to the "compeers" of the Cosmic Sense, they are the spiritual entities spoken of by Balzac. "Mysterious beings armed with wondrous faculties, who combine with other beings and penetrate them as active agents, beings which overpower others with the scepter and glory of a superior nature" [7 : 50]. Then in line nine "He" is the Cosmic Conscious Bacon, while the "affable familiar ghost" is Cosmic Consciousness. The expression, "Nightly gulls him with intelligence," may be compared with Whitman's "Message from the heavens whispering to me even in sleep" [193 : 324]. It may be noted here (most readers will observe it for themselves) that when speaking of the same experience Whitman's language is more moderate, lower toned, than Balzac's, Dante's or perhaps any other of the Cosmic Conscious writers.

SONNET XCV.

How sweet and lovely dost thou make the shame,
Which, like a canker in the fragrant rose,
Doth spot the beauty of thy budding name!
O, in what sweets dost thou thy sins enclose!
That tongue that tells the story of thy days,
Making lascivious comments on thy sport,
Cannot dispraise but in a kind of praise;
Naming thy name blesses an ill report.
O, what a mansion have those vices got
Which for their habitation chose out thee,
Where beauty's veil doth cover every blot,
And all things turn to fair that eyes can see!
    Take heed, dear heart, of this large privilege;
    The hardest knife ill-us'd doth lose his edge.

"How sweet and lovely dost thou make the shame." Helen Price says that in 1866 Walt Whitman (who wanted a publisher for "Leaves of Grass" badly enough at that time) was offered by a prominent house good terms on condition that he would consent to the deletion of a few lines of "Children of Adam." An hour or two after the offer was made he returned to her mother's house in New York, where he was then staying, and, after telling her and her mother of the offer, said: "But I dare not do it, I dare not leave out or alter what is so genuine, so indispensable, so lofty, so pure" [38 : 32]. So, as to an earlier episode in his life, he told the writer [38 : 26]: "When 'Leaves of Grass,' in 1855, roused such a tempest of anger and condemnation, I went off to the east end of Long Island and spent the late summer and all the fall—the happiest of my life—around Shelter Island and Peconic Bay. Then came back to New York with the confirmed resolution, from which I never afterwards wavered, to go on with my poetic enterprise in my own way and finish it as well as I could." A corresponding incident in Balzac's life occurred in connection with the publication of "Le Médecin de Campagne." In 1833 (shortly after illumination) he wrote to his much loved sister that that book would reach her next week: "It has cost me," he said, "ten times the work 'Louis Lambert' did. . . . That labor was frightful. I may now die in peace; I have done a great work for my country." Two months afterwards he writes again: "Do you know how 'Le Médecin' has been received? By a torrent of insults; . . . but I have chosen my path; nothing shall discourage me. . . . Never has the torrent which bears me onward been so rapid; no more terribly majestic work has ever compelled the human brain" [4 : 142-3]. Line four, ("O in what sweets," etc.) refers to the vices, crimes, meannesses in the plays (the acts of Regan, Goneril, Edmund, Iago, etc.). And does not a veil of beauty cover them all? That tongue, he says, that tells the visions, the revelations, which proceed from the Cosmic Sense, "cannot dispraise but in a kind of praise." ("And I say," says Whitman, "that there is in fact no evil") [193 : 22]. Then he cautions the Cosmic Sense to take "heed of this large privilege." And so we see Whitman "returning upon [his] poems, considering, lingering long," and striking out words and expressions that seem to him too free. This sonnet is one of the most difficult to fully enter into the meaning of, but when this is realized it is perhaps the most exquisite passage ever written by its author. The most exquisite in expression and in metaphysical subtlety. No comment, perhaps, certainly no comment by the present editor, can do it even the most meager justice.

SONNET XCVI.

Some say, thy fault is youth, some wantonness;
Some say, thy grace is youth and gentle sport;
Both grace and faults are lov'd of more and less;
Thou mak'st faults graces that to thee resort.
As on the finger of a throned queen

The plays (the offspring of the Cosmic Sense) are variously judged. What, for instance, seems "wantonness" to one to another is "gentle sport." Both faults and graces

The basest jewel will be well esteem'd,
So are those errors that in thee are seen
To truths translated, and for true things deem'd.
How many lambs might the stern wolf betray,
If like a lamb he could his looks translate!
How many gazers might'st thou lead away,
If thou would'st use the strength of all thy state!
But do not so; I love thee in such sort,
As, thou being mine, mine is thy good report.

are commended; for faults are made graces by the alchemy of the Cosmic Sense. "I am myself," says Whitman, "just as much evil as good, and my nation is, and I say there is in fact no evil" [193 : 22]. And Paul says: "I know and am persuaded in the Lord Jesus [that is, by the Cosmic Sense] that nothing is unclean of itself." As a base jewel on the hand of a queen passes for a rich gem, so all things in you (the Cosmic Sense) are beautiful, true and good. If you should give free expression to this revelation (using the strength of all your state) you would lead many astray (for they would misunderstand you), and you yourself (in your progeny—such as Paul's Epistles, the "Shakespeare" drama, the "Leaves of Grass," etc.) would be condemned and would be so hindered doing your proper work in the world, therefore "do not so."

SONNET XCVII.

How like a winter hath my absence been
From thee, the pleasure of the fleeting year!
What freezings have I felt, what dark days seen!
What old December's bareness everywhere!
And yet this time removed was summer's time;
The teeming autumn, big with rich increase,
Bearing the wanton burden of the prime,
Like widow'd wombs after their lord's decease:
Yet this abundant issue seem'd to me
But hope of orphans, and unfather'd fruit;
For summer and his pleasures wait on thee,
And, thou away, the very birds are mute;
Or if they sing, 'tis with so dull a cheer,
That leaves look pale, dreading the winter's near.

As to the absence of the Cosmic Sense—or, more properly speaking, its only occasional presence in even the greatest cases—see comment on Sonnet XXXIII. As elsewhere pointed out, even self consciousness, which has perhaps existed in the race for several hundred thousand years, and now appears in the individual at about three years of age, is liable to lapse. How *very* far from constant must then a new faculty like Cosmic Consciousness be! The writer speaks of a time when the Cosmic Sense was absent. But (as he puts it) it was he that was absent from the Cosmic Sense—that being considered the real person. So Whitman speaks of the Cosmic Sense as himself, and of the self conscious Whitman as "the other I am." And yet, he says, it was a period of very free production—as there is no reason it should not have been—for what is revealed by the Cosmic Sense remains clear and manifest even for months and years, supposing there should be no subsequent illumination. Compare Yepes, as quoted in comment on Sonnet XXXIII. But though a period of sufficient (reflected) light and of free production, it was joyless and bare as compared with periods during which the Cosmic Sense was actually present.

SONNET CXXVI.

O thou my lovely boy, who in thy power
Dost hold Time's fickle glass, his sickle, hour;
Who hast by waning grown, and therein show'st
Thy lovers withering, as thy sweet self grow'st;

This sonnet constitutes the close of the address to Cosmic Consciousness. It was probably written very shortly before publication (1609), after

If Nature, sovereign mistress over wrack,
As thou goest onwards, still will pluck thee back,
She keeps thee to this purpose, that her skill
May time disgrace, and wretched minutes kill.
Yet fear her, O thou minion of her pleasure!
She may detain, but not still keep, her treasure:
   Her audit, though delay'd, answer'd must be,
   And her quietus is to render thee.

the writer had been "illumined with the Brahmic Splendor" [155 : 232] nearly twenty years and had produced, under its influence, nearly the whole "Shakespeare" drama. O lovely boy, he says, addressing for the last time the Cosmic Sense, who in the hollow of thy hand doth hold time and death—who waning (as age advances within me) has grown (in the plays, thy products), and thereby showest thyself constantly augmenting as thy mortal lovers wither and die. If Nature should desire (as her way is) to destroy thee (the plays—children of Cosmic Consciousness) she yet will not, but will keep thee to show that she is able to disgrace time by making what he cannot kill. Not only so, but also to show that this product of Nature can even kill time (destroy wretched minutes). Yet do thou (Nature's favorite—the Cosmic Sense—the plays) still fear Nature, who may keep thee for a time, but perhaps not forever. As to her (Nature), though her rule is so strong, she must one day give an account of herself to a stronger power. That power is thee (Cosmic Consciousness), whom when evolution (which is Nature) has produced (that is, made general—as self consciousness is to-day), she (Nature) will have received her quietus. For the full apparition of the Cosmic Sense will destroy death, the fear of death, sin and space. "Then cometh the end, when he [Christ—Cosmic Consciousness] shall deliver up the kingdom to God even the Father, when he shall have abolished all rule, and all authority and power. For he must reign till he hath put all enemies under his feet. The last enemy that shall be abolished is death" [20 : 15 : 24-26]. For Cosmic Consciousness will throw the things of sense (of self consciousness—of Nature, as we know her to-day, which now absorb men's thoughts) so into the background as practically to abolish them. Nature, instead of being the Lord, as now, will be a slave—will effectually, in fact, receive her quietus.

SUMMARY.

In this case the ordinary details of proof of illumination are largely wanting. If William Shakespeare wrote the plays and "Sonnets," we have absolutely no external evidence to build upon. If Francis Bacon wrote them, we have the vague evidence of his seclusion at about the time his illumination (if at all) must have taken place, and Hawley's and his own seeming allusion to the possession by him of some such unusual, very exalted, faculty. Over and above these circumstances, which to most will seem very slight, the argument that the man who wrote the plays and "Sonnets" had Cosmic Consciousness must rest upon these writings themselves and would consist of two clauses. (1) The creator of the plays was perhaps the greatest intellect the world has seen. His moral intuitions were as true as his intellect was great. He was from all points of view a transcendently great spiritual force. Being so, he ought (according to the thesis maintained in this volume) to have had Cosmic Consciousness. (2) The first one hundred and twenty-six sonnets seem to show beyond doubt that their author had the Cosmic Sense and that these sonnets were addressed to it. It does not seem to the present writer that they can be made sense of (intelligently read) from any other standpoint.

CHAPTER 10.

Jacob Behmen (called The Teutonic Theosopher).

BORN 1575; died 1624.

His birthplace was at Alt Seidenberg, a place about two miles distant from Görlitz, in Germany. He came of a well-to-do family, but his first employment was that of a herd-boy on the Lands-Krone, a hill in the neighborhood of Görlitz. The only education he received was at the town school of Seidenberg, a mile from his home. Later he was apprenticed to a shoemaker in Seidenberg. By the year 1599 he was settled at Görlitz as a master shoemaker and married to Katharina, a daughter of Hans Kuntzschmann. a thriving butcher in that town.

I.

Behmen had two distinct illuminations. The first, in 1600 (when he was twenty-five years old), is thus described by Martensen:

Sitting one day in his room his eyes fell upon a burnished pewter dish, which reflected the sunshine with such marvellous splendor that he fell into an inward ecstasy, and it seemed to him as if he could now look into the principles and deepest foundation of things. He believed that it was only a fancy, and in order to banish it from his mind he went out upon the green. But here he remarked that he gazed into the very heart of things, the very herbs and grass, and that actual nature harmonized with what he had inwardly seen. He said nothing of this to any one, but praised and thanked God in silence. He continued in the honest practice of his craft, was attentive to his domestic affairs, and was on terms of good-will with all men [123].

Of this first illumination Hartmann says that by it or from it: "He learned to know the innermost foundation of nature, and acquired the capacity to see henceforth with the eyes of the soul into the heart of all things, a faculty which remained with him even in his normal condition" [97: 3]. And in the life prefixed to the works the same circumstance is mentioned in the words that follow:

About the year 1600, in the twenty-fifth year of his age, he was again surrounded by the divine light and replenished with the heavenly knowledge; insomuch as going abroad in the fields to a green before Neys Gate, at Görlitz, he there sat down and, viewing the herbs and grass of the field in his inward light, he saw into their essences, use and properties, which were discovered to him by their lineaments, figures and signatures. In like manner he beheld the whole creation, and from that foundation of revelation he afterwards wrote his book, "De Signatura Rerum." In the unfolding of those mysteries before his understanding he had a great measure of joy, yet returned home and took care of his family and lived in great peace and silence, scarce intimating to any these wonderful things that had befallen him till in the year 1610, being again taken into this light, lest the mysteries revealed to him should pass through him as a stream, and rather for a memorial than intending any publication, he wrote his first book, called "Aurora, or the Morning Redness" [40: 13-14].

The first illumination, in 1600, was not complete. He did not at that time really attain to Cosmic Consciousness; he passed into the dawn but not into the perfect day. Of his complete illumination, in 1610 (when thirty-five years old), Martensen says:

Ten years later [1610] he had another remarkable inward experience. What he had previously seen only chaotically, fragmentarily, and in isolated glimpses, he now beheld as a coherent whole and in more definite outlines [123].

Hartmann says of this latter experience:

Ten years afterwards, anno 1610, his third illumination took place, and that which in former visions had appeared to him chaotic and multifarious was now recognized by him as a unity, like a harp of many strings, of which each string is a separate instrument, while the whole is only one harp. He now recognized the divine order of nature, and how from the trunk of the tree of life spring different branches, bearing manifold leaves and flowers and fruits, and he became impressed with the necessity of writing down what he saw and preserving the record [97:3].

While he himself speaks of this final and complete illumination as follows:

The gate was opened to me that in one quarter of an hour I saw and knew more than if I had been many years together at a university, at which I exceedingly admired and thereupon turned my praise to God for it. For I saw and knew the being of all beings, the byss and abyss and the eternal generation of the Holy Trinity, the descent and original of the world and of all creatures through the divine wisdom: I knew and saw in myself all the three worlds, namely, (1) the divine [angelical and paradisical] (2) and the dark [the original of the nature to the fire] and (3) then the external and visible world [being a procreation or external birth from both the internal and spiritual worlds]. And I saw and knew the whole working essence, in the evil and the good and the original and the existence of each of them; and likewise how the fruitful-bearing-womb of eternity brought forth. So that I did not only greatly wonder at it but did also exceedingly rejoice [40:15].

The expression above, "He was again surrounded," refers to certain other visions which preceded this first (imperfect) oncoming of the Cosmic Sense at the age of twenty-five years. Such visions (it may be said) as seem to be common in the lives of men who afterward become illumined. They belong, no doubt, to such sensitive and highly-wrought nervous organizations as would be possessed by persons who had within them the "eligibility" (as Whitman would have expressed it) of rising to Cosmic Consciousness. Hartmann says of him:

Jacob Behmen was in possession of remarkable occult powers. He is known to have spoken several languages, although no one ever knew where he had acquired them. They had probably been learned by him in a previous life. He also knew the language of nature, and could call plants and animals by their own proper names [97:19].

Behmen says, himself, on this point:

I am not a master of literature nor of arts, such as belong to this world, but a foolish and simple minded man. I have never desired to learn any sciences, but from early youth I strove after the salvation of my soul, and thought how I might inherit or possess the kingdom of heaven. Finding within myself a powerful contrarium, namely, the desires that belong to the flesh and blood, I began to fight a hard battle against my corrupted nature, and with the aid of God I made up my mind to overcome the inherited evil will, to break it, and to enter wholly into the love of God in the Christ. I therefore then and there resolved to regard myself as one dead in my inherited form, until the spirit of God would take form in me, so that in and through Him I might conduct my life. This, however, was not possible for me to accomplish, but I stood firmly by my earnest resolution and fought a hard battle with myself. Now while I was wrestling and battling, being aided by God, a wonderful light arose within my soul. It was a light entirely foreign to my unruly nature, but in it I recognized the true nature of God and man, and the relation existing between them, a thing which heretofore I had never understood, and for which I would never have sought [97 : 50].

Frankenburg writes of him:

His bodily appearance was somewhat mean; he was tall of stature, had a low forehead but prominent temples, a rather aquile nose, a scanty beard, gray eyes sparkling into a heavenly blue, a feeble but genial voice. He was modest in his bearing, unassuming in conversation, lowly in conduct, patient in suffering, and gentle-hearted [123 : 15].

And Hartmann on the same subject says:

In his exterior appearance Behmen was little, having a short thin beard, a feeble voice and eyes of a grayish tint. He was deficient in physical strength; nevertheless there is nothing known of his having ever had any other disease than the one that caused his death [97 : 17].

His life may be read side by side with that of Gautama, Jesus, Paul, Las Casas, Yepes, or even Whitman, without fear that the gentle hearted Behmen should suffer by such comparison, while his death is worthy to stand on record with that of Yepes or Blake. It took place on Sunday, November 20th, 1624.

Before one A. M. Behmen called his son Tobias to his bedside and asked him whether he did not hear beautiful music, and then he requested him to open the door of the room so that the celestial song could be better heard. Later on he asked what time it was and when he was told that the clock struck two he said: "This is not yet time for me, in three hours will be my time." After a pause he again spoke and said: "Thou powerful God, Zabaoth, save me according to thy will." Again he said: "Thou crucified Lord Jesus Christ, have mercy upon me and take me into thy kingdom." He then gave to his wife certain directions regarding his books and other temporal matters, telling her also that she would not survive him very long (as indeed she did not), and, taking leave from his sons, he said: "Now I shall enter the Paradise." He then asked his eldest son, whose loving looks seemed to keep Behmen's soul

from severing the bonds of the body, to turn him round, and, giving one deep
sigh, his soul gave up the body to the earth to which it belonged and entered
into that higher state which is known to none except those who have experienced
it themselves [97:15].

II.

As utterances of the Cosmic Sense all the writings of Behmen
are well-nigh totally unintelligible to the merely self conscious mind. Nevertheless he who is willing to be at the necessary
pains will find that like those of Paul, Dante, Balzac, Whitman
and the rest, they are a veritable mine of wisdom, some of which
may be found by every earnest seeker, though undoubtedly the
whole may only be comprehended by those enlightened as he himself was.

To show what has been thought of these books by competent
men who have studied them it may be well to quote the words of
the editor of "The Three Principles" in the quarto [1764]
edition:

A man [he says] cannot conceive the wonderful knowledge, before he has
read this book diligently through, which he will find to be contained in it. And
he will find that *The Threefold* life is ten times deeper than this and the Forty
Questions to be tenfold deeper than that, and that to be as deep as a spirit is
in itself, as the author says; than which there can be no greater depth, for God
Himself is a spirit [42:3].

And those of Claude de Saint Martin, contained in his letters
to Kirchberger:

I am not young [he writes], being now near my fiftieth year; nevertheless
I have begun to learn German in order that I may read this incomparable
author in his own tongue. I have written some not unacceptable books myself,
but I am not worthy to unloose the shoestrings of this wonderful man, whom I
regard as the greatest light that has ever appeared upon the earth, second only
to Him who was the light itself. . . . I advise you by all means to throw yourself into this abyss of knowledge of the profoundest of all truths [97:32 and
199:30].

The extracts which follow (as all others in this volume) are
selected not so much for their intrinsic interest and excellence.

nor for what they reveal to us of the nature of the Cosmos, as for the light they assist in throwing on the characteristics of the faculty called Cosmic Consciousness; and for this purpose they are compared with like expressions of men whose spiritual position is similar to that of the inspired shoemaker of Görlitz.

III.

If you will behold your own self and the outer world, and what is taking place therein, you will find that you, with regard to your external being, are that external world [97 : 137].

You are a little world formed out of the large one, and your external light is a chaos of the sun and the constellations of stars. If this were not so you would not be able to see by means of the light of the sun [97 : 137].

Not I, the I that I am, know these things: But God knows them in me [97 : 34].

He alone, therefore, in whom Christ exists and lives, is a Christian, a man in whom Christ has been raised out of the wasted flesh of Adam [97 : 5].

Suddenly . . . my spirit did break through . . . even into the innermost birth of Geniture of the Deity, and there I was embraced with love, as a bridegroom embraces his dearly beloved bride. But the greatness of the triumphing that was in the spirit I

"Strange and hard that paradox true I give, objects gross and the unseen soul are one" [193 : 173], and Gautama, Plotinus and Carpenter are all equally definite upon the same point.

"Dazzling and tremendous, how quick the sunrise would kill me if I could not now and always send sunrise out of me" [193 : 50].

"The other I am" [193 : 32]. " 'Tis thee [myself] that for myself I praise" [176 : 62]. The recognition of the duplex individuality of the Cosmic Conscious person—i.e., the self conscious self and the Cosmic Conscious self.

"Christ" here was used as Paul constantly uses the word, as a name—that is, of Cosmic Consciousness.

The "breaking through" into the Cosmic Sense and the intense feeling of joy and exaltation which thereto belongs. The realization of "heaven, which is pure light; light intellectual, full of love, love of true good, full of joy; joy which transcends every sweetness" [72 : 193].

cannot express either in speaking or writing; neither can it be compared to anything, but with that wherein the life is generated in the midst of death, and it is like the resurrection from the dead. In this light my spirit suddenly saw through all, and in and by all the creatures, even in herbs and grass, it knew God, who he is, and how he is, and what his will is; and suddenly in that light my will was set on, by a mighty impulse, to describe the being of God. But because I could not presently apprehend the deepest births of God in their being and comprehend them in my reason, there passed almost twelve years before the exact understanding thereof was given me. And it was with me as with a young tree which is planted in the ground, and at first is young and tender, and flourishing to the eye, especially if it comes on lustily in its growing. But it does not bear fruit presently; and, though it blossoms, they fall off; also many a cold wind, frost and snow, puff upon it, before it comes to any growth and bearing of fruit [41:184].

If thou climbest up this ladder on which I climb up into the deep of God, as I have done, then thou hast climbed well: I am not come to this meaning, or to this work and knowledge through my own reason, or through my own will and purpose; neither have I sought this knowledge, nor so much as know anything concerning it. I sought only for the heart of God, therein to hide myself from the tempestuous storms of the devil [41:237].

None of those who have attained Cosmic Consciousness "sought" for it; they could not, for they did not know there was such a thing. But it would seem that all the pronounced cases were men who earnestly sought for the "heart of God"—i.e., for the highest and best life.

Now the will cannot endure the attracting and impregnation, for it would be free, and yet cannot, because it is desirous; and feeling it cannot be free, it entereth with the attracting into itself, and taketh (or conceiveth) in itself another will, which is to go out from the darkness into itself, and that other conceived will is the eternal mind, and entereth into itself as a sudden flash (or lightning) and dissipateth the darkness, and goeth forth into itself, and dwelleth in itself, and maketh to itself another (or second) principle of another quality (source or condition), for the sting of the stirring remaineth in the darkness [43:5]. The first eternal will is God the Father, and it is to generate His Son—viz., His Word—not out of anything else, but out of Himself; and we have already informed you about the essences, which are generated in the will, and also how the will in the essences is set in darkness, and how the darkness (in the wheel of the anxiety) is broken asunder by the flash of fire, and how the will cometh to be in four forms, whereas in the original all four are but one, but in the flash of fire appear in four forms; as also how the flash of fire doth exist, in that the first will doth sharpen itself in the eager hardness, so that the liberty of the will shineth in the flesh. Whereby we have given you to understand that the first will shineth in the flash of the fire and is consuming by reason of the anxious sharpness, where the will continueth in the sharpness, and comprehendeth the other will in itself (understand in the centre of the sharpness), which is to go out from the sharpness, and to dwell in itself in the eternal liberty without pain or source [43:15-16].

Two quaint expositions of the generating of the second (Cosmic Conscious) self in the first (self conscious) self.

For Jesus Christ, the Son of God, the Eternal Word in the Father (who is the glance, or brightness, and the power of the light eternity), must become man, and be born in you, if you will know God; otherwise you are in the dark stable, and go about groping and feeling, and look always for Christ at the right hand of God, supposing that he is a great way off; you cast your mind aloft above the stars and seek

"Christ," used as by Paul for the Cosmic Sense—"I live, yet not I, but Christ liveth in me" [22:2:20]. "Christ who is our life" [25:3:4]. "Jesus Christ is in you" [21:13:5].

God, as the sophisters teach you, who represent God as one afar off, in heaven [43:24].

I was as simple concerning the hidden mysteries as the meanest of all; but my virgin of the wonders of God taught me, so that I must write of His wonders; though indeed my purpose is to write this for a memorandum for myself, and yet I shall speak as for many, which is known to God [43:31].

The Cosmic Sense a virgin. Compare Dante's Beatrice and Balzac's Seraphita—Seraphitus—so also the youth—Cosmic Sense—in Bacon's "Sonnets" is a virgin. "For a memorandum." Compare Whitman: "Only a few hints I seek for my own use to trace out here" [193:14].

Thus we distinguish to you the substance in the darkness; and though we are very hard to be understood by you, and though also little belief may be afforded to it, we yet have a very convincing proof of it, not only in the created heaven, but also in the centre of the earth, as also in the whole principle of this world, which would be too long to set down here [43:33].

So as proof or argument for some of his most spiritual and recondite doctrines—optimism, immortality, unending growth, expansion and evolution—Whitman appeals to the common phenomena of nature and life. He says: "I hear you whispering there O stars of heaven, O suns—O grass of graves—O perpetual transfers and promotions, if you do not say anything how can I say anything" [193:77]?

The scholar said to his master: "How may I come to the supersensual life, that I may see God and hear Him speak?" His master said: "When thou canst throw thyself but for a moment into that where no creature dwelleth, then thou hearest what God speaketh."

So Balzac tells us: "From abstraction [self consciousness] are derived laws, arts, interests, social ideas. It is the glory and scourge of the world: Glorious, it creates societies; baneful, it exempts man from entering the path of specialism [Cosmic Consciousness], which leads to the Infinite" [5:142].

Scholar.—Is that near at hand or far off?

Master.—It is in thee, and if thou canst for awhile cease from all thy thinking and willing thou shalt hear unspeakable words of God.

Scholar.—How can I hear when I stand still from thinking and willing?

Master.—When thou standest still from the thinking and willing of self, the eternal hearing, seeing and speaking will be revealed to thee, and so God heareth and seeth through thee. Thine own hearing, willing and seeing hindereth thee, that thou dost not see nor hear God.

The same doctrine is repeated over and over in the Suttas. Compare also Carpenter [56:166-174].

Scholar.—Wherewithal shall I hear and see God, being He is above nature and creature?

Master.—When thou art quiet or silent, then thou art that which God was before nature and creature, and whereof He made thy nature and creature. Then thou hearest and seest with that therewith God saw and heard in thee before thy own willing, seeing and hearing began.

Scholar.—What hindereth or keepeth me back that I cannot come to that?

Master.—Thy own willing, seeing and hearing. And because thou strivest against that out of which thou art come, thou breakest thyself off with thy own willing from God's willing, and with thy own seeing thou seest in thy own willing only; and thy willing stoppeth thy hearing with thy own thinking of earthly natural things, and bringeth thee into a ground, and overshadoweth thee with that which thou willest, so that thou canst not come to that which is supernatural and supersensual [50: 75-6].

Master.—If thou rulest over all creatures outwardly only, then thy will and ruling is in a bestial kind, and is but an imaginary transitory ruling, and thou bringest also thy desire into a bestial essence, whereby thou becomest infected and captivated, and gettest also a bestial condition. But if thou hast left the imaginary condition, then thou art in the super-imaginariness, and rulest over all creatures, in that ground out of which they are created, and nothing on earth can hurt thee, for thou art like all things, and nothing is unlike to thee [50: 76].

His master said to him very kindly: Loving scholar, if it were that thy will could break off itself for one hour from all creatures and throw itself into that, where no creature is, it would be ever clothed with the highest splendor of God's glory, and would taste in itself the most sweet love of our Lord Jesus, which no man can express, and it would find in itself the unspeakable words of our Lord concerning his great mercy; it would feel in itself that the cross of our Lord Christ would be very pleasing to it, and it would love that more than the honor and goods of the world [50: 78].

Master.—Though thou lovest the earthly wisdom now, yet when thou art ever-clothed with the heavenly [wisdom] thou wilt see that all the wisdom of the world is but folly, and that the world hateth but thy enemy—viz., the

So says Whitman in respect to ownership: "As if one fit to own things could not at pleasure enter upon all and incorporate them into himself" [193 : 214]. And again: "To see no possession but you may possess it, enjoying all without labor or purchase, abstracting the feast yet not abstracting one particle of it, to take the best of the farmer's farm and the rich man's elegant villa, and the chaste blessings of the well married couple and the fruits of orchards and the flowers of gardens [193 : 127].

The "cross of Christ," from the point of view of what might be called the Pauline type of these men, means simply the deprivation of the good things of self consciousness and the bearing of the so-called evils of the self conscious life. But these goods are seen by them not to be good, and these evils not to be evils, and to reach that point of view (in Cosmic Consciousness) is the one good thing. "To arrive there is to depart hence, going away out of one's self as far as possible from this vile state to that which is the highest of all. Therefore, rising above all that may be known and understood temporally and spiritually, the soul must earnestly desire to reach that which in this life [the self conscious life] cannot be known and which the heart cannot conceive; and, leaving behind all actual and possible taste and feeling of sense and spirit, must desire earnestly to arrive at that which transcends all sense and all feeling" [203 : 74].

"We speak wisdom among the perfect; yet a wisdom not of this world" [20 : 2 : 6]. "If any man thinketh he is wise among you in this world let him become a fool that he may become wise. For the wisdom of this world is foolishness with God" [20 : 3 : 18-19]. The wisdom of self consciousness is mortal life; and when thou thyself comest to hate the will thereof, then thou also wilt begin to love that despising of the mortal life [50:80].

Scholar.—What is the virtue, power, height and greatness of love?

Master.—Its virtue is that nothing (whence all things proceed), and its power is (in and) through all things, its height is as high as God and its greatness is greater than God; whosoever findeth it findeth nothing, and all things.

Scholar.—Loving master, pray tell me how I may understand this.

Master.—That I said its virtue is that nothing, thou mayest understand thus: When thou art gone forth wholly from the creature, and art become nothing to all that is nature and creature, then thou art in that eternal one, which is God himself, and then thou shalt perceive and feel the highest virtue of love [50-1:81]. Also, that I said whosoever findeth it findeth nothing and all things; that is also true, for he findeth a supernatural, supersensual abyss, having no ground, where there is no place to dwell in; and he findeth also nothing that is like it, and therefore it may be compared to nothing, for it is deeper than anything, and is as nothing to all things, for it is not comprehensible; and because it is nothing, it is free from all things, and it is that only good, which a man cannot express or utter what it is. But that I lastly said, he that findeth it, findeth all things, is also true; it hath been the beginning of all things, and it ruleth all things. If thou findest it, thou comest into that ground from whence all things are proceeded, and wherein they subsist, and thou art in it a king over all the works of God [50:81].

Scholar.—Loving master, I can no more endure anything should divert me, how shall I find the nearest way to it?

Master.—Where the way is hardest there walk thou, and take up what the world rejecteth; and what the world doth, that do not thou. Walk contrary to the world in all things. And then thou comest the nearest way to it. . . .

Master.—That thou sayest also, thou shouldst be accounted a silly fool is true; for the way to the love of God is folly to the world, but wisdom to

foolishness from the point of view of the Cosmic Sense.

This extract and the next contain a definition of Cosmic Consciousness from the point of view of Nirvâna, its Buddhist name.

"O Bhikshu, empty this boat (i.e., empty yourself of the things of self consciousness); if emptied it will go quickly; having cut off passion and hatred, thou wilt go to Nirvâna" [156:86].

He who is fit (says Whitman) can enter into possession of all things [193:214].

If you wish to attain the divine life (Cosmic Consciousness), says Yepes, you must cast away every satisfaction, temporal and spiritual (of the self conscious man) [204:534], "forgetting the things which are behind [the things of self consciousness] and stretching forward to the things which are before" [24:3:13]. And this seems to be the universal dictum.

"The natural [merely self conscious] man receiveth not the things of the spirit of God; for they are foolishness unto him" [20:2:14].

the children of God.   When the world perceiveth this fire of love in the children of God, it saith they are turned fools, but to the children of God it is the greatest treasure, so great that no life can express it, nor tongue so much as name what the fire of the inflaming love of God is; it is whiter than the sun, and sweeter than anything; it is far more nourishing than any meat or drink, and more pleasant than all the joy of this world.   Whosoever getteth this is richer than any king on earth, more noble than any emperor can be, and more potent and strong than all authority and power.

Then the scholar asked his master further, saying: "Whither goeth the soul when the body dieth, be it either saved or damned?"

Master.—It needed no going forth. Only the outward moral life with the body do separate themselves from the soul; that soul hath heaven and hell in itself before, as it is written.   The kingdom of God cometh not with outward observation, neither shall they say, lo here, or lo there it is, for behold the kingdom of God is within you: And whether of the two, viz., either heaven or hell, shall be manifest in it, in that the soul standeth [50:82-3].

"There will never be any more heaven or hell than there is now" [193 : 30].

Scholar.—What, then, is the body of a man?

Master.—It is the visible world, an image and essence of all that the world is; and the visible world is a manifestation of the inward spiritual world, (come) out of the eternal darkness, out of the spiritual weaving (twining or connection) and it is an object or resemblance of eternity, wherewith eternity hath made itself visible; where self-will and resigned-will, viz., evil and good, work one with the other; and such a substance the outward man also is; for God created man out of the outward world, and breathed into him the inner spiritual world, for a soul and an understanding life, and therefore in the things of the outward world man can receive and work evil and good.

Says Whitman: "Not the types set up by the printer return their impression, the meaning, the main concern, any more than a man's substance and life, or a woman's substance and life, return in the body and the soul, indifferently before death and after death.   Behold the body includes and is the meaning, the main concern, and includes and is the soul; whoever you are, how superb and divine is your body or any part of it" [193 : 25].

Scholar.—What shall be after this world, when all things perish?

Master.—The material substance only ceaseth—viz., the four elements, the sun, moon, and stars, and then the inward world will be wholly visible and manifest.   But whatsoever hath been wrought by the spirit in this time, whether evil or good, I say, every work shall separate itself there in a spiritual manner, either into the eternal light, or into the eternal darkness; for that which is born from each will penetrateth again into that which is like itself [50:86].

"The soul is of itself, all verges to it, all has reference to what ensues, all that a person does, says, thinks, is of consequence, not a move can a man or woman make, that affects him or her in a day, month, any part of the direct lifetime, or the hour of death, but the same affects him or her onward afterwards through the indirect lifetime" [193 : 289].

IV.

SUMMARY.

a. In the case of Jacob Behmen there was the initial earnestness of character which belongs to the class of men of whom this book treats.

b. There was (almost certainly), though we are not told of it in so many words, the subjective light.

c. There was extraordinary intellectual illumination.

d. And equal moral elevation.

e. There was the sense of immortality.

f. Loss of the fear of death (if he ever had it, as is likely, since he seems to have been quite an ordinary boy and young man).

g. There was the suddenness, the instantaneousness, of the awakening of the new life.

h. At the time of his illumination he was at the typical age—namely, thirty-five years.

CHAPTER 11.

William Blake.

BORN 1757; died 1827.

If Blake had Cosmic Consciousness the words written above as to the vastly greater scope and variety of this than of self consciousness will receive from his case illustration. The few short extracts from his writings, below quoted, almost prove that he had the Cosmic Sense, which he called "Imaginative Vision" [95: 166], and he must have attained to it within a very few years after reaching the thirtieth of his age. There do not appear to be any details extant of his entrance into it, but his writings may fairly be allowed to prove the fact of possession.

I.

W. M. Rossetti, in the "Prefatory Memoir" to "The Poetical Works of William Blake" [52], gives an admirable sketch of

Blake's actual life and apparently a fair estimate of his abilities and defects. The following extracts therefrom will materially assist us in the inquiry now before us; that is: Had Blake Cosmic Consciousness?

The difficulty of Blake's biographers, subsequent to 1863, the date of Mr. Gilchrist's book, is of a different kind altogether. It is the difficulty of stating sufficiently high the extraordinary claims of Blake to admiration and reverence, without slurring over those other considerations which need to be plainly and fully set forth if we would obtain any real idea of the man as he was—of his total unlikeness to his contemporaries, of his amazing genius and noble performances in two arts, of the height by which he transcended other men, and the incapacity which he always evinced for performing at all what others accomplish easily. He could do vastly more than they, but he could seldom do the like. By some unknown process he had soared to the top of a cloud-capped Alp, while they were crouching in the valley: But to reach a middle station on the mountain was what they could readily manage step by step, while Blake found that ordinary achievement impracticable. He could not and he would not do it; the want of will, or rather the utter alienation of will, the resolve to soar (which was natural to him), and not to walk (which was unnatural and repulsive), constituted or counted instead of an actual want of power [139:9].

In the fact that Blake soared beyond, and far beyond, men of self consciousness merely, but could not see or do many things that these saw clearly and could do easily, we see a relationship between him and the great illuminati. For surely the very same thing could be said of all these. In worldly matters they are all, or nearly all, as little children, while in spiritual things they are as gods. Note Balzac contracting enormous debts for want of ordinary business common sense and laboring vainly for years to pay them while in the full exercise of enough genius to equip a regiment of Rothschilds. Bacon showered upon the human race intellectual and spiritual riches beyond all computation, but with every apparent advantage (position at court, hereditary prestige, influential friends) he labors in vain for years for position in the self conscious sphere, and after getting it cannot hold it. Buddha, Jesus, Paul, Las Casas, Yepes, Behmen and Whitman were wise: They saw that the things of the Cosmic Sense were enough, and they simply put by the things of self consciousness, but had they tried for these the chances are they would have failed to obtain them.

Rapt in a passionate yearning, he realized, even on this earth and in his mortal body, a species of Nirvâna: his whole faculty, his whole personality, the very essence of his mind and mould, attained to absorption into his ideal ultimate, into that which Dante's profound phrase designates "il Ben dell' intelletto" [139:11].

Blake, too, found the world of the Cosmic Sense enough, and wisely did not waste time and energy seeking for the so-called goods and riches of the self-conscious life.

William Blake's education was of the scantiest. being confined to reading

These men are independent of education, and most of them—like Blake himself—

and writing; arithmetic may also be guessed at, but is not recorded, and very probably his capacity for acquiring or retaining that item of knowledge was far below the average [139 : 14].

think it useless or worse. Blake says of it: "There is no use in education: I hold it to be wrong. It is the great sin; it is eating of the tree of the knowledge of good and evil. This was the fault of Plato. He knew of nothing but the virtues and vices, and good and evil. There is nothing in all that. Everything is good in God's eyes" [139 :

80]. This reminds us of what Rawley said of Bacon: "He had not his knowledge from books, but from some grounds within himself" [141 : 47], and of Whitman's "You shall no longer feed on the spectres in books" [193 : 30].

In the preface to "The Jerusalem" Blake speaks of that composition as having been "dictated" to him, and other expressions of his prove that he regarded it rather as a revelation of which he was the scribe than as the product of his own inventing and fashioning brain. Blake considered it "the grandest poem that this world contains;" adding, "I may praise it, since I dare not pretend to be any other than the secretary—the authors are in eternity." In an earlier letter (April 25th, 1803) he had said: "I have written this poem from immediate dictation, twelve or sometimes twenty or thirty lines at a time, without premeditation, and even against my will" [139 : 41].

This is the declaration of each possessor of the Cosmic Sense. It is not I, the visible man who speaks, but (as Jesus says) "As the Father hath said unto me so I speak" [14 : 12 : 50]; or as Paul writes: "I will not dare to speak of any things save those which Christ wrought through me" [16 : 15 : 18]. "Loose the stop from *your* throat" [193 : 32] says Whitman to the Cosmic Sense. And so universally.

Blake had a mental intuition, inspiration, or revelation—call it what we will; it was as real to his spiritual eye as a material object could be to his bodily eye; and no doubt his bodily eye, the eye of a designer or painter with a great gift of invention and composition, was far more than normally ready at following the dictate of the spiritual eye, and seeing, with an almost instantaneously creative and fashioning act, the visual semblance of a visionary essence [139 : 62].

"O I am *sure*," says Whitman, "they really came from Thee—the urge, the ardor, the potent, felt, interior, command, a message from the heavens" [193 : 324]. "The noble truths," Gautama said, "were not among the doctrines handed down, but there arose within him the eye to perceive them" [159 : 150].

His unworldliness, extreme as it was, did not degenerate into ineptitude. He apprehended the requirements of practical life, was prepared to meet them in a resolute and diligent spirit from day to day, and could on occasions display a full share of sagacity. He was of lofty and independent spirit, not caring to refute any odd stories that were current regarding his conduct or demeanor, neither parading nor concealing his poverty, and seldom accepting any sort of aid for which he could not and did not supply a full equivalent [139 : 69].

Each word of this passage is strictly true of Whitman, and allowing for difference of manners and customs in other times and countries, the paragraph could be read into the life of any one of the men discussed in this book.

He knows that what he does is not inferior to the grandest antiques. Superior it cannot be, for human power cannot go beyond either what he does or what they have done. It is the gift of God, it is inspiration and vision [139:72].

"Divine am I," says Whitman, "inside and out" [193 : 49].

It must be allowed that in many instances Blake spoke of himself with measureless and rather provoking self-applause. This is in truth one conspicuous outcome of that very simplicity of character of which I have just spoken; egotism it is, but not worldly, self-seeking [139:71].

"I conned old times," says Whitman; "I sat studying at the feet of the great masters, now if eligible O that the great masters might return and study me" [193 : 20].

That he was on the whole and in the best sense happy is, considering all his trials and crosses, one of the very

Happiness is one of the marks of the Cosmic Sense.

highest evidences in his praise. "If asked," writes Mr. Palmer, "whether I ever knew among the intellectual a happy man, Blake would be the only one who would immediately occur to me." Visionary and ideal aspirations of the intensest kind; the imaginative life wholly predominating over the corporeal and mundane life, and almost swallowing it up; and a child-like simplicity of personal character, free from self-interest, and ignorant or careless of any policy of self-control, though habitually guided and regulated by noble emotions and a resolute loyalty to duty—these are the main lines which we trace throughout the entire career of Blake, in his life and death, in his writings and his art. This it is which makes him so peculiarly lovable and admirable as a man, and invests his works, especially his poems, with so delightful a charm. We feel that he is truly "of the kingdom of heaven": above the firmament, his soul holds converse with archangels; on the earth, he is as the little child whom Jesus "sat in the midst of them" [139:70].

The essence of Blake's faculty, the power by which he achieved his work, was intuition: this holds good of his artistic productions, and still more so of his poems. Intuition reigns supreme in them; and even the reader has to apprehend them intuitively, or else to leave them aside altogether [139:74].

It is too bad that these "Prophetic Books" are not published. It seems almost certain that they embody (behind thick veils, doubtless) revelations of extraordinary value —news from "the kingdom of heaven"— from the better world—the world of the Cosmic Sense.

Ample evidence exists to satisfy us that Blake had real conceptions in the metaphysical or supersensual regions of thought—conceptions which might have been termed speculations in other people, but in him rather intuitions; and that the "Prophetic Books" embody these in some sort of way cannot be disputed [139:120].

As to his religious belief, it should be understood that Blake was a Christian in a certain way, and a truly fervent Christian; but it was a way of his own, exceedingly different from that of any of the churches. For the last forty years of his life he never entered a place of worship [139:76].

Blake's religion—his attitude toward the Church—toward God—toward immortality—is the characteristic attitude of the man who has attained to Cosmic Consciousness—as shown in each life and in all the writings of these men.

He believed—with a great profundity and ardor of faith—in God; but he believed also that men are gods, or that collective man is God. He believed in Christ; but exactly what he believed him to be is a separate question. "Jesus Christ," he said, conversing with Mr. Robinson, "is the only God, and so am I, and so are you" [139:77].

In immortality Blake seems to have believed implicitly, and (in some main essentials) without much deviation from other people's credence. When he heard of Flaxman's death (December 7th, 1826), he observes, "I cannot think of death as more than the going out of one room into another." In one of his writings he says: "The world of imagination is the world of eternity. It is the divine bosom into which we shall all go after the death of the vegetated body" [139:79].

His attitude toward death is that of all the illuminati. He does not believe in "another life." He does not think he will be immortal. He *has* eternal life.

Blake had in all probability read in his youth some of the mystical or cabalistic writers—Paracelsus, Jacob Böhme, Cornelius Agrippa; and there is a good deal in his speculations, in substance and tone, and sometimes in detail, which can be traced back to authors of this class [139:80].

So writes George Frederic Parsons about Balzac [6:11]. Thoreau makes a similar suggestion as to Whitman [38:143], and generally it is constantly being hinted or intimated that some of these men have been reading others of them. This may of course sometimes happen, but, speaking generally, it does not, for many of them are quite illiterate, and the studies of others, as, for instance, Bacon, do not lie in that direction. Blake, Balzac, Yepes, Behmen, Whitman, Carpenter and the rest has each seen for himself that other world of which he tells us. No one *can* tell of it at second hand, for no one who has not seen something of it can conceive it.

Blake's death was as noble and characteristic as his life. Gilchrist [94:360-1] gives us the following simple and touching account of it:

"His illness was not violent, but a gradual and gentle failure of physical powers which nowise affected the mind. The speedy end was not foreseen by his friends. It came on a Sunday, August 12, 1827, nearly three months before completion of his seventieth year. 'On the day of his death,' writes Smith, who had his account from the widow, 'he composed and uttered songs to his

Maker so sweetly to the ear of his Catharine that when she stood to hear him he, looking upon her most affectionately, said: "My beloved, they are not mine—*no, they are not* mine!" He told her they would not be parted; he should always be about her to take care of her. To the pious songs followed, about six in the summer evening, a calm and painless withdrawal of breath; the exact moment almost unperceived by his wife, who sat by his side. A humble female neighbor, her only other companion, said afterwards: "I have been at the death, not of a man, but of a blessed angel." ' "

II.

It remains to quote certain declarations emanating from Blake and which seem to bear upon the point under consideration —viz., upon the question, Was Blake a case of Cosmic Consciousness?

The world of imagination is the world of eternity. It is the divine bosom into which we shall all go after the death of the vegetated body. This world of imagination is infinite and eternal, whereas the world of generation, of vegetation, is finite and temporal.

Blake's name for Cosmic Consciousness. With this paragraph compare Whitman's "I swear I think now that everything without exception has an eternal soul! The trees have rooted in the ground! The weeds of the sea have! The animals" [193 : 337].

There exist in that eternal world the permanent realities of everything which we see reflected in this vegetable glass of nature [95 : 163].

We are in a world of generation and death, and this world we must cast off if we would be artists such as Raphael, Michael Angelo and the ancient sculptors. If we do not cast off this world we shall be only Venetian painters, who will be cast off and lost from art [95 : 172].

The world of self consciousness. Balzac says: (Self conscious) "man judges all things by his abstractions—good, evil, virtue, crime. His formulas of right are his scales, and his justice is blind; the justice of God [i.e., of the Cosmic Sense] sees—in that is everything" [5 : 142].

The player is a liar when he says: Angels are happier than men because they are better! Angels are happier than men and devils because they are not always prying after good and evil in one another and eating the tree of knowledge for Satan's gratification [95 : 176].

"Showing the best and dividing it from the worst *age vexes age. Knowing the perfect fitness and equanimity of things,* while they discuss I am silent" [193 : 31].

The last judgment is an overwhelming of bad art and science [95 : 176].

true career; the infinite dawns upon him" delayed, must be answered, and her quietus [176 : 126].

Some people flatter themselves that there will be no last judgment. . . . I will not flatter them. Error is created; truth is eternal. Error or creation will be burned up, and then, and not till then, truth or eternity will appear. It [error] is burned up the moment men cease to behold it. I assert for myself that I do not behold outward creation, and that to me it is hindrance and not action. "What!" it will be questioned, "when the sun rises do you not see a round disc of fire somewhat like a guinea?" "Oh, no, no! I see an innumerable company of the heavenly host crying: 'Holy, holy, holy is the Lord God Almighty!'" I question not my corporeal eye any more than I would question a window concerning a sight. I look through it and not with it [95 : 176].

Beneath the figures of Adam and Eve (descending the generative stream from there) is the seat of the harlot, named mystery [self conscious life], in the Revelations. She (*mystery*) is seized by two beings (life and death), each with three heads; they represent vegetative existence. As it is written in Revelations, they strip her naked and burn her with fire [i.e., death strips her naked, and the passions of the self conscious life burn it as with fire]. It represents the eternal consumption of vegetable life and death [the life and death of the merely self conscious] with its lusts. The wreathed torches in their hands [in the hands of life and death] represent eternal fire, which is the fire of generation or vegetation; it is an eternal consumption. Those who are blessed with imaginative vision [Cosmic Consciousness] see this eternal female [mystery—the self conscious life] and tremble at what others fear not; while they despise and laugh at what others fear [95 : 166].

I am not ashamed, afraid or averse to tell you what ought to be told—that I am under the direction of messengers from heaven, daily and nightly. But

I.e., it is the advent of universal Cosmic Consciousness. "Specialism [the Cosmic Sense] opens to man," says Balzac, "his true career; the infinite dawns upon him" [5 : 144]. "The audit of nature, though delayed, must be answered, and her quietus is to render thee" [Cosmic Consciousness] [176 : 126].

Blake says his self conscious faculties are a hindrance to him, not a help. So Balzac: "Baneful, it [self consciousness] exempts man from entering the path of specialism [Cosmic Consciousness], which leads to the infinite" [5 : 142]. So the Hindoo experts teach and have always taught, that suppression and effacement of many of the self conscious faculties are necessary conditions to illumination [56 : 166 et seq.].

So Carpenter asks (knowing well the answer): "Does there not exist in truth . . . an inner illumination . . . by which we can ultimately see things *as they are*, beholding all creation . . . in its true being and order [57 : 98].

"Their worm dieth not and the fire is not quenched" [12 : 9 : 48], said by Jesus of the self conscious life, which (also) is the hell of Dante.

So Whitman: "I laugh at what you call dissolution."

"He [my other self], nor that affable, familiar ghost [the Cosmic Sense] which nightly gulls him with intelligence" [176 : 86].

the nature of such things is not, as   "A message from the heavens whispering
some suppose, without trouble or care   to me even in sleep" [193 : 324].
[95 : 185].

III.

SUMMARY.

a. Blake seems to have entered into Cosmic Consciousness
when a little more than thirty years of age.

b. The present editor does not know anything of the occurrence of subjective light in his case.

c. The fact of great intellectual illumination seems clear.

d. His moral elevation was very marked.

e. He seems to have had the sense of immortality that belongs
to Cosmic Consciousness.

f. Specific details of proof are in this case, as they must inevitably often be, largely wanting, but a study of Blake's life,
writings (he is not in a position nor is he competent to judge
Blake from his drawings) and death convinces the writer that he
was a genuine and even probably a great case.

CHAPTER 12.

Honoré de Balzac.

I.

BORN 1799; died 1850.

"Perhaps the greatest name in the post-Revolutionary literature of France" [78 : 304].

And well summed up by a still more recent writer, W. P. Trent
[3 : 566]:

"The unexpected," he tells us, "sometimes happens, as I discovered recently when I finished the fiftieth volume of M. Calmann Levy's popular edition of the works of Balzac. I had
thought that the completion of Horace's odes and Shakespeare's

plays, and of the 'Odyssey,' marked the three chief epochs in my own intellectual life, and that I might not likely be so stirred, so swept away again, by any book or by any author. But I had erred. Balzac, whose novels taken singly had moved me powerfully, but had not often swept me away, whom I had made a companion of for years without fully comprehending—this Balzac, when viewed in the light of his total and stupendous achievements, suddenly stood out before me in his full stature and might, as one of the few genuine world geniuses that our race can point to with legitimate and unshakable pride. I had emerged from the 'Comédie Humaine' just as I had emerged from the Homeric poems and from the plays of Shakespeare, feeling that I had traversed a world and been in the presence of a veritable creator."

Still another and even more recent writer may be quoted to the same effect. H. T. Peck [128a: 245] sums up the result of his studies as follows: "The place which this great genius must ultimately hold in literary history has not yet been definitely settled. French critics link his name with that of Shakespeare, while English critics seem to think that a comparison like this is very daring. My own belief is that at the last his name will be placed higher still than Shakespeare's, at the very apex of a pyramid of literary fame."

"Search as one may, there is no complete life of Balzac. There are still unpublished letters and papers in the possession of the Vicomte de Spoelberch de Lovenjoul, a compatriot who thoroughly understood him; but adding these to all that has been written, it is still doubtful if the real man will be found behind them. Expansive at times, yet he withdrew from the knowledge of others. There are periods in his life when he disappears, lies concealed from sight, and each must interpret for himself the secret that made his power and insures his fame."

Balzac put the following words into the mouth of Dante, who he tells us was a "Specialist." Balzac was himself a "Specialist." The words will therefore apply as well to him as to Dante: "And so that poor lad thinks himself an angel exiled from heaven Who among us has the right to undeceive him? Is it I? I who

am so often lifted above this earth by magic power; I who belong
to God; I who am to myself a mystery?   Have I not seen the most
beautiful of all angels [the Cosmic Sense] living on this base
earth?   Is the lad either more or less beside himself than I am?
Has he taken a bolder step into faith?   He believes; his belief
will doubtless lead him into some luminous path like that in which
I walk" [9: 263].

That Balzac stood apart from and on a higher plane than ordinary men was divined during his life and has been perceived by
thousands since his death.   Taine, groping after an explanation
of the obvious fact, says: "His instrument was intuition, that
dangerous and superior faculty by which man imagines or discovers in an isolated fact all the possibilities of which it is capable; a kind of second sight proper to prophets and somnambules,
who sometimes find the true, who often find the false, and who
commonly attain only verisimilitude" [6: 12].

G. F. Parsons, in his introduction to "Louis Lambert," comes
nearer it when he asks: "Whether the condition [of chronic
ecstasy, in which the patient—i. e., Louis Lambert—really Balzac
himself—seems withdrawn] may not be the consequence of an
illumination so much higher than that vouchsafed mankind at
large as to transcend expression—to separate the recipient from
intellectual contact with his fellows by revealing to his inner sense
untranslatable things" [6: 11].

This last seems to be the simple truth, Balzac, very clearly,
having been a well marked case of Cosmic Consciousness.   The
evidence that he was so resides (1) in the fact of his life as observed by others, and (2) in his own revelations as to his inner
self.   The first series of facts may be gathered from his biography, compiled by K. P. Wormeley, largely from memoirs written by Balzac's sister Laure—Madame Surville; the second from
Balzac's own writings, and chiefly from "Louis Lambert" and
"Seraphita."   And first as to his outer life as revealing the inner:
Miss W. says: "A complete life of Balzac cannot be written at
the present time and possibly never can be.   Nearly the whole
of what he was to himself, what his own being was, what were the

influences that molded it, how that eye that saw the manifold lives
of others saw his own life, how that soul which crowned its earthly
work with a vision of the living word was nurtured—what that
soul was, in short, has been concealed from sight" [4:1]. "In
all estimates of Balzac's nature attention must be paid to the fact
that he was eminently sound and healthy in mind and body.
Though his spirit rose to regions that could be reached only by intuition, and ruminated over problems the study of which we associate with fragility of body and aloofness from things of life, he
was at the same time, and quite as thoroughly, a man with human
instincts, loving life and enjoying it. In this lies, no doubt, one
of the secrets of his power. It was a part of the many-sidedness
of his genius; it enabled him to actually live and have his being
in the men and women whom he evoked from the depths and
heights of human nature. His temperament was, above all
things, genial and his humor gay; no pressure of worldly anxiety
and debt, no crushing toil, no hidden grief, with which the man,
like the child in his cell, was acquainted, could destroy that healthy
cheerfulness or prevent the rebound into hearty or even jovial
gaiety. 'Robust' is the word that seems to suit him on the material side of his nature, applying even to his mental processes. He
was gifted with a strong common sense, which guided his judgment on men and circumstances" [4:58-9].

While still very young Balzac decided to be a writer. It
seems that he felt, even as a boy, that he was destined to do something great in that line, and he composed at school, among other
things, a treatise on the will and an epic poem. Later he wrote
at Paris, in the course of ten years, mostly over the pseudonym
of "Horace de Saint Aubin," some forty volumes, said to be almost entirely valueless. A good authority [106:87] sums up this
episode in Balzac's history as follows: "Before he was thirty
years old he had published, under a variety of pseudonyms, some
twenty long novels, veritable Grub Street productions, written in
sordid Paris attics, in poverty, in perfect obscurity. Several of
these "œuvres de jeunesse' have lately been republished, but the
best of them are unreadable. No writer ever served harder ap-

prenticeship to his art, or lingered more hopelessly at the base of the ladder of fame.''

Then, at the age of thirty, his genius began to dawn in ''Les Chouans'' and ''Physiologie du Marriage.'' He must have entered Cosmic Consciousness about the early part of 1831, when thirty-two years of age, since ''Louis Lambert'' (which was undoubtedly conceived immediately after illumination) was written in 1832. By 1833, when he was thirty-four years of age, he had entered into full possession of his true life, a presentiment of which had dominated him from early boyhood.

Madame Surville says: ''It was not until 1833, about the time of the publication of the ''Médecin de Campagne,'' that he first thought of collecting all his personages together and forming a complete society. The day when this idea burst upon his mind was a glorious day for him. He started from the Rue Cassini, where he had taken up his abode after leaving the Rue de Tournon, and rushed to the faubourg Poissonniere, where I was then living.

'' 'Make your bow to me,' he said to us, joyously; 'I am on the highroad to become a genius!'

''He then unfolded his plan, which frightened him a little, for no matter how vast his brain might be, it needed time to work out a scheme like that.

'' 'How glorious it will be if I succeed,' he said, walking up and down the room. He could not keep still; joy radiated from every feature. 'I'll willingly let them call me *a maker of tales,* all the while that I am cutting stones for my edifice. I gloat in advance over the astonishment of those nearsighted creatures as they see it rise' '' [4:83].

It seems likely, judging from Madame Surville's report, that Balzac was either in the state of Cosmic Consciousness during this visit to her, or had recently been so.

A writer already quoted [106:87] describes, no doubt correctly, in the following words, what Balzac's scheme now was, and it is worth noting that to all intents and purposes it was the same as that conceived and attempted (each for his own world) by Dante, "Shakespeare" and Whitman:

"Balzac proposed to himself to illustrate by a tale or a group of tales every phase of French life and manners during the first half of the nineteenth century. To be colossally and exhaustively complete—complete not only in the generals but in the particulars—to touch upon every salient point, to illuminate every typical feature, to reproduce every sentiment, every idea, every person, every place, every object, that has played a part, however minute, however obscure, in the life of the French people."

Here is a description of him in the early thirties by Lamartine:

Balzac was standing before the fireplace of that dear room where I have seen so many remarkable men and women come and go. He was not tall, though the light on his face and the mobility of his figure prevented me from noticing his stature. His body swayed with his thought; there seemed at times to be a space between him and the floor; occasionally he stooped as though to gather an idea at his feet, and then he rose on them to follow the flight of his thought above him. At the moment of my entrance he was carried away by the subject of a conversation then going on with Monsieur and Madame de Girardin, and only interrupted himself for a moment to give me a keen, rapid, gracious look of extreme kindness.

He was stout, solid, square at the base and across the shoulders. The neck, chest, body and thighs were powerful, with something of Mirabeau's amplitude, but without heaviness. His soul was apparent, and seemed to carry everything lightly, gaily, like a supple covering, not in the least like a burden. His size seemed to give him power, not to deprive him of it. His short arms gesticulated easily; he talked as an orator speaks. His voice resounded with the somewhat vehement energy of his lungs, but it had neither roughness nor sarcasm nor anger in it; his legs, on which he rather swayed himself, bore the torso easily; his hands, which were large and plump, expressed his thought as he waved them. Such was the outward man in that robust frame. But in presence of the face it was difficult to think of the structure. That speaking face, from which it was not easy to remove one's eye, charmed and fascinated you; his hair was worn in thick masses; his black eyes pierced you like darts dipped in kindliness; they entered confidingly into yours like friends. His cheeks were full and ruddy; the nose well modeled, though rather long; the lips finely outlined, but full and raised at the corners; the teeth irregular and notched. His head was apt to lean to one side, and then, when the talk excited him, it was lifted quickly with an heroic sort of pride.

But the dominant expression of his face, greater than even that of intellect, was the manifestation of goodness and kindheartedness. He won your mind when he spoke, but he won your heart when he was silent. No feeling of envy or hatred could have been expressed by that face; it was impossible that it should seem otherwise than kind. But the kindness was not that of indifference; it was loving kindness, conscious of its meaning and conscious of others; it inspired gratitude and frankness, and defied all those who knew him not to love him. A childlike merriment was in his aspect; here was a soul at play; he had dropped his pen to be happy among friends, and it was impossible not to be joyous where he was [4 : 123 : 5].

It has been said of Balzac: "He was an illumination thrown upon life."

He was an illustration of his own dictum: "All we are is in the soul" ("nous ne sommes que par l'ame"), and a question of his to a friend touches closely upon the thesis of this volume:

Are you certain [he said] that your soul has had its full development? Do you breathe in air through every pore of it? Do your eyes see all they can see [4 : 126].

This recalls Whitman's: "The eyesight has another eyesight, and the hearing another hearing, and the voice another voice" [193 : 342].

A glance at a few of his letters to an intimate friend at the period will throw light on our present inquiry:

"August, 1833. The 'Médecin de Campagne' will reach you next week. It has cost me ten times the work that 'Louis Lambert' did. There is not a sentence, not an idea, which has not been viewed and reviewed, read and reread, and corrected; the labor was frightful. I may now die in peace. I have done a great work for my country. To my mind it is better to have written this book than to have made laws and to have won battles. It is the gospel in action" [4 : 143].

"October, 1833. Do you know how the 'Médecin' has been received? By a torrent of insults. The three newspapers of my own party which have spoken of it have done so with the utmost contempt for the work and its author" [4 : 143].

"December, 1835. Never has the torrent which bears me onward been so rapid; no more terribly majestic work has ever compelled the human brain. I go to my toil as a gambler to cards. I sleep only five hours and work eighteen; I shall end by killing myself" [4 : 145].

Like all men of his class—i. e., like all men glorified by the divine spark which is the subject of this poor volume—Balzac was greatly loved by those who were brought in contact with him.

His servants loved him. Rose, the cook, a true cordon bleu (we called her La Grande Nanon), used to go into despair when her master, in his working months, neglected her dainty dishes. I have seen her come into his room on tiptoe, bringing a delicious consommé, and trembling with eagerness to see him drink it. Balzac would catch sight of her; perhaps the fumes of the soup would reach his olfactories; then he would toss back his mane of hair with an impatient jerk of his head, and exclaim in his roughest and most surly voice: "Rose, go away; I don't want anything; let me alone!" "But mossieu will ruin his health if he goes on in this way; mossieu will fall ill!" "No, no! Let me alone, I say!" in a thundering voice. "I don't want anything; you worry me; go away!" Then the good soul would turn to go slowly, very slowly, muttering: "To take such pains to please mossieu! and such a soup—how good it smells! Why should mossieu keep me in his service if he doesn't want what I do for him?" This was too much for Balzac. He called her back, drank the soup at a gulp and said in his kindest voice, as she went off radiant to her kitchen: "Now, Rose, don't let this happen again!" When his microscopic groom, a poor little orphan whom he called Gain de mil, died, Balzac took extreme care of him, and never failed to go and see him daily during his illness. Yes, God had given my great writer a heart of gold; and those who really knew him adored him. He possessed the art of making others love him to such a degree that in his presence they forgot any real or fancied complaint against him, and only remembered the affection they bore him [4: 162-3].

It has been said: "Few writers have been greater than Balzac in the exhibition of the moral qualities." But says Goethe: "Wenn ihr nicht füllt ihr Werdet's nicht erjagen." If a man is destitute of a given faculty it is useless for him to attempt to describe it.

How is it that, as Hugo says, "A genius is an accursed man?" That the men having the greatest qualities are precisely those men who are accredited with the absence of these? And, to come back to Balzac, why should it be doubted that this man—who gave *every* proof of moral greatness—was great by his moral as well as his intellectual qualities? Simply because it is easier to misunderstand than to understand men of his class, and because when we do not understand we incline to infer the worst rather than the best.

The *fact* is, as has been said: "Balzac is a moralist, the greatest moralist of the nineteenth century, one who does not preach but *shows* the truth" [4: 178].

So Bacon, although in his prose works he may be said to *preach,* yet these works were intended as merely introductory to others which were to *show* the truth.   In the "Plan" of his life work, the "Instauratio Magna," he divides this last into six parts: (I) The division of the sciences, represented by the "De Augmentis"; (II) "The New Organon"; (III) "The Phenomena of the Universe," represented by his natural history books; (IV) "The Ladder of the Intellect," represented by the "Comedies"; (V) "The Forerunners," represented by the "Histories," and (VI) "The New Philosophy," represented by the "Tragedies."

Speaking now [34: 51] of IV (the "Comedies"), and describing the aim of that part, he says that this does not consist of precepts and rules (for, he says, I have given plenty of these in the "Novum Organum"), but of actual "types and models" by which those things which are to be taught are "set as it were before the eyes."   Then of VI (the "Tragedies") he says that this part consists not in "mere felicity of speculation," but that it presents (as we know it does) "the real business and fortunes of the human race."   "For God forbid," he continues, "that we should give out a dream of our own imagination for a pattern of the world; rather may he graciously grant to us to write an apocalypse or true vision of the footsteps of the Creator imprinted on his creatures."   Neither did Jesus, nor Whitman, nor any of these men, preach, but they all showed the truth, each in his own way, in his life and in his spoken or written word.

Another trait that seems common to these men—absorption in their own time—has been noted of Balzac.   Theophile Gautier dwells at length on what he calls the absolute modernity of Balzac's genius.   "Balzac owes nothing," he says, "to antiquity. For him there are neither Greeks nor Romans, nor any trace in the composition of his talent of Homer, or Virgil, or Horace— no one was ever less classic" [4: 170].

"One might suppose that his feelings would have been hurt

when he found the way barred against his entrance to the Academy. But he behaved with dignity and withdrew his name when failure seemed probable. 'The matter does not stir my feelings very much,' he said; 'some persons think not at all, but they are mistaken. If I do get there, so much the better; if I do not, no matter' " [4:190].

George Sand bears witness of him as follows:

"He searched for treasures and found none but those he bore within him—his intellect, his spirit of observation, his marvellous capacity, his strength, his gaiety, his goodness of heart—in a word, his genius."

"Sober in all respects, his morals were pure; he dreaded excesses as the death of talent; he cherished women by his heart or his head, and his life from early youth was that of an anchorite" [4:201].

"He has seen all and said all, comprehended all and divined all—how, then, can he be immoral? . . .

"Balzac has been reproached for having no principles because he has, as I think, no positive convictions on questions of fact in religion, art, politics or even love" [4:203].

This is a highly significant statement. Every one of these people has been judged in the same way by contemporaries. Why? Because they *have* no opinions or principles in the sense in which their neighbors have them. The things that seem vital to those about them seem to them of no import. And the things that are of value to them are out of sight of the rest.

Here is Gautier's evidence as to the kind of man he was (it ought to be quoted in full, but that is impossible in this place):

When I saw Balzac for the first time he was about thirty-six, and his personality was one of those that are never forgotten. In his presence Shakespeare's words came to my memory—before him "nature might stand up and say to all the world: This was a man." He wore the monk's habit of white flannel or cashmere, in which, some time later, he made Louis Boulanger paint him. What fancy had led him to choose, in preference to all other costumes, this particular one, which he always wore, I do not know. Perhaps it symbolized to his eyes the cloistral life to which his work condemned him; and,

benedictine of romance, he wore the robe. However that may be, it became
him wonderfully.

He boasted, .showing me his spotless sleeves, that he never dropped the least
spot of ink upon it; "for," he added, "a true literary man ought to be clean at
his work."

Then, after describing other features, Gautier goes on:

As to his eyes, there were never any like them; they had a life, a light, an
inconceivable magnetism; the whites of the eyeballs was pure, limpid, with a
bluish tinge, like that of an infant or a virgin, enclosing two black diamonds,
dashed at moments with gold reflections—eyes to make an eagle drop his lids—
eyes to read through walls and into bosoms or to terrify a furious wild beast—
the eyes of a sovereign, a seer, a subjugator. The habitual expression of the
face was that of puissant hilarity, of Rabelaisian and monachal joy.

Strange as it may seem to say so in the nineteenth century, Balzac was a
seer. His power as an observer, his discernment as a physiologist, his genius
as a writer, do not sufficiently account for the infinite variety of the two or
three thousand types which play a rôle more or less important in his human
comedy. He did not copy them: he lived them ideally. He wore their clothes,
contracted their habits, moved in their surroundings, *was themselves*, during
the necessary time [4: 204-8].

As another man of the same class says of himself: "I am a
free companion." "My voice is the wife's voice." "I am the
hounded slave." "I am an old Artillerist." "I am the mashed
fireman." "It is I let out in the morning and barred at night."
"Not a youngster is taken for larceny but I go up, too, and am
tried and sentenced." "Not a cholera patient lies at the last gasp
but I also lie at the last gasp. My face is ash colored, my sinews
gnarl, away from me people retreat." "Askers embody themselves in me and I am embodied in them. I project my hat, sit
shamefaced and beg." Gautier goes on:

And yet Balzac, immense in brain, penetrating physiologist, profound observer, intuitive spirit, did not possess the literary gift. In him yawned an
abyss between thought and form [4: 209].

Here is a curious thing. How is it that these men who form
the mind of the race can seldom or never (at least according to
their contemporaries) write their own language decently? According to Renan (and he does not seem to be contradicted) Paul's

style was about as bad as possible ("sans charme; la forme, en est apre est presvue toujour dénuée de grace") [143: 568].

Mohammed can hardly be said to have written, and in his day and country there was no recognized standard with which to compare his language. The author of the "Shakespeare" drama was for long ranked as a writer below the meanest pamphleteer. And down to the present moment scarcely a man has defended Walt Whitman from the purely literary point of view, while thousands have utterly condemned him.

But the writings of Paul dominate whole continents. Mohammed's utterances hold in spiritual subjection two hundred millions of people. The author of "Hamlet" has been called, and rightly called, "The Lord of Civilization." And Walt Whitman's will probably eventually be seen to be the strongest voice of the nineteenth century.

The seeming anomaly is perhaps easily explained. In each generation there are certain men, who are never large in number, who possess the literary instinct, and there are also certain men who are endowed with Cosmic Consciousness, but there is no reason whatever why the two endowments should unite. If they do so it is a mere accident. The man with the literary instinct writes for the sake of writing. He feels that he has the faculty, and, looking about for a subject, or for one subject after another, he writes upon it or them. The man endowed with Cosmic Consciousness has almost certainly no literary instinct (the chance is millions to one against it), but he sees certain things which he feels he must tell. He simply, with might and main, does the best he can. The importance of his message causes him to be read. His personality, as it becomes recognized, causes everything in immediate connection with him to be admired, and in the end he is perhaps held up as a model of style.

Madame Surville continuing, says: "The attacks against my brother increased rather than lessened; the critics, unable to repeat the same things forever, changed their batteries and accused him of immorality. These accusations were very injurious to my brother; they grieved him deeply, and sometimes they disheart-

ened him" [4:242].   The old, old story, but never worn out, never
threadbare, always as ready for service, as fresh and, alas! as
fatal as ever.

The foregoing few brief extracts suggest the kind of man Balzac was as seen from the outside.   It is clear from them, to any
one in a position to judge, that he was such a person as might very
probably be so endowed, and it only remains to show from his own
words—words that could not otherwise have been written—that
he was really one of the illuminati—a man possessing the rare
and splendid faculty called Cosmic Consciousness.

And first a few short extracts, written by Balzac of himself,
and which give us glimpses of the inner man before the oncoming
of the Cosmic Sense.

It will be noticed that he, like all men of the class to which he
belongs, was religious, though not quite in the orthodox way;
these men seldom adhere to a church.   A "specialist" may *found*
a religion; he seldom belongs to one.   "Specialists" are for *religion,* not for *a religion.*   So Balzac tells us of himself, under the
name of "Louis Lambert:"

Though naturally religious, he did not share in the minute observances of
the Roman Church; his ideas were more particularly in sympathy with those
of St. Theresa, Fénelon, several of the fathers and a few saints, who would be
treated in our day as heretics or atheists.   He was unmoved during the church
services.   Prayer, with him, proceeded from an impulse, a movement, an elevation of the spirit, which followed no regular course; in all things he gave himself up to nature, and would neither pray nor think at settled periods [5:73].
The limit which most brains attain was the point of departure from which
his was one day to start in search of new regions of intelligence [5:79].

Later he makes this remark about himself:

The seed has swelled and germinated.   Philosophers may regret the foliage,
struck with frost ere it burgeoned, but they shall one day see the perfect
flower blooming in regions higher far than the highest places of the earth [5:84].

In his further fragmentary, veiled and mystic narration of the
actual oncoming of the Cosmic Sense, it is important, for the present argument, to notice that: (*a*) He had no idea what had happened to him.   (*b*) He was seized with terror [5:129].   (*c*) He

debated seriously with himself whether he was not insane. (*d*) He considers (or reconsiders) the question of marriage—doubts that it will be "an obstacle to the perfectability of his interior senses and to his flight through the spiritual worlds" [5: 131] and seems to decide against it. And, in fact, when we consider the antagonistic attitude of so many of the great cases toward this relation (Gautama, Jesus, Paul, Whitman, etc.), there seems little doubt that anything like a general possession of Cosmic Consciousness must abolish marriage as we know it to-day.

II.

Balzac must have attained to Cosmic Consciousness about 1831 or 1832, at the age of thirty-two or thirty-three. It was at this time he began writing his great books. But it is especially important at present to note that in 1832 he wrote "Louis Lambert" and in 1833 "Seraphita."

In these two books he describes the new sense more fully than it had ever been described elsewhere. In "Louis Lambert" he gives a bold, plain common sense description of it which is especially valuable for our present purpose. Then the next year, after writing that work, he composed "Seraphita," the object of which was to delineate a person who was possessed of the great faculty. The two taken together prove the possession of the faculty by their author. "Seraphita" must be read entire to be understood and appreciated, and so, of course, ought "Louis Lambert"; but the evidence now needed may be obtained from the latter within the compass of a few pages. The extracts are from K. P. Wormley's translation, which has been compared with the original and found faithful.

The world of ideas divides itself into three spheres—that of instinct; that of abstraction; that of specialism [5: 141].

The greater part of visible humanity—that is, the weaker part—inhabits the sphere of instinctivity. The in-

There are in the intellect three stages—simple consciousness, self consciousness and Cosmic Consciousness.

It is, of course, not true that the bulk of the race has simple and *not* self consciousness. It is in fact the latter that constitutes a given creature a man. But it is true

stinctives are born, work and die without rising to the second degree of human intelligence—namely, abstraction
[5:142].

At abstraction society begins.
Though abstraction as compared with
instinct is an almost divine power, it
is infinitely feeble compared with the
endowment of specialism, which alone
can explain God. Abstraction com-
prises within it a whole nature in germ,
as potentially as the seed contains the
system of a plant and all its products.
From abstraction are derived laws, arts,
interests, social ideas. It is the glory
and scourge of the world. Glorious, it
creates societies; baneful, it exempts
man from entering the path of specialism which leads to the infinite.
Man judges all things by his abstrac-

(what Balzac means) that with the mass
simple consciousness plays a far greater part
than self consciousness. The "weaker part"
do live in simple far more than in self consciousness.

At abstraction—i.e., at self consciousness
—humanity, and therefore human society, begins. "Specialism alone can explain God."
Let it be noted in this connection that all
religion worthy of the name—Buddhism, Mohammedanism, Christianity and possibly
others—has sprung from specialism—i.e.,
Cosmic Consciousness. "I" [Christ, Cosmic Sense] "am the way, the truth and the
life, *no one comes to God but by me.*" It
is not so clear how self consciousness bars
the way to Cosmic Consciousness. It *seems*,
on the contrary, the necessary and only road
which could lead there. Many of the illuminated, however, take the same view as
Balzac, and they ought to be the best judges.

tions—good, evil, virtue, crime. His formulas of right are his scales, and his
justice is blind; the justice of God sees—in that is everything. There are,
necessarily, intermediate beings who separate the kingdom of instinctives from
the kingdom of the abstractives, in whom instinctivity mixes with abstractivity
in endless variety of proportion. Some have more of the former than of the
latter, and vice versa. Also there are beings in whom the action of each is
neutralized, because both are moved by an equal force [5:142].

Specialism consists in seeing the
things of the material world as well as
those of the spiritual world in their
original and consequential ramifica-
tions. The highest human genius is
that which starts from the shadows of
abstraction to advance into the light of

Note that Balzac is only speaking of Cosmic Consciousness from the point of view of
"ideas." He therefore does not tell us here
of the moral exaltation which is an essential part of it. He gives that aspect, however, very fully in "Seraphita."

specialism. (Specialism, *species*, sight, speculation, seeing all, and that at one
glance; *speculum*, the mirror or means of estimating a thing by seeing it in its
entirety). Jesus was a specialist. He saw the deed in its roots and in its
products; in the past, which begot it; in the present, where it is manifested;
in the future, where it develops;* his sight penetrated the understanding of
others. The perfection of the inward
sight gives birth to the gift of specialism. Specialism carries with it intuition. Intuition is a faculty of the
inner man, of whom specialism is an
attribute.

* As says Dante: "Even as earthly minds
see that two obtuse angles are not contained
in a triangle, so thou [the Cosmic Sense],
gazing upon the point to which *all times are
present*, seest contingent things ere in themselves they are" [72:111].

Between the sphere of specialism and the sphere of abstraction, and likewise between those spheres and that of instinctivity, we find beings in whom the diverse attributes of the two kingdoms are mingled, producing a mixed nature—the man of genius [5:143].

The specialist is necessarily the loftiest expression of *man*—the link which connects the visible to the superior worlds. He acts, he sees, he feels through his *inner being*. The abstractive thinks. The instinctive simply acts [5:144].

Hence three degrees for man. As an instinctive he is below the level; as an abstractive he attains to it; as a specialist he rises above it. Specialism opens to man his true career: the Infinite dawns upon him—he catches a glimpse of his destiny [5:144].

"Natura non facit saltum:" There must be a gradual passage from simple to self and from self to Cosmic Consciousness—i.e., there must be *a way* of passing gradually. Nevertheless nothing is more sure than that the passage from simple to self and from self to Cosmic Consciousness is commonly made with a sudden and often terribly startling jump. But that the conditions may not blend and overlap one another, as Balzac says, it would be well not to be too positive.

The state of Cosmic Consciousness is undoubtedly the highest that we can at present conceive, but it does not follow that there are not higher nor that we may not eventually attain to higher.

With simple consciousness only man is not yet man—he is the alalus homo. With self consciousness he is what we know him. With Cosmic Consciousness he is as we see him (or rather do *not* see him; for who of us really sees these men?) in Jesus, Mohammed, Balzac, Whitman. When the race shall have attained to Cosmic Consciousness, as in the far past it attained to self consciousness, another start will be made on another level. Man will enter into his heritage and into his true work.

Balzac proceeds as follows:

There exists three worlds—the *natural world*, the *spiritual world*, the *divine world*. Humanity moves hither and thither in the *natural world*, which is fixed neither in its essence nor in its properties. The *spiritual world* is fixed in its essence and variable in its properties. The *divine world* is fixed in its properties and its essence. Consequently there is a material worship, a spiritual worship, a divine worship; which three are manifested by *action, word* and *prayer*, or (to express it otherwise) *deed, understanding, love*. The *instinctive* desires deeds; the abstractive turns to ideas; the *specialist* sees the end, he aspires to God, whom

In other words: The men who live entirely or almost entirely in simple consciousness float on the stream of time as do the animals—drift with the seasons, the food supply, etc., etc., as a leaf drifts on a current, not self-moved or self-balanced, but moved by outer influences and balanced by the natural forces as are the animals and the trees. The fully self-conscious man takes stock of himself and is, so to say, self-centered. He feels that he is a fixed point. He judges all things with reference to that point. But outside of himself (we know) there is nothing fixed. He trusts in what he calls God and he does not trust in him—he is a deist, an atheist, a Christian, a Buddhist. He believes in science, but science is constantly changing and will rarely tell him, in any case, anything worth knowing. He is fixed, then, at one point and moves freely on that. The man with Cosmic Conscious-

he inwardly perceives or contemplates [5:144].

ness being conscious of himself and conscious of the Cosmos, its meaning and drift, is fixed both without and within, "in his essence and in his properties." The creature with simple consciousness only is a straw floating on a tide, it moves freely with every influence. The self-conscious man is a needle pivoted by its centre—fixed in one point but revolving freely on that. The man with Cosmic Consciousness is the same needle magnetized. It is still fixed by its centre, but besides that it points steadily to the north—it has found something real and permanent outside of itself toward which it cannot but steadily look.

Therefore perhaps one day the inverse sense of *et verbo caro factum* will be the epitome of a new gospel which will read: *and the flesh shall be made the word;* it shall become the utterance of God [5:145].

When the whole race shall have attained to Cosmic Consciousness our idea of God shall be realized in man.

The resurrection is brought about by the winds of heaven which sweep the worlds. The angel born upon the blast saith not: "Ye Dead, arise;" he saith, "Arise, ye living" [5:145].

The "resurrection" is not of the so-called dead, but of the living who are "dead" in the sense of never having entered upon true life.

III.

SUMMARY OF THE CASE OF BALZAC.

a. We do not know of any day and hour when the Cosmic Sense declared itself.

b. We know nothing about a subjective light.

c. We know that Balzac had the intensely earnest nature and the spiritual aspiration which seems necessarily to precede, though it often exists without leading up to, illumination.

d. We know that Balzac, after a certain age, had the almost preternatural intellectual and moral qualities which are characteristic of the Cosmic Sense.

e. But the proof that Balzac was a case of Cosmic Consciousness rests upon the fact that he has accurately defined and described the mental status so named, and he could not have described the condition if he had not experienced it.

f. He not only describes it in great detail, as in "Louis Lambert," and ascribes it there to himself—for that book is openly autobiographic; but still more, in "Seraphita" he creates a personality in which the Cosmic Sense is the chief element and in the course of the narrative brings in every characteristic feature of the same, and to do this the possession of the Cosmic Sense was an absolute prerequisite.

g. To any one who realizes what the Cosmic Sense is it is as certain that Balzac possessed it as that he possessed eyesight.

CHAPTER 13.

Walt Whitman.

I.

BORN 1819; died 1892.

In each of these instances of so-called Cosmic Consciousness it would be proper to give a fairly exhaustive account of the external life of the man as well as of his teaching, since the one does, and ought to be shown to, corroborate the other. It would not, however, be possible to do this and still keep the argument within reasonable limits. Fortunately, too, it is not absolutely necessary; most of the men in question being so well known. Also it may be said that the present volume is intended not so much to teach anything as to show that there exists a certain lesson to be learned and to indicate where it may be studied. This volume is not so much a road as a finger post on a road. Its greatest value (if it have any) will be to lead to the serious study of certain men of an exceptional type; not one or the other of them, but as a group and from a particular standpoint. While it is necessary, then, to say a few words about Walt Whitman here, it will be well for the reader to be far from satisfied with these but to seek elsewhere a much more complete statement of the life and thought of this remarkable man. The following brief description is taken from the writer's "Life of Whitman" [38], written in the summer of 1880, while he was visiting the author. Walt Whitman was then sixty-one years of age:

At first sight he looks much older, so that he is often supposed to be seventy or even eighty. He is six feet in height, and quite straight. He weighs nearly two hundred pounds. His body and limbs are full-sized and well proportioned. His head is large and rounded in every direction, the top a little higher than a semicircle from the front to the back would make it. Though his face and head give the appearance of being plentifully supplied with hair, the crown is moderately bald; on the side and back the hair is long, very fine, and nearly snow white. The eyebrows are highly arched, so that it is a long distance from the eye to the centre of the eyebrow (this is the facial feature that strikes one most at first sight). The eyes themselves are light blue, not large—indeed, in proportion to the head and face they seem rather small; they are dull and heavy, not expressive—what expression they have is kindness, composure, suavity. The eyelids are full, the upper commonly droops nearly half over the globe of the eye. The nose is broad, strong, and quite straight; it is full-sized, but not large in proportion to the rest of the face; it does not descend straight from the forehead, but dips down somewhat between the eyes with a long sweep. The mouth is full-sized, the lips full. The sides and lower part of the face are covered with a fine white beard, which is long enough to come down a little on the breast. The upper lip bears a heavy moustache. The ear is very large, especially long from above downwards, heavy and remarkably handsome. I believe all the poet's senses are exceptionally acute, his hearing especially so; no sound or modulation of sound perceptible to others escapes him, and he seems to hear many things that to ordinary folk are inaudible. I have heard him speak of hearing the grass grow and the trees coming out in leaf. His cheeks are round and smooth. His face has no lines expressive of care, or weariness, or age—it is the white hair and beard, and his feebleness in walking (due to paralysis) that make him appear old. The habitual expression of his face is repose, but there is a well-marked firmness and decision. I have never seen his look, even momentarily, express contempt, or any vicious feeling. I have never known him to sneer at any person or thing, or to manifest in any way or degree either alarm or apprehension, though he has in my presence been placed in circumstances that would have caused both in most men. His complexion is peculiar—a bright maroon tint, which, contrasting with his white hair and beard, makes an impression very striking. His body is not white like that of all others whom I have seen of the English or Teutonic stock—it has a delicate but well-marked rose color. All his features are large and massive, but so proportioned as not to look heavy. His face is the noblest I have ever seen.

No description can give any idea of the extraordinary physical attractiveness of the man. I do not speak now of the affection of friends and of those who are much with him, but of the magnetism exercised by him upon people who merely see him for a few minutes or pass him on the street. An intimate friend of the author's, after knowing Walt Whitman a few days, said in a letter: "As for myself, it seems to me now that I have always known him and loved him."

And in another letter, written from a town where the poet had been staying for a few days, the same person says: "Do you know every one who met him here seems to love him?"

The following is the experience of a person well known to the present writer: He called on Walt Whitman and spent an hour at his home in Camden, in the autumn of 1877. He had never seen the poet before, but he had been profoundly reading his works for some years. He said that Walt Whitman only spoke to him about a hundred words altogether, and these quite ordinary and commonplace; that he did not realize anything peculiar while with him, but shortly after leaving a state of mental exaltation set in, which he could only describe by comparing to slight intoxication by champagne, or to falling in love, and this exaltation, he said, lasted at least six weeks in a clearly marked degree, so that, for at least that length of time, he was plainly different from his ordinary self. Neither, he said, did it then or since pass away, though it ceased to be felt as something new and strange, but became a permanent element in his life, a strong and living force (as he described it), making for purity and happiness. I may add that this person's whole life has been changed by that contact—his temper, character, entire spiritual being, outer life, conversation, etc., elevated and purified in an extraordinary degree. He tells me that at first he used often to speak to friends and acquaintances of his feeling for Walt Whitman and the "Leaves," but after a time he found that he could not make himself understood, and that some even thought his mental balance impaired. He gradually learned to keep silence upon the subject, but the feeling did not abate, nor its influence upon his life grow less.

Walt Whitman's dress was always extremely plain. He usually wore in pleasant weather a light gray suit of good woolen cloth. The only thing peculiar about his dress was that he had no necktie at any time, and always wore shirts with very large turndown collars, the button at the neck some five or six inches lower than usual, so that the throat and upper part of the breast were exposed. In all other respects he dressed in a substantial, neat, plain, common way. Everything he wore and everything about him was always scrupulously clean. His clothes might (and often did) show signs of wear, or they might be torn or have holes worn in them, but they never looked soiled. Indeed, an exquisite aroma of cleanliness has always been one of the special features of the man; it has always belonged to his clothes, his breath, his whole body, his eating and drinking, his conversation, and no one could know him for an hour without seeing that it penetrated his mind and life, and was in fact the expression of a purity which was physical as much as moral and moral as much as physical.

Walt Whitman, in my talks with him at that time, always disclaimed any lofty intention in himself or his poems. If you accepted his explanations they were simple and commonplace. But when you came to think about these explanations, and to enter into the spirit of them, you found that the simple and commonplace with him included the ideal and the spiritual. So it may be said that neither he nor his writings are growths of the ideal from the real, but are the actual real lifted up into the ideal. With Walt Whitman his body, his outward life, his inward spiritual existence and his poetry were all one; in every respect each tallied the other, and any one of them could always be inferred from any other. He said to me one day (I forget now in what connection): "I have imagined a life which should be that of the average man in average circumstances, and still grand, heroic." There is no doubt that such an ideal had been constantly before his mind, and that all he did, said, wrote, thought and felt, had been and were, from moment to moment, molded upon it. His manner was curiously calm and self-contained. He seldom became excited in conversation, or at all events seldom showed excitement; he rarely raised his voice or used any gestures. I never knew him to be in a bad temper. He seemed always pleased with those about him. He did not generally wait for a formal introduction; upon meeting any person for the first time he very likely stepped forward, held out his hand (either left or right, whichever happened to be disengaged), and the person and he were acquainted at once. People could not tell why they liked him. They said there was something attractive about him; that he had a great deal of personal magnetism, or made some other vague explanation that meant nothing. One very clever musical person, who spent a couple of days in my house while Walt Whitman was there, said to me on going away: "I know what it is; it is his wonderful voice that makes it so pleasant to be with him." I said: "Yes, perhaps it is; but where did his voice get that charm?"

Though he would sometimes not touch a book for a week, he generally spent a part (though not a large part) of each day in reading. Perhaps he would read on an average a couple of hours a day. He seldom read any book deliberately through, and there was no more (apparent) system about his reading than in anything else that he did; that is to say, there was no system about it at all. If he sat in the library an hour, he would have half a dozen to a dozen volumes about him, on the table, on chairs and on the floor. He seemed to read a few pages here and a few pages there, and pass from place to place, from volume to volume, doubtless pursuing some clue or thread of his own. Sometimes (though very seldom) he would get sufficiently interested in a volume to read it all. I think he read almost. if not quite the whole, of Renouf's "Egypt," and Bruschbey's "Egypt," but these cases were exceptional. In his way of reading he dipped into histories, essays, metaphysical, religious and scientific treatises, novels and poetry—though I think he read less poetry than anything else. He read no language but English, yet I believe he knew a great deal more French, German and Spanish than he would own to. But if you took his own word for it, he knew very little of any subject.

His favorite occupation seemed to be strolling or sauntering about outdoors by himself, looking at the grass, the trees, the flowers, the vistas of light, the varying aspects of the sky, and listening to the birds, the crickets, the tree-frogs, the wind in the trees, and all the hundreds of natural sounds. It was evident that these things gave him a feeling of pleasure far beyond what they give to ordinary people. Until I knew the man it had not occurred to me that anyone could derive so much absolute happiness and ample fulfilment from these things as he evidently did. He himself never spoke of all this pleasure. I dare say he hardly thought of it, but anyone who watched him could see plainly that in his case it was real and deep.

He had a way of singing, generally in an undertone, wherever he was or whatever he was doing, when alone. You would hear him the first thing in the morning while he was taking his bath and dressing (he would then perhaps sing out in full, ballads or martial songs), and a large part of the time that he sauntered outdoors during the day he sang, usually tunes without words, or a formless recitative. Sometimes he would recite poetry, generally, I think, from Shakespeare or Homer, once in a while from Bryant or others. He spent very little time in writing. It is probable that he never did give much time to that occupation. He wrote few private letters. While he was with us he would write a letter to a Canadian paper, about his travels, his condition, and his latest doings and thoughts, and get fifty or a hundred copies and send them to his friends and relations, especially the girls and young folks, and make that do for correspondence. Almost all his writing was done with a pencil in a sort of loose book that he carried in his breast pocket. The book consisted of a few sheets of good white paper, folded and fastened with a pin or two. He said he had tried all sorts of note-books and he liked that kind best. The literary work that he did was done at all sorts of times, and generally on his knee, impromptu, and often outdoors. Even in a room with the usual conveniences for writing he did not use a table; he put a book on his knee, or held it in his left hand, laid his paper upon it and wrote so. His handwriting was clear and plain, every letter being perfectly formed.

He was very fond of flowers, either wild or cultivated; would often gather and arrange an immense bouquet of them for the dinner-table, for the room where he sat, or for his bed-room; wore a bud or just-started rose, or perhaps a geranium, pinned to the lapel of his coat, a great part of the time; did not seem to have much preference for one kind over any other; liked all sorts. I think he admired lilacs and sunflowers just as much as roses. Perhaps, indeed, no man who ever lived liked so many things and disliked so few as Walt Whitman. All natural objects seemed to have a charm for him; all sights and sounds, outdoors and indoors, seemed to please him. He appeared to like (and I believe he did like) all the men, women and children he saw (though I never knew him to say that he liked anyone), but each who knew him felt that he liked him or her, and that he liked others also. He was in this and in everything entirely natural and unconventional. When he did express a preference for any person (which was very seldom) he would indicate it in some indirect way; for instance, I have known him to say: "Goodbye, my love," to a young married lady he had only seen a few times.

He was especially fond of children, and all children liked and trusted him at once. Often the little ones, if tired out and fretful, the moment he took them up and caressed them, would cease crying, and perhaps go to sleep in his arms. One day several ladies, the poet and myself, attended a picnic given to hundreds of poor children in London. I lost sight of my friend for perhaps an hour, and when I found him again he was sitting in a quiet nook by the river side, with a rosy-faced child of four or five years old, tired out and sound asleep in his lap.

For young and old his touch had a charm that cannot be described, and if it could the description would not be believed except by those who knew him either personally or through "Leaves of Grass." This charm (physiological more than psychological), if understood would explain the whole mystery of the man, and how he produced such effects not only upon the well, but among the sick and wounded.

It is certain, also, perhaps contrary to what I have given, that there is another phase, and a very real one, to the basis of his character. An elderly gentleman I talked with (he is a portrait painter and a distant relative of the poet), who was much with him, particularly through the years of his middle age and later (1845 to 1870), tells me that Walt Whitman, in the elements of his character, had deepest sternness and hauteur, not easily aroused, but coming forth at times, and then well understood by those who knew him best as something not to be trifled with. The gentleman alluded to (he is a reader and thorough accepter of "Leaves of Grass") agrees with me in my delineation of his benevolence, evenness and tolerant optimism, yet insists that at the inner framework of the poet there has always been, as he expresses it, "a combination of hot blood and fighting qualities." He says my outline applies more especially to his later years; that Walt Whitman has gradually brought to the front the attributes I dwell upon, and given them control. His theory is, in almost his own words, that there are two natures in Walt Whitman. The one is of immense suavity, self-control, a mysticism like the occasional fits of Socrates, and a pervading Christ-like benevolence, tenderness and sympathy (the sentiment of the intaglio frontispiece portrait, which I showed him, and he said he had seen exactly that look "in the old man," and more than once during 1863-'64, though he never observed it before or since). But these qualities, though he has enthroned them and for many years governed his life by them, are duplicated by far sterner ones. No doubt he has mastered the latter, but he has them. How could Walt Whitman (said my interlocutor) have taken the attitude toward evil, and things evil, which is behind every page of his utterance in "Leaves of Grass" from first to last—so different on that subject from every writer known, new or old—unless he enfolded all that evil within him.

Then there was another side to the picture—the indispensable exception that proved the rule. This man, the sight of whom excited such extraordinary affection, whose voice had for most of those who heard it such a wonderful charm, whose touch possessed a power which no words can express—in rare instances, this man, like the magnet, repelled as well as attracted. As there were those who instinctively loved him, so there were others, here and there, who instinctively disliked him. As his poetic utterances were so ridiculous to many, even his personal appearance, in not a few cases, aroused equally sarcastic remark. His large figure, his red face, his copious beard, his loose and free attire, his rolling and unusually ample shirt-collar, without necktie and always wide open at the throat, all met at times with jeers and explosive laughter.

He did not talk much. Sometimes, while remaining cheery and good-natured, he would speak very little all day. His conversation, when he did talk, was at all times easy and unconstrained. I never knew him to argue or dispute, and he never spoke about money. He always justified, sometimes playfully, sometimes quite seriously, those who spoke harshly of himself or his writings, and I often thought he even took pleasure in those sharp criticisms, slanders and the opposition of enemies. He said that his critics were quite right, that behind what his friends saw he was not at all what he seemed, and that, from the point of view of his foes, his book deserved all the hard things they could say of it—and that he himself undoubtedly deserved them and plenty more.

When I first knew Walt Whitman I used to think that he watched himself, and did not allow his tongue to give expression to feelings of fretfulness, antipathy, complaint and remonstrance.

It did not occur to me as possible that these mental states could be absent in him.   After long observation, however, and talking to others who had known him for many years, I satisfied myself that such absence or unconsciousness was entirely real.   His deep, clear and earnest voice made a good part, though not all, of the charm of the simplest things he said—a voice not characteristic of any special nationality or dialect.   If he said (as he sometimes would involuntarily on stepping to the door and looking out), "Oh, the beautiful sky!" or, "Oh, the beautiful grass!" the words produced the effect of sweet music.

He said, one day, while talking about some fine scenery and the desire to go and see it (and he himself was very fond of new scenery): "After all, the great lesson is that no special natural sights —not Alps, Niagara, Yosemite or anything else—is more grand or more beautiful than the ordinary sunrise and sunset, earth and sky, the common trees and grass."   Properly understood, I believe this suggests the central teaching of his writings and life— namely, that the commonplace is the grandest of all things; that the exceptional in any line is no finer, better or more beautiful than the usual, and that what is really wanting is not that we should possess something we have not at present, but that our eyes should be opened to see and our hearts to feel what we all have.

He never spoke deprecatingly of any nationality or class of men, or time in the world's history, or feudalism, or against any trades or occupations—not even against any animals, insects, plants or inanimate things, nor any of the laws of nature, or any of the results of those laws, such as illness, deformity or death. He never complained or grumbled either at the weather, pain, illness or at anything else.   He never in conversation, in any company, or under any circumstances, used language that could be thought indelicate (of course he has used language in his poems which has been thought indelicate, but none that is so).   In fact, I have never known of his uttering a word or a sentiment which might not be published without any prejudice to his fame.   He never swore; he could not very well, since as far as I know he never spoke in anger, and apparently never was angry.   He never exhibited fear, and I do not believe he ever felt it. His conversation, mainly toned low, was always agreeable and usually instructive. He never made compliments, very seldom apologized, used the common forms of civility, such as "if you please" and "thank you," quite sparingly, usually made a smile or a nod answer for them. He was, in my experience of him, not given to speculating on abstract questions (though I have heard others say that there were no subjects in which he so much delighted). He never gossiped. He seldom talked about private people, even to say something good of them, except to answer a question or remark, and then he always gave what he said a turn favorable to the person spoken of.

His conversation, speaking generally, was of current affairs, work of the day, political and historical news, European as well as American, a little of books, much of the aspects of nature—as scenery, the stars, birds, flowers and trees. He read the newspapers regularly, liked good descriptions and reminiscences. He did not, on the whole, talk much anyhow. His manner was invariably calm and simple, belonged to itself alone, and could not be fully described or conveyed.

II.

Walt Whitman is the best, most perfect, example the world has so far had of the Cosmic Sense, first because he is the man in whom the new faculty has been, probably, most perfectly developed, and especially because he is, par excellence, the man who in modern times has written distinctly and at large from the point of view of Cosmic Consciousness, and who also has referred to its facts and phenomena more plainly and fully than any other writer either ancient or modern.

He tells us plainly, though not as fully as could be wished, of the moment when he attained illumination, and again towards the end of his life of its passing away. Not that it is to be supposed that he had the Cosmic Sense continuously, for years, but that it came less and less frequently as age advanced, probably lasted

less and less long at a time, and decreased in vividness and
intensity.

Moreover, in the case of Whitman, we have means of knowing
the man thoroughly from youth till death—both before and after
illumination—and so (better than in any other. case, except, perhaps, that of Balzac) can compare the fully developed man with
his earlier self. The line of demarcation (between the two Whit-
mans) is perfectly drawn.

On the one hand the Whitman of the forties, writing tales and
essays (such as "Death in a School-room," 1841; "Wild Frank's
Return," id.; "Bervance, or Father and Son," id.; "The Tomb
Blossoms," 1842; "The Last of the Sacred Army," id.; "The
Child Ghost, a Story of the Last Loyalist," id.; "The Angel of
Tears," id.; "Revenge and Requital," 1845; "A Dialogue," id.;
etc.), which even his present splendid fame cannot galvanize into
life; on the other the Whitman of the fifties, writing the first
(1855) edition of the "Leaves."

We expect and always find a difference between the early and
mature writings of the same man. What an interval, for instance, between Shelley's romances and the "Cenci"; between
Macaulay's earliest essays and the history. But here is something quite apart from those and similar cases. We can trace a
gradual evolution of aptitude and power from "Zastrozzi" to
"Epipsychidion," from Macaulay's "Milton" to his "Massacre
of Glencoe." But in the case of Whitman (as in that of Balzac)
writings of absolutely no value were *immediately* followed (and,
at least in Whitman's case without practice or study) by pages
across each of which in letters of ethereal fire are written the
words ETERNAL LIFE; pages covered not only by a masterpiece but
by such vital sentences as have not been written ten times in the
history of the race. It is upon this instantaneous evolution of the
Titan from the *Man,* this profound mystery of the attainment of
the splendor and power of the kingdom of heaven, that this present volume seeks to throw light.

And it is interesting to remark here that Whitman seems to
have had as little idea as had Gautama, Paul or Mohammed what

it was that gave him the mental power, the moral elevation and the perennial joyousness which are among the characteristics of the state to which he attained and which seem to have been to him subjects of continual wonder. "Wandering amazed," he says, "at my own lightness and glee" [193:36].

Let us see, now, what Whitman says about this new sense which must have come to him in June, 1853 or 1854, at the age, that is, of thirty-four or thirty-five. The first direct mention of it is on page 15 of the 1855 edition of the "Leaves" [191:15]. That is to say, it is upon the third page of his first writing after this new faculty had come to him—for the long preface in this volume was written after the body of the book. The lines are found essentially unaltered in every subsequent edition. In the current (1891-92) edition they are upon page 32.

As given here the quotation is from the 1855 edition, as it is important to get as near the man at the time of writing the words as possible. He says:

I believe in you my soul, . . . the other I am must not abase itself to you,
And you must not be abased to the other.
Loaf with me on the grass, . . . loose the stop from your throat,
Not words, not music or rhyme I want, . . . not custom or lecture, not even the best,
Only the lull I like, the hum of your valved voice.
I mind how we lay in June, such a transparent summer morning;
You settled your head athwart my hips and gently turned over upon me,
And parted the shirt from my bosom-bone, and plunged your tongue to my bare-stript heart,
And reached till you felt my beard, and reached till you held my feet.
Swiftly arose and spread around me the peace and joy and knowledge that pass all the art and argument of the earth;
And I know that the hand of God is the elder hand of my own,
And I know that the spirit of God is the eldest brother of my own,

The new experience came in June, probably in 1853, when he had just entered upon his thirty-fifth year. It would seem that he was at first in doubt what it meant, then became satisfied and said: I believe in its teaching. Although, however, it is so divine, the other I am (the old self) must not be abased to it, neither must it (the new self) ever be overridden by the more basic organs and faculties. He goes on: Stay with me, loaf with me on the grass, instruct me, speak out what you mean, what is in you, no matter about speaking musically, or poetically, or according to the rules, or even using the best language, but just use your own words in your own way. He then turns back to tell of the exact occurrence. The illumination (or whatever it was) came to him or upon him one June morning, and took

And that all the men ever born are also my brothers,
    . . . and the women my sisters and lovers,
And that a kelson of creation is love.

(though gently) absolute possession of him, at least for the
time.

Henceforth, he says, his life
received its inspiration from
the newcomer, the new self, whose tongue, as he expresses it, was plunged to his bare-stripped
heart.

His outward life, also, became subject to the dictation of the new self—*it held his feet*.
Finally he tells in brief of the change wrought in his mind and heart by the birth within
him of the new faculty. He says he was filled all at once with peace and joy and knowledge transcending all the art and argument of the earth. He attained that point of view
from which alone can a human being see something of God ("which alone," says Balzac,
"can explain God;" which point, unless he attains, "he cannot," says Jesus, "see the
kingdom of God"). And he sums up the account by the statement that God is his close
friend, that all the men and women ever born are his brothers and sisters and lovers and
that the whole creation is built and rests upon love.

Add now to this the following four lines [192:207], written at
another time but certainly referring to the same or to a similar
experience:

As in a swoon, one instant,
Another sun, ineffable full-dazzles me,
And all the orbs I knew, and brighter, unknown orbs;
One instant of the future land, Heaven's land.

So Dante: "Day seemed to
be added to day as if he who
is able had adorned the heavens
with another sun."

At the same time and in the same connection consider this
passage:

Hast never come to thee an hour,
A sudden gleam divine, precipitating, bursting all these bubbles, fashions,
    wealth?
These eager business aims—books, politics, arts, amours,
To utter nothingness [193:218]?

For the purpose now of aiding to bring before the mind of
the earnest reader (and any other has little business with this
book) a hint, a suggestion (for what more is it possible to give
here?) of what this Cosmic Consciousness is, it may be well to
quote from a prose work of Whitman's certain passages that
seem to throw light on the subject. Speaking of the people, he
says: "The rare, cosmical, artist mind, lit with the infinite, alone
confronts his manifold and oceanic qualities" [195:215]. Again:
"There is yet, to whoever is eligible among us, the prophetic
vision, the joy of being tossed in the brave turmoil of these times

—the promulgation and the path, obedient, lowly reverent to the voice, the gesture of the god, or holy ghost, which others see not, hear not'' [195:227]. Once more: "The thought of identity. . . . Miracle of miracles, beyond statement, most spiritual and vaguest of earth's dreams, yet hardest basic fact, and only entrance to all facts. In such devout hours, in the midst of the significant wonders of heaven and earth (significant only because of the *Me* in the centre), creeds, conventions, fall away and become of no account before this simple idea. Under the luminousness of real vision, it alone takes possession, takes value. Like the shadowy dwarf in the fable, once liberated and looked upon, it expands over the whole earth and spreads to the roof of heaven'' [195:229]. Yet another: "I should say, indeed, that only in the perfect uncontamination and solitariness of individuality may the spirituality of religion positively come forth at all. Only here and on such terms, the meditation, the devout ecstasy, the soaring flight. Only here communion with the mysteries, the eternal problems, *whence? whither?* Alone and identity and the mood—and the soul emerges, and all statements, churches, sermons, melt away like vapors. Alone, and silent thought, and awe, and aspiration —and then the *interior consciousness,* like a hitherto unseen inscription, in magic ink, beams out its wondrous lines to the sense. Bibles may convey and priests expound, but it is exclusively for the noiseless operation of one's isolated *Self* to enter the pure ether of veneration, reach the divine levels, and commune with the unutterable'' [195:233]. The next passage seems prophetical of the coming race: "A fitly born and bred race, growing up in right conditions of outdoor as much as indoor harmony, activity and development, would probably, from and in those conditions, find it enough merely *to live*—and would, in their relations to the sky, air, water, trees, etc., and to the countless common shows, and in the fact of *life* itself, discover and achieve happiness—with Being suffused night and day by wholesome ecstasy, surpassing all the pleasures that wealth, amusement, and even gratified intellect, erudition, or the sense of art, can give'' [195:249]. And finally, and best of all, the following: "Lo! *Nature* (the only complete, actual poem) existing calmly in the divine scheme, containing all, content, careless of the criticisms of a day, or these endless and wordy chatterers. And lo! to the consciousness of the soul, the permanent identity, the thought, the something, before which the magnitude even of Democracy, art, literature, etc., dwindles, becomes partial, measurable—something that fully satisfies (which those do not). That something is the *All* and the idea of *All,* with the accompanying idea of eternity, and of itself, the soul, buoyant, indestructible, sailing Space forever, visiting every region, as a ship the sea. And again lo! the pulsations in all matter, all spirit, throbbing forever—the eternal beats, eternal systole and dyastole of life in things—wherefrom I feel and know that death is not the ending, as we thought, but rather the real beginning—and that nothing ever is or can be lost, nor even die, nor soul nor matter" [195:253]. Here we have brought out strongly the consciousness of the Cosmos, its life and eternity—and the consciousness of the equal grandeur and eternity of the individual soul, the one balancing (equal to) the other. In a word, we have here the expression (as far, perhaps, as it can be expressed) of what is called in this volume Cosmic Consciousness.

Those who so far have been endowed with Cosmic Consciousness have been, almost to a man, carried away and subjugated by it; they have looked upon it—most of them—as being a preterhuman, more or less supernatural faculty, separating them from other men. They have almost, if not quite, always sought to help men, for their moral sense has been inevitably purified and elevated by the oncoming of the new sense, to an extraordinary degree; but they have not realized the need, nor, probably, felt the possibility of using their unusual insight and power in any systematic manner. That is, *THE MAN* has not mastered, taken possession of, and used, the new faculty, but has been (on the contrary) largely or entirely mastered and used by it. This was clearly the case with Paul, who was led away by the grandeur and glory of the new sense to underrate the really equal divinity of his previous human faculties. The same words could with nearly equal truth be applied to the case of Gautama. The evils that humanity has suffered and is to-day suffering simply because these two men took this mistaken view—the evils, namely, that have come upon us through despising "the flesh"—i. e., through despising the so-called "natural man"—the evils, in fine, that have come from the teaching that one part of man is good and to be cultivated, while another part is bad and (if possible) to be extirpated, or, if that is not possible, covered up and hidden away —the evils that have come upon us from this false view are entirely incalculable and would sometimes almost tempt us to forget the even greater benefits bestowed upon the race by the men from whom the evils specified have come.   Not that Gautama and Paul are by any means entirely responsible for the monasticism and asceticism of their followers.   It is doubtless true, as Lecky [114: 108] tells us, that this movement had already begun.   But no one can or will deny that the influence of these two men in intensifying and directing the passion for abnegation of pleasure and so-called purity (in other words, in setting aside the things of the self conscious life in favor of those of the Cosmic Conscious) was incalculably great.

The evils in question have been clearly seen, lucidly portrayed and traced back to their predominant source in these great teachers by many writers.   Among the rest Kidd [108:125f] has indicated with great force and truth the immense impulse toward self denial that marked the early centuries of Christianity; has shown that the impulse in question, though "irrational," had a meaning deeper than reason; that if the race is to advance such anti-social instincts are a necessity (though it is neither necessary nor well that they should often have the force they possessed in the centuries referred to); that they have their place in this scheme just as have their complement, the social instincts.   What Kidd does *not* see is—whence the great teachers derived the insight from which was born the assurance that so moved them and through them the world.

This antagonism between the higher and the lower life, between the life for self and the life for others, between the life of the flesh and the life of the spirit, between the life of the individual and the life of the race, between the self conscious life and the Cosmic Conscious life, is, perhaps, the supreme fact of the modern world—giving to it both motion and stability, just as the opposite forces, the centrifugal and the centripetal, give both motion and stability in the sphere of the astral universe. And from this point of view it is clear why it should be that: Le sort des grands hommes est de passer tour à tour pour des fous et pour des sages. La gloire est d'etre un de ceux que choisit successivement l'humanité par les aimer et les haïr [138: 182].

It may be that Walt Whitman is the first man who, having Cosmic Consciousness very fully developed, has deliberately set himself against being thus mastered by it, determining, on the contrary, to subdue it and make it the servant along with simple consciousness, self consciousness and the rest of the united, individual SELF. He saw, what neither Gautama nor Paul saw, what Jesus saw, though not so clearly as he, that though this faculty is truly Godlike, yet it is no more supernatural or preternatural than sight, hearing, taste, feeling, or any other, and he consequently refused to give it unlimited sway, and would not allow it to tyrannize over the rest. He believes in it, but he says the other self, the old self, must not abase itself to the new; neither must the new be encroached upon or limited by the old; he will see that they live as friendly co-workers together. And it may here be said that whoever does not realize this last clause will never fully understand the "Leaves."

The next reference made by Walt Whitman to Cosmic Consciousness, to be noted here, is in a poem called the "Prayer of Columbus" [193: 323], a few words on the history of which will be in order. It was written about 1874-5, when the condition of the poor, sick, neglected spiritual explorer was strikingly similar to that of the heroic geographical explorer shipwrecked on the Antillean island in 1503, at which time and place the prayer is supposed to be offered up. Walt Whitman—a very common trick with him—used this agreement of circumstance to put his own words (ostensibly) into the mouth of the other man. The prayer is in reality, of course, Walt Whitman's own and all the allusions in it are to his own life, work, fortunes—to himself. In it he refers specifically and pointedly to the present subject matter. Speaking to God, he says:

Thou knowest my manhood's solemn and visionary meditations.

O I am sure they really came from Thee,
The urge, the ardor, the unconquerable will,
The potent, felt, interior command, stronger than words,
A message from the Heavens, whispering to me even in sleep,
These sped me on.

One effort more, my altar this bleak sand;
That Thou O God my life hast lighted,
With ray of light, steady, ineffable, vouchsafed of Thee,
Light rare untellable, lighting the very light,
Beyond all signs, descriptions, languages;
For that O God, be it my latest word, here on my knees,
Old, poor, and paralyzed, I thank Thee.

My hands, my limbs grew nerveless,
My brain feels rack'd, bewilder'd,
Let the old timbers part, I will not part,
I will cling fast to Thee O God, though the waves buffet me,
Thee, Thee at least I know.

At the time of writing these lines Walt Whitman is fifty-five or fifty-six years of age. For over twenty years he has been guided by this (seeming) supernatural illumination. He has yielded freely to it and obeyed its behests as being from God Himself.

He has "loved the earth, sun, animals, despised riches, given alms to every one that asked, stood up for the stupid and crazy, devoted his income and labor to others" [193: 273], as commanded by the divine voice and as impelled by the divine impulse, and now for reward he is poor, sick, paralyzed, despised, neglected, dying. His message to man, to the delivery of which he has devoted his life, which has been dearer in his eyes (for man's sake) than wife, children, life itself, is unread or scoffed and jeered at. What shall he say to God? He says that God knows him through and through, and that he is willing to leave himself in God's hands. He says that he does not know men nor his own work, and so does

not judge what men may do with, or say to, the "Leaves."   But
he says he does know God, and will cling to him though the waves
buffet him.   Then about the inspiration, the illumination, the
potent, felt, interior command stronger than words?   He is sure
that this comes from God.   He has no doubt.   There can be no
doubt of that.

He goes on to speak of the ray of light, steady, ineffable, with
which God has lighted his life, and says it is rare, untellable, beyond all signs, descriptions, languages.   And this (be it well remembered) is not the utterance of wild enthusiasm, but of cold,
hard fact by a worn-out old man on (as he supposed) his deathbed.

This acknowledgment by Whitman of God's goodness recalls
forcibly Bacon's gratitude to God for his "gifts and graces," his
circumstances in the summer of 1621 (both outwardly and inwardly) being as parallel as they could possibly be with those of
Whitman in 1875.

The next direct allusion to Cosmic Consciousness to be noted
is embodied in a poem called "Now Precedent Songs, Farewell"
[193:403], written in June, 1888, when he again, and with good
reason, supposed himself dying.   The poem was written as a hasty
good-bye to the "Leaves."   At the end of it he refers to his songs
and their origin in these words:

O heaven! what flash and started endless train of all! compared indeed to that!
What wretched shred e'en at the best of all!

He says: Compared to the flash, the divine illumination from
which they had their origin, how poor and worthless his poems
are.   And it must be borne in mind that Whitman never had a
bad opinion of the "Leaves."   He used to say (in a semi-jocular
manner, but fully meaning it all the same) that none of the fellows
(meaning out-and-out admirers), not even O'Conner, Burroughs
or Bucke, thought as highly of them as he did.   But thinking that
way of them he could still exclaim how poor they were compared
to the illumination from which they sprang.   But he did not die
at that time.   He rallied, and again, it seems, from time to time

the vision appeared and the voice whispered. Doubtless the vision grew more dim and the voice less distinct as time passed and the feebleness of age and sickness advanced upon him. At last, in 1891, at the age of seventy-two, the "Brahmic Splendor" finally departed, and in those mystic lines, "To the Sunset Breeze" [193: 414], which the Harpers returned to him as "a mere improvisation," he bids it farewell:

Thou hast O Nature! elements! utterance to my heart beyond the rest—and this
    is of them. . . .
Thou art spiritual, Godly, most of all known to my sense,
Minister to speak to me, here and now, what word has never told, and cannot tell,
Art thou not universal, concrete's distillation?

As a man with Cosmic Consciousness *sees* the Cosmic order, and that, as Paul says, "all things work together for good"* [19: 8: 28], so every such man is what is called "an Optimist," and it may be freely stated that the *knowledge* of the friendliness of the universe to man is a distinctive mark of the class of men considered in this volume. That Whitman has this mark needs saying only to those who have not read him. Again and again in ever-varying words he says and repeats: "And I say there is in fact no evil" [193: 22]. "Clear and sweet is my soul, and clear and sweet is all that is not my soul" [193: 31]. "Is it lucky to be born?" he asks, and answers: "It is just as lucky to die" [193: 34].

So Dante, in summing up, declares that, seen by the light of the Cosmic Sense, all is perfect, including that which outside that light is (or seems) imperfect [72: 213].

It is not supposed that in the case of any man so far born has the Cosmic Sense been constantly present for years, months, or even weeks—probably not even for days or hardly hours. In many cases it appears only once and for a few moments only, but that flash is sufficient to light up (more or less brightly) all the subsequent years of life. In the greatest cases it may be present for many minutes at a time and return at intervals of weeks,

---

*In the passage Paul seems to limit the statement "to them that love God" (to those who have Cosmic Consciousness), but what he really intends is doubtless: All things work together for good; but this is only really seen and known by those who have been endowed with the Cosmic Sense.

months or years.   Between these extremes there would seem to be a vast range of greater and less cases.

It has already been stated more than once that while Cosmic Consciousness is actually present there is a profound change in the appearance of the subject of it.   If one thinks how the countenance is lit up by ordinary great joy, it will be seen that the change spoken of must happen.   Not only so, but it is within the personal knowledge of the writer that (at all events, in some cases) a man does not altogether return (at least permanently) to his old expression and appearance for months or even years after a period of illumination.

This is as much as to say that the face of a man who had occasional periods of illumination, extending through years, would wear, habitually, a more or less exalted and noble expression, and this is true.

It is, however, of course, while Cosmic Consciousness is actually present that the change in the aspect of the subject is the greatest.   The following seems to be a description of this change. Either Cosmic Consciousness was actually present at the hour mentioned or it had been present immediately before it.   The account is by an eye witness—Miss Helen Price—a lady well known to the person who writes these lines:

One evening in 1866, while Walt Whitman was stopping with us in New York, the tea bell had been rung ten minutes or more when he came down from his room, and we all gathered around the table.   I remarked him as he entered the room; there seemed to be a peculiar brightness and elation about him, an almost irrepressible joyousness, which shone from his face and seemed to pervade his whole body.   It was the more noticeable as his ordinary mood was one of quiet, yet cheerful serenity.   I knew he had been working at a new edition of his book, and I hoped if he had an opportunity he would say something to let us into the secret of his mysterious joy.   Unfortunately most of those at the table were occupied with some subject of conversation; at every pause I waited eagerly for him to speak; but no, some one else would begin again, until I grew almost wild with impatience and vexation.   He appeared to listen, and would even laugh at some of the remarks that were made, yet he did not utter a single word during the meal; and his face still wore that singular brightness and delight, as though he had partaken of some divine elixir.   His expression was so remarkable that I might have doubted my own observation had it not been noticed by another as well as myself [38:32].

III.

SUMMARY.

a. The subjective light appeared strongly to Whitman.

b. The moral elevation and

c. Intellectual illumination were extreme, and in his case stand out very clearly, since we know the man so well both before and after the oncoming of the Cosmic Sense.

d. In no other man who ever lived was the sense of eternal life so absolute.

e. Fear of death was absent. Neither in health nor in sickness did he show any sign of it, and there is every reason to believe he did not feel it.

f. He had no sense of sin. This must not be understood as meaning that he felt himself to be perfect. Whitman realized his own greatness as clearly and fully as did any of his admirers. He also realized how immeasurably he was below the ideal which he constantly set up before himself.

g. The change of the self conscious man into the Cosmic Conscious was instantaneous—occurring at a certain hour of a certain day.

h. It occurred at the characteristic age and at the characteristic time of the year.

i. The altered appearance of the man while in the Cosmic Conscious state was seen and noted.

CHAPTER 14.

Edward Carpenter.

I.

WAS born August 29th, 1844, at Brighton, where he spent his early youth. His father came from Cornwall. He went for several years to Brighton College, and in 1864 entered Trinity Hall,

Cambridge, where he obtained a scholarship, graduated in 1868 as tenth wrangler, and afterwards was elected a fellow of the college.   In due course he was ordained, and for some years acted as curate of St. Edward's Church, Cambridge, of which at the time Frederic Dennison Maurice was vicar.   He never profoundly believed in the historical accuracy of the Bible.   His father was a Broad Churchman, and brought him up to think for himself. When quite young he had made up his mind to take orders and stuck to that notion largely from an idea that the church could be *widened from the inside*.   Once fairly inside, however, he found it would take a precious long time.   In fine, he soon felt himself so ill at ease that a complete break with the whole thing became absolutely necessary.   He was in orders from 1869 to 1874.

We find him immediately after this working with approved success in a new field—that of university extension.   He was at this time, from 1874 to 1880, especially known and loved in and about York, Nottingham and Sheffield.

About the same time he began to study deeply social questions, and became convinced that society was on a wrong basis and moving in a wrong direction.

It was early in 1881, as he tells us, when in his thirty-seventh year, that Carpenter entered into Cosmic Consciousness.   The evidence of the fact is perfectly clear, but it is not within the power of the writer to give details of illumination in the case beyond those given below.   As a direct result of the oncoming of the Cosmic Sense he practically resigned his social rank and became a laborer; that is to say, he procured a few acres of land not many miles from Dronfield, in Derbyshire, built upon it a small house and lived there with the family of a working man as one of themselves.   Dressing in the common corduroy of the country side, he took up his spade and worked steadily with the others.   It seemed to him that the manners and habits of the rich were less noble than those of the poor; that the soul and life of the rich were less noble. He preferred to live with the comparatively poor and to be himself comparatively poor, in that respect (not following the example of, but) participating in the instinct of Gautama. Jesus,

Paul, Las Casas and Whitman. He retains his piano, and after his hours of manual toil will refresh himself with a sonata of Beethoven, for he is an accomplished and original musician. It is needless to say that he is a pronounced and advanced socialist —perhaps an anarchist. He is *one* with the people, the "common" people (made so numerous, so *common,* said Lincoln, because God loves them and likes to see many of them). It is childish to say (as some have thought and said) that men of this stamp live as poor men with the poor for the sake of influencing these and as an example to the rich. They simply live as poor men with the poor, as laboring men with laborers, because they prefer the life, the manners, the habits, the surroundings, the personality of these to the life, the manners, the habits, the surroundings and the personality of the rich. Occasionally he descends into so-called "good society" (having close and dear relations there), but does not remain in it for any length of time. He loves above all things, in himself and others, honesty, candor, sincerity and simplicity, and he says he finds more of these in the poor, common, working people than he finds in the rich men and women who constitute "society."

In 1873 Carpenter published "Narcissus and Other Poems," and in 1875 "Moses: A Drama." He began reading Whitman in 1869, and read the "Leaves" continuously for ten years thereafter. Whether Carpenter would have acquired Cosmic Consciousness if he had never read Whitman cannot perhaps be said, either by himself or by any one else, but there seems little doubt that the study of the "Leaves" was a material factor leading up to his illumination. He is not the only man who has been helped forward by the same agency, and it is probable that in the world's future many thousand men and women will be in similar manner helped to the same goal. For (and in this fact is the raison d'être of the present volume), next to the necessary heredity and the right constitution (bodily and mental), association with the minds of those who have passed the boundary into "Specialism" is of supreme importance. He began to write "Towards Democracy" (the book in which he attempted to embody the teachings of the

Cosmic Sense) immediately after his illumination. The first edition, small and thin, was published in 1883; the second, a good deal enlarged, in 1885; the third, grown into a stout, handsome volume, in 1892; and the fourth, in 1896. No better book can be read from which to obtain an idea as to what Cosmic Consciousness is and in what it differs from self consciousness. Besides "Towards Democracy," Carpenter published, in 1887, "England's Ideal"; in 1889, "Civilization, its Cause and Cure," and in 1893, "From Adam's Peak to Elephanta"; all of which are exceedingly well worth attention.

II.

In a letter to the present writer, who had asked for certain facts about the new sense, he says:

I really do not feel that I can tell you anything without falsifying and obscuring the matter. I have done my best to write it out in "Towards Democracy." I have no experience of physical light in this relation. The perception seems to be one in which all the senses unite into one sense. In which *you become* the object. But this is unintelligible, mentally speaking. I do not think the matter can be defined as yet; but I do not know that there is any harm in writing about it.

In the Vagasaneyi-Samhita-Upanishad occurs the following verse: "When, to a man who understands, the *self has become all things*, what sorrow, what trouble can there be to him who once beheld that unity" [150 : 312]?

In another place he has the following clear and explicit passage on the subject:

Notwithstanding, then, the prevalence of the foot régime (inductive science) and that the heathen so furiously rage together in their belief in it, let us suggest that there is in man a divine consciousness as well as a foot consciousness. For as we saw that the sense of taste may pass from being a mere local thing on the tip of the tongue to pervading and becoming synonymous with the health of the whole body; or as the blue of the sky may be to one person a mere superficial impression of color, and to another the inspiration of a poem or picture, and to a third, as to the "God-intoxicated" Arab of the desert, a living presence like the ancient Dyaus or Zeus—so may not the whole of human consciousness gradually lift itself from a mere local and temporary consciousness to a divine and universal? There is in every man a local consciousness connected with his quite external body; that we know. Are there not also in every man the making of a universal consciousness? That there are in us phases of consciousness which transcend the limit of the bodily senses is a matter of daily experience; that we perceive and know things which are not conveyed to us by our bodily eyes and heard by our bodily ears is certain; that there rise in us waves of consciousness from those around us—from the people, the race, to which we belong—is also certain. May there, then, not be in us the makings of a perception and knowledge which shall not be relative to this body which is here and now, but which shall be good for all time and everywhere? Does there not exist, in truth, as we have already hinted, an inner illumination, of which what we call light in the outer world is the partial expression and manifestation, by which we can ultimately see things *as they are,* beholding all creation—the animals, the angels, the plants, the figures of our friends and all the ranks and races of human kind, in their true being and order—not by any local act of perception, but by a cosmical intuition and presence, identifying ourselves with what we see? Does there not exist a perfected sense of hearing—as of the morning stars singing together—an understanding of the words that are spoken all through the universe, the hidden meaning of all things, the word which is creation itself—a profound and far-pervading sense, of which our ordinary sense of sound is only the first novitiate and initiation? Do we not become aware of an inner sense of health and of holiness—the translation and final outcome of the external sense of taste—which has power to determine for us absolutely and without any ado, without argument, and without denial, what is good and appropriate to be done or suffered in every case that can arise? If there are such powers in man, then, indeed, an exact science is possible. Short of it there is only a temporary and phantom science. "Whatsoever is known to us by (direct) consciousness," says Mill in his "Logic," "is known to us without possibility of question." What is known by our local and temporary consciousness *is known for the moment* beyond possibility of question; what is known by our permanent and universal consciousness is permanently known beyond possibility of question [57:97-8].

In a later book, Carpenter has a chapter, "Consciousness Without Thought" [56:153], written expressly to give to the uninitiated an idea of what is meant by the words used as the title of the present volume. Here follows that chapter entire. Those interested in the subject had better see the book itself, as it contains other chapters almost equally important. The chapter begins:

The question is: What is this experience? or rather—since an experience can really only be known to a person who experiences it—we may ask: What is the nature of this experience? And in trying to indicate an answer of some kind to this question I feel considerable diffidence, just for the very reason (for one) already mentioned—namely, that it is so difficult or impossible for one person to give a true account of an experience which has occurred to another.

If I could give the exact words of the teacher, without any bias derived either from myself or the interpreting friend, the case might be different; but that I cannot pretend to do; and if I could, the old-world scientific form in which his thoughts were cast would probably only prove a stumbling block and a source of confusion, instead of a help, to the reader. Indeed in the case of the sacred books, where we have a good deal of accessible and authoritative information, Western critics, though for the most part agreeing that there is some real experience underlying, are sadly at variance as to what that experience may be.

For these reasons I prefer not to attempt or pretend to give the exact teaching, unbiased, of the Indian Gurus or their experiences, but only to indicate, so far as I can, in my own words, and in modern thought-form, what I take to be the direction in which we must look for this ancient and world-old knowledge which has had so stupendous an influence in the East, and which indeed is still the main mark of its difference from the West.

And first let me guard against an error which is likely to arise. It is very easy to assume, and very frequently assumed, in any case where a person is credited with the possession of an unusual faculty, that such person is at once lifted out of our sphere into a supernatural region, and possesses every faculty of that region. If, for instance, he or she is, or is supposed to be, clairvoyant, it is assumed that everything is or ought to be known to them; or if the person has shown what seems a miraculous power at any time or in any case, it is asked by way of discredit why he or she did not show a like power at other times or in other cases. Against all such hasty generalizations it is necessary to guard ourselves. If there is a higher form of consciousness obtainable by man than that which he can for the most part claim at present, it is probable—nay, certain—that it is evolving and will evolve but slowly, and with many a slip and hesitant pause by the way. In the far past of man and the animals consciousness of sensation and consciousness of self have been successively evolved—each of these mighty growths with innumerable branches and branchlets continually spreading. At any point in this vast experience a new growth, a new form of consciousness might well have seemed miraculous. What could be more marvellous than the first revealment of the sense of sight, what more inconceivable to those who had not experienced it, and what more certain than that the first use of this faculty must have been fraught with delusion and error? Yet there may be an inner vision which again transcends sight, even as far as sight transcends touch. It is more than probable that in the hidden births of time there lurks a consciousness which is not the consciousness of sensation and which is not the consciousness of self—or at least which includes and entirely surpasses these—a consciousness in which the contrast between the ego and the external world, and the distinction between subject and object, fall away. The part of the world into which such a consciousness admits us (call it supermundane or whatever you will) is probably at least as vast and complex as the part we know, and progress in that region at least equally slow and tentative and various, laborious, discontinuous and uncertain. There is no sudden leap out of the back parlor onto Olympus; and the routes, when found, from one to the other, are long and bewildering in their variety.

And of those who do attain to some portion of this region we are not to suppose that they are at once demi-gods or infallible. In many cases indeed the very novelty and strangeness of the experience give rise to phantasmal trains of delusive speculation. Though we should expect, and though it is no doubt true on the whole, that what we should call the higher types of existing humanity are those most likely to come into possession of any new faculties which may be flying about, yet it is not always so, and there are cases well recognized, in which persons of decidedly deficient or warped moral nature attain powers which properly belong to a higher grade of evolution, and are correspondingly dangerous thereby.

All this, or a great part of it, the Indian teachers insist on. They say— and I think this commends the reality of their experience—that there is nothing abnormal or miraculous about the matter; that the faculties acquired are on the whole the result of long evolution and training, and that they have distinct laws and an order of their own. They recognize the existence of persons of a demoniac faculty, who have acquired powers of a certain grade without corresponding moral evolution, and they admit the rarity of the highest phases of consciousness and the fewness of those at present fitted for its attainment. With these little provisos, then, established I think we may go on to say that what the Gñáni seeks and obtains is a new order of consciousness—to which, for want of a better, we may give the name universal or Cosmic Consciousness, in contradistinction to the individual or special bodily consciousness with which we are all familiar. I am not aware that the exact equivalent of this expression "universal consciousness" is used in the Hindu philosophy; but the Sat-chit-ánanda Brahm, to which every yogi aspires, indicates the same idea: "sat," the reality, the all pervading; "chit," the knowing, perceiving; "ánanda," the blissful—all these united in one manifestation of Brahm.

The West seeks the individual consciousness—the enriched mind, ready perceptions and memories, individual hopes and fears, ambition, loves, conquests —the self, the local self, in all its phases and forms—and sorely doubts whether such a thing as an universal consciousness exists. The East seeks the universal consciousness, and in those cases where its quest succeeds individual self and life thin away to a mere film, and are only the shadows cast by the glory revealed beyond.

The individual consciousness takes the form of Thought, which is fluid and mobile like quicksilver, perpetually in a state of change and unrest fraught with pain and effort; the other consciousness is not in the form of Thought. It touches, hears, sees, and is those things which it perceives—without motion, without change, without effort, without distinction of subject and object, but with a vast and incredible Joy.

The individual consciousness is specially related to the body. The organs of the body are in some degree its organs. But the whole body is only as one organ of the Cosmic Consciousness. To attain this latter one must have the power of knowing one's self separate from the body—of passing into a state of ecstasy, in fact. Without this the Cosmic Consciousness cannot be experienced.

It is said: "There are four main experiences in initiation—(1) the meeting with a Guru; (2) the consciousness of Grace or Arul—which may perhaps be interpreted as the consciousness of a change—even of a physiological change—working within one; (3) the vision of Siva (God), with which the knowledge of one's self as distinct from the body is closely connected; (4) the finding of the universe within.'' ''The wise,'' it is also said, ''when their thoughts become fixed, perceive within themselves the Absolute consciousness, which is Sarva sakshi, Witness of all things.''

Great have been the disputes among the learned as to the meaning of the word Nirvâna—whether it indicates a state of no-consciousness or a state of vastly enhanced consciousness. Probably both views have their justification; the thing does not admit of definition in the terms of ordinary language. The important thing to see and admit is that under cover of this and other similar terms there does exist a real and recognizable fact (that is, a state of consciousness in some sense), which has been experienced over and over again, and which to those who have experienced it in ever so slight a degree has appeared worthy of lifelong pursuit and devotion. It is easy of course to represent the thing as a mere word, a theory, a speculation of the dreamy Hindu; but people do not sacrifice their lives for empty words, nor do mere philosophical abstractions rule the destinies of continents. No, the word represents a reality, something very basic and inevitable in human nature. The question really is not to define the fact—for we cannot do that—but to get at and experience it. It is interesting at this juncture to find that modern Western science, which has hitherto—without much result—been occupying itself with mechanical theories of the universe, is approaching from its side this idea of the existence of another form of consciousness. The extraordinary phenomena of hypnotism—which no doubt are in some degree related to the subject we are discussing, and which have been recognized for ages in the East—are forcing Western scientists to assume the existence of the so-called secondary consciousness in the body. The phenomena seem really inexplicable without the assumption of a secondary agency of some kind, and it every day becomes increasingly difficult not to use the word consciousness to describe it. Let it be understood that I am not for a moment assuming that this secondary consciousness of the hypnotists is in all respects identical with the Cosmic Consciousness (or whatever we may call it) of the Eastern occultists. It may or may not be. The two kinds of consciousness may cover the same ground, or they may only overlap to a small extent. That is a question I do not propose to discuss. The point to which I wish to draw attention is that Western science is envisaging the possibility of the existence in man of another consciousness of some kind beside that with whose workings we are familiar. It quotes (A. Moll) the case of Barkworth, who ''can add up long rows of figures while carrying on a lively discussion, without allowing his attention to be at all diverted from the discussion''; and asks us how Barkworth can do this unless he has a secondary consciousness which occupies itself with the figures while his primary consciousness is in the thick of argument. Here is a lecturer (F. Myers) who for a whole minute allows his mind to wander entirely away from the subject in hand, and imagines himself to be sitting beside a friend in the audience and to be engaged in conversation with him, and who wakes up to find himself still on the platform lecturing away with perfect ease and coherency. What are we to say to such a case as that? Here, again, is a pianist who recites a piece of music by heart, and finds that his recital is actually hindered by allowing his mind (his primary consciousness) to dwell upon what he is doing. It is sometimes suggested that the very perfection of the musical performance shows that it is mechanical or unconscious, but is this a fair inference? and would it not seem to be a mere contradiction in terms to speak of an unconscious lecture or an unconscious addition of a row of figures?

Many actions and processes of the body, e.g., swallowing, are attended by distinct personal consciousness; many other actions and processes are quite unperceived by the same; and it might seem reasonable to suppose that these latter, at any rate, were purely mechanical and devoid of any mental substratum. But the later developments of hypnotism in the West have shown— what is well known to the Indian fakirs—that under certain conditions consciousness of the internal actions and processes of the body can be obtained; and not only so, but consciousness of events taking place at a distance from the body and without the ordinary means of communication.

Thus the idea of another consciousness, in some respects of wider range than the ordinary one, and having methods of perception of its own, has been gradually infiltrating itself into Western minds.

There is another idea, which modern science has been familiarizing us with, and which is bringing us towards the same conception—that, namely, of the fourth dimension. The supposition that the actual world has four space-dimensions instead of three makes many things conceivable which otherwise would be incredible. It makes it conceivable that apparently separate objects, e.g., distinct people, are really physically united; that things apparently sundered by enormous distances of space are really quite close together; that a person or other object might pass in and out of a closed room without disturbance of walls, doors, or windows, etc.; and if this fourth dimension were to become a factor of our consciousness it is obvious that we should have means of knowledge which to the ordinary sense would appear simply miraculous. There is much, apparently, to suggest that the consciousness attained to by the Indian gñanis in their degree, and by hypnotic subjects in theirs, is of this fourth-dimensional order.

As a solid is related to its own surfaces, so, it would appear, is Cosmic Consciousness related to ordinary consciousness. The phases of the personal consciousness are but different facets of the other consciousness; and experiences which seem remote from each other in the individual are perhaps all equally near in the universal. Space itself, as we know it, may be practically annihilated in the consciousness of a larger space of which it is but the superficies; and a person living in London may not unlikely find that he has a back door opening quite simply and unceremoniously out in Bombay.

"The true quality of the soul," said the Guru one day, "is that of space, by which it is at rest, every-

Cf. Whitman: "Dazzling and tremendous, how quick the sunrise would kill me, if I could not now and always send sunrise

where. But this space (Akása) within   out of me. We also ascend dazzling and tre-
the soul is far above the ordinary ma-   mendous as the sun.''
terial space. The whole of the latter, including all the suns and stars, appears
to you then as it were but an atom of the former''—and here he held up his
fingers as though crumbling a speck of dust between them.

"At rest everywhere," "Indifference," "Equality." This was one of the
most remarkable parts of the Guru's teaching. Though (for family reasons)
maintaining many of the observances of caste himself, and though holding and
teaching that for the mass of the people caste rules were quite necessary, he
never ceased to insist that when the time came for a man (or woman) to be
"emancipated" all these rules must drop aside as of no importance—all distinction of castes, classes, all sense of superiority or self-goodness—of right and
wrong even—and the most absolute sense of equality must prevail towards
everyone, and determination in its expression. Certainly it was remarkable
(though I knew that the sacred books contained it) to find this germinal principle of Western Democracy so vividly active and at work deep down beneath
the innumerable layers of Oriental social life and custom. But so it is; and
nothing shows better the relation between the West and East than this fact.

This sense of equality, of freedom from regulations and confinements, of
inclusiveness, and of the life that "rests everywhere," belongs, of course, more
to the Cosmic or universal part of a man than to the individual part. To the latter it is always a stumbling-block and an offense. It is easy to show that men are
not equal, that they cannot be free, and to point the absurdity of a life that is
indifferent and at rest under all conditions. Nevertheless to the larger consciousness these are basic facts, which underlie the common life of humanity,
and feed the very individual that denies them.

Thus repeating the proviso that in using such terms as Cosmic and universal consciousness we do not commit ourselves to the theory that the instant
a man leaves the personal part of him he enters into absolutely unlimited and
universal knowledge, but only into a higher order of perception—and admitting
the intricacy and complexity of the region so roughly denoted by these terms,
and the microscopical character of our knowledge about it—we may say once
more, also as a roughest generalization, that the quest of the East has been
this universal consciousness, and that of the West the personal or individual
consciousness. As is well known the East has its various sects and schools of
philosophy, with subtle discriminations of qualities, essences, godheads, devil-
hoods, etc., into which I do not propose to go, and which I should feel myself
quite incompetent to deal with. Leaving all these aside, I will keep simply to
these two rough Western terms, and try to consider further the question of
the methods by which the Eastern student sets himself to obtain the Cosmic
state, or such higher order of consciousness as he does encompass.

Later [62] Carpenter has made still another attempt to explain
or at least indicate the nature of the new sense. He says:

I have sometimes been asked questions about "Towards Democracy" which I found it difficult to answer: and I will try and shape a few thoughts about it here.

It is important to notice that all through this exposition, as well as in Carpenter's other writings on the same subject (as whoever has read this book so far will see without further repetition), his testimony as to the phenomena of Cosmic Consciousness constantly runs parallel to, is often even identical with, that of the Suttas, of Behmen, of Yepes, and of other writers of the same class dealing with this subject (especially, perhaps, the author of the Bagavat Gita), though it does not appear that he has, and probably he has not studied these writers.

Quite a long time ago (say when I was about twenty-five, and living at Cambridge) I wanted to write some sort of a book which should address itself very personally and closely to any one who cared to read it—establish, so to speak, an intimate personal relation between myself and the reader; and during successive years I made several attempts to realize this idea—of which beginnings one or two in verse (one, for instance, I may mention, called "The Angel of Death and Life") may be found in a little volume entitled "Narcissus and Other Poems," now well out of print, which I published in 1873. None of my attempts satisfied me, however, and after a time I began to think the quest was an unreasonable one—unreasonable because, while it might not be difficult for anyone with a pliant and sympathetic disposition to touch certain chords in any given individual that he met, it seemed impossible to hope that a book—which cannot in any way adapt itself to the idiosyncrasies of its reader—could find the key of the personalities into whose hands it might come. For this it would be necessary to suppose, and to find, an absolutely common ground to all individuals (all, at any rate, who might have reached a certain stage of thought and experience), and to write the book on and from that common ground; but this seemed at that time quite unfeasible.

Years followed, more or less eventful, with flight from Cambridge and university lectures carried on in the provincial towns, and so forth; but of much dumbness as regards writing, and inwardly full of extreme tension and suffering. At last, early in 1881, no doubt as the culmination and result of struggles and experiences that had been going on, I became conscious that a mass of material was forming within me, imperatively demanding expression—though what exactly its expression would be I could not then have told. I became for the time overwhelmingly conscious of the disclosure within me of a region transcending in some sense the ordinary bounds of personality, in the light of which region my own idiosyncrasies of character—defects, accomplishments, limitations, or what not—appeared of no importance whatever—an absolute freedom from mortality, accompanied by an indescribable calm and joy.

I also immediately saw, or felt, that this region of self existing in me existed equally (though not always equally consciously) in others. In regard to it the mere diversities of temperament which ordinarily distinguish and divide people dropped away and became indifferent, and a field was opened in which all might meet, in which all were truly equal. Thus the two words which controlled my thought and expression at that time became Freedom and

Equality. The necessity for space and time to work this out grew so strong
that in April of that year I threw up my lecturing employment. Moreover
another necessity had come upon me which demanded the latter step—the
necessity, namely, for an open air life and manual work. I could not finally
argue with this any more than with the other; I had to give in and obey. As
it happened, at the time I mentioned I was already living in a little cottage on
a farm (at Bradway, near Sheffield) with a friend and his family, and doing
farm work in the intervals of my lectures. When I threw up the lecturing I
had everything clear before me. I knocked together a sort of wooden sentinel
box in the garden, and there, or in the fields and the woods, all that spring and
summer and on through the winter, by day and sometimes by night, in sunlight or in rain, in frost and snow, and all sorts of gray and dull weather, I
wrote "Towards Democracy"—or at any rate the first and longer poem that
goes by that name.

By the end of 1881 this was finished—though it was worked over and patched
a little in the early part of 1882; and I remember feeling then that, defective
and halting and incoherent in expression as it was, still if it succeeded in rendering even a half the splendor which inspired it, it would be good, and I need
not trouble to write anything more (which, with due allowance for the said
"if," I even now feel was a true and friendly intimation).

The writing of this and its publication (in 1883) got a load off my mind
which had been weighing on it for years, and I have never since felt that sense
of oppression and anxiety which I had constantly suffered from before—and
which I believe, in its different forms, is a common experience in the early part
of life.

In this first poem were embodied, with considerable alterations and adapta-
tions, a good number of casual pieces, which I had written (merely under stress
of feeling and without any particular sense of proportion) during several pre-
ceding years. They now found their interpretation under the steady and clear
light of a new mood or state of feeling which previously had only visited me
fitfully and with clouded beams. The whole of "Towards Democracy"—I may
say, speaking broadly and including the later pieces—had been written under
the domination of this mood. I have tested and measured everything by it; it
has been the sun to which all the images and conceptions and thoughts used
have been as material objects reflecting its light. And perhaps this connects
itself with the fact that it has been so necessary to write in the open air.
The more universal feeling which I sought to convey refused itself from me
within doors; nor could I at any time or by any means persuade the rhythm
or style of expression to render itself up within a room—tending there always
to break back into distinct metrical forms; which, however much I admire them
in certain authors, and think them myself suitable for certain kinds of work,
were not what I wanted and did not express for me the feeling which I sought
to express. This fact (of the necessity of the open air) is very curious, and I
cannot really explain it. I only know that it is so, quite indubitable and
insurmountable. I can feel it at once, the difference, in merely passing through
a doorway—but I cannot explain it. Always, especially the *sky*, seemed to

contain for me the key, the inspiration; the sight of it more than anything gave what I wanted (sometimes like a veritable lightning flash coming down from it on to my paper—I a mere witness, but agitated with strange transports).

But if I should be asked—as I have sometimes been asked—What is the exact nature of this mood, of this illuminant splendor, of which you speak? I should have to reply that I can give no answer. The whole of "Towards Democracy" is an endeavor to give it utterance; any mere single sentence, or direct definition, would be of no use—rather indeed would tend to obscure by limiting. All I can say is that there seems to be a vision possible to man, as from some more universal standpoint, free from the obscurity and localism which specially connect themselves with the passing clouds of desire, fear, and all ordinary thought and emotion; in that sense another and separate faculty; and a vision always means a sense of light, so here is a sense of inward light, unconnected of course with the mortal eye, but bringing to the eye of the mind the impression that it *sees*, and by means of the medium which washes, as it were, the *interior* surfaces of all objects and things and persons—how can I express it? And yet this is most defective, for the sense is a sense that one *is* those objects and things and persons that one perceives (and the whole universe)— a sense in which sight and touch and hearing are all fused in identity. Nor can the matter be understood without realizing that the whole faculty is deeply and intimately rooted in the ultra-moral and emotional nature, and beyond the thought-region of the brain.

And now with regard to the "I" which occurs so freely in this book. In this and in other such cases the author is naturally liable to a charge of egotism, and I personally do not feel disposed to combat any such charge that may be made. That there are mere egotism and vanity embodied in these pages I do not for a moment doubt, and that so far as they exist they mar the expression and purpose of the book I also do not doubt. But the existence of these things do not affect the real question: What or who in the main is the "I" spoken of?

To this question I must also frankly own that I can give no answer. I do not know. That the word is not used in the dramatic sense is all I can say. The "I" is myself, as well as I could find words to express myself; but what that self is and what its limits may be—and therefore what the self of any other person is and what *its* limits may be—I cannot tell. I have sometimes thought that perhaps the best work one could do—if one felt at any time enlargements and extensions of one's *ego*—was to simply record these as faithfully as might be, leaving others—the scientist and the philosopher—to explain, and feeling confident that what really existed in oneself would be found to exist either consciously or in a latent form in other people. And I will say that I have in these records above all endeavored to be genuine. If I have said "I, Nature," it was because at the time, at any rate, I felt "I, Nature"; If I have said "I am equal with the lowest," it was because I could not express what I felt more directly than by those words. The value of such statements can only appear by time; if they are corroborated by others, then they help to form a body of record which may well be worth investigation, analysis and explanation. If they are not so corroborated, then they naturally and properly fall away as mere vagaries of self-deception. I have not the least doubt that anything which is really genuine will be corroborated. It seems to me more and more clear that the word "I" has a practically infinite range of meaning—that the ego covers far more ground than we usually suppose. At some points we are intensely individual, at others intensely sympathetic; some of our impressions (as the tickling of a hair) are of the most momentary character, others (as the sense of identity) involve long periods of time. Sometimes we are aware of almost a fusion between our own identity and that of another person. What does all this mean? Are we really separate individuals, or is individuality an illusion, or, again, is it only a part of the *ego* or soul that is individual and not the whole? Is the *ego* absolutely one with the body, or is it only a part of the body, or again is the body but a part of the self—one of its organs, so to speak, and not the whole man? Or, lastly, is it perhaps not possible to express the truth by any direct use of these or other terms of ordinary language? Anyhow, what am I?

These are questions which come all down Time, demanding solution—which humanity is constantly endeavoring to find an answer to. I do not pretend to answer them. On the contrary I am sure that not one of the pieces in "Towards Democracy" has been written with the view of providing an answer. They have simply been written to express feelings which insisted on being expressed. Nevertheless it is possible that some of them—by giving the experiences and affirmations even of one person—may contribute material towards that answer to these and the like questions which will one day most assuredly be given. That there is a region of consciousness removed beyond what we usually call mortality, into which we humans can yet pass, I practically do not doubt; but granting that this is a fact, its explanation still remains for investigation. I have said in these few notes on "Towards Democracy" nothing about the influence of Whitman—for the same reason that I have said nothing about the influence of the sun or the winds. These influences lie too far back and ramify too complexly to be traced. I met with William Rosetti's little selection from "Leaves of Grass" in 1868 or 1869, and read that and the original editions continuously for ten years. I never met with any other book (with the exception perhaps of Beethoven's sonatas) which I could read and re-read as I could this one. I find it difficult to imagine what my life would have been without it. "Leaves of Grass" "filtered and fiber'd" my blood; but I do not think I ever tried to imitate it or its style. Against the inevitable drift out of the more classic forms of verse into a looser and freer rhythm I fairly fought, contesting the ground ("kicking against the pricks") inch by inch during a period of seven years in numerous abortive and mongrel creations—till in 1881 I was finally compelled into the form (if such it can be called) of "Towards Democracy." I did not adopt it because it was an approximation to the form of "Leaves of Grass." Whatever resemblance there may be between the rhythm, style, thoughts, construction, etc., of the two books, must, I think, be set down to a deeper similarity of emotional atmosphere and intention in the two authors—even though that similarity may have sprung and no doubt largely did spring out of the personal influence of one upon the other.

Anyhow our temperaments, standpoints, antecedents, etc., are so entirely diverse and opposite that, except for a few points, I can hardly imagine that there is much real resemblance to be traced. Whitman's full-blooded, copious, rank, masculine style must always make him one of the world's great originals—a perennial fountain of health and strength, moral as well as physical. He has the amplitude of the Earth itself, and can no more be thought away than a mountain can. He often indeed reminds me of a great quarry on a mountain side—the great shafts of sunlight and the shadows, the primitive face of the rock itself, the power and the daring of the men at work upon it, the tumbled blocks and masses, materials for endless buildings and the beautiful tufts of weed or flower on inaccessible ledges—a picture most artistic in its very incoherence and formlessness. "Towards Democracy" has a milder radiance, as of the moon compared with the sun—allowing you to glimpse the stars behind. Tender and meditative, less resolute and altogether less massive, it has the quality of the fluid and yielding air rather than of the solid and uncompromising earth.

All the above passages from the writings of Edward Carpenter are to be looked upon as utterances of the self conscious mind about Cosmic Consciousness. In "Towards Democracy" it must be understood that the Cosmic Sense itself speaks; sometimes about itself, sometimes about nature, man, etc., from the point of view of itself. As for instance:

Lo! What mortal eye hath not seen nor ear heard— *A suggestion of what the Cosmic Sense shows him.*

All sorrow finished—the deep, deep ocean of joy opening within—the surface sparkling.

The myriad-formed disclosed, each one and all, all things that are, transfigured—

Being filled with joy, hardly touching the ground, reaching cross-shaped with outstretched arms to the stars, along of the mountains and the forests, habitation of innumeral creatures, singing, joy unending—

As the sun on a dull morning breaking through the clouds—so from behind the sun another sun, from within the body another body—these shattered falling—

Lo! now at last or yet awhile in due time to behold that which ye have so long sought—

O eyes, no wonder you are intent [61 : 200].

That day—the day of deliverance— shall come to you in what place you know not; it shall come but you know not the time. *As it came to him so shall it come to others.*

In the pulpit while you are preaching   Almost literally true of Las Casas.
     the sermon, behold! Suddenly the
     ties and bands—in the cradle, in the coffin, cerements and swathing-clothes
     —shall drop off;

In the prison One shall come; and the chains which are stronger than iron, the
     fetters harder than steel, shall dissolve—you shall go free forever.

In the sick room, amid life-long suffering and tears and weariness, there shall
     be a sound of wings—and you shall know that the end is near—

(O loved one arise, come gently with me—be not too eager—lest joy itself
     should undo you.)

In the field with the plow and the chain-harrow; by the side of your horse in
     the stall;

In the brothel amid indecency and idleness and repairing your and your com-
     panions' dresses;

In the midst of fashionable life, in making and receiving morning calls, in idle-
     ness, and arranging knick-knacks in your drawing-room—even there who
     knows?

It shall duly, at the appointed hour, come [61:231].

There is no peace except where I am,   The Cosmic Sense speaks.
     saith the Lord—

Though you have health—that which is called health—yet without me it is only
     the fair covering of disease;

Though you have love, yet if I be not between and around the lovers, is their
     love only torment and unrest;

Though you have wealth and friends and home—all these shall come and go—
     there is nothing stable or secure, which shall not be taken away.

But I alone remain—I do not change,

As space spreads everywhere, and all things move and change within it, but it
     moves not nor changes,

So I am the space within the soul, of which the space without is but the simili-
     tude and mental image;

Comest thou to inhabit me, thou hast the entrance to all life—death shall no
     longer divide thee from whom thou lovest.

I am the sun that shines upon all creatures from within—gazest thou upon me
     thou shalt be filled with joy eternal.

Be not deceived. Soon this outer world shall drop off—thou shalt slough it
     away as a man sloughs his mortal body.

Learn even now to spread thy wings in that other world—the world of equal-
     ity—to swim in the ocean, my child, of me and my love.

(Ah! have I not taught thee by the semblance of this outer world, by its aliena-
     tions and deaths and mortal sufferings—all for this?

For joy, ah! joy unutterable!) [61:343-4].

III.

SUMMARY.

a. Illumination occurred at the characteristic age—in the thirty-seventh year.

b. And in the characteristic season—in the spring.

c. There was a sense of "inward light," but not strictly the usual experience of subjective light.

d. There was the usual sudden intellectual illumination,

e. And the usual sudden moral elevation.

f. His life was absolutely governed henceforth by the new light that had dawned upon him—"it held his feet."

g. He lost, absolutely, upon illumination, the sense of sin.

h. He clearly saw himself to be immortal.

i. But the best proof of Cosmic Consciousness in his case is his description thereof, which could only be drawn (as he tells us it was) from his own experience.

PART V.

ADDITIONAL—SOME OF THEM LESSER, IMPERFECT AND DOUBTFUL INSTANCES

CHAPTER 1.

The Twilight.

THE main purpose of this Fifth Part is to illustrate the inevitable fact that granted that there is such a mental faculty as Cosmic Consciousness and that it has been brought forth, as were the others, by gradual evolution, there must exist minds on all intermediate planes between mere self consciousness and the fullest Cosmic Consciousness so far produced by the onward and upward march of the race.

If we think of the oncoming of the Cosmic Sense as the rising of a sun in the individual life it becomes clear, carrying out the analogy as we may probably do without fear of material error, that between the comparative darkness of the night of mere self consciousness and the light of the day which is Cosmic Consciousness there must exist an.interval of what may fairly be called twilight—a region in which the sun of the Cosmic Sense will give more or less light, although not yet risen and perhaps never to rise in the life of that person. This twilight is often distinctly traceable (as in the case of Dante and Behmen) in lives that later become fully illumined. After momentary illumination, too, in the lesser cases a glow is left lasting for years, as if the sun, after appearing for a few moments above the horizon, remained immediately below it, very slowly descending, like the physical sun in northern latitudes about the time of the summer solstice. In another class of cases the individual spiritual life may be compared to a winter day within the arctic circle. The sun slowly approaches the horizon, its path slanting gradually upward until the fiery ball nearly touches the earth's rim, passes slowly along the southeast, south, southwest, lighting the landscape but never showing its dazzling face—effecting a genuine illumination but without rising—yielding a glow which is in strong contrast to the darkness of night but which is yet infinitely short (in splendor and especially in fructifying power) of that of the direct solar rays. Such a case was one of the most noteworthy in this Fifth Part, that, namely, of Richard Jefferies.

To-day innumerable men and women must be living in this twilight. Undoubtedly many cases of so-called conversion are simply instances of, generally sudden, spiritual ascent from the average self conscious level into the region of greater or less splendor, according to the altitude reached, which lies between that and Cosmic Consciousness. And if Carlyle's opinion [59:150], which is in full accord with what we know of mental evolution—that "conversion," namely, "was not known to the ancients but has come to light for the first time in our modern era," be accepted, does this not clearly indicate a gradual spiritual ascent of a vast section of the human mind? Cases of conversion occurring in the young are not here noticed. These are probably generally, if not always, cases of more or less sudden spiritual ascent within the region strictly belonging to self consciousness and do not therefore concern us. But cases of so-called conversion occurring at thirty or thirty-five years of age (such as that of C. G. Finney, chapter 13, infra) are in themselves more striking phenomena and are doubtless always, or nearly always, instances of ascent into the region which lies beyond the limits of the ordinary self conscious mind.

One word may be said in this place to guard against a possible suspicion. In the reporting of *no case* was the reporter (the person having the experience) prompted by word or sign. Every one of the following reports (as is manifestly true of those which are included in Part IV) is given absolutely spontaneously and nearly always without any knowledge of the phenomena belonging to other cases, and *certainly* without being influenced in narration by a knowledge of other cases. In view of the extraordinary uniformity of the accounts given (as far as these go) it is important that this fact should be clearly realized.

CHAPTER 2.

Moses.

RENAN tells us that the oldest documents in which Moses is mentioned are four hundred to five hundred years posterior to the date of the Exodus, at which time Moses lived, if he lived at all: "Les documents les plus anciens sur Moise sont posterieurs de quatre cents ou cinq cents ans á l'époque ou ce personage a du vivre" [137: 160]. Could there have been older, lost, written narratives, upon which those we have were based? Or could the long interval of over four hundred years have been bridged by tradition in such manner as to make the accounts we have of any value? It is hard to say. But if we should dare believe that the incidents in this man's personal history given in Exodus are in any sense reliable (they cannot, of course, be expected to be accurate), then we have in the great Egypto-Israelitish lawgiver a probable case of Cosmic Consciousness. The burning bush that he saw in Horeb, which was not consumed by the fire, would then be the form taken in tradition by the subjective light: "And the angel of the Lord appeared unto him in a flame of fire out of the midst of a bush; and he looked, and behold the bush burned with fire and the bush was not consumed" [11: 3: 2]. And the shining of his face: "And it came to pass, when Moses came down from Mount Sinai with the two tables of the testimony in Moses' hand when he came down from the mount, that Moses wist not that the skin of his face shone or sent forth beams by reason of his speaking with Him. And when Aaron and all the children of Israel saw Moses, behold the skin of his face shone; and they were afraid to come nigh him" [11: 34:

29-30]. This shining of Moses' face, when he descended Sinai, would be the "transfiguration" characteristic of Cosmic Consciousness.

At the time that Moses saw the "fire," it would seem that he was already married and had sons [11:4:20], but he was, however, still young, for he lived and labored for forty years thereafter. It seems likely that he was at or near the usual age of illumination at the time. He was at first alarmed at the "fire," or light, as is usual: "And Moses hid his face, for he was afraid to look upon God" [11:3:6]. He distrusted his fitness for the task laid upon him: "Who am I that I should go unto Pharaoh" [11:3:11]? just as Mohammed distrusted himself. The "voice" giving more or less explicit commands is a common phenomenon. It is doubtful if this voice is ever heard with the outward ear—perhaps occasionally—more likely never. The light is almost certainly always subjective, and no doubt the voice also. But with the Cosmic Sense comes a consciousness of certain facts, and the impression made upon the person is that he has been told these, and if so, then by some one—some person (but, of course, not by a human being)—hence the voice of God to Moses, the voice of the Father to Jesus, the voice of Christ to Paul, the voice of Gabriel to Mohammed, the voice of Beatrice to Dante. Who the person thought to be heard (into whose mouth the teaching is put), shall be supposed to be, will be determined by the mental habitudes of the subject and of his age and nation.

What, now, was actually "told" Moses—if we may believe the report—and it seems credible—is (as far as the present writer can judge) exactly what would have been told him by the Cosmic Sense: The unity, power and goodness of God, namely, and that he should work for the people, of whom he was one. It seems likely, moreover, that there came upon Moses at about the epoch of the "burning bush" a great intellectual and moral expansion. The tables of the law (doubtless composed by him) go to prove this—so does the recognition of his superiority and authority, apparently so freely rendered by a people not especially inclined (it would seem) to surrender their own ideas and place themselves under the control of a leader having no hereditary or priestly jurisdiction.

Since the above was written the editor has had a letter from C. M. C., whose case is included in this volume (Chapter 29, infra), in which she gives an experience so very similar to that of "the burning bush," that it is impossible to resist the temptation to quote it. She says: "Two lady friends and I were out driving a few days ago. It was a lovely, perfect morning. As we passed along the shaded country road, we got out of the carriage to gather the purple aster, which was blooming in all its perfection by the wayside. I was in a strangely joyous mood—all nature seemed sweet and pensive. The asters had never before seemed so beautiful to me. I looked at the large bunches we had gathered with growing amazement at their brightness, and it was some little time before I realized that this was unusual. But I soon found that I was seeing the aura of the flowers. A wonderful light shone out from every little petal and flower, and the whole was a blaze of splendor. I trembled with rapture—it was a 'burning bush.'[2] It cannot be described. The flowers looked like gems or stars, the color of amethysts, so clear and transparent, so still and intense, a subtle living glow. The veil almost parted; not quite, or I should have seen them smiling and conscious and looking at me. What a moment that was! I thrill at the thought of it."

CHAPTER 3.

Gideon, Surnamed Jerubbaal.

Thirteenth century B. C.

And the angel of the Lord came and sat under the oak which was in Ophrah, that pertained unto Joash the Abiezrite: and his son Gideon was beating out wheat in the winepress, to hide it from the Midianites. And the angel of the Lord appeared unto him, and said unto him: The Lord is with thee, thou mighty man of valor. And Gideon said unto him, Oh, my Lord, if the Lord be with us, why then is all this befallen us? and where be all his wondrous works which our fathers told us of, saying, Did not the Lord bring us

up from Egypt? but now the Lord hath cast us off, and delivered us into the
hand of Midian. And the Lord looked upon him, and said, Go in this thy
might, and save Israel from the hand of Midian: have not I sent thee? And
he said unto him, Oh, Lord, wherewith shall I save Israel? behold, my family
is the poorest in Manasseh, and I am the least in my father's house. And the
Lord said unto him, Surely I will be with thee, and thou shalt smite the
Midianites as one man. And he said unto him, If now I have found grace in
thy sight, then show me a sign that it is thou that talkest with me. Depart
not hence, I pray thee, until I come unto thee, and bring forth my present,
and lay it before thee. And he said, I will tarry until thou come again. And
Gideon went in, and made ready a kid, and unleavened cakes of an ephah of
meal: the flesh he put in a basket, and he put the broth in a pot, and brought
it out unto him under the oak, and presented it. And the angel of God said
unto him, Take the flesh and the unleavened cakes, and lay them upon this
rock, and pour out the broth. And he did so. Then the angel of the Lord put
forth the end of the staff that was in his hand and touched the flesh and the
unleavened cakes; and there went up fire out of the rock and consumed the
flesh and the unleavened cakes; and the angel of the Lord departed out of his
sight. And Gideon saw that he was the angel of the Lord; and Gideon said,
Alas, O Lord God! forasmuch as I have seen the angel of the Lord face to face.
And the Lord said unto him, Peace be unto thee; fear not: thou shalt not die.
Then Gideon built an altar there unto the Lord, and called it Jehovahshalom:
unto this day it is yet in Ophrah of the Abiezrites [12:6:11-24].

Renan's comment on the life of this man would, were it taken
seriously, make him, if not a great, at all events a case of Cosmic
Consciousness. He says: ''Circumstances of which we are ignorant inclined him to the exclusive worship of Jahveh. This conversion was attributed to a vision, and it is possible that in the
case of Gideon, as in that of Moses, a sensible experience may have
intervened. It would appear that there occurred to him one of the
apparitions of flame in which Jahveh is supposed to reveal Himself'' [137:320].

Nothing definite can be said in this case. Gideon's age at the
time is not known. The subjective light (if he experienced it),
his sudden conversion from a lower to a higher religious plane
(which seems pretty certain), his rapid elevation in the esteem
of his countrymen, his long and strenuous life, his marked recognition of God, his refusal to reign in any other sense than as the
agent of Jahveh—all these point to the possibility of his illumination.

CHAPTER 4.

Isaiah.

HAD "the greatest of the Hebrew prophets" the Cosmic Sense? It does not seem unlikely. As Isaiah lived and wrote for thirty-nine years after his "vision" it might easily be that he was something over thirty years of age at that time—that is to say, in the year of the death of Uzziah, B. C. 740. The vision itself, as he describes it, suggests illumination—the oncoming of Cosmic Consciousness. Isaiah writes:

In the year that King Uzziah died I saw the Lord sitting upon a throne, high and lifted up, and his train filled the temple. Above him stood the seraphims: each one had six wings; with twain he covered his face, and with twain he covered his feet, and with twain he did fly. And one cried unto another, and said, Holy, Holy, Holy is the Lord of hosts; the whole earth is full of his glory. And the foundations of the threshold were moved at the voice of him that cried, and the house was filled with smoke. Then said I, Woe is me! for I am undone; because I am a man of unclean lips, for mine eyes have seen the King, the Lord of hosts. Then flew one of the seraphim unto me, having a live coal in his hand, which he had taken with the tongs from off the altar: and he touched my mouth with it and said, Lo, this hath touched thy lips; and thine iniquity is taken away, and thy sin purged. And I heard the voice of the Lord, saying, Whom shall I send, and who will go for us? Then I said, Here am I; send me [Isaiah: 6: 1-8].

The chief points to be noticed are: (1) He saw God. (2) He saw that God *is* the Cosmos. (3) The expression "the house was filled with smoke" ought (if the hypothesis is correct) rather to read "with light" or "with flame," since it should refer to the subjective light; but it seems doubtful whether the Hebrew word Ashan ever means "light" or "flame." If, however, it is connected philologically with the Sanskrit Arman it ought to be capable of bearing an analogous interpretation. (4) He loses the sense of sin.

CHAPTER 5.

The Case of Lî R.

THE above named, who is commonly called Lâo-tsze (the old philosopher), was born about 604 B. C., in Honan, China. For part of his life, perhaps a large part, he was curator in the Royal

Library. Kung-fu-tse (Confucius) visited Lî in 517, when he (Lî) was in his eighty-eighth year. In the course of their conversation Lî said to Kung: "The men about whom you talk are dead and their bones are mouldered to dust; only their words are left. Moreover when the superior man gets his opportunity he mounts aloft; but when the time is against him he is carried along by the force of circumstances. I have heard that a good merchant, though he have rich treasures safely stored, appears as if he were poor; and that the superior man, though his virtue be complete, is yet to outward seeming, stupid. Put away your proud air and many desires—your insinuating habit and wild will. They are of no advantage to you; this is all I have to tell you." Kung is made to say to his disciples after the interview: "I know birds can fly, fish swim and animals run. But the runner may be snared, the swimmer hooked, and the flyer shot by the arrow. But there is the dragon: I cannot tell how he mounts on the wind through the clouds and rises to heaven. To-day I have seen Lâo-tsze, and can only compare him to the dragon" [166:34]. It seems to have been after this meeting that Lâo-tsze wrote his book on the Tâo and its attributes in five thousand characters. After writing the book he is said to have gone away toward the northwest. It is not known when or where he died.

What is this Tâo? It is said to keep those who possess it young. A famous Tâoist, an old man, is represented as being addressed as follows: "You are old, sir, while your complexion is like that of a child; how is it so?" And the reply is: "I became acquainted with the Tâo" [166:24]. In the first translation of the Tâo Teh King into any Western language Tâo is taken in the sense of Ratio or the Supreme Reason. Abel Remusat's account of the character Tâo is: "It does not seem possible to me to translate this word except by Logos in the triple sense of Sovereign Being, Reason and the Word." Remusat's successor in the chair of Chinese at Paris, Stanislas Julien, who made a translation of the Tâo Teh King, decided that it was impossible to understand by Tâo Primordial Reason or Sublime Intelligence, and concluded that the Tâo was devoid of action, of thought, of judgment and of intelligence—in fact, he seems (without saying so) to have made the word synonymous (as it doubtless is) with Nirvâna [166 : 12]. Finally he translates it "a way" or "the way," in the sense of "I am the way, the truth and the life," and so again it becomes synonymous with "Christ," with "Nirvâna" and with Cosmic Consciousness.

Lâo-tsze speaks of certain results which flow from the cultivation of the Tâo, and if we will rightly understand his language we shall find that it holds good of those who have the Cosmic Sense. He says: "He who is skillful in managing his life travels on land without having to shun rhinoceros or tiger, and enters a host without having to avoid buff coat or sharp weapon. The rhinoceros finds no place in him into which to thrust its horn, nor the tiger a place in which to fix its claws, nor the weapon a place to admit its point. And for what reason? Because there is in him no place of death." And again: "He who has in himself abundantly the attributes (of the Tâo) is like an infant. Poisonous insects will not sting him; fierce beasts will not seize him; birds of prey will not strike him" [166 : 25].

To come down to our own day, here in America, to illustrate this passage. The writer has seen Walt Whitman on Long Island, New York, remain on a verandah a whole long summer evening, the air being literally loaded with mosquitoes. These would settle upon him in large numbers, but he did not appear to notice them. From time to time he waved a palm leaf fan which he held in his hand, but did not use it or his other hand to drive away or kill any of the mosquitoes. He did not appear to be bitten or in any way annoyed by the small creatures, who were driving the rest of the party almost wild. It is well known that Walt Whitman came and went freely and with impunity for years, off and on as he pleased, among the most dangerous people of New York. It has never been said that he was at any time molested or even spoken roughly to. As to the life of the possessor of the Tâo (if that is Cosmic Consciousness) being indestructible by tigers, or other wild beasts or armed men, that is the simple truth.

Again it is said of the Tâo that its "highest excellence is like that of water. The excellence of water appears in its benefiting all things, and in its occupying, without striving to the contrary, the low ground which all men dislike. Hence (its way) is near to that of the Tâo. There is nothing in the world more soft and weak than water, and yet for attacking things that are firm and strong there is nothing that can take precedence of it. Every one in the world knows that the soft overcomes the hard, and the weak the strong, but no one is able to carry it out in practice" [166: 30-1].

So Whitman says of the Cosmic Sense: "What is commonest, cheapest, meanest, easiest, is Me." And again: "There is nothing so soft but it makes a hub for the wheeled universe."

It is said further that: "It is the way of the Tâo to act without (thinking of) acting, to conduct affairs without (feeling) the trouble of them, to taste without discerning any flavor, to consider the small as great, and the few as many, and to recompense injury with kindness" [166: 31].

Here follow a few passages from Lî R's book, the Tâo Teh King, accompanied by parallel passages from the sayings or writings of other men possessed of Cosmic Consciousness:

Ordinary men look bright and intelligent, while I alone seem to be benighted. They look full of discrimination, while I alone am dull and confused. I seem to be carried about as on the sea, drifting as if I had nowhere to rest. All men have their spheres of action, while I alone seem dull and incapable, like a rude borderer. (Thus) I alone am different from other men, but I value the nursing-mother [the Tâo] [166: 63].

"Behold this swarthy face, these gray eyes, This beard, the white wool unclipt upon my neck, My brown hands and the silent manner of me without charm" [193 : 105].

"The foxes have holes, and the birds of the heaven have nests; but the Son of man hath not where to lay his head" [14 : 8 : 20].

The partial becomes complete; the crooked, straight; the empty, full; the worn out, new. He whose (desires) are few gets them; he whose (desires) are many goes astray [166: 65].

"The felon steps forth from the prison, the insane becomes sane . . . the throat that was unsound is sound, the lungs of the consumptive are resumed, the poor distressed head is free" [193 : 332].

The Tâo, considered as unchanging, has no name. Though in its primordial simplicity it may be small, the whole world dares not deal with (one embodying) it as a minister. If a feudal

"It is like a grain of mustard seed, which, when it is sown upon the earth, though it be less than all the seeds that are upon the earth, yet when it is sown, groweth up and becometh greater than all the herbs, and putteth out great branches; so that the birds

prince or king could guard or hold it, all would spontaneously submit themselves to him. Heaven and earth (under his guidance) unite together and send down the sweet dew, which, without the directions of men, reaches equally everywhere as of its own accord [166 : 74].

To him who holds in his hands the Great Image (of the invisible Tâo) the whole world repairs. Men resort to him, and receive no hurt, but (find) rest, peace, and the feeling of ease. Music and dainties will make the passing guest stop (for a time). But though the Tâo as it comes from the mouth seems insipid and has no flavor, though it seems not worth being looked at or listened to, the use of it is inexhaustible [166 : 77].

"The natural man receiveth not the things of the spirit of God [of the Cosmic Sense], for they are foolishness unto him" [20 : 2 : 14]. The teachings of the Cosmic Sense are always tasteless and insipid at first, but their use "is inexhaustible."

of the heaven can lodge under the shadow thereof" [15 : 4 : 31].

Without going outside his door, one understands (all that takes place) under the sky; without looking out from his window, one sees the Tâo of heaven. The farther that one goes out (from himself) the less he knows [166 : 89].

"In vain the speeding or shyness,
In vain objects stand leagues off and assume manifold shapes" [193 : 54].
"I but use you a minute, then I resign you, stallion,
Why do I need your paces when I myself out-gallop them?
Even as I stand or sit passing faster than you" [193 : 55].

"What is commonest, cheapest, meanest, easiest, is Me" [193 : 39].
"Will you seek afar off? You surely come back at last" [193 : 175].

He who gets as his own all under heaven does so by giving himself no trouble (with that end). If one takes trouble (with that end) he is not equal to getting as his own all under heaven [166 : 90].

"To see no possession but you may possess it, enjoying all without labor or purchase, abstracting the feast yet not abstracting one particle of it,
To take the best of the farmer's farm and the rich man's elegant villa, and the chaste blessings of the well married couple, and the fruits of orchards and the flowers of gardens,
To gather the minds of men out of their brains, the love out of their hearts" [193 : 127].

He who has in himself abundantly the attributes (of the Tâo) is like an infant. Poisonous insects will not sting him; birds of prey will not strike him [166 : 99].

He who knows (the Tâo) does not (care to) speak (about it); he who is (ever ready to) speak about it does not know it. He (who knows it) will keep his mouth shut and close the portals

"Whosoever shall not receive the kingdom of God as a little child, he shall in no wise enter therein" [15 : 10 : 15].

It is curious that men with Cosmic Consciousness will not speak of it. Years ago, when the writer was as intimate with Walt Whitman as he ever was with any of his brothers he tried hard to get Whitman to tell him something about it (for he knew

(of his nostrils). He will blunt his sharp points and unravel the complications of things; he will attemper his brightness, and bring himself into agreement with the obscurity (of others). This is called "the Mysterious Agreement." (Such an one) cannot be treated familiarly or distantly;

well there was something special to tell and Whitman knew that he knew), but he could never extract a word from the poet. These men put it in their writings in an impersonal manner, but will hardly ever speak face to face of their personal experiences; these are too sacred to be dealt with in that manner.

he is beyond all consideration of profit or injury—of nobility or meanness; he is the noblest man under heaven [166:100].

(Its) admirable words can purchase honor; (its) admirable deeds can raise their performer above others. Even men who are not good are not abandoned by it [166:105].

"Then came Peter and said to him, Lord, how oft shall my brother sin against me and I forgive him? Until seven times? Jesus said unto him, I say not unto thee, until seven times, but until seventy times seven" [14:18:21].

(It is the way of the Tâo) to act without (thinking of) acting; to conduct affairs without (feeling the) trouble of them; to taste without discerning any flavor;

"But I say unto you, Love your enemies, and pray for them that persecute you" [14:5:44].

to consider what is small is great, and a few as many; and to recompense injury with kindness [166:106].

That whereby the rivers and seas are able to receive the homage and tribute of all the valley streams, is their skill in being lower than they; it is thus that they are the kings of them all.

"Whosoever would become great among you shall be your minister; and whosoever would be first among you shall be your servant" [14:20:26].

So it is that the sage (ruler), wishing to be above men, puts himself by his words below them, and, wishing to be before them, places his person behind them [166:109].

All the world says that, while my Tâo is great, it yet appears to be inferior (to other systems of teaching). Now it is just its greatness that makes it seem to be inferior.

Consider and compare the lives and teachings of Gautama, Jesus, Paul, Whitman, Carpenter and nearly all the great cases.

If it were like any other (system), for long would its smallness have been known!

But I have three precious things which I prize and hold fast. The first is gentleness; the second is economy, and the third is shrinking from taking precedence of others.

With that gentleness I can be bold; with that economy I can be liberal; shrinking from taking precedence of others, I can become a vessel of the highest honor. Nowadays they give up gentleness and are all for being bold; economy, and are all for being liberal; the hindmost place, and seek only to be foremost; (all of which the end is) death [166:110].

Sincere words are not fine; fine words are not sincere; those who are skilled (in the Tâo) do not dispute

"Logic and sermons never convince" [193:53].
"I cannot beguile the time with talk.

(about it); the disputatious are not skilled in it. Those who know (the Tâo) are not extensively learned; the extensively learned do not know it [166 : 123].

In the learned coterie sitting constrained and still, for learning inures not to me" [193 : 249].

"If any man thinketh that he is wise among you in this world, let him become a fool, that he may become wise" [20 : 3 : 18].

CHAPTER 6.

Socrates.

BOTH by his moral qualities and intellectual gifts, Socrates seems to take rank with the foremost men of all history. But it would be obviously absurd to argue that because of these facts he was a case of Cosmic Consciousness, and that among the marks of Cosmic Consciousness are moral elevation and intellectual enlightenment. Xenophon tells us that Socrates claimed that "intimations were given him by a God" [201: 350]. He says that "Socrates had been admired beyond all men for the cheerfulness and tranquillity with which he lived" [201: 505], and he further quotes Socrates as saying: "I would not admit to any man that he has lived either better or with more pleasure than myself" [201: 506]. These indications, without being absolute, suggest strongly that Socrates had the Cosmic Sense. It is well known that he had exceptional health and constitutional strength, and it seems that at the time of his death, though over seventy years of age, both his mind and body were as vigorous as ever. Also it seems clear that he had a very strong conviction of immortality, though possibly this did not amount to the *sense* of immortality which belongs to Cosmic Consciousness. His optimism, also one of the marks of the Cosmic Sense, must not be forgotten, nor must his far more than average personal attractiveness. The phenomenon of the "sign," "voice," "god," "genius" or "dæmon" is said to have dated from his early years.

On the other hand, Lelut [88: 313] dates what he considers as Socrates' insanity* from the siege of Potidæa, B. C. 429, when

---

* For Lelut is a typical "common sense" man and to him all mystics are lunatics.

Socrates would have been about forty years old. What happened on this occasion is given as follows in the "Symposium" [127: 71]: "One morning he was thinking about something which he could not resolve; he would not give it up, but continued thinking from early dawn until noon. There he stood, fixed in thought; and at noon attention was drawn to him, and the rumor ran through the wondering crowd that Socrates had been standing and thinking about something ever since the break of day. At last, in the evening, after supper, some Ionians, out of curiosity (I should explain that this was not in winter but in summer), brought out their mats and slept in the open air that they might watch him and see whether he would stand all night. There he stood all night until the following morning; and, with the return of light, he offered up a prayer to the sun and went his way."

If, now, we accept this narrative as fact we shall possibly prefer Elam's explanation of it to that of Lelut. It runs: "It is not impossible that he who had turned his back upon an old, worn-out, effete system of philosophy, and who out of the depths of his own thought had eliminated the great truths of the immortality of the soul, and the certainty of a future state of rewards and punishments; who from a chaotic polytheism had arrived at the belief in One God, the Creator and upholder of all things—it is not impossible that such a man may have been so wrapt and lost in the opening immensity and profundity of these considerations as to become insensible to surrounding objects for even so long a time as is here mentioned" [88: 314].

Let us add the testimony of Balzac in "Louis Lambert" [5: 127], in which a state analogous to catalepsy is described as accompanying illumination in that case.

If we put all the facts together—the age of Socrates at the time, the character of the man physically, intellectually and morally—we may not be far wrong if we conclude that he belonged to the order of men of which this volume treats.

CHAPTER 7.

Roger Bacon.

1214-1294 (?).

NEITHER this nor any other man should be classed among the members of the new race because he had an extraordinary wit, for some of the greatest human intellects are clearly outside Cosmic Consciousness; neither would any extraordinary development of this faculty alone lead a man into it. It is not, then, because of his intelligence, extraordinary as this seems to have been, that the question, Was Roger Bacon a case of Cosmic Consciousness? is raised here. On the other hand, unfortunately, no details, such as instantaneous illumination or the subjective light, have come down to us as having existed in this case. All we have are references of Bacon's to a certain "Master Peter," from whom he received extraordinary assistance in his philosophical work. And the question is, Does not this Master Peter bear the same relation to Bacon that Christ bore to Paul, Beatrice to Dante, Seraphita to Balzac, Gabriel to Mohammed? For we must never forget the essential quality of the Cosmic Conscious mind.

This, then, according to Charles [58], is the way matters stood between Bacon and Master Peter. Let each judge for himself who or what Master Peter may have been. Charles has been speaking of the intellectual stir and life of the time, and goes on: "In the midst of it all under what flag shall the Oxford student fight? What master shall he choose among so many illustrious doctors? He contemplates at its most brilliant focus this science of which his contemporaries are so proud, and the sentiment he feels is not enthusiasm but scorn. He listens to the most eloquent voices, but for master he chooses not an Alexander of Hales, or an Albert, but an obscure person of whom history knows nothing. This apparent renaissance seems to him a veritable decadence. To him these Dominicans and Franciscans are ignorant men when compared with Robert de Lincoln and his friends, and the moderns generally barbarians as contrasted with the Greeks and the Arabs. Experience, he thinks, is worth more than all the writings of Aristotle, and a little grammar and mathematics more useful than all the metaphysics of the schools. So he applied himself passionately to these disdained sciences. He learns Arabic, Greek, Hebrew, Chaldee—four languages—in an age in which Albert knew only one of them and in which St. Thomas is glad to use the bad translations of William de Morbeke. He reads with avidity the books of the ancients, studies mathematics, alchemy, optics. Before reforming the education of his age he reconstructs his own education, and to this end associates himself with mathematicians and obscure savants in preference to the most renowned philosophers. Alexander de Hales inspires him with nothing but scorn. Albert, in his eyes, is ignorant and presumptuous, and his influence fatal to the epoch over which its dominance extends. William of Auvergne alone merits respect. The friends whom he values are less celebrated persons—William of Shirwood, according to him, much more learned than Albert; Campano de Novarre, mathematician and arithmetician; Nicolas, tutor of Amansy de Montfort; John of London, believed by Jeff to be John Peckham, and, above all, the most unknown, according to him, the most learned of the men of that time, him whom he venerates as his master, admires as the living example of true science and whom he names 'Master Peter.'

"If we judge by the portrait Bacon has drawn of him, this is a singular person. Master Peter is a solitary, as careful to avoid renown as others to seek it; taking pains to veil and hide his science from men, and who refuses men the truth which they are not worthy to receive. Master Peter does not belong to any of the powerful church orders of the day; he does not teach, and desires neither students nor admirers; he shuns the importunity of the vulgar. He is proud, and to his disdain of the crowd he unites an immense faith in himself. He lives isolated, content with the mental wealth he has, which he could multiply many times if he desired so to do. Did he deign to fill a professor's chair the whole world would come to Paris to hear him; should he be willing to

attach himself to some sovereign no treasury could pay the value
of his marvellous science. But he despises the mass made up of
madmen tainted with the subtleties of law, charlatans who by
their sophisms dishonor philosophy, render medicine ridiculous
and falsify theology itself. The most clear-sighted of them are
blind, or should they make vain efforts to use their eyes the truth
dazzles them. They are like bats in the twilight—the less light
there is the better they see. He alone looks face to face at the
radiant sun. Hidden in a retreat which gives him security with
silence, Master Peter leaves to others long discourses and the war
of words to give himself up to the study of chemistry, the natural
sciences, mathematics, medicine, and, above all, experience, of
which he alone in this age realizes the importance. His disciple
salutes him by the name of 'Master of Experience,' which re-
places in his case the ambitious and sonorous titles of the other
doctors.

"Experience reveals to him the secrets of nature, the curative
art, celestial phenomena and their relation to those of earth; he
disdains nothing and does not shrink from applying science to
the realities of the common earth; he would blush if he found
a layman, an old woman, a soldier or a peasant better informed
than himself in matters that concern each.

"To cast and forge metals, to manipulate silver, gold and all
minerals,* to invent deadly instruments of war, new arms, to make
a science of agriculture and of the labor of the rustic, not to neglect surveying nor the art of building, to seek with diligence the
basis of truth hidden even under the charms of the sorcerer, under
the impostures and artifices of jugglers—this is the work to which
he has devoted his life. He has examined all, learned all, separated everywhere the true from the false, and through the void
and sterile wilderness has discovered a practicable route. Is it
desired to hasten the progress of science? Here is the only man
equal to the task. Should he make up his mind to divulge his
secrets, kings and princes would crown him with honors and gifts,

---

* "In the labor of engines and trades and the labor of fields I find the developments,
and find the eternal meanings" [193 : 169].

and in an expedition against the infidel he would render more service to St. Louis than half—yes, than all—his army.*

"It is from this great unknown, this undiscovered genius, whose name has remained unregistered in the history of science, that (according to him) Bacon learned languages, astronomy, mathematics, experimental science, everything, in fact, that he knew. Compared with this Master Peter, the students, professors, writers, masters, thinkers of the universities were dull, lumpish, insensate [compare Paul, Bacon, Behmen, Mohammed; it is indeed the universal testimony that when the Cosmic Sense appears the wisdom of self consciousness is reduced to dust and ashes]. The piety of Bacon toward his unknown master ought to rescue this latter from the obscurity in which he is buried, but it seems impossible to identify him among the infinite number of savants of the same name who are to be found in the catalogues" [58: 14 et seq.].

CHAPTER 8.

Blaise Pascal.

1623-1772.

HE was born on the 19th of June, 1623. As a child, boy and young man, he was exceptionally precocious—in this respect comparable to Bacon. It is said that, although his parents endeavored to restrain his mental development, yet "at the age of ten he had propounded an acoustic theory in advance of the views then entertained; at twelve he had evolved geometry from his own reflections; and at fifteen he composed a treatise on conic sections which Descartes refused to believe in as having proceeded from so young a mind" [88: 329].

Pascal's health was all his life delicate. He was probably always a perfectly moral man, though fond of gaiety and the social pleasures of his time and country.

---

*The above account of Master Peter is collected by Charles from Bacon's "Opus Tertium," "Opus Minus," his "De Septem Peccatis," and other works.

He gave abundant evidence throughout his whole life that he possessed in an unusual degree the mental honesty and earnestness that seems always to belong to those who attain to the Cosmic Sense.

In November, 1654, he being then thirty-one and a half years old, something happened which radically altered Pascal's life. From that date he practically abandoned the world and became and remained, until his death, markedly religious and charitable. From that date, however, his life was very secluded and few details appear to be known.

Bright as his intellect was before November, 1654, it was still brighter afterwards. About a year subsequent to that date he began the "Provincial Letters," and later wrote his "Pensées," both of which works (though the latter is only a series of notes for a book to be written) show extraordinary mental qualities. It is safe to say that he could not have written either of them before the above date.

A few days after Pascal's death a servant felt by chance something hard and thick under the cloth of his doublet. Ripping the seam in the neighborhood he found a folded parchment, and within this a folded paper. These both bore writing in Pascal's hand, the words of which are those here given. Both parchment and paper were taken to Pascal's sister, Madame Périer, who showed them to some friend. They all saw at once that these words thus written by Pascal in duplicate and preserved by him with so much care and trouble(removing them himself, as he did, from garment to garment), must have had in his eyes a profound meaning. Some time after the death of Madame Périer (which happened twenty-five years after the death of her brother), her children communicated the documents to a friar, who was an intimate friend of the family. He copied the document and wrote some pages of commentary upon it, to which Marguerite Périer added some further pages. These commentaries are now lost, as is also the parchment. The paper copy, however, in Pascal's hand, is still extant in the Bibliotheque Nationale, Paris. It was Cordocet who gave the document the name of "Pascal's Mystic Amulette" [112a: 156].

Translated into English the words of the amulet are as follows: "The year of grace 1654, Monday, 23 November, day of St. Clement, Pope and Martyr. From about half-past ten in the evening until about half-past twelve, midnight, FIRE. God of Abraham, God of Isaac, God of Jacob, not of the philosophers nor of the Wise. Assurance, joy, assurance, feeling, joy, peace. GOD OF JESUS CHRIST, my God and thy God. Thy God shall be my God. Forgotten of the world and of all except GOD. He is only found in the ways taught in the Gospel. THE SUBLIMITY OF THE HUMAN SOUL. Just Father, the world has not known thee but I have known thee. Joy, joy, joy, tears of joy. I do not separate myself from thee. They left me behind, me a fountain of living water. My God, do not leave me. Let me not be separated from thee eternally. This is eternal life that they should know thee the only true God and him whom thou hast sent. JESUS CHRIST—JESUS CHRIST. I have separated myself from him; I have fled, renounced, crucified him. Let me not be forever separated from him. One is saved only by the teaching of the Gospel. RECONCILIATION TOTAL AND SWEET. Total submission to JESUS CHRIST and to my DIRECTOR. Continual joy for the days of my life on earth. I shall not forget what you have taught me. Amen." *

---

* Lelut [112a : 154] gives the exact words of the amulet, their *form and arrangement*, as follows

L'an de grace 1654
Lundy 23e novbre jour de St Clement
Pape et m. et autres au martirologe Romain
veille de St. Crisogone m. et autres, etc. . . .
Depuis environ dix heures et demi du soir
jusques environ minuit et demi.

_____FEU_____

Dieu d'Abraham.   Dieu d'Isaac.   Dieu de Jacob
non des philosophes et des savans

No one who has read this book so far will have, I think, the least doubt as to the meaning of the words of the amulet.

The subjective light was evidently strongly marked. Immediately following it comes the sense of liberation, salvation, joy, content, intense thankfulness. Then the realization of the grandeur of the human soul, immediately followed by the rapture of the realization of God. He glances back and sees how futile his life and ambitions have so far been. Then realizes his present reconcilement with the cosmos and that the rest of his life must be continual joy.

The words of the amulet, the care and secrecy with which it was preserved, its date in reference to Pascal's age, Pascal's splendid intellect and previous character so far as known to us, the change in his life, synchronous with the date of the amulet,

---

Certitude joye certitude, sentiment, veue joye paix.
Dieu de Jésus christ
Deum meum et Deum vestrum
Jeh. 20. 17.
Ton Dieu sera mon Dieu.   Ruth.
Oubly du monde et de tout hormis Dieu
Il ne se trouve que par les voyes enseignées
dans l'Evangile. Grandeur de l'ame humaine.
Père juste, le monde ne t'a point
connu. mais je t'ai connu.   Jeh. 17
Joye, joye, joye, et pleurs de joys_____
Je m'en suis separé_____
Dereliquerunt me fontem aquæ vivæ_____
mon Dieu me quitterez vous_____
que je n'en sois pas separé éternellement.

Cette est la vie éternelle qu'ils te connaissent
Seul vray Dieu et celuy que tu as envoyé
Jésus christ_____
Jésus christ_____
Je m'en suis separé je l'ay fuy renoncé, crucifé,_____
que je n'en sois jamais separé_____
Il ne se conserve que par les voyes ensignées
dans l'Evangile
Renonciation totale et douce_____
Soûmission totale à Jésus christ et à mon Directeur.
éternellement en joye pour un jour d'exercice sur la terre
non obliviscar sermones tuos. Amen.

his moral exaltation and intellectual illumination from and after that time; above all, the subjective light, which seems to have been more than usually pronounced and longer than usually continued, though in the case of John Yepes it is said to have lasted a whole night [112:108]. All these taken together make it certain to the mind of the writer that Pascal was a case of Cosmic Consciousness. Of course, it has been said of him, as it was of Jesus, Paul, Blake, and others, that Pascal was insane; but I see no evidence of anything of the kind. The words of the amulet bear testimony to having been written immediately after illumination (before he went to bed that night, it would seem). They are, therefore, naturally somewhat incoherent. They bear witness to joy, triumph, enlightenment, not to disease. The man who writes them has just seen the Brahmic Splendor and felt the Brahmic Bliss. That is all.

CHAPTER 9.

Benedict Spinoza.

1632-1677.

BORN at Amsterdam, November 24th, 1632, the son of a Portuguese Jew and a Jew himself until the age of twenty-four, when he was "solemnly cut off from the Commonwealth of Israel" [87b:400]. He was an accomplished Latinist and an enthusiastic disciple of Descartes, though he ceased to be his follower by the end of the five years of concentrated thought and study that followed his excommunication. This is not the place to insist on the greatness of Spinoza, which indeed should be known to all who read serious books.

Few moderns indeed have been so endorsed by the discipleship of great men as he—by that of Goethe, for instance, and Coleridge, of Novalis, Hegel, Lessing, Herder, Schelling, Scheiermacher and many others. So true is this that "it is admitted that Spinoza was the founder of modern philosophy" [133:372].

It will not be possible to show that Spinoza was a case of Cos-

mic Consciousness in the same sense that it can be shown, for instance, that John Yepes was a case; we have not the necessary
details of his illumination. All that can be done is to set down
such facts as we have and let the reader judge for himself. We
shall consider first the nature of his philosophic teaching and then
the facts of his actual life. We shall find that both point almost
inevitably to the same conclusion. Spinoza (for instance) "cannot allow that sin and evil have any positive reality, much less
that anything happens contrary to God's will. Nay, it is only an
inexact and human fashion of speech to say that man can sin
against or offend God" [133: 47]. Again: "The Universe is governed by divine laws, which, unlike those of man's making, are
immutable, inviolable and an end to themselves, not instruments
for the attainment of particular objects. The love of God is man's
only true good. From other passions we can free ourselves, but
not from love, because for the weakness of our nature we could
not subsist without the enjoyment of something that may
strengthen us by our union with it. Only the knowledge of God
will enable us to subdue the hurtful passions. This, as the source
of all knowledge, is the most perfect of all; and inasmuch as all
knowledge is derived from the knowledge of God, we may know
God better than we know ourselves. This knowledge in time leads
to the love of God, which is the soul's union with Him. *The union
of the soul with God is its second birth, and therein consists man's
immortality and freedom*" [133: 86]. The last clause of the above
sentence, italicized by the present editor, if taken absolutely, settles the question—for the union of the soul with God is illumination, is the second birth, and in it is immortality and freedom.
Again he says: "Love toward a thing eternal and infinite feeds
the mind with pure joy, and is wholly free from sorrow; this is
to be greatly desired and strenuously sought for" [133: 116].
This is the Brahmic Bliss—the joy that Whitman, Carpenter,
Yepes and the rest never tire of celebrating. Then farther on he
tells us that the chief good is to be endowed with a certain character. "What that character is we shall show in its proper place—
namely, that it consists in knowledge of the union which the mind

has with the whole of nature" [133:118]. But such knowledge does not exist apart from illumination, while on the other hand all those who have entered Cosmic Consciousness possess it. So Spinoza, instead of seeking in the usual way an artificial explanation for the correspondence of two such (apparently) different things as body and mind pronounces boldly that "they are the same thing and differ only as aspects" [133:180]. So Whitman (and all the rest in varying language): "Was somebody asking to see the soul? See your own shape and countenance, etc." [193:25]. So, again, Spinoza more than once classifies the kinds of our knowledge in such manner as to necessitate the inclusion of what is called in this book intuition, which is that form which belongs to the Cosmic Conscious mind and to that mind only. He says, for instance: "We may learn things (1) by hearsay or on authority; (2) by the mere suggestion of experience; (3) by reasoning; (4) by immediate and complete perception" [133:119 and 188]. And he says further that this last mode of knowing "proceeds from an adequate idea of the absolute nature of some attribute of God to an adequate knowledge of the nature of things." That is to say, the man enters into conscious relation with God (in the act of illumination), and through that contact— as far as it goes—he has an "adequate knowledge of things." It is doubtful whether any merely self conscious man could have used this language, for to such a man nothing seems more absurd than a claim to knowledge by simple intuition, and yet nothing is more certain than that such a knowledge is thus acquired. The following is equally characteristic: "To know God—in other words, to know the order of nature and regard the universe as orderly—is the highest function of the mind; and knowledge, as the perfect form of the mind's normal activity, is good for its own sake and not as a means" [133:241]. If Spinoza means here (as it seems likely he does) the same as Balzac meant when he said of specialism that it "alone can explain God," then Spinoza was a specialist. So when he says that "clear and distinct knowledge of the intuitive kind engenders love towards an immutable and eternal being, truly within our reach" [133:268], he implies in himself the possession of Cosmic Consciousness and teaches that this is within reach of all. Equally characteristic is the following: "In all exact knowledge the mind knows itself under the form of eternity; that is to say, in every such act it is eternal and knows itself as eternal. This eternity is not a persistence in time after the dissolution of the body, no more than a pre-existence in time, for it is not commensurable with time at all. And there is associated with it a state or quality of perfection called *the intellectual love of God*" [133: 269]. Spinoza, as Whitman, taught that "there is in fact no evil" [193: 22]; he says: "The perfection of things is to be reckoned only from their own nature and power; and things are not therein more or less perfect that they delight or offend the sense of men, or that they are convenient for the nature of man or repugnant thereto. If any ask why God hath not so created all men that they should be governed only by reason? I give them no answer but this: Because he lacked not matter for creating all things, even from the highest degree of perfection into the lowest. Or more exactly thus: Because the laws of his own nature were so vast as to suffice for producing all things which can be conceived by an infinite understanding" [133: 327]. As Pollock remarks, this is "a hypothetical infinite mind, which must be distinguished from the infinite intellect, which we have met with as one of the things immediately produced by God" [133: 328].

Finally Spinoza sums up in the following noble passage: "I have finished everything I wished to explain concerning the power of the mind over the emotions and concerning its liberty. From what has been said we see what is the strength of the wise man and how much he surpasses the ignorant who is driven by blind desire. For the ignorant man [the self conscious mind—compare Balzac —supra and [5: 144] where he classifies the human mind as Spinoza does here] is not only agitated by external causes in many ways, and never enjoys true peace of soul, but lives also ignorant, as it were, both of God and of things, and as soon as he ceases to suffer ceases also to be. On the other hand, the wise man [the Cosmic Conscious man], in so far as he is considered as such, is scarcely ever moved in his mind, but, being conscious by a certain eternal necessity of himself, of God, and of things, never ceases to be and always enjoys true peace of soul. If the way which, as I have shown, leads hither [i. e., to Cosmic Consciousness] seems very difficult, it can nevertheless be found. It must indeed be difficult, since it is so seldom discovered; for if salvation lay ready to hand and could be discovered without great labor, how could it be possible that it should be neglected almost by everybody? But all noble things are as difficult as they are rare" [170a : 283].

A few words now as to the personal characteristics of the man. John Colerus, minister of the Lutheran church, at that city, during Spinoza's residence at The Hague, knew him well, and what follows will be taken largely from his narrative, which is included in Sir Frederick Pollock's volume. Colerus says: "Spinoza was of middle size, had good features, complexion dark, black curly hair, long black eyebrows, so that one might easily know by his looks that he was descended from Portuguese Jews. As for his clothes, he was very careless of them; they were not better than those of the meanest citizen" [133 : 394].

Spinoza was in fact very poor. Like Thoreau, Whitman, Carpenter, Buddha, Jesus and many other men of his class, he seemed to prefer poverty. He made a very plain living by grinding glasses for telescopes. He was several times offered money by well-off persons who knew and liked him, but always refused until a friend, de Vries, from whom he had refused during his life to accept money, dying, charged his brother, who was his heir, to pay to Spinoza out of his estate a suitable maintenance. The brother wanted to pay Spinoza five hundred florins a year, but Spinoza would only accept three hundred—about one hundred and fifty dollars [87b : 401]. Spinoza lived in the plainest possible way; he was never married; most of his life he lived with others, paying his board; the rest of the time he lived alone in lodgings, buying what he needed and keeping very retired. "It is scarcely credible how sober and frugal he was all the time. Not that he was reduced to so great a poverty as not to be able to spend more if he had been willing. He had friends enough who offered him their purses and all manner of assistance. But he was naturally very sober and could be satisfied with little, and he did not care that people should think that he had lived, even but once, at the expense of other men. What I say about his sobriety and good husbandry may be proved by several small reckonings which have been found among his papers after his death. It appears by them that he lived a whole day upon a milk soup done with butter, which amounted to three-pence, and upon a pot of beer of three halfpence. Another day he ate nothing but gruel done with raisins and butter, and that dish cost him four-pence halfpenny. There are but two half-pints of wine at most for one month to be found among these reckon-ings, and though he was often invited to eat with his friends he chose rather to live upon what he had at home, though it were ever so little, than to sit down at a good table at the expense of another man'' [133: 393]. ''His conversation was very sweet and easy. He knew admirably well how to be master of his passions, and was never seen very melancholy nor very merry. He was very courteous and obliging, and would often discourse with his land-lady and the people of the house when they happened to be sick or afflicted—never failing to comfort them. He would put the chil-dren often in mind of going to church and taught them to be obe-dient and dutiful to their parents. One day his landlady asked him whether he believed she could be saved in the religion she pro-fessed? He answered: *'Your religion is a good one; you need not look for another, nor doubt that you may be saved in it pro-vided while you apply yourself to piety you live at the same time a peaceable and quiet life.'* When he stayed at home he was trou-blesome to nobody; he spent the greater part of his time quietly in his own chamber. When he happened to be tired by having applied himself too much to his philosophical meditations he went downstairs to refresh himself and discoursed with the people of the house about anything that might afford matter for an ordinary conversation and even about trifles. He also took pleasure in smoking a pipe of tobacco'' [133: 395].

Spinoza was never a robust man. ''Consumption had been making its insidious inroads upon him for many years, and early in 1677 he must have been conscious that he was seriously ill. On

Saturday, 20th of February, he sent to Amsterdam for his friend, Dr. Meyer. On the following day the people of the family with whom he lived, having no thought of immediate danger, went to afternoon service. When they came back Spinoza was no more; he had died about three in the afternoon, with Meyer for the only witness of his last moments" [87b: 403]. At the time of his death Spinoza was forty-four years and three months old.

All that remains is to show that, as in his life and teachings, so in his reception by the world, is Spinoza closely allied to the class of men with whom it is here sought to associate him. "The first effect of his writings in Holland was to raise a storm of controversial indignation" [133: 349]. And the man whom Novalis truly described as "God intoxicated," was pronounced "blasphemous, atheistic, deceitful," while his books were described as the "soul-destroying works of Spinoza" [ib.]. For a hundred years after his death he was little read, but since then more and more, and he now takes rank where he belongs, as one of the great spiritual leaders of the race.

CHAPTER 10.

Colonel James Gardiner.

1688-1745.

BORN January 10, 1688. Is said to have fought three duels before he was grown up. Entered the army young and fought with great bravery. His relations with women said to have been free, even licentious. Was not religious, even the reverse of that, but at times suffered "inexpressible remorse," on account of his life, which seemed to him evil. In the middle of July, 1719, when he was thirty-one and a half years of age, occurred the event which gives him a place in this volume: "He had spent the evening in some gay company and had an unhappy assignation with a married woman, whom he was to attend exactly at twelve. The company broke up at eleven, and, not judging it convenient to anticipate the time appointed, he went into his chamber to kill the tedious hour, perhaps with some amusing book, or some other way. But it very accidentally happened that he took up a religious book, which his good mother or aunt had, without his knowledge, slipped into his portmanteau. It was called, if I remember the title exactly, 'The Christian Soldier, or Heaven Taken by Storm,' and it was written by Mr. Thomas Watson. Guessing by the title of it that he would find some phrases of his own profession spiritualized in a manner which he thought might afford him some diversion, he resolved to dip into it; but he took no serious notice of anything it had in it.* And yet while this book was in his hand an impression was made upon his mind (perhaps God only knows how) which drew after it a train of the most important and happy consequences. He thought he saw an unusual blaze of light fall upon the book which he was reading, which he at first imagined might happen by some accident in the candle; but lifting up his eyes, he apprehended, to his extreme amazement, that there was before him, as it were suspended in the air, a visible representation of the Lord Jesus Christ upon the cross, surrounded upon all sides with a glory, and was impressed as if a voice, or something equivalent to a voice,† had come to him to this effect (for he was not confident as to the words): '𝔒𝔥, 𝔰𝔦𝔫𝔫𝔢𝔯, 𝔡𝔦𝔡 𝔍 𝔰𝔲𝔣𝔣𝔢𝔯 𝔱𝔥𝔦𝔰 𝔣𝔬𝔯 𝔱𝔥𝔢𝔢, 𝔞𝔫𝔡 𝔞𝔯𝔢 𝔱𝔥𝔢𝔰𝔢 𝔱𝔥𝔭 𝔯𝔢𝔱𝔲𝔯𝔫𝔰?' Struck with so amazing a phenomenon as this, there remained hardly any life in him,‡ so that he sank down in the armchair in which he sat and continued, he knew not how long, insensible" [107 : 286]. The immediate effect of Gardiner's experience is said to have been a *knowledge,* or rather a *sight,* of the "majesty and goodness of God," and his after life (a period of twenty-six years) was of distinguished excellence. The "new man" was as virtuous and pure and godly as the "old" had been licentious and profane [107 : 71].

---

* He was wide awake—probably extra wide awake—and at the same time his mind (for the moment) was a blank. This is the condition which we are told by all the authorities from Gautama to the present is *sine qua non* for the oncoming of illumination.

† As to the objectivity or subjectivity of the "voice" in such cases see remarks under head of "Moses"—what the person *sees* comes, of course, under the same category.

‡ "Less than a drachm of blood remains in me that does not tremble," says Dante, under similar circumstances [71 : 192].

CHAPTER 11.

Swedenborg.

1688-1772.

INDEPENDENTLY of illumination, Swedenborg was one of the great men of all time—a great thinker, a great writer, a great scientist, a great engineer.   In 1743, at the age of fifty-four years, something happened—some change took place in him; it does not seem to have been any form of insanity, since he was not sick, maintained and even increased all his friendships, was apparently entirely unsuspected by those about him of any mental alienation. His own account of his illumination to his friend Robsahm, as far as it goes, is very characteristic; he reports that God appeared to him and said, "𝕴 𝖆𝖒 𝕲𝖔𝖉 𝖙𝖍𝖊 𝕷𝖔𝖗𝖉, 𝖙𝖍𝖊 𝕮𝖗𝖊𝖆𝖙𝖔𝖗 𝖆𝖓𝖉 𝕽𝖊𝖉𝖊𝖊𝖒𝖊𝖗 𝖔𝖋 𝖙𝖍𝖊 𝖜𝖔𝖗𝖑𝖉.   𝕴 𝖍𝖆𝖛𝖊 𝖈𝖍𝖔𝖘𝖊𝖓 𝖙𝖍𝖊𝖊 𝖙𝖔 𝖚𝖓𝖋𝖔𝖑𝖉 𝖙𝖍𝖊 𝖘𝖕𝖎𝖗𝖎𝖙𝖚𝖆𝖑 𝖘𝖊𝖓𝖘𝖊 𝖔𝖋 𝖙𝖍𝖊 𝕳𝖔𝖑𝖞 𝕾𝖈𝖗𝖎𝖕𝖙𝖚𝖗𝖊𝖘.   𝕴 𝖜𝖎𝖑𝖑 𝖒𝖞𝖘𝖊𝖑𝖋 𝖉𝖎𝖈𝖙𝖆𝖙𝖊 𝖙𝖔 𝖙𝖍𝖊𝖊 𝖜𝖍𝖆𝖙 𝖙𝖍𝖔𝖚 𝖘𝖍𝖆𝖑𝖙 𝖜𝖗𝖎𝖙𝖊" [87a: 759].

It is admitted by all students of Swedenborg's life that the change was in reality an illumination, that putting aside his visions of angels and demons he actually had thereafter a spiritual insight beyond that of ordinary men, and if he was a visionary he also "led the most real life of any man then in the world" [87a: 96].   As for his visions, it may be said that they were not fundamentally different from those of Blake, Behmen, Dante and others.   It must be remembered that these men see things that we do not see—things that are outside of our language; if, then, they use this language (which is all they have) to set them before us, it seems inevitable that we should not understand their words as they understand them.   The result, in the case of every such expositor, however common-sense he tries to be—in the case of Jesus, Gautama, Paul and all the rest—is terrible misunderstanding and confusion; and yet, in spite of all, something passes from these men to us of more importance than all that we could get from the ordinary scientists and philosophers.

Many facts indicate that Swedenborg may have belonged to the class of men here in question. "He was never married. He had great modesty and gentleness of bearing. His habits were simple; he lived on bread, milk and vegetables" [87a: 98]. "He was a man who won the respect, confidence and love of all who came in contact with him" [87a: 759]. Though many of those about him did not believe in his visions they respected him too much to make light of these in Swedenborg's presence. His teaching at bottom is that of all the great seers—that God in himself is infinite love—that his manifestation, form or body is infinite wisdom—that divine love is the self-subsisting life of the universe [87a: 759].

Swedenborg departs from the norm of these cases especially by his age (fifty-four years) at illumination. It seems incredible that a man could go on growing to such an age; still this is what we must believe if we include him. Mohammed was thirty-nine, Las Casas forty, C. M. C. forty-nine; these were undoubted cases, and it does not seem as if Swedenborg's personal history can be explained on any other hypothesis.

CHAPTER 12.

William Wordsworth.

1770-1850.

THAT the mind of this writer (nearly if not quite a poet) in his loftier moods attained a very close neighborhood to Cosmic Consciousness, if he did not actually enter the magic territory of the kingdom of heaven, no one will deny who knows what these words mean and who also has read him with any sympathy. In fact the following short passages, from lines written at Tintern Abbey in his twenty-ninth year, prove as much. In the first he speaks of "that blessed mood"

> In which the burden of the mystery,
> In which the heavy and the weary weight
> Of all this unintelligible world,

Is lightened :—that serene and blessed mood
In which the affections gently lead us on,—
Until, the breath of this corporeal frame
And even the motion of our human blood
Almost suspended, we are laid asleep
In body, and becomes a living soul.
While with an eye made quiet by the power
Of harmony, and the deep power of joy,
We see into the life of things [198:187].

This passage indicates plainly the relief (approaching to joy) and the enlightenment (approximating illumination) which belong to the unrisen sun of the Cosmic Sense. But there is no evidence that upon him, at any time, the sun actually rose—that the veil was ever rent and the splendor let through; in fact it may be considered as quite clear that this did not happen. Then, next line, follows the usual doubt:

If this but be a vain belief

(whether or not the revelation can be relied on)—a question never asked, at least after the first few minutes or hours, by a person who has obtained even one glimpse of the "Brahmic Splendor."

Later, in the same poem, is another passage describing in other words the same mental condition, which may be properly called the twilight of Cosmic Consciousness:

I have felt
A presence that disturbs me with the joy
Of elevated thought; a sense sublime
Of something far more deeply interfused,
Whose dwelling is the light of setting suns,
And the round ocean and the living air,
And the blue sky, and in the mind of man—
A motion and a spirit, that impels
All thinking things, all objects of all thought,
And rolls through all things [198:189].

CHAPTER 13.

Charles G. Finney.

1792-1875.

THIS case is of more than usual interest from the fact that although in it occurred almost certainly, although not strongly marked, the phenomenon of the subjective light, together with pronounced moral exaltation and probably some intellectual illumination, yet it was not crowned by the Cosmic vision—the Brahmic Splendor. It is not therefore complete, but only partial or imperfect.

That the illumination of Charles G. Finney was not accompanied by the consciousness of the Cosmos is certain because the account of the Cosmic vision, had this been present, could not have been omitted from his relation of his "conversion," of which it would have been the most striking feature—the very core and centre. What he did see and feel was wonderful and striking enough. How surprised, and probably how incredulous, would he have been if he could have been told that although he had reached the threshold of and strongly felt the Divine Presence to which he was so close, that yet the vision which would have meant so much to him was still hidden behind the veil of sense and for the time denied to him!

So this man's life, though by the experience of that autumn day infinitely exalted as compared with that of the average self conscious man, is yet just as markedly below that of the men who have not only felt the Infinite One as Charles G. Finney felt him, but have passed into His presence and seen His inconceivable glory.

The distinction pointed out may be clearly realized by making a comparison of the book Charles G. Finney has left us with the epoch-making books—the Suttas (for instance), the Gospels, the Epistles, the Qur'an, the "Divine Comedy," the "Shakespeare" works, the "Comédie Humaine," the "Leaves of Grass" and the rest—inspired or written by the men to whom has been shown the Brahmic Splendor as a visible fact.

The illumination of Charles G. Finney took place early in his thirtieth year—that is, in October, 1821. He had the usual earnest religious temperament, and for some time had been greatly troubled about his spiritual state, eagerly desiring, but unable to reach assurance of, salvation. Then occurred what he calls his "conversion." He says:

The rising of my soul was so great that I rushed into the room behind the front office, to pray.

There was no fire and no light in the room; nevertheless it appeared as if it were perfectly light. As I went in and shut the door it seemed as if I met the Lord Jesus Christ face to face. It did not occur to me that it was wholly a mental state; it seemed that I saw him as I would see any other man. He said nothing, but looked at me in such a manner as to break me right down at his feet. I have always since regarded this as a most remarkable state of mind; for it seemed that he stood before me, and I fell down at his feet and poured out my soul to him. I wept aloud like a child, and made such confessions as I could with my choked utterance.

I must have continued in this state for a good while; but my mind was too much absorbed to recollect anything I said. But I know, as soon as my mind became calm, I returned to the front office, and found that the fire, that I had made of large wood, was nearly burned out. But as I turned and was about to take a seat by the fire, I received a mighty baptism of the Holy Ghost. Without any expectation of it, without ever having the thought in my mind that there was any such thing for me, without any recollection that I had ever heard the thing mentioned by any person in the world, the Holy Spirit descended upon me in a manner that seemed to go through me, body and soul.

No words can express the wonderful love that was shed abroad in my heart. I wept aloud with joy and love; and I do not know, but I should say, I literally bellowed out the unutterable gushings of my heart. These waves came over me, and over me, and over me, one after the other, until I recollect I cried out, "I shall die if these waves continue to pass over me." I said, "Lord, I cannot bear any more;" yet I had no fear of death.

How long I continued in this state I do not know. But it was late in the evening when a member of my choir came to see me. He was a member of the church. He found me in this state of loud weeping, and said, "Mr. Finney, what ails you?" I could make him no answer for some time. He then said, "Are you in pain?" I gathered myself up and replied, "No, but so happy that I cannot live" [104: 17-18].

The long, laborious and beneficent after life of this man proved, if proof was necessary, that his "conversion" was no accidental excitement that might have happened to any man, but an unmistakable mark of spiritual superiority.

Mr. Finney had, too, to an extraordinary degree, the personal magnetism that is so characteristic of the class of men to which he belonged. The effect of his preaching was indescribable, and yet it is doubtful whether the words uttered had much to do with its exceptional power. His presence, his touch, the sound of his voice, seemed often sufficient to arouse unutterable feelings—to uplift and regenerate in what may fairly be called a miraculous manner.

Not actually having Cosmic Consciousness, he had not the duplex personality which thereto belongs, and yet he had a feeling of that other self within himself which upon full illumination would have stood out as the "I am," while the self conscious man would have taken second place as "The other I am." As illustrating this inchoate duplex personality, he says: "Let no man think that those sermons which have been called so powerful were productions of my own brain or of my own heart unassisted by the Holy Ghost. They are not mine, but from the Holy Spirit in me."

Finally it should be noted that the life and the life work of Charles G. Finney were on strictly parallel lines, though on a less high plane, with the life and life work of the great religious initiators, he, as they, expending all his time and energy laboring to place his brothers and sisters on a higher moral plane than that on which they had heretofore lived, the only difference being that they worked on a somewhat higher moral level than that upon which he worked.

CHAPTER 14.

Alexander Pushkin.

BORN May 26, 1799; died January 29, 1837.

If Pushkin traced the following lines after his own personal experience he was almost certainly a case of Cosmic Consciousness. Be this as it may, their descriptive power makes them worth quoting.   The translation into English is by Dana, of the "New York Sun":

Tormented by thirst of the spirit,
I was dragging myself through a gloomy
    forest,*
When a six-winged seraph †
At the cross-roads appeared to me.
With fingers light as a dream
My eyes he touched,
And my eyes opened wide,
Like those of a frightened she eagle.
My ears he touched,
And roaring and noise filled them;
And I heard the trembling of the heavens;
And the high flight of the angels,
And the movement of the creatures beneath the sea,
And the growing of the grass in the valleys!
And he laid hold of my lips,
And tore out my sinful tongue—
Sinful, frivolous and cunning;
And the sting of a wise serpent,
Between my unconscious lips,
With bloody right hand he planted.
And he cut through my breast with a sword,
And took out the trembling heart,
And a coal blazing and flaming,
Into the open breast he thrust.
Like a corpse I lay in the desert,*
And the voice of God called me:
Rise up, Prophet, and see, and under-
    stand! †
Filled full of My Will,
Going forth over sea and land,
Set men's hearts afire with the Word.

* Dante's dark forest in which he was lost.
† Compare Isaiah's vision.

* The dazed condition which is so common following illumination.

† Intellectual illumination.

CHAPTER 15.

Ralph Waldo Emerson.

BORN May, 1803; died April, 1882.

Spiritually eminent as was this great American, it does not appear that he belonged to the class of men discussed in this volume. He was perhaps as near Cosmic Consciousness as it is possible to be without actually entering that realm. He lived in the light of the great day, but there is no evidence that its sun for him actually rose. Emerson's "Oversoul" was printed in 1841, when the author was thirty-eight years old. In it he tells us plainly where he stood at that time, and it is as good as certain that in later years he did not advance beyond that position. In it he says, for instance:

There is a difference between one and another hour of life, in their authority and subsequent effect.

There is a depth in those brief moments which constrains us to ascribe more reality to them than to all other experiences.

Every man's words, who speaks from that life, must sound vain to those who do not dwell in the same thought on their own part.

If he had had experience of the Cosmic Vision—the Brahmic Splendor—he could not have used this exceedingly moderate, even cold, language when referring thereto. Neither could he omitting that, be here referring to other experiences.

These passages show how deep, however short of the bottomless deep, Emerson's spiritual experience was.

Only itself can inspire whom it will, and behold! their speech shall be lyrical, and sweet, and universal as the rising of the wind.

In ascending to this primary and aboriginal sentiment, we have come from our remote station on the circumference instantaneously to the centre of the world, where, as in the closet of God, we see causes, and anticipate the universe, which is but a slow effect.

This energy does not descend into individual life, or any other condition than entire possession. It comes to the lowly and simple; it comes to whomsoever will put off what is foreign and proud; it comes as insight; it comes as serenity and grandeur. When we see those whom it inhabits we are apprized of new degrees of greatness. From that inspiration the man comes back with a changed tone. He does not talk with men, with an eye to their opinion. He tries them. It requires of us to be plain and true. The vain traveler attempts to embellish his life by quoting my lord, and the prince, and the countess, who thus said or did to *him*. The ambitious vulgar show you their spoons, and brooches, and rings, and preserve their cards and compliments. The more cultivated, in their account of their own experience, cull out the pleasing poetic circumstance; the visit to Rome, the man of genus they saw; the brilliant friend they know; still further on, perhaps, the gorgeous landscape, the mountain lights, the mountain thoughts, they enjoyed yesterday—and so seek to throw a romantic color over their life. But the soul that ascendeth to worship the great God is plain and true; has no rose color; no fine friends; no chivalry; no adventures; does not want admiration; dwells in the hour that now is, in the earnest experience of the common day—by reason of the present moment, and the mere trifle having become porous to thought, and bibulous of the sea of light.

CHAPTER 16.

Alfred Tennyson.

THIS poet (for though not absolutely entitled to rank in the divine order, yet he has worthily served for and must be allowed that name) passed the greater part of a long life in that region of self consciousness which lies close upon the lower side of the Cosmic Sense. His "weird seizures" mentioned in "The Princess," in which he seemed to "move among a world of ghosts, and feel (himself) the shadow of a dream" [185: 11], belong to that spiritual realm; but far more certainly a condition well described in the following lines of the "Ancient Sage":

> More than once when I
> Sat all alone, revolving in myself
> The word that is the symbol of myself,
> The mortal limit of the Self was loosed,
> And passed into the nameless, as a cloud
> Melts into heaven.   I touch'd my limbs, the limbs
> Were strange, not mine—and yet no shade of doubt,
> But utter clearness, and thro' loss of Self
> The gain of such large life as matched with ours
> Were sun to spark—unshadowable in words,
> Themselves but shadows of a shadow-world [186: 48].

And again in the "Holy Grail":

> Let visions of the night, or of the day
> Come as they will; and many a time they come
> Until this earth he walks on seems not earth,
> This light that strikes his eyeball is not light,
> This air that smites his forehead is not air,
> But vision—yea his very hand and foot—
> In moments when he feels he cannot die,
> And knows himself no vision to himself,
> Nor the high God a vision, nor that one
> Who rose again; ye have seen what ye have seen [184: 290].

And yet once more in plain prose:

A kind of walking trance I have frequently had, quite up from boyhood, *"Repeating my own name."* Tennyson quite unconsciously was using the means laid

when I have been all alone. This has often come upon me through *repeating my own name* to myself silently till, all at once, as it were, out of the intensity of the consciousness of individuality, the individuality itself seemed to dissolve and fade away into boundless being; and this not a confused state, but the clearest of the clearest, the surest of the surest, the weirdest of the weirdest, utterly beyond words, where death was an almost laughable impossibility, the loss of personality (if so it were) seeming no extinction, but the only true life [182:320].

down from immemorial time for the attainment of illumination: "He who thinking of nothing, making the mind cease to work, adhering to uninterrupted meditation, *repeating the single syllable, Om*, meditating on me, reaches the highest goal" (i.e., Cosmic Consciousness) [154 : 79]. Of course it makes no difference what word or name is used. What is required is that the action of the mind should be as far as possible suspended, especially that all desires of every kind be stilled, nothing wished or feared, the mind in perfect health and vigor, but held quiescent in a state of calm equipoise!

"Religion was no nebulous abstraction for him. He consistently emphasized his own belief in what he called the eternal truths, in an omnipotent, omnipresent and all-loving God, who has revealed himself through the human attribute of the highest self-sacrificing love, and in the immortality of the soul" [182: 311].

"He invariably believed that humility is the only true attitude of the human soul, and therefore spoke with the greatest reserve of what he called 'these unfathomable mysteries,' as befitting one who did not dogmatize but who knew that the finite can by no means grasp the infinite, and yet he had a profound trust that when all is seen face to face all will be seen as the best" [182: 316].

"He said again, with deep feeling, in January, 1869: 'Yes, it is true there are moments when the flesh is nothing to me, when I feel and know the flesh to be the vision, God and the spiritual—the only real and true. Depend upon it, the spiritual *is* the real; it belongs to one more than the hand and the foot. You may tell me that my hand and my foot are only imaginary symbols of my existence. I could believe you, but you never, never can convince me that the *I* is not an eternal reality, and that the spiritual is not the true and real part of me.' These words he spoke with such passionate earnestness that a solemn silence fell on us as he left the room" [182a: 90].

It was written of Tennyson just after his death: "It is understood that he believed that he wrote many of the best and truest things he ever published under the direct influence of higher intelligences, of whose presence he was distinctly conscious. He felt them near him, and his mind was impressed by their ideas" [170], the meaning of which, if the report, as it probably is, is true, is that the veil between him and the Cosmic Sense was so thin that he felt the teachings of the latter through it, but there is no evidence known to the present writer that it was ever torn away so that he *saw* the other world. In other words, there is no evidence that he ever actually entered into Cosmic Consciousness.

CHAPTER 17.

J. B. B.

J. B. B., Doctor of Medicine, born 1817. Entered into Cosmic Consciousness 1855, at the age of thirty-eight years. An informant says of him: "He is not a refined man," and he goes on: "It is one of the strange things in this whole matter that the attainment of the truth seems to leave a man in this respect about as it finds him. Dr. B. was an example. He seemed content to live in a cheap, bare house, and he rather courted coarseness in dress, talk and life." As regards coarseness in dress, food and surroundings, our informant need not have looked upon J. B. B. as so exceptional. He might have compared him with Tilleinathan Swamy [56:142], with Edward Carpenter, or even with Jesus, Mohammed or Walt Whitman. "At the same time," our informant continues, "touch him on the subject of the inner vision and he was alive to the core. He had been a spiritualist, but after illumination, while seeming to know that much that spiritualism taught was true, its importance was dwarfed by the much greater truths to which he had access." "He once told me," the informant continues, "a curious thing: He said he died, his spirit left his body for twenty minutes, and he looked at, hovered over, and finally went back into it. He told this in a grave, convincing way, which caused in the hearer a gruesome feeling. No one who heard him tell it could help believing it."

CHAPTER 18.

Henry David Thoreau.

BORN July 12, 1817; died May 6, 1862. There are several reasons for suspecting Thoreau to have been a case of Cosmic Consciousness, such as his addiction to solitude, his love of mysticism and the mystics, the almost preternatural acuteness of his senses, his love for and fellowship with animals, his intellectual keenness and his moral elevation. The present editor has, however, searched in vain for data which might convert this presumption into anything like a certainty, and Thoreau is so close to us that, had he experienced illumination, the evidence thereof ought to be forthcoming and decisive. But what do these eight lines mean, if not that their author had passed through some such experience as is here treated of?

I hearing get who had but ears,
And sight who had but eyes before,
I moments live who lived but years,
And truth discern who knew but learn-
    ing's lore.

I hear beyond the range of sound,
I see beyond the range of sight,
New earths, and skies and seas around,
And in my day the sun doth pale his
    light.

"Have you ever asked for that instruction by which we hear what cannot be heard, by which we perceive what cannot be perceived, by which we know what cannot be known?" [148 : 92].

"Hearing ye shall hear and shall in no wise understand, and seeing ye shall see and shall in no wise perceive" [14 : 13 : 14].

"The eyesight has another eyesight and the hearing another hearing and the voice another voice" [193 : 342].

If Thoreau experienced illumination at the usual age, evidence of the fact should be found in "Walden," which was written between 1845 and 1854, when its author was twenty-eight to thirty-seven years of age. As a matter of fact, we do find passages in that book which suggest that the writer of it, if not an actual case of Cosmic Consciousness, was yet well on the way thereto. For instance:

Our manners have been corrupted by communication with the saints. Our hymn books resound with a melodious cursing of God and enduring him forever. One would say that even the prophets and redeemers had rather consoled the fears than confirmed the hopes of man. There is nowhere recorded a simple and irrepressible satisfaction with the gift of life, any memorable praise of God [199a: 85].

He finds God and human life greater and better than has ever been said, as indeed they are greater and better than any one has said or can say.

The millions are awake enough for physical labor; but only one in a million is awake enough for effective intellectual exertion, only one in a hundred millions for a poetic or divine life [199a: 97].

Compare Whitman: ''I cannot be awake, for nothing looks to me as it did before, or else I am awake for the first time, and all before has been a mean sleep'' [124a : 49].

Sometimes, when I compare myself with other men, it seems as if I were more favored by the gods than they, beyond any deserts that I am conscious of; as if I had a warrant and surety at their hands which my fellows have not, and were especially guided and guarded. I do not flatter myself, but if it be possible they flatter me. I have never felt lonesome, or in the least oppressed by a sense of solitude, but once, and that was a few weeks after I came to the woods, when, for an hour, I doubted if the near neighborhood of man was not essential to a serene and healthy life. To be alone was something unpleasant. But I was at the same time conscious of a slight insanity in my mood and seemed to foresee my recovery. In the midst of a gentle rain, while these thoughts prevailed, I was suddenly sensible of such sweet and beneficent society in Nature, in the very pattering of the drops, and in every sound and sight around my house, an infinite and unaccountable friendliness all at once, like an atmosphere, sustaining me, as made the fancied advantages of human neighborhood insignificant, and I have never thought of them since. Every little pine needle expanded and swelled with sympathy and befriended me. I was so distinctly made aware of the presence of something kindred to me, even in the scenes which we are accustomed to call wild and dreary, and also that the nearest of blood to me and humanest was not a person nor a villager, that I thought no place could ever be strange to me again.

Some of my pleasantest hours were during the long rain storms in the spring and fall, which confined me to the house for the afternoon as well as the forenoon, soothed by their ceaseless roar and pelting; when an early twilight ushered in a long evening, in which many thoughts had time to take root and unfold themselves. In those driving northeast rains, which tried the village houses so, when the maids stood ready with mop and pail in front entries to keep the deluge out, I sat behind my door in my little house, which was all entry, and thoroughly enjoyed its protection. In one heavy thunder shower the lightning struck a large pitch-pine across the pond, making a very conspicuous and perfectly regular spiral groove from top to bottom, an inch or more deep and four or five inches wide, as you would groove a walking stick. I passed it again the other day and was struck with awe on looking up and beholding that mark, how more distinct than ever, where a terrific and resistless bolt came down out of the harmless sky eight years ago. Men frequently say to me: "I should think you would feel lonesome down there and want to be nearer to folks, rainy and snowy days, and nights especially." I am tempted to reply to such: This whole earth, which we inhabit, is but a point in space. How far apart, think you, dwell the two most distant inhabitants of yonder star, the breadth of whose disk cannot be appreciated by our instruments? Why should I feel lonely? Is not our planet in the Milky Way? This which you put seems to me not to be the most important question. What sort of space is that which separates a man from his fellows and makes him solitary? I have found that no exertion of the legs can bring two minds much nearer to one another. What do we want most to dwell near to? Not to many men, surely, the depot, the post office, the barroom, the meeting house, the schoolhouse, the grocery, Beacon Hill, or the Five Points, where men most congregate, but to the perennial source of our life, whence in all our experience we have found that to issue, as the willow stands near the water and sends out its roots in that direction. This will vary with different natures, but this is the place where a wise man will dig his cellar. . . . I one evening overtook one of my townsmen, who has accumulated what is called "a handsome property"— though I never got a fair view of it—on the Walden Road driving a pair of cattle to market, who inquired of me how I could bring my mind to give up so many of the comforts of life. I answered that I was very sure I liked it passably well; I was not joking. And so I went home to my bed and left him to pick his way through the darkness and the mud to Brighton—or Brighttown—which place he would reach some time in the morning.

Any prospect of awakening or coming to life to a dead man makes indifferent all times and places. The place where that may occur is always the same, and indescribably pleasant to all our senses. For the most part we allow only outlying and transient circumstances to make our occasions. They are, in fact, the cause of our distraction. Nearest to all things is that power which fashions their being. Next to us the grandest laws are continually being executed. Next to us is, not the workman whom we have hired, with whom we love so well to talk, but the workman whose work we are [199a: 143-5].

I only know myself as a human entity; the scene, so to speak, of thoughts and affections; and am sensible of a certain doubleness by which I can stand as remote from myself as from another. However intense my experience, I am conscious of the presence and criticism of a part of me, which, as it were, is not a part of me, but spectator, sharing no experience, but taking note of it; and that is no more I than it is you [199a: 146].

Cf. Whitman: "Trippers and askers surround me, people I meet, the effect upon me of my early life or the ward and city I live in, or the nation, the latest dates, discoveries, inventions, societies, authors old and new, my dinner, dress, associates, looks, compliments, dues, the real or fancied indifference of some man or woman I love, the sickness of one of my folks or of myself, or ill-doing or loss or lack of money, or depressions or exaltations, battles, the horrors of fratricidal war, the fever of doubtful news, the fitful events; these come to me days and nights and go from me again, but they are not the Me myself.

"Apart from the pulling and hauling stands what I am, stands amused, complacent, compassionating, idle unitary, looks down, is erect, or bends an arm on an impalpable certain rest, looking with side-curved head curious what will come next, both in and out of the game and watching and wondering at it" [193 : 31].

CHAPTER 19.

J. B.

BORN 1821. Entered Cosmic Consciousness 1859, aet. thirty-nine years. Was a Methodist and in high standing in his church. He prayed fervently for light, for assurance of salvation, etc. Seemed no use, so he ceased praying—then light broke gradually; no subjective light, but a steady, continuous intellectual illumination, and with it a deeper and deeper feeling of moral peace, rest and happiness. This intellectual illumination and moral peace steadily grew until the whole man was transformed. He became an acknowledged authority among enlightened and able men on all spiritual matters. Consciousness of immortality came shortly after intellectual and moral new birth. It really came with the others, but took longer to attain to its full growth. He had had the hope of immortality all along, in common with other members of his church, but never the thing itself or anything approaching it. Now (that is, since illumination) he does not look forward to immortality, but is conscious that he has attained to it, entered into possession and enjoyment of it. He was born in England; was a weaver; in America has for years been an undertaker. Is, from the point of view of the schools, entirely uneducated. The present writer passed several hours in his company, about 1890, and was impressed by his intellectual enlightenment, but far more by his perfect happiness, his absolute moral peace.

An informant, himself an able and thoughtful man, a dweller in a great capital, who all his life has seen, heard and read the best men and books, and who for years has been an earnest seeker for the truth, saw J. B. first in 1870 and has been intimate with him ever since. He says: "I had not heard him talk ten minutes before I knew that I was now for the first time in the presence of a

man who had what I wanted. I have never met a man who was
so mighty in the Scriptures. He knew the Bible almost by heart
and had the same inspiration as Paul and John. There never was
a time when I met J. B. that he did not by a word, a sentence, or
a long talk, make it clear that he stood on a rock of solid truth.''

CHAPTER 20.

C. P.

BORN 1822. Has been all his life a laboring man. Was, and
is, esteemed as a saint and sage by every man who knew and knows
him. His conversation is enlightened to an extraordinary degree.
Is, of course, uneducated. Attained to Cosmic Consciousness in
the year 1859, when he was in his thirty-seventh year. An informant, who knew C. P. well, says: "He has been a great
dreamer of curious and remarkable dreams. His chief charm is
his wonderful exposition of the Scriptures. He is the very embodiment of the living Christ. He despises money. One feels in
his presence that here is a brother. His letters are the most
charming I have ever received. The most curious and strange
thing in his case is that he believes that death ends all. He has
been a fine public speaker for forty years; first in the Methodist
church, then for a time in a semi-infidel vein, but since his enlightenment his talks have been mostly Biblical. He has strong
socialistic views.''
The writer of the present volume has had two long talks with
C. P. and can testify to his extraordinary intelligence. His want
of faith in the continuance of the individual life seems at first
sight to set him apart from the class of men having Cosmic Consciousness; but, first, as before noted, we must make great allowance for range of spiritual life on that plane; and, second, it must
be noted that his conviction was, probably, to him, more opti-
mistic than would have been that of the usual eternal life. He
believes, is indeed sure, that after death he will be absorbed into
God, and that in losing his individuality he will gain something

much more valuable. His feeling, his conviction, his *knowledge* (as in all these cases) is that the *best* will happen. He gives a slightly different interpretation to this *best*—that is all.

In July, 1895, C. P. published a book, in which he endeavored to set forth some of the spiritual results of illumination in his case. Such a task is no light one, as many besides C. P. have found. It is, in fact, in all cases really an impossible task, as Paul, Whitman and others have testified. C. P. was less qualified than have been some other men of the class for the enterprise, and his attempt, though exceedingly interesting, cannot be pronounced a perfect success. The following quoted passages will show, however, to whoever can understand them, that C. P., beyond all doubt, belongs to the order of men treated of in this volume—a fact which was positively known to the present writer long before the book quoted was written. C. P. says:

Paul said "the Jews missed the kingdom of heaven because they sought it by the deeds of the law of Moses"—by the righteousness of the moral law—"instead of seeking it through righteousness of faith" in the perfection of the order of existence—the faith of the Christ. They could not see that there are two separate and distinct kinds of righteousness, or laws—one imperfect, for the imperfect or carnal mind, and the other perfect, for the perfect or spiritual mind, which two states are as separate and distinct from each other as sheep are from goats [132: 13].

The same misconception is universal, or almost universal, to-day. To every man who has had the smallest flash of Cosmic Consciousness this is as clear as day, "Unless your righteousness," says Jesus, "shall exceed the righteousness of the scribes and Pharisees." And he does not mean to exceed in degree, but in kind. "Except a man be born anew." "If any man is in Christ he is a new creature"—not the old creature bettered, but another, a new, creature.

The life is not in believing there is a divinity somewhere, but in knowing it. To know the Word of the Truth, and to have its spirit generated in the mind and heart, is to have its pure offspring—its Son—begotten within, consciously crying "Father" with certitude [132: 19].

Here again is a distinct and absolute mark proving the writer to have had the Cosmic Sense. No merely self conscious man knows of God as he knows of mundane matters of fact. Every Cosmic Conscious man does so. He knows by actual inward vision just as he knows (by self consciousness) that he is a distinct entity.

The government of the carnal mind, which hath not the Son of Divinity begotten in it, hath no *actual knowledge* of what the only true Divinity is. No one knoweth the names of the actual

In other words: The merely self conscious mind may believe in God but cannot know Him—has never seen God, can never see Him. The only men who can and do know the Deity are the Cosmic Conscious men (the consciousness of the Deity and of the Cosmos being

Divinity and its Lamb until these are written in their understandings by special revelation to each one individually. On this Rock of the actual revelation of the Christ in the mind by its eternal Father the congregation of the true Christ is built. This is the sole immovable basis of certitude; and the world may continue to divide indefinitely into disagreeing sects until it receives this revelation, because it can have no certitude until then; but all who receive it see eye to eye, and they cannot disagree [132:20].

the same thing). What C. P. very properly calls the congregation of Christ is simply made up of those who have been illumined. This illumination is the sole basis of certainty in these matters. If all the world had Cosmic Consciousness all would agree on many basic questions of religion and philosophy which are now disputed—though doubtless other questions, many of which are not in sight at the present time, would arise and be disputed upon.

It was of this very part—this Son begotten in him—which was the spiritual mind, that the Spirit of Truth said, "Thou art my Son: this day have I begotten thee." And he knew the very day he was begotten—the very day he became conscious of being made alive to this Father of his understanding, because this spiritual Son in him spontaneously "cried Father" with natural certitude as it had not cried before. And thus this begotten Son of the eternal Spirit of Truth so cries in every one in whom it is begotten, so that they, and they only, know how the first born was begotten. And these only know what the dominion of the Divinity is, for, "Except a man be thus born again he cannot see it" [132:22].

Needs no comment; is simply a statement of the definiteness of the new birth—that is, of the oncoming of Cosmic Consciousness.

The carnal mind can talk about the "Fatherhood of God and the brotherhood of man," but it realizes nothing of either, because this Son of God is not begotten in it [132:23].

God is the Father of each one of us; but no one, without illumination, can realize what these words mean.

Moreover, he said, "At that day" —the day when they should be conscious of this Spirit's having come to them—"ye shall know that I am in the Father, and ye in me, and I in you." And as it was impossible for the man to be personally in them, and they in him, it is clear that when the Spirit of Truth had written itself clearly in their consciousness this would be both the Father and the Son in them, and they in that, and the work was purely that of a spiritual mental state [132:24].

Needs no comment.

"He that was least in the kingdom of heaven was greater than John," because those who entered into that were made perfect by the fullness of Light of the eternal Spirit. Hence "the law of the prophets were until John, but with him began the preaching of the kingdom of God" [132:31].

Jesus looked upon himself as the first man of the new (Cosmic Conscious) race. Among merely self conscious men none ranked higher than John, but the least man of the new order would be greater than he.

And to these (the enlightened) it is entirely clear that this Divinity, be-

One aspect of the Cosmic vision.

ing eternal, all existence must be eternal, because all Truth is simply the **Truth** of existence. To these existence is one eternal immensity of infinite existence, acting with infinite force, in an inevitable, infinite, therefore absolutely perfect order, in whose perfection, or truth, all things and their action must of necessity be included, and this Paul expressed in the one comprehensive, basic sentence, "All things are of the Divinity" [132: 68].

The apostles were ministers of the new Covenant, which was based on this Rock, which was an entirely new basis of ratiocination, and they were not ministers of the old covenant of the moral law at all. The moral law, being the knowledge of good and evil, is the "ministration of death," while the new law is the ministration of life.

The "Rock" is, of course, the Cosmic Sense. Whether or not any of the apostles, besides Paul, had themselves Cosmic Consciousness, their work was on that plane, since the object of it was to preserve and extend the teaching of Jesus. In Cosmic Consciousness there is no condemnation, no sin, no evil, no death. This may be a hard saying, but it is true.

The old is the minister of condemnation, which is the death, and the new is the minister of justification, which is the life, hence those who pass into the dominion of the new necessarily pass out of the dominion of the old, and thus they must be "made free from the old," and it is thus that there is no condemnation, no death, to those who are in the Covenant of the Christ" [132: 73].

This reveals the boundless radiance of the infinite face of the real Divinity, beaming on him who sees it its equipoise of "Mercy and Truth" [132: 75].

"This" refers to the Cosmic Vision, the "Brahmic Splendor."

And when this Christ is formed in the mind and heart it is known to be the "Spirit of faith" in the infinite order of all existence as all true, and

"This Christ," i.e., Cosmic Consciousness. When that comes to a man he can say, as Whitman says: "There is in fact no evil" [193 : 22].

for this reason it "resisteth not the evil" which is an inevitable part of the Order, and seen in the Light of the whole Truth to be all good, having a perfect use [132: 140].

And it is thus that this Spirit of Faith in the whole Order is the Christ formed in the mind, and this is the "Lamb of God which taketh away all sin"—by taking away all resistance of the natural Order of existence. When this Christ is formed in the mind then it has the perfect Light by which all the things of the Divinity of all Truth are clearly understood. Then, and only then, it knoweth how all the things of the new Covenant are spiritually discerned, for then, and only then, it knoweth the only true Divinity and its Christ. And then the mind knoweth

To the self conscious mind there is good in the world but also a great deal of evil. To the Cosmic Conscious mind all is good; there is no evil. The chief function of those few Cosmic Conscious minds that so far the world has had has been to reconcile (as far as may be) the self conscious mind to the Cosmic order, which seemed to the one perfect, to the other imperfect. Whitman expresses this very well in a short poem [193 : 416]:
"When the full-grown poet came,
Out spake pleased Nature (the round impassive globe, with all its shows of day and night), saying, *He is mine:*
But out spake too the soul of men, proud, jealous, and unreconciled, *Nay, he is mine alone;*

with entire certitude, by its own experience, that all that the first-born, Paul, or any of the believers, had of the knowledge of the Truth (and they had its fullness) came to them by internal revelation, and not by any external "signs and wonders" [132: 140-1].

—Then the full-grown poet stood between the two, and took each by the hand;
And to-day and ever so stands, as blender, uniter, tightly holding hands,
Which he will never release until he reconciles the two,
And wholly and joyously blends them.''

By being perfectly enlightened by the Spirit of all existence he was reconciled to it all, therefore could not resist any part of it as if it had no right to be; and he cheerily saw that the way to the peace and harmony of mankind with each other was through the reconciliation to, or harmony with, the infinite Order, which he saw to be all Truth, therefore infinite perfection [132:247].

CHAPTER 21.

The Case of H. B. in His Own Words.

"MY early home was one of quite narrow limitations. I did not find myself among books, though such was my desire for them that nothing else had any attractions for me. My mental activity must have been noticeable, as I can now see it, in comparison with that of others about me. I never found much pleasure in the ordinary amusements of boyhood. I preferred to be alone, and in summer I loved most of all to be in the woods. I found companionship in the trees; they seemed nearer to me than human beings. I used to talk to them, and think they said something to me. All my life the woods have thus drawn me to themselves, and now, if I could, I would live among the trees. All my life I have loved to be alone and still do. Whether, according to Byron's dictum, I am 'a wild beast or a God' I will not stop to guess. It is also true that I love the society of congenial spirits in domestic and general life.

"I soon learned that men regulated their intercourse with each other by conventional rules and not by what I now understand as spiritual laws, but which I could not then name and could not understand, though I felt their presence, as Wordsworth felt 'an outward presence' in nature.

"The shocks that my spiritual consciousness experienced as I came in contact with rough men were such as no language can reach. There has been a gradual development of this perception, or spiritual vision, all through life. I early began to inquire how things came to be as they are, and that is what I am now trying to do. As things look to me now, I must always regard it as a misfortune that I was born into the atmosphere of the Calvinistic theology. I lived for a score of years under the shadow of that black cloud—years which might have otherwise been spent in healthy growth. This theology I tried to accept intellectually because everybody about me did; but my soul never endorsed it. At the age of forty I was quite free from the dwarfing influence of such a line of thought, and since then have breathed freely.

"What I am I owe mostly to books. I have been but little in contact with men who could have taught me and given me strength. A year or two at an academy and twenty weeks in college is all I have known in those directions. As I came out from the shadow of that dark theology I chanced to hear Emerson. I then got his books. I have been a close student of them for fifty years. I owe more to him than to, I almost might say, all other men beside. Next I found my way to Darwin. Mine was the only copy of the 'Origin of Species' to be found in my community for ten years.

"The first real mental illumination I remember to have experienced was when I saw that the universe exists in each of its individual atoms—that is, the universe is the result of a few simple processes infinitely repeated. When a drop of water has been mathematically measured, every principle will have been used which would be called for in the measurement of the heavens. All life on the globe is sustained by digestion and assimilation; when by voluntary and traumatic action these stop death follows. The history of an individual mind is the history of the race. Know one thing in its properties and relations and you will know all things. All crystallography is in one grain of sand, all animal life in one insect, all vegetable in a single bud. I was then about forty.

"My next was when I saw there was no boundary line between

vegetable and animal life, and hence no beginning nor end to either. The first of these experiences came to me long before I found what Thales said on this point. These statements are perhaps enough to indicate the direction in which my intellect has developed.

"Whatever calm delights have come to me through the intellect the true grandeur of my days has been found in the atmosphere of the moral sentiment—a grandeur which reduces all material happenings to the value of toys. I felt this when a boy as an overshadowing presence that was constantly drawing me away from all that seemed to make up the life of those about me—drawing me away I knew not how or whither. What I then saw dimly, or as 'through a glass darkly,' now shines all about me with a brightness exceeding that of the sun. In its light I see that love and justice cannot be limited by what, in the poverty of our ignorance, we call time and space. Hence all the thinking and all the teaching that has been done in the world, founded in our ideas of time and space, are blown away like chaff, or are consumed like 'wood, hay and stubble.'

"I was nearly sixty when I came to see that what is true at any time and in any place is also true at all times and in all places, or, what we call law, found anywhere will be found everywhere, though men may give it different names. What men call gravity holds in mental no less than in physical phenomena, and all physical phenomena, at their best, are dull and murky till they come up into spiritual life. As an illustration that every law has its universality take the familiar law or principle that action and reaction are equal. What is this but reaping the whirlwind after one has sown the wind, or how does that natural law differ from this teaching: 'Whatsoever a man soweth that shall he also reap?' Are they aught but different strains in the great cosmic melody?

"Soon after I began to understand the paradoxical teachings of Jesus, as when he declared that 'he that would save his life must lose it and he that would lose it (for Jesus' sake) alone shall find it.' The same in Paul, 'as having nothing yet possessing all things.' From this it was but a step to a knowledge of the central principle of all spiritual life—namely, the giving of one's self for others.

"About ten years ago, at the age of sixty, I found myself tormented with that question with which intelligence has wrestled since there was any of that commodity in the earth—namely, the beginning of things. When in deep agony, a side light was flashed upon my soul, with almost blinding suddenness—'If you could find a beginning, would not that beginning be itself an end?' Hence, if you could find one end of things, would not that show you that there must also be another end? What! an end of all things, beyond which there could be only blankness, as there must have been before things began to be, if they did begin. No! 'There was no beginning and there can be no end!' Since that moment's experience I have not been troubled as to the immortality of the soul, and I now think I never shall be again.

"Five years ago I had an experience which has proved more fruitful to me perhaps than all others combined. I had a fall, striking on my head. I lost consciousness. In regaining possession of myself I passed through all the experiences of the race! In the first stage I simply was aware of the fact that I was something; what that was, I neither knew nor cared to know. I did not know what knowing was. I was calm, blissfully happy, and to me there was no past nor any future. There was to me no time, no place, no anything, save that tiny speck of consciousness—myself. As there was nothing to note duration—that stage might have been in duration incomprehensible. At any rate, such was its lesson to me.

"This stage of blissful existence was ended by my discovering that there was something about me which was not myself. I began to see and seeing I began to reason, and so I at length found my objective world. As in the previous stage, I had no use for time, and so, to me, there was none. This stage might have lasted an eternity, so far as I took note of it. I was busy in studying myself first, and then the things about me, and so the infinite peace of my first experience was broken up.

"Unable to think otherwise, I concluded that what I saw must be like myself, and so I began my acquaintance with this outer world by transferring to its objects what I found in myself. This stage lasted in my experience from the moment I saw things about me to the dawn of experimental science. I then became acquainted with the beginning of all knowledge and especially of all religion. Of course, self consciousness soon returned and I came back into my old world again. Since that hour my experience has seemed more than that of all my previous life. Nothing is now any longer dim or obscure. My spiritual expansion has been rapid in these three or four past years. I live in the world, but I seem to myself not of it!

"I enjoy what I must call spiritual vision. No sooner does the intellect seize upon a fact than I see it in its spiritual relations, no less than in its material, only much more clearly. The perfection of mathematics is simply a demonstration of the spiritual truth that God cannot lie.

"Natural phenomena are but the shadows of the spirit from which they spring, as the human face changes under the influence of love, hatred or fear. Color in nature, which washes all things in its warm waves, shows us what spiritual love would do if once let loose in the world. The Bible is simply a picture, which I see with infinite clearness. This vision seems to extend to the atomdance in nature, no less than through all laws, all knowledge, all science, all history and all religion.

"You set me a hard task when you bid me give 'the difference I perceive in myself' since these experiences. I find no language in which I can tell of the things in this realm where I now am. I have not even discovered an alphabet. When, O when, shall I be able to reveal its poetry? I see everywhere and in every object unceasing motion, and in that motion a creative force forever and forever repeating and re-repeating the same simple process as to infinity. Through all nature the grand rhythms roll and heaven and earth are filled with the melody. Men are but boys chasing shadows. The spiritual significance of the world none seem to see—the infinite simplicity of its processes none care to understand."

SUMMARY.

This seems to the editor to be probably, though not certainly, a true case of Cosmic Consciousness, in which the cosmic plane was reached gradually, and not as usually happens per saltum. If it is not that, then it is a case of gradual ascent to the extreme limit of the self conscious mind. In any case, the experience of H. B. is interesting and instructive and well deserves a place in this book.

CHAPTER 22.

R. P. S.

BORN 1830; died 1898.

In a letter to the editor R. P. S. says: "I was about thirty when this marvellous transforming baptism came to me. To it I attribute results* immensely disproportioned to my very moderate natural ability or knowledge. A scientific, accurate diagnosis of it all would be a most valuable contribution to human knowledge."

The experience may now be given in R. P. S.'s own words, beginning [140: 135]:

"Having always known that upon conversion the believer received the Holy Spirit, and that his guidance and power would be known, when needed, in unfolding the treasures of Scriptures, in service or in trials, I had not looked for any other special manifestations of His presence. And yet there was a large class of passages in the Old and New Testament the conditions of which were not fully met by any consciousness of my own, full as had been the knowledge of pardon, adoption and standing in Christ, nor yet by a later experience, which came to me ten years after my conversion, of the wonderful inward cleansing of the blood 'from all sin.'

"I had read 'Whosoever drinketh of the water that I shall give

---

* Referring to work done by him almost miraculous in character and quantity but which cannot be further specified here.

him, shall never thirst; but the water that I shall give him shall be in him a well of water springing up into everlasting life.' This was not true in my experience, in the full meaning evidently intended by the words. There did not always from my heart 'flow rivers of living water' freely and spontaneously. Too often the force-pump, rather than the fountain, would have represented my condition. As I gazed in the mirror of the Word, upon the glorious person of my Lord, my soul was often bowed in adoring love, but I had never come to 'know' [17:14:17] the Comforter in such a fullness that I could realize His indwelling presence as even better than that of the visible person of Jesus. I had read that as men were 'possessed' by an evil spirit and led to do things far beyond their natural powers, so these 'filled with the spirit,' seemed to be carried out of, and beyond, themselves. I had read the charge against the apostles, of being 'drunken,' and that afterwards Paul brought the same thought of the elevation of wine, as the illustration of being 'filled with the Spirit.' This seemed to be an ordained condition, since God's commands are always promises; just as his promises are commands; the promises being always larger than the commands. As yet I had never known, in my consciousness, a being thus 'filled with the Spirit,' or the meaning of John the Baptist's declaration, 'He shall baptise you with the Holy Ghost and with fire.'

"So ignorant was I, even in the matters of the greatest importance to my spiritual interests, that, in finding the inward cleansing and the outward 'victory' over sin—that 'faith which overcometh' the world—I did not press beyond my educational habits of thought to recognize that a far more glorious manifestation of God was yet to be known by the Spirit. I then scarcely noticed that it was after our Lord had breathed on his disciples, with the words 'Receive ye the Holy Ghost,' they had yet to wait ten days at one time in prayerful expectation for the more full baptism of the Spirit; nor that it was some time after this event that, 'When they had prayed, the place was shaken where they were assembled together, and they were all filled with the Holy Ghost.' I was not, indeed, in the condition of the 'disciples' who

as yet had 'not so much as heard whether there be any Holy
Ghost'; and yet I had formed no conception of what the promised
baptism 'with the Holy Ghost and with fire' could be.

"Deeply thankful for the privileges of 'sanctification through
faith,' realized in an unexpected fullness a few months before, I
one day joined in the woods a few Christians who had met to wait
before God for the baptism of the Spirit. Except a few low hymns
or brief prayers, the half-hour was spent in solemn silence. At
length 'there came a sound from heaven as of a rushing, mighty
wind, and it filled all the (place) where they were sitting.' No
uninspired words could so describe my impressions. And yet no
leaf above or blade of grass below was moved—all nature was
still. It was to our souls, not to our senses, that the Lord revealed
himself by the Spirit. My whole being seemed unutterably full
of the God upon whom I had long believed. The perception of my
senses could bring no such consciousness as now was mine. I
understood the supersensual visions of Isaiah, Ezekiel and Paul.
No created thing was now so real to my soul as the Creator Himself. It was awful, yet without terror. I lost no part of my
senses, and yet they were all wrapped up in the sublime manifestation. A question put to me was answered as briefly as possible,
that my soul might lose nothing of the Heavenly Presence en-
wrapping and filling my being. I do not remember to have then
told anyone of it, but days afterwards, when I rejoined my wife,
she burst into tears as we met, before we had spoken a word, so
great was the change in my appearance. 'Songs in the night season,' the living waters welling up from my heart, came with the
consciousness of waking. An awe, sweet but not burdensome,
shadowed my spirit, as every moment was filled with the presence
of God; nor did it leave me in the midst of the most engrossing
occupations. Life became a psalm of praise.

"This elevation of feeling necessarily subsided after a season,
but it left me with an inner consciousness of God which is expressed by the words: 'I will dwell in them and walk in them.'
'We will come to him and make our abode with him.' The scene
upon the Cross of Calvary became often more real than the senses

could make it. Without the materiality of bodily sight, the holy countenance of Jesus, in its tender, suffering humanity, lightened by the glory of divinity, seems now to me to look down from the cross, upon assemblies, as I tell of redemption for sinners. It is painful to endeavor to speak of these things. My poor words seem rather to cover than to reveal them. Would that the glorious reality would be conveyed to other hearts!''

Here is a case of ascent into the full light of the morning *before* the actual rising of the sun. This man was highly privileged, but it was not given to him to see "the heavens opened.'' He passed into the "Brahmic Bliss,'' but did not see (as far as it appears) the "Brahmic Splendor.''

CHAPTER 23.

E. T.

BORN 1830. Entered Cosmic Consciousness 1860, aet. thirty years. The writer has (at present) no details to give in this case and only includes it for the age of illumination.

CHAPTER 24.

Case of Ramakrishna Paramahansa.

WE are indebted to Max Mueller and to Protap Chunder Mozoomdar for such scanty details as we have in this case. Their evidence is perhaps all the more valuable, since the first named, at least, who is the principal reporter [116: 306], has never shown in his writings any knowledge or appreciation of the faculty here called Cosmic Consciousness, although his lifework in Indian literature has brought him in contact with the more or less perfect expression of it a thousand times. All that is done here is to epitomize such information as the reporters above named have given us.

Ramakrishna Paramahansa was born in 1835, in a village near Jahanabad (Hooghly district), near Kamarpukur. His chief place of residence is said to have been at a temple of the Goddess Kali, on the bank of the Ganges, near Calcutta. He died 1886, in the Kasipur Garden, two miles north of Calcutta. He is said to have exercised an extraordinary influence upon a large number of intelligent and highly educated men, including Protap Chunder Mozoomdar and Keshub Chunder Sen. A score of young men, who attached themselves closely to him, have, since his death, become ascetics. They follow his teaching by giving up the enjoyment of wealth and carnal pleasure, living together in a college and retiring at times to holy and solitary places. Besides these, we are told that a great number of men with their families are ardently devoted to his cause.

Ramakrishna never moved in the world or was a man of the world. He seems, from the first, to have practiced severe asceticism. He was a Brahmin by caste, well formed in body, but the austerities through which his character developed seemed to have permanently disordered his system, leaving upon his features an appearance of debility, paleness and shrunkenness which excited compassion. Yet, in the midst of his emaciation, his face retained a fullness, a childlike tenderness, a profound visible humbleness, an unspeakable sweetness of expression, and a smile such as Mozoomdar says he never saw on any other face. A Hindu saint is always particular about his externals. He wears the Garua cloth, eats according to strict forms, refuses to have intercourse with men, is a rigid observer of caste, is always proud and professes secret wisdom; he is always a universal counsellor and dispenser of charms. But the man Ramakrishna was singularly devoid of any such claims. His dress and diet did not differ from those of other men, except in the general negligence he showed towards both, and as to caste, he openly broke it every day. He repudiated the title of a teacher, showed displeasure at any exceptional honor which people tried to pay him, and he emphatically disclaimed the knowledge of secrets and mysteries. He worshiped no particular Hindu deity, neither Siva, Vishnu, or the

Saktis, and yet he accepted all the doctrines, the embodiments, the usages and devotional practices of every religious cult. Each in turn was infallible to him. His religion meant ecstasy, his worship transcendental insight, his whole nature burnt day and night with the permanent fire and fever of a strange faith and feeling. His conversation was a ceaseless breaking forth of his inward fire and lasted for long hours. He was often merged in rapturous ecstasy and outward unconsciousness during the day, particularly when he spoke of his favorite spiritual experiences or heard any striking response to them. Krishna became to him the incarnation of loving devotion, and we are told that, while meditating on him, his heart full of the burning love of God, his features would suddenly become stiff and motionless, his eyes lose their sight, and while completely unconscious himself, tears would run down his rigid, pale, yet smiling face; and while in that state he would sometimes break out into prayers, songs and utterances, the force and pathos of which would pierce through the hardest heart and bring tears to eyes that never wept before through the influence of religion.

What is most extraordinary, his religion was not confined to the worship of Hindu deities. For long days he subjected himself to various kinds of discipline to realize the Mohammedan idea of all-powerful Allah. He let his beard grow, he fed on Moslem diet, he continually repeated sentences from the Koran. For Christ his reverence was deep and genuine. He bowed his head at the name of Jesus, honored the doctrine of his sonship, and once or twice attended Christian places of worship. He showed how it was possible to unify all the religions of the world by seeing only what is good in each one of them, and by sincere reverence for every one who has suffered for the truth, for their faith in God and for their love of men. He left nothing in writing. His friends wrote some of his sayings. He did not desire to found a sect.

Here follow a few more or less characteristic passages from his teachings:

How to get rid of the lower self.   The blossom vanishes of itself as the fruit grows, so will your lower self vanish as the divine grows in you.

So long as the heavenly expanse of the heart is troubled and disturbed by the gusts of desire, there is little chance of our beholding therein the luminary God.   The beatific godly vision occurs only in the heart which is calm and wrapped in divine communion.

The soiled mirror never reflects the rays of the sun; so the impure and the unclean in heart that are subject to Maya (illusion) never perceive the glory of Bhagavan, the Holy One.   But the pure in heart see the Lord as the clear mirror reflects the sun.   So be holy.

A recently married young woman remains deeply absorbed in the performance of domestic duties, so long as no child is born to her.   But no sooner is a son born to her than she begins to neglect household details, and does not find much pleasure in them.   Instead thereof she fondles the new-born baby all the livelong day and kisses it with intense joy.   Thus man in his state of ignorance is ever busy in the performance of all sorts of works, but as soon as he sees in his heart the Almighty God he finds no pleasure in them.   On the contrary, his happiness consists now only in serving God and doing his works. He no longer finds happiness in any other occupation, and cannot draw himself from the ecstasy of the Holy Communion.

As one can ascend to the top of a house by means of a ladder, or a bamboo, or a staircase, or a rope, so divers are the ways and means to approach God, and every religion in the world shows one of these ways.

Why can we not see the Divine Mother?   She is like a high-born lady, transacting all her business from behind the screen—seeing all, but seen by none.   Her devout sons only see Her by going near Her, behind the screen of Maya.

You see many stars at night in the sky, but find them not when the sun rises.   Can you say there are no stars in the heavens of day?   So, O man, because you behold not God in the days of your ignorance say not that there is no God.

In the play of hide-and-seek, if the player succeeds in touching the grand dame (Boori), he is no longer liable to be made a thief of by the seeker. Similarly, by once seeing God, man is no longer bound down by the fetters of the world.   Just as the person touching the Boori is free to go about wherever he chooses without being pursued and made a thief of, so also in this world's playground there is no fear to him who has once touched the feet of God. He attains freedom from all worldly cares and anxieties, and nothing can ever bind him again.

The pearl-oyster that contains the precious pearl is in itself of very little value, but it is essential for the growth of the pearl.   The shell itself may prove to be of no use to the man who has got the pearl.   So ceremonies and rites may not be necessary for him who has attained the Highest Truth—God.

A little boy wearing the mask of the lion's head looks indeed very terrible. He goes where his little sister is at play and yells out hideously, which at once shocks and terrifies his sister, making her cry out in the highest pitch of her voice in the agony of despair to escape from the clutch of the terrible being. But when her little tormentor puts off the mask the frightened girl at once recognizes her loving brother and flies up to him, exclaiming, "Oh, it is my dear brother, after all!" Even such is the case of all the men of the world who are deluded and frightened and led to do all sorts of things by the nameless power of Maya, or Nescience, under the mask of which Brahman hides himself. But when the veil of Maya is taken from Brahman, the men then do not see in him a terrible and uncompromising Master, but their own beloved Other Self.

It cannot, perhaps, be proved (in the usual way) that Ramakrishna was a case of Cosmic Consciousness. We cannot point to the presence of the subjective light or to sudden illumination at a certain age. Still there is little doubt about the diagnosis, and we can readily understand our want of definite information, which is probably due to the fact that those who reported the case to us had no conception of its real nature, or what were the characteristic and essential symptoms. To them subjective light (if they knew of it) would probably seem a matter of no consequence, and equally so the age and the more or less suddenness of the oncoming of such features in the case as they did report.

CHAPTER 25.

Case of J. H. J.

A MERCHANT in a pretty large way of business. The advent of the Cosmic Sense—which was momentary and incomplete—made no visible change in his life, and very few of the hundreds who knew him had the least suspicion that he ever had any experience out of the common. He is not regarded as a saint nor exactly as a sage, but he has many warm friends and is in several respects remarkably intelligent. He was born May 25, 1837. On the night of December 31, 1868, in the middle of his thirty-second year, he had the following dream. It is not at all clear that the dream had any connection with the subsequent illumination. I give it in his own language as part of the case, and each reader may form his own opinion as to its importance. The writer, however, may say that it seems to him that the sense of intense light experienced in it, if not actually the subjective light that belongs to the oncoming of Cosmic Consciousness, bore some close relation to it:

"I thought," he writes, "I was standing behind the counter of my shop in the middle of a bright, sunshiny afternoon, and instantly, in a flash, it became darker than the darkest night, darker than a mine, and the gentleman who was talking with me ran out into the street. Following him, although it was so dark, I could see hundreds and thousands of people pouring into the street, all wondering what had happened. Just then I noticed in the sky, in the far southwest, a bright light like a star, about the size of the palm of my hand, and in an instant it seemed to grow larger and larger and nearer and nearer, until it began to light up the darkness. When it got to the size of a man's hat, it divided itself into twelve smaller lights with a larger one in the centre, and then very rapidly it grew much larger, and instantly I knew that this was the coming of Christ. The moment this thought occurred to me the whole southwestern heavens became filled with a shining host, and in the centre of it Christ and the twelve apostles. By this time it was lighter than the lightest day that could possibly be imagined, and as the shining host advanced toward the zenith, the friend with whom I was talking, exclaimed; 'That is my Saviour!' and I thought he immediately left his body and ascended into the sky, and I thought I was not good enough to accompany him. Then I awoke.

"For some days afterwards I was very strongly impressed by this dream and could not tell it to anyone. In about a fortnight I told it to my family; afterwards to my Sunday school class, and since I have frequently repeated it. It was the most vivid dream I ever had."

The rest of his experience is drawn from a letter, dated June 4, 1892:

"I had been for three years or more in the 'wine press.' I knew there must be a place of rest, or else the whole Bible was a lie. I had, from a boy, read and thought much about 'the second coming,' and, while I laughed at the 'Millerites' and knew that they were idiotic in their expectations, yet I still had enough of the *marvelous* in me to be looking for a sudden change of some sort. One day, in the late spring of 1871 [he was then just thirty-four years old], Mr. B. [the J. B. of this volume] told my wife that my case was a very curious one. Said he: 'Your husband is born again and don't know it. He is a little spiritual baby, with eyes not yet open, but he will know it in a very short time.' And about three weeks after that, about a quarter to eight o'clock, while walking on Second Avenue (N. Y.) with my wife, on my way to a lecture at the Liberal Club, I suddenly exclaimed to my wife: 'A., I have eternal life!' I cannot say there was a tremendous, though there was a marked, exaltation. The prominent feeling was a sort of undying assurance that the Christ in me had arisen and would remain in everlasting consciousness—and it has. There was a time after this, three years later, in August, 1874, on a Long Branch boat, when in a crowd of people, sitting, leaning back in my chair, I had an experience of the greatest mental and spiritual exaltation—when it seemed as if my whole soul, *and body, too,* were suffused with light; but this never made me forget the first experience, which, while something like the latter, was not so transporting."

CHAPTER 26.

T. S. R.

BORN 1840. Entered Cosmic Consciousness in 1872, at the age of thirty-two years. Was a member of a Presbyterian Church in good standing. Upon illumination left the church and has had no connection with any similar organization since. Was always an earnest, thoughtful man. "In 1872 [an informant says] his friends thought for a time that he was becoming insane. He passed through a grave spiritual crisis, the exact nature of which is not known to me.* Whatever it was, it, to all appearance,

* Louis Lambert—that is, Balzac—was supposed by his friends to be insane at the time of illumination [5 : 126 et seq.]. Mohammed feared he was becoming insane. In the case of M. C. L. (infra) the same question came up. This question has undoubtedly presented itself to the mind of almost every person who has experienced illumination.

passed over, and he has been ever since not only sane but exceptionally intelligent and rightminded. He is the best read Emerson scholar that I know. In all his home relations—by wife, children and friends—he is greatly beloved. He has a positive certainty of individual immortality. He is a very modest man, but has a certain air or manner which impresses those who meet him that he (being a mere clerk) is a richer man than his millionaire employers, *and that he knows it.*"

CHAPTER 27.

W. H. W.

BORN 1842. Entered Cosmic Consciousness 1877, at the age of thirty-five years. Had a very strong and original mind and a wonderful memory. A gentleman who knew him writes: "He was an extraordinary conversationalist; it was as if he had absorbed the minds and works of Darwin, Huxley and Spencer, and spoke with the authority and knowledge of all three; their works, thought, language, were at his tongue's end; it was an education to be with him for a few days. He was a wonderful violinist—the equal of the best not known as a star. He heard of J. B. [the J. B. of this volume] in 1877, sent for him and had a five hours' talk with him (he had a capacity of taking in a case, subject, book, musical composition, what not, and retaining permanently all he heard or read about it). He asked for another interview, and after a second talk of two hours said: 'Now, Mr. B., I have done. I have just one more question to ask you and only one. Have you got what the scientists might call "a New Prime"?' 'I have,' replied B., 'and I can further add that you will get it, too. I don't know when, but you will get it.' J. B. went back to his own city that afternoon. The following afternoon he received a telegram from W. H. W. 'I have got that Prime.' I afterwards heard him describe the experience. He said: 'I went into the yard to the pump, and just as I got there it came—a shock, a flood of light, and along with, or immediately following, the shock and the subjective glow—like a great internal blaze—came the feeling of absolute harmony with the power that made all things and is in all things. All striving stopped—there was nothing to strive for— I was at peace.' "

CHAPTER 28.

Richard Jefferies.

BORN November 6th, 1848; died August 14th, 1887.

This case is given as that of a man who spent several years in what has been called above the twilight of Cosmic Consciousness but upon whom the sun did not rise. In this connection the man is an exceedingly interesting study to all those who care about the subject matter of the present volume, and the more so because he has written a book in which he gives us what is undoubtedly a straightforward and candid account of his spiritual life down to his thirty-fifth year [105]. He seems to have entered early into the twilight above referred to, and it seems probable that Jefferies would have entered into at least momentary Cosmic Consciousness at about the usual age had it not been that before that time came, when thirty-three years old, he was seized with a fatal sickness which weakened and tortured him from that time until his death, which took place in his thirty-ninth year. Be this as it may, the book named represents the highest spiritual altitude attained by Jefferies—a spiritual altitude clearly above that of mere self consciousness and as clearly below the mental status of complete Cosmic Consciousness.

The book, of course, should be read as a whole—and it will well repay perusal—but for the purposes of the present volume the passages found below must suffice.

The story of my heart commences seventeen years ago [105 : 1]. I was not more than eighteen when an inner and esoteric meaning began to come to me from all the visible universe, and undefinable aspirations filled me [105 : 181].

At eighteen years of age he enters into the twilight of the Cosmic Sense. But neither then nor afterwards present themselves any of the characteristic phenomena of entrance into Cosmic Consciousness.

I was utterly alone with the sun and the earth. Lying down on the grass, I spoke in my soul to the earth, the sun, the air, and the distant sea far beyond sight. I thought of the earth's firmness—I felt it bear me up; through the grassy couch there came an influence as if I could feel the great earth speaking to me. I thought of the wandering air—its pureness, which is its beauty; the air touched me and gave me something of itself [105:4]. By all these I prayed; I felt an emotion of the soul beyond all definition [105:5].

I thought of my inner existence, that consciousness which is called the soul. These—that is, myself—I threw into the balance to weigh the prayer the heavier. My strength of body, mind and soul, I flung into it; I put forth my strength; I wrestled and labored and toiled in might of prayer. The prayer, this soul-emotion, was in itself—not for an object—it was a passion. I hid my face in the grass, I was wholly prostrated, I lost myself in the wrestle, I was rapt and carried away [105:7].

Jefferies is always longing, always aspiring, always reaching out and striving. He intensely feels that there is something infinitely desirable just beyond his outstretched hand, but he never actually touches it.

Had any shepherd accidentally seen me lying on the turf he would only have thought that I was resting a few minutes; I made no outward show. Who could have imagined the whirlwind of passion that was going on within me as I reclined there! I was greatly exhausted when I reached home [105:8].

Having drunk deeply of the heaven above and felt the most glorious beauty of the day, and remembering the old, old sea, which (as it seemed to me) was but just yonder at the edge, I now became lost, and absorbed into the being or existence of the universe. I felt down deep into the earth under, and high above into the sky, and farther still to the sun and stars. Still farther beyond the stars into the hollow of space, and losing thus my separateness of being came to seem like a part of the whole [105:8-9].

With all that time and power I prayed that I might have in my soul the intellectual part of it—the idea, the thought [105:17]. Now, this mo-

Of such passages as these Salt [172:53] says: "Jefferies now writes without disguise, as one who has received a solemn revelation of the inner beauty of the universe." But note especially his love of external nature is always a longing, becoming intense but never fulfilled, to become the object. But perhaps the essence of the Cosmic Sense, from the point of view of the intellect, is the realization that the subject and object *are one.* See supra the words of E. C. and of the Vaga-Saneyi-Samhita-Upanishad also [193:173]: "Strange and hard that paradox true I give, objects gross and the unseen soul *are one.*" But Gautama says that "within him there arose the eye to perceive, the knowledge, the understanding, the wisdom that lights the true path, the light that expels darkness."

ment gives me all the thought, all the idea, all the soul expressed in the Cosmos around me [105:18]. Gives me fullness of life like to the sea and the sun, to the earth and the air; gives me fullness of physical life, mind, equal and beyond their fullness; gives me a greatness and perfection of soul higher than all things; gives me my inexpressible desire which swells in me like a tide—gives it to me with all the force of the sea [105:103]. I realize a soul-life illimitable; I realize the existence of a Cosmos of thought [105:51]. I believe in the human form; let me find something, some method, by which that form may achieve the utmost beauty. Its beauty is like an arrow, which may be shot any distance according to the strength of the bow. So the idea expressed in the human shape is capable of indefinite expansion and elevation of beauty. Of the mind, the inner consciousness, the soul, my prayer desired that I might discover a mode of life for it, so that it might not only conceive of such a life, but actually enjoy it on the earth. I wished to search out a new and higher set of ideas on which the mind should work. The simile of a new book of the soul is the nearest to convey the meaning—a book drawn from the present and future, not the past. Instead of a set of ideas based on tradition, let me give the mind a new thought drawn straight from the wondrous present, direct this very hour [105:30].

Recognizing my own inner consciousness, the psyche, so clearly, death did not seem to me to affect the personality. In dissolution there was no bridgeless chasm, no unfathomable gulf of separation; the spirit did not immediately become inaccessible, leaping at a bound to an immeasurable distance [105:34].

He has the feeling of continuous life—it *does not seem* that he can die. If he had attained to Cosmic Consciousness he would have entered into eternal life, and there would be no "seems" about it.

To me everything is supernatural [105:42]. It is impossible to wrest the mind down to the same laws that rule pieces of timber [105:42].

When I consider that I dwell this moment in the eternal Now that has ever been and will be, that I am in the midst of immortal things this moment, that there probably are souls as infinitely superior to mine as mine to a piece of timber—what, then, is a "miracle" [105:44]?

"Why, who makes much of a miracle? To me every hour of the light and dark is a miracle, every cubic inch of space is a miracle" [193:301], etc.

I feel on the margin of a life unknown, very near, almost touching it—on the verge of powers which, if I could grasp, would give me an immense breadth of existence [105:45]. Sometimes a very ecstasy of exquisite enjoyment of the entire universe filled me [105:182]. I want more ideas of soul-life. I am certain that there are more yet to be found. A great life—an entire civilization—lies just outside the pale of common thought [105:48].

There is an Entity, a Soul-Entity, as yet unrecognized [105:48].

He feels that he has not realized—that there is something just out of reach; his contentment is never complete or only so by flashes. On the other hand, those who have fully entered Cosmic Consciousness—upon whom the sun has risen—who have achieved Nirvâna—the kingdom of heaven—are at rest and happy. "I am satisfied," says Whitman, "I exist as I am. That is enough." "I know I am solid and sound." "I know I am deathless;" and all the fully illumined from Gautama down to E. C., both inclusive, declare the same complete fulfillment of desire.

Yes, the Cosmic Sense which Jefferies felt but did not enter upon.

Man has a soul, as yet it seems to me lying in abeyance, by the aid of which he may yet discover things now deemed supernatural [105:144].

I believe, with all my heart, in the body and the flesh, and believe that it

"I believe in the flesh and the appetites. Seeing, hearing, feeling, are miracles, and should be increased and made more beautiful by every means [105:114]; each part and tag of me is a miracle. Divine am I inside and out!'' that the organs of the body may be stronger in their action, perfect, and lasting; that the exterior flesh may yet be more beautiful; that the shape may be finer, and the motions more graceful [105:29]. I believe all manner of asceticism to be the vilest blasphemy—blasphemy towards the whole of the human race. I believe in the flesh and the body, which is worthy of worship [105:114].

How can I adequately express my contempt for the assertion that all things occur for the best, for a wise and beneficent end, and are ordered by a human intelligence! It is the most utter falsehood and a crime against the human race [105:134].

In these passages is positive evidence that Jefferies never really attained to the Cosmic Sense—that is, he never became conscious of the Cosmic order—the vision of the ''eternal wheels'' of the ''chain of causation'' was not granted him.

Nothing is evolved. There is no evolution any more than there is any design in nature. By standing face to face with nature, and not from books, I have convinced myself that there is no design and no evolution. What there is, what was the cause, how and why, is not yet known; certainly it was neither of these [105:126]. There is nothing human in any living animal. All nature, the universe as far as we can see, is anti- or ultra-human, outside, and has no concern with man [105:62]. There being nothing human in nature in the universe, and all things being ultra-human and without design, shape, or purpose, I conclude that no deity has anything to do with nature [105:63]. Next, in human affairs, in the relations of man with man, in the conduct of life, in the events that occur, in human affairs generally, everything happens by chance [105:64]. But as everything in human affairs obviously happens by chance, it is clear that no deity is responsible [105:66].

I have been obliged to write these things by an irresistible impulse which has worked in me since early youth. They have not been written for the sake of argument, still less for any thought of profit; rather, indeed, the reverse. They have been forced from me by earnestness of heart, and they express my most serious convictions [105:181]. One of the greatest difficulties I have encountered is the lack of words to express ideas [105:184].

So Blake said of ''Jerusalem'': ''I have written this poem from immediate dictation, twelve or sometimes twenty or thirty lines at a time, without premeditation and even against my will.'' This feeling of external or internal domination by something or somebody is common if not universal with men having the Cosmic Sense. Even as in the case of those who have entered the holy of holies, so Jefferies, though the revelation to him was far from complete, saw more than he found it easy to express in our language of the self conscious mind.

CHAPTER 29.

Case of C. M. C. in Her Own Words.

IT is important to clearly realize that in writing the following pages C. M. C. (and the same may be truly said of every person whose evidence is included in this volume) had no prior or contemporary case before her mind upon which, if she were capable of so doing, she could have modeled her narrative. This latter is, beyond all question, a faithful account (as simple and straightforward as she could make it) of her actual psychological experience as she lived through it.

I was born in the year 1844. I have been told that as a child I never seemed young—that is, that along with my youth there was an air of thoughtfulness that belongs to more advanced years. I cannot remember a time when I did not think and wonder about God. The beauty and sublimity of nature have always, from early childhood, impressed me deeply. Went to church and Sunday school, listened attentively to the prayers and sermons—thought over the latter more than was probably supposed. The sermons were old-time Presbyterian—the day of judgment, the sinner's lost condition, the unpardonable sin, and all those things so dreadful to a serious, imaginative child. The older I grew and the more I thought the more puzzled and bewildered I became. Over the sufferings of Jesus I wept bitter tears, grieving that my sins should have nailed him to the cross. How he could be God I could not understand, yet never doubted but that it must be true. I studied the Bible and catechism and especially the "Confession of Faith," not only because it was a duty but because I felt as if I must find out the truth about things. How terribly I felt when I learned that without the gospel the heathen could not be saved. The cruelty and injustice of it made me almost hate God for making the world so. I joined the church, however, thinking that it might bring me peace and rest; but although feeling more *safe* I was just as far as ever from being satisfied. While still quite a girl we began taking some rather liberal church papers which I read and which were to a certain extent a comfort to me, since they showed me that the narrow doctrines in which I had been brought up were not the whole of Christianity. At this time "Paradise Lost," Pollock's "Course of Time" and "Pilgrim's Progress" were favorite books. The "Course of Time," however, left me depressed for many weeks. The vastness and grandeur of the God which I felt in nature I could never reconcile with the God in the Bible, try as I would, and of course I felt myself a wicked skeptic in conse-

C. M. C. seems to have had the mental constitution (as far as the evidence goes) of persons who, when the proper age arrives, reach Cosmic Consciousness.

quence. So it went on and though to all appearance I was happy and full of life like other girls, there was always that undercurrent—a vein of sadness deep down, out of sight. Often as I have walked out under the stars, looking up into those silent depths with unspeakable longing for some answer to the wordless questions within me, I have dropped down upon the ground in a perfect agony of aspiration. But if the stars knew the secret I sought they gave no sign. My experience was no doubt ordinary—largely that of the average girl living the average commonplace life—with aspirations and ideals to all appearance beyond any hope of fulfillment. At twenty-two I was married. Ten years later a change of place broke up the old routine of my life, giving me new associates and new interests. I was thrown into relation with people of more liberal tendencies, and soon began reading the books and magazines ("Popular Science Monthly," etc.) which I found in the hands of my new acquaintances. Tyndall's "Belfast Address," one of the books in question, was the first really thoughtful book (from the point of view of modern science) I had ever read, and it was a revelation to me. From that time, without my going very deeply into the subject, a general idea of evolution was gained, and gradually the old conceptions gave place to more rational ones, and more in accordance with my own feelings. The questions of design or purpose in nature, of individual immortality, etc., were left for scientific research to discover, if to be discovered at all. My attitude was that of an agnostic.

There I rested, not altogether content, it is true. Something in life had been missed which it seemed *ought* to be there; depths in my own nature which had never been sounded; heights I could see, which had not been reached. The chasm between what I was and what I needed to be was deep and wide, but as this same incompleteness was obvious in the lives of others, it was accepted as my share in the common lot. But now into this life, past its meridian and apparently fixed for good or ill, was to come a new element, which should transform me, my life and the world to me. The soul, the deeper self, was to awake, and *demand its own!*

All readers of this book will have noticed the apparent incompatibility between the so-called religions—in other words, the churches—and Cosmic Consciousness. The man who enters or is to enter the latter either never belonged to a church, as Walt Whitman, or leaves the church before illumination, as C. M. C. did, or immediately upon illumination. Almost the only exception to this rule was John Yepes—an exception to be explained by the great breadth of the Catholic Church, which allowed him to interpret his experience in terms of the current religion. Churches are inevitable and doubtless indispensable on the plane of self consciousness, but are probably (in any shape) impossible on the Cosmic Conscious plane.

An irresistible force was to be aroused which should, with mighty throes, rend the veil behind which nature hides her secrets. An illness, combining extreme bodily prostration with equally extreme mental and emotional disturbance, revealed to me the depths in my own nature. After some months my strength was restored and my mental condition to some extent improved, but the deep unrest remained. With the power to suffer came the power of sympathy with all suffering. What I had hitherto known or realized of life was as the prick of a pin to the thrust of a dagger. I had been living on the surface; now I was going down into the depths, and as I went deeper and deeper the barriers which had separated me from my fellow men were broken down, the sense of kinship with every living creature had deepened, so that I was oppressed with a double burden. Was I never to know rest or peace again? It seemed not. Life had many blessings—home, husband, children, friends—yet it was with dismay that I thought of the coming years till death should set me free.

Walt Whitman, in "Leaves of Grass," had portrayed with wonderful power and sublimity this phase of mental and spiritual development, as those who look deeply into their own natures must see. In those wonderful poems nature herself utters her voice, pouring out the elemental pain and passion in living, burning words as lava is poured in torrents from the crater of a volcano—not his voice alone, but that of the soul of humanity imprisoned, struggling to break the bonds which enclose and hold it in. How sweet to lean upon that great soul! to feel that tender human sympathy! and seeing what heights he had reached, and knowing the road he had traveled, what courage!

Passing over the interval between this time and September, 1893, as unimportant, except for the constant struggle within me, I proceed to describe, as well as may be, the supreme event of my life, which undoubtedly is related to all else, and is the outcome of those years of passionate search.

I had come to see that my need was greater even than I had thought. The pain and tension deep in the core and centre of my being was so great that I felt as might some creature which had outgrown its shell, and yet could not escape. What it was I knew not, except that it was a great yearning—for freedom, for larger life—for deeper love. There seemed to be no response in nature to that infinite need. The great tide swept on uncaring, pitiless, and strength gone, every resource exhausted, nothing remained but *submission.* So I said: There must be a reason for it, a purpose in it, even if I cannot grasp it. The Power in whose hands I am may do with me *as it will!* It was several days after this resolve before the point of complete surrender was reached. Meantime, with every internal sense, I searched for that principle, whatever it was, which would hold me when I let go.

At last, subdued, with a curious, growing strength in my weakness, *I let go of myself!* In a short time, to my surprise, I began to feel a sense of physical comfort, of rest, as if some strain or tension was removed. Never before had I experienced such a feeling of perfect health. I wondered at it. And how bright and beautiful the day! I looked out at the sky, the hills and the river, amazed that I had never before realized how divinely beautiful the world was! The sense of lightness and expansion kept increasing, the wrinkles smoothed out of everything, there was nothing in all the world that

I let go! Carpenter tells us [56 : 166 et seq.] that the "suppression of thought" and the "effacement of projects and purposes" are the chief things insisted upon by the Indian experts or yogis in the attainment of the Siddhi or miraculous powers (meaning illumination—Nirvâna). The same doctrine has evidently been taught in India for ages. In the Bhagavad Gita it is laid down [154 : 68] that the "working of the mind and senses" must be restrained—that, in fact, an absolute mental vacancy or blank is *the* condition in which to receive illumination. This seems to be the basis of the teaching of Jesus, that we shall not allow ourselves to be preoccupied with care for money, food, clothing, household needs [14 : 6 : 25—16 : 10 : 42]. But one thing is need-

seemed out of place. At dinner I re-marked: "How strangely happy I am to-day!" If I had realized then, as I did afterwards, what a great thing was happening to me, I should doubtless have dropped my work and given my-self up to the contemplation of it, but it seemed so simple and natural (with all the wonder of it) that I and my affairs went on as usual. The light and color glowed, the atmosphere seemed to quiver and vibrate around and within me. Perfect rest and peace and joy were everywhere, and, more strange than all, there came to me a sense as of some serene, magnetic presence—

ful, he says: Nirvâna, the kingdom of God. And worrying about these worldly matters only tends to keep us from that, while if we attain to the worldly things which we seek nothing is gained, for they are valueless. So Balzac says: The self conscious life "is the glory and scourge of the world; glorious, it creates societies; baneful, it exempts man from entering the path of specialism, which leads to the Infinite." So Whitman: "What do you seek?" he says. "Do you think it is love?" "Yes," he continues, "love is great, but," he says (referring to the Cosmic Sense), "there is something else very great: it makes the whole coincide; it, magnificent, beyond materials, with continu-ous hands, sweeps and provides for all." If you have that you want nothing else.

grand and all pervading. The life and joy within me were becoming so in-tense that by evening I became restless and wandered about the rooms, scarcely knowing what to do with myself. Retiring early that I might be alone, soon all objective phenomena were shut out. I was seeing and comprehending the sublime meaning of things, the reasons for all that had before been hidden and dark. The great truth that life is a spiritual evolution, that this life is but a passing phase in the soul's progression, burst upon my astonished vision with overwhelming grandeur. Oh, I thought, if this is what it means, if this is the outcome, then pain is sublime! Welcome centuries, eons, of suffering if it brings us to this! And still the splendor increased. Presently what seemed to be a swift, oncoming tidal wave of splendor and glory ineffable came down upon me, and I felt myself being enveloped, swallowed up.

I felt myself going, losing myself. Then I was terrified, but with a sweet terror. I was losing my consciousness, my identity, but was powerless to hold myself. Now came a period of rapture, so intense that the universe stood still, as if amazed at the unutterable majesty of the spectacle! Only one in all the infinite universe! The All-loving, the Perfect One! The Perfect Wisdom, truth, love and purity! And with the rapture came the insight. In that same wonderful moment of what might be called supernal bliss, came illumination. I saw with intense inward vision the atoms or molecules, of which seemingly the universe is composed—I know not

The fear that has been noted a dozen times in this volume:

whether material or spiritual—rear-ranging themselves, as the cosmos (in its continuous, everlasting life) passes from *order to order*. What joy when I saw there was no break in the chain— not a link left out—everything in its place and time. Worlds, systems, all blended in one harmonious whole. Uni-

Order to order: This is the cosmic vision —the Brahmic Splendor—the sense or con-sciousness of the cosmos, which lies (ap-parently) at the root of this whole business, just as the sense or consciousness of *self* is the central fact in humanity as we see it to-day about us. It is the "Chain of Causa-tion" of Gautama, the "eternal wheels" of Dante, the "measured and perfect motion"

versal life, synonymous with universal love!

How long that period of intense rapture lasted I do not know—it seemed an eternity—it might have been but a few moments. Then came relaxation, the happy tears, the murmured, rapturous expression. I was safe; I was on the great highway, the upward road which humanity had trod with bleeding feet, but with deathless hope in the heart and songs of love and trust on the lips. I understood, now, the old eternal truths, yet fresh and new and sweet as the dawn. How long the vision lasted I cannot tell. In the morning I awoke with a slight headache, but with the spiritual sense so strong that what we call the actual, material things surrounding me seemed shadowy and unreal. My point of view was entirely changed. Old things had passed away and all had become new. The ideal had become real, the old *real* had lost its former reality and had become shadowy. This *shadowy unreality* of *external things* did not last many days. *Every longing of the heart was satisfied*, every question answered, the "pent-up, aching rivers" had reached the ocean—I loved infinitely and was infinitely loved! The universal tide flowed in upon me in waves of joy and gladness, pouring down over me as in torrents of fragrant balm.

of the "procession of the universe" [193 : 85] of Whitman.

"At other times," says John Yepes, "the divine light strikes the soul with such force that the darkness is unfelt and the light unheeded; the soul seems unconscious of all it knows and is therefore lost, as it were, in forgetfulness, knowing not where it is nor what happened to it, *unaware of the lapse of time*" [203 : 127].

Every longing of the heart was satisfied: The abolition or extinction of the passions and desires belonging to the self conscious life (hence the name Nirvâna) is one of the characteristic features (as we have seen many times already) of the kingdom of heaven—the Cosmic Sense. This point is noted in *every* genuine case, but is nowhere better expressed than in the following words: "Jesus said unto her, If thou knewest the gift of God, and who it is that saith unto thee, Give me to drink: thou wouldest have asked of him and he would have given thee living water. The woman saith unto him, Sir, thou hast nothing to draw with, and the well is deep: from whence hast thou that living water? Jesus answered and said unto her, Every one that drinketh of this water [that is, whoever seeks to quench, by satisfying them, the appetites, passions and desires of the self conscious life] shall thirst again [for these cannot be satisfied and quieted by gratification]: but whosoever drinketh of the water [the kingdom of heaven—the Cosmic Sense] that I shall give him shall never thirst; but the water that I shall give him shall become in him a well of water springing up unto eternal life" [17 : 4 : 10-14].

This describes an actual sensation. The infinite love and tenderness seemed to really stream down over me like holy oil healing all my hurts and bruises.

Our light affliction (which is for the moment) *worketh for us* more and more exceedingly an eternal weight of glory [21 : 4 : 17].

How foolish, how childish, now seemed petulance and discontent in presence of that serene majesty! I had learned the grand lesson, that suffering is the price which must be paid for all that is worth having; that in some mysterious way we are refined and sensitized, doubtless largely by it, so that we are made susceptible to nature's higher and finer influences—this, if true of one, is true of all. And feeling and knowing this, I do not now rave as once I did, but am "silent" "as I sit and look out upon all the sorrow of the world"—"upon all the meanness and agony without end." That sweet eternal smile on nature's face! There is nothing in the universe to compare with it—such joyous repose and sweet unconcern— saying to us, with tenderest love: All

"That which I was seeing," says Dante, under the same circumstances, "seemed to me *a smile of the universe*. O joy! O ineffable gladness!"

is well, always has been and will always be. The "subjective light" (it seems to me) is magnetic or electric—some force is liberated in the brain and nervous system—some explosion takes place—the fire that burned in the breast is now a mounting flame. On several occasions, weeks after the illumination described, I distinctly felt electric sparks shoot from my eyes. In my experience the "subjective light" was not something *seen*—a sensation as distinct from an emotion—it was emotion itself—ecstasy. It was the gladness and rapture of love, so intensified that it became an ocean of living, palpitating light, the brightness of which outshone the brightness of the sun. Its glow, warmth and tenderness filling the universe. That infinite ocean was the eternal love, the soul of nature and all one endless smile!

Outshone the brightness of the sun: "Above the brightness of the sun," says Paul. Mohammed saw "a flood of light of such intolerable splendor that he swooned away." Yepes was for some days partially blinded by it. In Dante's experience, "On a sudden, day seemed to be added to day, as if He who is able had adorned the heaven with another sun;" and Whitman was dazzled by "Another sun ineffable, and all the orbs I knew, and brighter, unknown orbs."

What astonished me beyond all else was, as the months went on (from that September), a deepening sense of a Holy Presence. There was a hush on everything, as if nature were holding her breath in adoration. There were times when the feeling came over me with such force as to become oppressive, almost painful. It would not have surprised me if the very rocks and hills had burst forth in one great anthem of praise. At times I felt as if they *must*, to relieve my feelings.

"The rent veil," "the holy of holies," "the cherubim with folded wings," "tabernacles" and "temples"—I saw that they were symbols—the attempts of man to give expression to an inward experience. Nature touched me too closely; I sometimes felt oppressed by it, such extreme exaltation exhausted me, and I was glad when I could have a common day. I looked forward with somewhat of dread to the summer, and when it came its light and its profusion of color, although delightful, were almost more than I could bear. We think we see, but we are really blind—if we could see!

One day, for a moment, my eyes were opened. It was in the morning, in the early summer of 1894, I went out in happy, tranquil mood, to look at the flowers, putting my face down

A parallel experience is related of Behman. He sat down in a green field, "and, viewing the herbs and grass, he saw into their essences, uses and properties" [40 : 13].

into the sweet peas, enjoying their fragrance, observing how vivid and distinct were their form and color. The pleasure I felt deepened into rapture; I was thrilled through and through, and was just beginning to wonder at it, when *deep within me* a veil, or curtain, suddenly parted, and I became aware that the flowers were alive and conscious! They were in commotion! And I knew they were emitting electric sparks! What a revelation it was! The feeling that came to me with the vision is indescribable—I turned and went into the house, filled with unspeakable awe.

There was and is still, though not so noticeable as earlier, a very decided and peculiar feeling across the brow above the eyes, as of tension gone, a feeling of *more room*. That is the physical sensation. The mental is a sense of *majesty*, of serenity, which is more noticeable *when out of doors*. Another very decided and peculiar effect followed the phenomena above described —that of being *centred*, or of being *a* centre. It was as if surrounding and touching me closely on all sides were the softest, downiest pillows. Lean in what direction I might there they were. A pillow or pillows which fitted *every*

When out of doors: So Carpenter [56] tells us that in transcribing the thoughts and emotions of the Cosmic Sense he found it "necessary to write in the open air," for he says: "What I sought to convey refused itself from me within doors." So also the Cosmic Sense, speaking through Whitman, says [193 : 75]: "I will never translate myself at all only to him or to her who privately stays with me in the open air."

tired spot, so that though I was distinctly conscious of that lightest touch there was not the least resistance or obstruction to movement, and yet the support was as permanent and solid as the universe. It was "the everlasting arms." I was anchored at last! But to what? To something outside myself?

The consciousness of completeness and permanence in myself is one with that of the completeness and permanence of nature. This feeling is quite

The sense of immortality, eternal life, which belongs to Cosmic Consciousness.

distinct from any that I had before illumination and has sprung from that. I often ponder on it and wonder what has happened—what change can have taken place in me to so poise and individualize me. My feeling is as if I were as distinct and separate from all other beings and things as is the moon in space and at the same time indissolubly one with all nature.

Out of this experience was born an unfaltering trust. Deep in the soul, below pain, below all the distraction of life, is a silence vast and grand—an infinite ocean of calm, which nothing can disturb; Nature's own exceeding peace, which "passes understanding."

That which we seek with passionate longing, here and there, upward and outward, we find at last *within ourselves*. The kingdom within! The indwelling God! are words whose sublime meaning we never shall fathom.

The subjoined note was sent the editor by a younger sister of C. M. C. in reply to inquiry made by him as to whether or not any change in the appearance of C. M. C. had been noticed at the time of or subsequent to her experiences given above. The note is dated February 2d, 1895, and is, word for word, as follows:

It was in December, three months after, that I saw my sister for the first time after the experience described, and her changed appearance made such a deep impression on me that I shall never forget it. Her looks and manner were so changed that she scarcely seemed the same person. There was a clear, bright, peaceful light in her eyes, lighting her whole face, and she was so happy and contented—so satisfied with things *as they were*. It seemed as though some heavy weight had been lifted and she was free. As she talked to me I felt that she was living in a new world of thought and feeling unknown to me. Sincerely, P. M.

CHAPTER 30.

The Case of M. C. L. in His Own Words.

BORN about January, 1853.

It is a difficult matter to write about myself, especially touching an experience which for four or five years has been one of the most sacredly guarded events of my life. Dr. M. described to me your theory of Cosmic Consciousness, which I at once recognized as defining, in a general way, a certain experience in my own life. I did not communicate the details to the doctor. I never had to anyone, lest I should be charged with superstition or madness.

Early in my career a reputation as a popular preacher was won, and the power to interest and hold an audience achieved. As a minister I wrestled with the intellectual problems of the age, not only in the theological but in the physical, sociological and psychical realms. My desire for information was eager, and the search for truth honest and persistent.

In the month of February, 1890, just following my thirty-seventh birthday, Rev. J. E. L., of Canada, came to assist me in a series of special meetings in my church. My affection for him gained during his stay. He had been gone three days when, thinking of him far through the night—the gray of the morning was already in the heavens—the conviction came to me that in him I had met an incarnation of Christ. I stood a moment transfixed with the thought. Was that which I had held as a theory to be realized as a fact? My friend was forgotten in the vision of Christ, who had come to me, not from without, but through the gates which open inwardly. I knew him, was conscious of him in my own spirit, soul and body. Then with that unfolding consciousness there came a suffusion, as of a delicate cloud or haze, which searched the entire body, was more invasive than light, more penetrating than heat, more inreaching than electricity. It was as if I had been plunged into a bath of fluid more subtle and permeating than ether. Against the inflow and outflow of that enswathing essence the body was not as resistant as the air to a bird's wing or a morning mist to the sunbeam. The rapture, the exaltation, the divinity of that moment passes knowledge. Then swiftly came the awe of the mysterious presence that filled me, and the consciousness of the whole creation, universe, went thrilling through me, not as a thought, a sensation, an emotion, but as the vital breath of God. This grew until I found myself rising and expanding into the Infinite, being diffused and lost therein, and the mind and body reeled. Feeling myself falling, I exclaimed: "The vision is too much! I cannot look upon the face of God and live! Father in heaven, it is enough!" And the voice answered. I sank on my bed and slept like a child. A few hours later I woke in joy which was unspeakable and full of glory. I knew what Paul meant by the "unspeakable gift." The experience was to me the "election"—the calling of sonship to do the Father's will. I went to my pulpit vibrant from subjection to the holy breath, and preached upon the text: "And I, if I be lifted up, will draw all men unto me." The sermon became intense. I saw the cross before me as the necessity of my life. Its agony and fear possessed me, the mind could not bear up under it, I staggered from my pulpit, the congregation awed by the anguish on my face and in my words.

My family were alarmed and a physician was called. He pronounced that I was suffering from nervous prostration, but found no symptoms of insanity, the horror of which had oppressed me. The exhaustion was such that I felt the need of rest and went to my mother, in the old homestead among the hills of Connecticut. To her I told the story. She said: "My boy, I have been expecting this. Now you know the truth of a Living Christ."

The character of my preaching completely changed. The old popularity has waned, but larger powers of mind have come and the perception of truth is clearer. The holy breath kills lust, passion, hate; fills the heart with laughter and the soul with peace.

Compare Bhagavad Ghita: "Objects of sense draw back from a person who is abstinent; not so the *taste for these objects*. But even the taste departs from him *when he has seen the Supreme*" [154 : 50].

I know the eternal Christ of Paul and John, the Christ manifested in the Nazarene, and who in the manifestation was the interpretation of the Cosmic Consciousness of the past and the typal form of the new race in whom that consciousness is evolved. It is the race of the Sons of God, who, like Moses, have stood in the presence and been bathed in the glory of His beauty and the blessedness of His joy. Cosmic Consciousness is the light of the glory of God in the face of Jesus Christ.

In answer to a request for further particulars M. C. L. adds:

The haze or light was more felt than seen. The nearest approach to the sensation I ever knew was experienced when I was at Niagara and visited the Cave of the Winds. And also when, from my window, at Hotel Coutet, in Chamouni, I saw the sun rise on Mt. Blanc. The tinge, subtler than the waves of color, was that of these experiences—a fluid beryl or watery emerald.

The mind slowly passed from fear into a distinct consciousness of some seemingly extra-natural event. At first my thought was, "This is a stroke of paralysis," and I tested every function of body and mind; then the mind opened to understand something of what was going on. It kept pace with the sensation, and each progress of experience involved a mental process.

I am inclined to locate the point of contact in the mind. I use the word mind as synonymous with the psyche, which of course involves the personality. I always have believed that the event primarily was subjective, but a subjective experience which was in perfect accord with the entire objective universe. It was the exaltation of the subjective in me to a new relation with the objective in earth and heaven.

This is the first attempt I have ever made to give a verbal history of that holy hour, and it has been with something of a feeling of hesitancy that I have written; but what is written is written.

CHAPTER 31.

Case of J. W. W., Largely in His Own Words.

HE was born August 11th, 1853. The date of his illumination was January 20th, 1885. He is an architect. He has always been an earnest man, anxious to know the right and to do it. After the momentary attainment of Cosmic Consciousness he became still more bent upon pursuing the same path. Before his illumination he was an agnostic and sceptic, as the annexed autobiographic sketch will show. Not only did he not believe but he had no hope. After illumination he never again doubted the infinite beneficence of the central and over-ruling power of the universe. Although in this case the Cosmic Sense came for a moment only and then passed away, probably for the remainder of life, yet was the man by it incredibly ennobled. That seems the best term for the change that took place in him. Though not a Buddha, a Christ or a Whitman, he was, from that time, clearly superior to the average man. In proof of which statement the fact may be cited that a number of the best young men of his town sought him out and constituted him, under the name of "Master," their spiritual leader. These men have, as the present writer can personally testify, for years tendered this man their personal affection and reverence for no other reason than that they saw clearly in him a superior spiritual nature, which superiority was never detected or suspected in him until after the oncoming of the Cosmic Sense in 1885. J. W. W. has since his illumination devoted his life to the intellectual and moral elevation of himself and his friends.

Here follows an autobiographic sketch, written for the purpose of showing in what manner and under what circumstances he entered into the new life. The pages were not written for this book nor at the instigation of the writer of it. They were, in fact, written before the present writer knew J. W. W., and for·that reason are all the more valuable in this place. Neither were they written to illustrate or support any theory. J. W. W. had and has no theory on the subject. All he knows, or perhaps cares to know, in this connection is that he at that moment entered into relation with a higher form of life, and learned, as Paul says, "unspeakable things"—such things, at all events, as were and are of quite unspeakable importance to him, any doubt of the truth of which things has been, and (as he thinks) always will be, entirely out of the question.

J. W. W., then, addressing his intimate friends, the young and middle-aged men mentioned above, who surround him, and, as said, call him "Master," spoke as follows:

To-day, the 20th of January, 1890, is the anniversary of my mother's death, five years ago. I have decided to celebrate it by giving you some account of circumstances which I have hitherto kept to myself, and sacred in the recesses of my own heart and memory.

I need not tell you, I think, that my mother's last illness and death were, by immeasurable odds, the heaviest grief and pain I have ever known, or shall, probably, ever know. But it is also true that the memory of them is for all time my most precious and priceless possession.

That period was the supreme moment of my life and its deepest experience. In ordinary life we live only on the surface of things, our attention distracted endlessly by the shallowest illusions and baubles.

We discuss with a light heart, and very much at our own ease, the great problems we have been discussing lately in the college (of immortality and the infinite goodness), but are not deeply concerned in them, and care but little what their solutions may be.

But a great bereavement strips the scales from our eyes and compels us, in the intense solitude of our own souls, to gaze into the unfathomable depths in which we float and to question their vast and solemn meanings. It comes upon us clothed in thick darkness and mystery, and pierces our hearts with un-utterable agony and grief, but it may be that the darkest hours of its visitation, the supreme moment itself, may also prove a revelation to our souls of the

Highest and bring us into the very presence of the Infinite Love and Tenderness.

For myself I cannot doubt that this was my own experience. To speak of it is to profane it. I am unworthy to so much as hint at it. But it has been the comfort of my life ever since.

Alas, for the years that have followed! One momentary glimpse into the ineffable brightness, followed by gathering clouds and darkness, painful stumblings and wide errors, unsupported by any recognizable spiritual aid or presence, the heavens deaf and careless to my most earnest prayers and agonizings, nay, even slighting them, so far as appeared. But through it all, like the steadfast shining of a clear star, the memory of that sacred time has remained deep in my heart, and I have never really doubted for a moment that an Infinite Wisdom and Love *does* encircle all our lives—tender, pitying and sympathizing. We may pass our lives without ever realizing it, doubting it, nay, flatly denying it. But it is *there;* and he to whom the vision has ever come at all, though in the briefest transient flash of momentary consciousness, can never again forget it, though his whole after path may be enveloped in darkness and he himself may fall into gross error and backsliding.

I received the ordinary orthodox training of the Presbyterian Church. I was baptized and was a regular attendant at church and Sunday school till well on in my teens.

I attribute at least equal importance, in the formative elements of my religious training, to the daily practice at home, while I was a boy, of family worship. I recall now, as I write, with reverent emotion, the tender tones of my mother's voice, as it pleaded especially for her only deeply loved child.

I was always a lover of books, and I was not far in my teens before I began to learn something of the opposition between the teaching of science and many of the beliefs I had been taught. This discovery was a gradual one, and I will only give a brief outline of the position in which I was ultimately landed.

I learned that the first chapter of Genesis was, at least, a very crude statement of the actual fact. At one time I was an ardent and enthusiastic student of Hugh Miller's books and rested content with the reconciliation he sought to establish between the teaching of his beloved science, Geology, and the Biblical record. But I had to give it up when I came to read and study Darwin's and other books and to acquaint myself with the most recent geological discoveries. I remember well the enthusiasm with which I copied in writing Professor Huxley's famous address to the Geological Section of the British Association, in which he traced the pedigree of the horse to its progenitors in the Eocene period and the clear evidence of its evolution.

Darwinism demolished for me the Biblical account of creation, the authority of the Bible and the account it gives of the origin of evil and the fall of man. This last clearly involves the whole theological superstructure based upon it, including the so-called scheme of redemption and the doctrine of the atonement. The legends of the flood, the tower of Babel, the dispersion of man and the origin of different languages were minor matters of comparatively trifling importance.

I remember the delight with which I read Tyndall's book on "Heat as a

Mode of Motion," and re-read it again and again. I read, too, his lectures on "Sound." These were my introduction to physics, from which I learned the great doctrines of the conservation and correlation of forces, as I had previously learned to realize in some degree the unity and uniformity of nature. In presence of such majestic and august conceptions the ordinary ideas of prayer and miracles seemed childish. I remember reading Tyndall's "Fragments of Science" and feeling this yet more strongly. I came in time to abandon the habit of prayer entirely.

One cannot read much in physiological science without serious reflection on the nature of consciousness, the relation between mind and physical structure and the bearings of all this on the belief in personal immortality. It has always seemed clear to me that the only logical outcome of the considerations put forward by science are flatly and altogether opposed to such belief.

To sum up: Science destroyed for me all belief in the Biblical legends of the creation and the fall of man, etc., and in the doctrine of the atonement, and at least gravely questioned all narratives of miracle, the probability of answer to prayer and the idea of personal immortality. The whole idea, too, of the divine incarnation of Christ on our insignificant atom of a world seemed out of keeping with the august spectacle of the infinite universe and its immeasurable duration. But my reading was never exclusively scientific, and my thoughts accordingly were always modified by other considerations.

I learned something of Descartes, Kant, Fichte, Schelling, Hegel and Spinoza. What the effect of it all was upon me it is impossible for me now to analyze or to tell. But let a man once get fairly into his head the teaching of Kant that time and space only exist as the condition of our consciousness, and the discussion of immortality will seem irrelevant—he will feel the very basis of his speculations crumble beneath his feet. From my earliest youth I have acknowledged two masters, to whom I continually turned and whom I have studied with ever-fresh interest and delight—Carlyle and Emerson—two widely different men but fundamentally alike in the absolute honesty and sincerity of their teaching, their noble and heroic character, and their steady, life-long consecration to the service of the highest. Both of them rejected the materialistic conception of the world, which they regarded as spiritual in its essence, and each believed in his own way in a divine purpose—Emerson with genial and growing optimism, Carlyle with an accompanying Hebraic sense of the mystery and terror of evil.

But neither from Carlyle nor Emerson will a student derive any firm conviction on the subject of individual immortality. Carlyle preferred to leave it a mystery, about which nothing can be definitely said with true assurance, but about which much may be hoped. Emerson, in the main, really believed it, but may be quoted on both sides of the subject. "The questions we lust to have answered are," he declared, "a confession of sin." He preached an unconditional submission and trust. Believe with all your heart and soul that all is well and ask no questions. If it is best that you should continue you will do so; if not, you should not wish it. And the whole subject, he believed, belongs to a much higher plane than that on which it is usually discussed.

It is fifteen years since I carefully studied Tennyson, and especially his "In Memoriam." His arguments, however, seemed to me unconvincing though powerful. I came to prize the two volumes I had of Browning's selections, but could not give complete adhesion to his views either. My judgment was suspended with a leaning of the heart to the "Larger Hope." George Macdonald did me great and growing service, though I could never accept all his conclusions nor admire greatly his logic. On the other hand, the logic of George Eliot's creed seemed to me faultless, and her sympathy with opposite views complete. And her rigid and faithful devotion to truth and fact alone seemed to me to be rewarded in her art. George Macdonald's creations as a rule seem ghostly abstractions. George Eliot's are *alive;* prick them and they bleed. But the melancholy which her books create is undeniable, and the *heart* instinctively revolts from her creed. Matthew Arnold did me immense service by his theological books, and opened the Bible for me again as a book of living interest. But his famous axiom that miracles do not happen, and his elimination of the supernatural element, are unmistakable. But a careful study of Isaiah, with the help of his notes, gave me a clue to a higher view, in my judgment, than the one he himself arrived at. He, too, deprecates the ascription of personality to God, and so does away with the impulse to pray. For who can pray to a "stream of tendency"? Here, again, however, the light which he throws upon the character and teaching of St. Paul helps one also to realize better the teaching of Paul himself, which is higher than that of the critic. Ruskin believed in these things, but his authority is weakened by the evangelical teaching which he himself in time discarded. The great masters seemed to me inconclusive. The whole value of Dante's teaching is vitiated by his false and horrible presentations of eternal punishment. Shakespeare holds himself aloof from the subject, and his opinions do not lie on the surface. Goethe I believed to more explicitly teach the efficacy of prayer and individual immortality than he actually did. I had long had a slight knowledge of and much curiosity about Whitman, and twelve months before my mother died I read for the first time complete copies of "Leaves of Grass" and "Specimen Days," and felt the deep thrill of contact with a mighty spirit. And it seemed a great thing that he, of all men, taught the doctrine of immortality with quite new emphasis and authority.

The foregoing are only very crude and sketchy outlines of the intellectual gropings, questionings, studies and complex, many-sided experiences and difficulties of many years. But they will help you to partially understand my position at the time I write of.

And now to my narrative: I will not trouble you with any particulars which do not seem to me necessary for my purpose. And these I will give as briefly as is consistent with the clearness and right coloring of the picture I want to present. I feel, however, that I must, at the outset, make a disclaimer. I do not want you to judge of my character as a son from my devotion to my mother on her deathbed. As a matter of fact I was *never* in the true sense "a good son." I have too many grave faults and strong opposing idiosyncrasies for that. And I have innumerable bitter memories of harshness, temper, selfish want of consideration and sympathy, things left undone that I ought to have done and things done that I ought to have left undone. They are past recall or expiation now, and I can only pray and strive for a better nature in future.

It is perhaps hardly necessary to speak of my mother. She was not without faults or weaknesses either. She had *good* qualities in an exceptional degree that I need not analyze or speak of. But it is necessary for my purpose that I should refer to what was her ruling passion—a deep, constant, absorbing and self-sacrificing love for her only son. Every one knows something of the sacred depths of a mother's love. But very few can sound their profound abysses as it has been *my* lot to do.

Many circumstances threw us more together than is usual. For one thing, my father was much from home. My own tastes and pursuits kept me more closely at home than is the case with most young men. Our natures, too, were similar in many ways. Naturally I was in many things my mother's confidant. Her sufferings and declining strength made her more and more dependent upon me and knit our hearts together more closely as time went on.

She suffered excruciating pains at times. She became lame and lost the power to stand. If my father was at home he would carry her upstairs at night to bed; if not, she crept to the foot of the stairs and pulled herself up step by step. But on no account would she let me carry her, fearing that I might strain or hurt myself. But eventually she *had* to allow me, and after that I always carried her upstairs.

She was always poorly in the morning and suffered great internal pain. I used to regularly take her up a cup of tea to breakfast, but she ate next to nothing.

Some eighteen months before she died she told me that she believed she suffered from an internal cancer. I had long urged her to let me call in a doctor, and I now insisted upon it.

For a long time she would not allow it, but finally yielded, and Dr. R. was called in. She seemed more bright and cheerful after his visit. She told me that his verdict was that it was *not* a cancer, but the facts which led her to think it was were the results of her rheumatism. It was a happy relief to me, and I dismissed altogether the dreadful ideas which had weighed like lead upon my heart. As a matter of fact it *was* a cancer, and my mother soon came to *know* it without a shadow of a doubt. But in her self-sacrificing regard for me she kept all knowledge back from me, and in the weary, painful and gloomy months that followed I lived in absolute ignorance of the real facts of the case. Perhaps it was better so. I really believe that if I *had* known, the dreadful knowledge would have killed me. As it was I was supported by groundless hopes. And even *so*, the pain of it and the daily strain on my heart and mind were almost more than I could bear, and their effects have remained with me ever since.

I will say as little as possible of that time. I will only note her visibly declining strength, the solitude and many miseries of her lot, her absorbing and endless solicitude for me, her complete indifference to self and her constant

spirit of loving self-sacrifice and a love in *both* our hearts that grew more tender and profound as we realized more and more the coming and inevitable end.
The countless heartaches and pains of those days only revealed more clearly
the depth and strength of a love which was mightier than all adverse circumstances, even death itself.

So the days and weeks and months dragged on in ever-deepening gloom,
till the fateful month of January, 1885. As my mother's strength became less
and less her time for going to bed grew earlier, from ten to half-past nine, to
nine, to half-past eight, to eight. It pained me excessively to note this, and
every night after she had gone I felt unspeakably sad and wretched as I thought
of the future. I could not bear to part with her. I used to keep her as long as
possible, joke with her and do my best to cheer her as well as myself. But her
weariness getting too great she would often lose patience and say, with pathetic
entreaty, "Willie, *do* take me," "Why don't you take me?" or "Willie, *do*
let me go." After that there was nothing for it but to take her at once.

On the 9th of January, 1885, I went to a birthday party. I was far from
well, and I had no heart for it, but I went to tea, came home at eight to take
my mother to bed (for the last time it turned out) and went back, not returning till between one and two. During the night I was awakened by my mother
knocking at the wall. She felt faint, she said, and asked me to bring her a
glass of water. I asked if I should make tea, and she said she preferred water,
which I got her. I grieve to say that I was altogether harsh, unsympathetic
and ungracious. I ought to have *known* that she needed more, and without a
moment's thought for myself should have got it. She thanked me with her
usual tenderness and I went to bed again.

Next morning when I took her tea it all came out. During the night she
had crept out of bed and fainted on the floor. On recovery she had managed
with much painful effort to get into bed again. She would not disturb or
trouble *me*, knowing what she did, but felt compelled at last to rouse me and
ask for a glass of water. Fancy it! Cold water! and rendered with unsympathetic grumbling at that. I have never forgiven myself for my far worse
than stupidity and callousness. My mother, however, in her sweet, serene
charity and loving kindness forgave me from the first.

I will not go into details of the illness that followed. She did not get up
that day, though serenely cheerful, hopeful and loving. My father came home in
the afternoon and she seemed a little better, but at night grew worse and slightly
delirious. Early next morning (Sunday) I brought the doctor, and I learned
for the first time, what others knew, that she had been really suffering from
cancer all the time and that recovery was impossible, though the inevitable end
might possibly be averted for a time. It was a horrible blow to me. I hunted
up a nurse and was in constant attendance on her myself till the end came—
nine days after.

On Sunday, Monday and Tuesday she continued to improve, and my heart
grew lighter and more cheerful. Then she began to grow worse and went step
by step down, *down* into the Valley of the Shadow.

I will pass on rapidly to the closing scenes. But I must note first the following traits of my mother's behavior: An utter and complete forgetfulness of self, unfailing love and charity to all, serene cheerfulness and even gaiety, exerting herself always to cheer *me* with bright and loving smiles and consoling, hopeful words. This, of course, only while she was able. At night she always grew delirious, of which, more anon.

I am sorry to give you painful details, and I only do so where it is necessary for my ultimate purpose. But I am compelled to give you some details of closing scenes.

The night but one before she died was the most horrible night I ever spent. As usual, in such wasting diseases, the waste of the body, after devastating the muscular system, attacks the *nervous* system. When this stage is reached the patient enters on a period of horrible unrest and weariness, passionately longing for rest and incessantly and vainly seeking it by a change of position. Every night, in the delirium of her illness, she felt something of this weariness and would, at the close of the day, call on me, in the old familiar words, "Willie, *do* take me upstairs; do take me." On this particular night, similar cries rang in my ears the whole horrible night long—"Willie, do take me," "Do let me go," "Why don't you let me go?" The words pierced my heart. I *knew* that the rest she sought could only come in death, and my heart was hot in angry rebellion. I *could not let* her go. Fate was too much for me. But it was an unspeakable cruel fate, and every faculty in me rose in passionate protest and resentment. I changed her position again and again, adjusted and smoothed her pillow, and for a few brief moments she would lie quiet. Then again the old, incessant, heart-piercing cries, "Willie, *do* let me go," "*Do* take me," "*Why* don't you let me go?" And so, again and again, through the whole length of the horrible night.

Next day she was quieter. The doctor said it was only a question of hours. In the afternoon she seemed utterly exhausted and for a time we thought she was dying. My father, Mrs. D. (the nurse) and I stood looking on in momentary expectation of the end. I was quite tired out, heart and body, sullen and resentful. It was of a piece with the whole horrible thing that she should die *thus*, without any sign or leave taking. But it was not to be so and she revived again. About seven o'clock that night I was alone with her. She was unconscious. I kneeled at her bedside, my face down on the bed. My brain felt *scorched* and the whole thing a horrible nightmare. It was no longer my mother lying there but a ghastly automaton, I myself an automaton, both alike driven in a vast world *machine*, remorseless, brainless and heartless, crushing all before it. Later on, my father, coming upstairs, must have been alarmed about me and compelled me to go an errand, which he declared absolutely necessary. I think it probable that my going out for a short time saved my reason. Late at night my father drove me to bed. I refused. I *could* not go, or lose any of the precious time now left me with my mother, but I agreed ultimately to go for two hours at most, if he would rouse me sooner in case of change. Very reluctantly I went, but I was quite spent and I slept soundly till six, my father letting me sleep on. I at once hastened to the room and stayed there till the end, about one o'clock.

My mother was apparently the same, but weaker. She welcomed me with the sweet old smile, and responded always, as before, with loving kisses to mine. She was quite conscious but too weak to speak. The morning dragged on till noon, when I heard Mr. T. in the kitchen with my father. I asked her if she would like him to come up, and she nodded a pleased expression of her wish. He came and prayed at her bedside, my mother following it all with full appreciation, her head supported by my arm, shaking with the extreme palsy of coming death. She tried to express her thanks and followed him with grateful eyes as he left the room. Later, about one o'clock, my father and the nurse went downstairs. Mrs. D. remained, but I asked her to go, too, and leave me alone with my mother. I then asked mother if she would like me to pray with her. I had never done so, but I fancied that she wished it, and she assented with evident satisfaction. Standing at the foot of the bed I prayed briefly to God, our Father, to mercifully release my mother from her suffering and take her to Himself and guide and help me in the lonely path that lay before me. I then turned away a minute or two to the window. Looking around, I saw instantly that the last change had come. I hastened to moisten her lips, but her tongue was rigid. I went to the top of the stair and called to my father. He hastened up and was just in time to catch the last futile attempt at breath. In an access of strong emotion I cried out: "Thanks be to God, that giveth us the victory," and it seemed to my excited fancy that my mother's spirit nodded assent. It seemed to me for the moment that I stood in the very presence of the Infinite Love and felt it through my being.

I went downstairs and told Mrs. D. and the nurse that all was over, and they went upstairs to render the last sad offices. I came into *this room* (the room in which this paper was read) and gave myself up to a long, heavy fit of sobbing—sobbing, however, no longer of grief, but of great *relief*, recognition of the mighty *comfort* that had come into my heart and of resigned and loving *farewell*.

During the days that followed and until after the funeral I felt a great calm and peace of mind and heart, a peace of mind which I venture to say was no other than "the peace of God that passeth all understanding." It passed away, but the memory of it remained. Grief and the sense of irrecoverable loss had their natural course, and I spent many weeks of sleeplessness and tears.

I have no hope that my words will convey more than a poor fraction of the real facts. At best I can only sketch these in rudest outline. But I will ask you to consider a few of the most prominent in the narrative I have given you.

Remember what I have said of the spiritual questionings of many years and their results. Consider how my mother's long and frightful suffering revealed and strengthened as nothing else could, not only the sweet and lovable qualities of her heart and mind and the strength of the hope and faith which sustained her through it all, but also the length and breadth and depth of her wonderful self-sacrificing love for *me*, which grew only stronger, deeper and more tender as she advanced further into the shadow of our inevitable parting. And when the last stroke fell upon her and she was confined to her bed never to rise again, think how grateful and sweet to me were those days of slight improvement, when I was privileged to attend her constantly and show her, as I never could before, the reality and depth of my responding love and receive her entire forgiveness for all the thoughtlessness and wrongdoing of the past and her heartfelt blessing. And hastening on to the closing scene: Think of the horrible night, when her incessant cries rang out to me to "let her go," and *I knew that it meant* let her go to the last rest of death, and my heart stood out in passionate resentment and protest against a cruel and merciless fate. Think of that scene next day, when her strength seemed gone and we watched for the end and I felt, with sullen resentment, that it was only of a piece with all the rest that she should die *thus,* without any sign or leave taking, in the presence of comparative aliens, not of her own household, while *I,* her son, born of her body, bone of her bone and flesh of her flesh, the one person whom she loved with all the mighty love of her great heart, stood as an outsider beyond her consciousness. Think of the hour that evening when, with scorched brain, I felt through and through my being the dreadful significance of the materialistic creed, that we were mere automatic parts of a vast machine, brainless, heartless, merciless and cruel. Think of the providence by which restoring and healing sleep was granted me to make me capable of a truer vision. Think of the tender grace of our next morning's communion, my mother's full consciousness and the sweet tokens of her undying love. Think of the providence which led Mr. T. to come within an hour of the end and offer up solemn prayer, in which my mother could join with full appreciation in company with my father and myself. Think of the fitness of the arrangement by which, at the last moment, my mother and I were left alone, as she would have wished. Think of the divine training by which my rebellious heart was bowed into acquiescence and resignation. Think of the course by which my antagonism and scepticism were laid low, and I was led, with my mother's pleased concurrence, *at last* to "let her go" and to call audibly on the Divine Father of all to take her to Himself. And think how *immediately* the prayer was answered and God revealed himself to me and I felt through all my being, in the moment of her death, the presence of the Infinite Love, the Divine Comforter, soothing me with a strange and ineffable peace.

Human words are poor instruments for the expression of such realities. But beyond the touch of all possible argument, despite the apparent experiences of my life since and my backslidings, I knew that a divine providence was at work in my hour of utmost need summing up the long gropings and processes of the past, and despite all earthly darknesses and sin illumining all my future course with an infinite hope.

I no longer trouble myself with the difficulties raised by metaphysics and philosophy about the personality of God, for, however that may be, I know that there is that in Him to which I may address myself as to a loving friend and father. I no longer trouble myself with the discussions about God's providence and the contrary evidences of life and experiences, for I have *seen* His providence visibly at work, summing up in a crowning experience the processes of long years, in events which were entirely *natural* in their order and course, but were also visibly *super*natural and miraculous, too. I no longer trouble myself with doubts about *God's love*, and the contrary evidences furnished by the world's sin and endless miseries, for in the midst of the heaviest grief of my own life I *have seen* an ineffable tenderness and love revealed, which crowned and justified the sufferings which preceded it, and illumined much that lay dark and mysterious in the past. However this poor outline may strike *you*, I *know* that the actual facts were more fit and beautiful than any earthly poet could have conceived in his most gracious and tender mood. I no longer trouble my-self with the current discussions about immortality, for I know that my mother is secure and that all is well with her, for, unworthy as I am, I have *myself seen* the ineffable glory of the love which received her when she was taken from me.

SUMMARY.

a. J. W. W.'s narrative makes it quite clear that he had the earnestness of mind and desire for spiritual growth which, as we have seen, seem to be prerequisites to illumination.

b. His age, upon the occurrence of this last, was thirty-one and a half years.

c. There was no experience of subjective light.

d. Intellectual illumination was well marked.

e. And moral exaltation still more so.

f. Although he does not give details (perhaps could not do so), it is clear that he experienced something very near akin to the Cosmic vision, if he did not even see the Brahmic Splendor itself.

g. The "peace and knowledge" spoken of by Whitman and referred to by all the cases as one of the chief results of the attainment of Nirvâna—the Cosmic Sense—came to J. W. W. unmistakably, instantaneously.

h. The strict parallelism of this case with all the others given will be recognized by every careful reader.

CHAPTER 32

Case of J. William Lloyd, in His Own Words.

You ask for a brief statement of my life and spiritual evolution. I was born in Westfield, N. J., June 4, 1857. My parents were English, and had had but a few months' schooling apiece. My father was a carpenter, my mother a seamstress. My mother was a woman of broad, gentle nature, spiritual, poetic, a great reader. My father was an intense abolitionist. My schooling was scant, at a district school. We lived near a great wood. I cared not much for other children, but spent my time with books and the trees. I loved the trees like conscious friends.

The disagreeable side of religion was never shown me. I talked with God when an infant as naturally as with my mother. Some old book on philosophy (I do not know its name) fell into my hands, and I commenced to think to the core. I read the Bible, commentaries, a book on "All Religions." At thirteen I was atheist, then turned quickly, experienced conversion, and, as I read, became Calvinist, Arminian, Swedenborgian. At fifteen I was apprenticed to a carpenter, but work failed in 1873, and I became a gardener. At seventeen I was a leader in prayer-meetings, an exhorter, a disputant with ministers on points of orthodoxy. At eighteen I went to Trall's Hygienic College at Florence, N. J., as a working student. All radical questions met me here, and the woman who became my wife. Trall died, the college failed, I went to Kansas as a pioneer, was a herder, a homesteader, married in 1879, acted as hygienic physician for my neighbors, read the Boston "Index" and Theodore Parker, and became a member of the Free Religious Association. Three years' drouth drove me from Kansas to a sanitarium in Vinton, Iowa, where I was assistant. Became agnostic. Read Ingersoll and the scientists. Joined a hygienic colony in Tennessee in January, 1883. Again a pioneer in the woods. Accepted Karl Heingen's Democracy, and grew more confirmed in writing poems, which I had first commenced just before going to Kansas. Accepted free-love, which I had fought for years. Colony failed, and I went to another similar one in Florida. Many spiritualists here. Read Tucker's "Liberty" and became an enthusiastic anarchist. Orange grower, farm laborer and pioneer. Colony and work failed, and went to Palatka. Poultry farmer. Wife died in September, 1888, after nearly a decade of most happy married life. Came North to old home, with two little children, and became a professional nurse. Here found more books, and read the poets—Emerson, Whitman, Thoreau, Spencer, Darwin, Carpenter, William Morris. I loved the Transcendentalists, but did not understand them very well. I lived mostly in poetry and sociologic science.

As to my illumination: I was going to New York City one morning in January, 1897, on a train, to do some hospital work. I was reading Carpenter. It was a beautiful winter morning. I think I was near the Bay Bridge, or on it, when the Thought came. There was no particular sensation, except that something beautiful and great seemed to have happened me, which I could only describe in terms of light. Yet it was purely mental. But everything looked different to me. I went about the city that day calm, but glad and uplifted. The thing I remember most was a wonder how soon the sensation, or impression, would leave me. I was latently sceptical, and thought it a temporary inspiration, like that of a poem. But days, weeks, months, passed, and I found the shoot which had broken ground that winter morning was ever growing, strengthening and changing all the scenery of my life. I continually questioned and tested, and at last, after a year's trial, began to write. All the early part of the book was written at night, while I nursed and guarded a lunatic boy, whose yells, laughs, curses and filthy jests made the room ring as I wrote. Yet I wrote easily, swiftly, without any conscious cerebration, and with a sort of wonder at the words I wrote, as if they had no connection with me. Part of the book was written in the following summer, when at home, part of it in the winter of 1899-1900, while getting ready for the press, but always with the same sensations of ease and inspiration. And still, when I read the book, it seemed to me something apart, in whose construction I had had no hand. As to *how* I felt when I received the Thought, you have yourself most accurately described the symptoms on pages 10 and 11 of your pamphlet: "With the intellectual illumination comes an indescribable moral elevation, an intense and exalted joyfulness, and, along with this, a sense of immortality; not merely a belief in a future life—that would be a small matter—but a consciousness that the life now being lived is eternal, death being seen as a trivial incident which does not affect its continuity. Further, there are annihilation of the sense of sin and an intellectual competency not simply surpassing the old, but on a new and higher plane." Also many of the marks of Arahatship, as taught by Buddha, describe accurately the feeling.

What proves J. William Lloyd to be a case of Cosmic Consciousness is not so much the above account of himself (although that could hardly have been written without some such an experience as illumination) as the volume [110a] which he produced after the occurrence in question. This volume, which contains overwhelming evidence of the fact, is easily accessible and will doubtless be read by every person who feels an interest in the subject.

The oncoming of Cosmic Consciousness in this case was very similar to the same fact in the case of Edward Carpenter. There was a clearly-marked moment when the light began to break through, but illumination came gradually. There was no subjective light. There was well-marked intellectual illumination and moral elevation, but the Cosmic vision, the Brahmic Splendor, of the great cases does not appear to have been present. If not, this cannot be said to be a complete case, and still J. William Lloyd's book shows a most excellent insight into the cosmic order. It must be remembered that illumination that comes gradually may be as complete as that which comes instantly. Why there should be such difference in the awakening in different cases cannot at present be explained.

As far as our facts will carry us it would appear that the cases in which the Cosmic Sense makes its appearance full grown, instantly and, as it were, in a flash, are those in which there is marked subjective light—such cases as that of Dante, Yepes, Paul, Pascal and others. When, on the contrary, the new sense comes more gradually there may be no subjective light, as in the cases of Carpenter and Lloyd. It seems tolerably certain that with illumination there occurs actual, physical, molecular rearrangement somewhere in the cerebral centres and that it is this molecular rearrangement which, when considerable and sudden, gives rise to the phenomenon of the subjective light.

CHAPTER 33.

Horace Traubel.

WAS born December 19, 1858, and was therefore in his thirty-first year at time of his first illumination. His experience is here given in his own words. It is all of it full of interest, but perhaps the most significant thing about it is the manner the intelligence of it was received by Walt Whitman, whose matter of fact, simple words, "I knew it would come to you," carry a depth of meaning quite out of the common. H. T. tells the story of his awakening in this colloquial and direct way, in answer to the inquiries of the editor:

You are quite familiar with the path of my spiritual development—with the course taken by my mental self in arriving at its present state. You know I have come to my own, whatever that may be, mostly by immediate contact with experience rather than through books, though I have read in books of the most miscellaneous character and at one period in appalling numbers. But, somehow, the scholar in me never seems to have obscured the man. I suppose my intenser early reading was in Emerson, Carlyle, Hugo and whatever else I could get hold of having to do with the world of myth and the ante-Christian Scriptures of the race. I do not seem to have known a time when I have not read "Leaves of Grass." But previous to May, 1889, I do not seem to have got that (in a sense) final grasp of its mystery which now imparts to it its primary and supernatural significance. May, 1889. Then, again, two years later, 1891. A third time, 1893 or 4, on the historic night ⟨historic to me⟩.

when circumstance made me the spokesman of the dissentient group of Ethicists, in Philadelphia, on the occasion of the split of the Ethical Society there. May, 1889. That overwhelming night, as I leaned over the railing of the ferryboat, lost this world for another, and in the anguish and joy of a few minutes saw things heretofore withheld from me revealed. Those who have had such an encounter will understand what this means, others will not, or will perhaps only realize it by intimation. I could not separate the physical and spiritual of that moment. My physical body went through the experience of a disappearance in spiritual light. All severe lines in the front of phenomena relaxed. I was one with God, Love, the Universe, arrived at last face to face with myself. I was sensible of peculiar moral and mental disturbances and readjustments. There was an immediateness to it all—an indissoluble unity of the several energies of my being in one force. I was no more boating it on a river than winging it in space or taking star leaps, a traveler from one to another on the peopled orbs. While I stood there the boat had got into the slip and was almost ready to go out again. A deckhand who knew me came up and tapped me on the shoulder. "Don't you intend going off the boat?" he asked. And he added when I faced him and said "Yes:" "You look wonderfully well and happy to-night, Mr. Traubel." I did not see Walt till the next day, evening. In the meantime I had lived through twenty-four hours of ecstasy mixed with some doubts as to whether I had not had a crack in the skull and gone mad rather than fallen under some light and made a discovery. But the first words Walt addressed to me when I sallied into his room were reassuring: "Horace, you have the look of great happiness on your face to-night. Have you had a run of good luck?" I sat down and tried in a few words to indicate that I had had a run of good luck, though not perhaps the good luck he had in mind for me at the moment. He did not seem at all surprised at what I told him, merely remarking, as he put his hand on my shoulder and looked into my eyes: "I knew it would come to you." I suggested: "I have been wondering all day if I am not crazy." He laughed gravely: "No, sane. Now at last you are sane."

It was a month before the immediate effect of this experience wore off. The reflex effect was of course fixed. I can say now (writing 1901) that from that day to this I have never known one moment of despair concerning my spiritual relations to man and the universe. I have my earth troubles and my earth foibles. But the essential faith is adamantine. I have never had any suspicion of immortality. The glimpse of that minute—and of the repeated experiences on the two after occasions mentioned above—into the eternal law left no blot or qualification. I had often said before, in speaking of Whitman (making in a way a true guess): "Whitman's notion of immortality is not one of logic but is pictorial. He does not believe in immortality. He *sees* it." Many times Whitman had said to me regarding that explanation: "It is every word true. You hit the nail on the head." Now I knew better than I had before—not only better but in a way I could not have known before—what I myself meant when I used the expression: "Whitman *sees*." I see around and through phenomena. Phenomena is never a wall or a veil. I have been able to do my work as never before. It has brought me friends and the cheer of sympathetic greetings from all parts of the world. One feature of my writing I ought to mention. I think I told you long ago that I become in effect automatic when I am engaged in any serious composition. I do not seem to write. The writing seems done through me. I take up my pen and hardly know what I write. After I have written I am often surprised at the things I have said. They are as new to me as to any reader. All the writing which has brought me any returns—congratulations—has been done in that mood.

On the night of the Ethical split I was in a position which forced me to be the main spokesman of the party of freedom. I made a speech upon which my enemies even more than my friends congratulated me. Yet when I got on my feet on the floor and plunged into talk I was instantly immersed in the strange light which had visited me on the first experience and simply uttered without thought or reason, formally speaking, the words of the mightier power that possessed me. I have found since that on occasions of crisis I have merely to throw myself back again on this resource to discover that every strength— spiritually speaking—it imparted once it imparts again. In my very busy life, which has its temporal distresses, this is more than a balance in bank and contributes more than any ephemera of material prosperity could towards my victories: in fact is the first and last letter of my power. When the little affairs of every day seem most mixed up, most to be past solution, I am sure finally to make my escape by the avenue of these ameliorating revelations. Not once has the spirit deserted me—not once has the light, in some degree of its radiance, not always of course in full power, failed to appear. The difference it makes in one's life is the difference between preparation and consummation. On the occasion of my second experience (April, 1891), which was not outwardly momentous, I found that my initial self suspicion—my question, Am I unbuilt or built?—did not reappear.

If you take my verse "Illumination" [and a great deal of H. T.'s verse and prose written since that year], and try to get it statistically languaged, you will find that I have expressed a series of experiences of profound significance to all who have been similarly blessed. I find that my members are no longer at war with each other. When I was a youngster I read my way vigorously and sympathetically back especially into Oriental literature of the religious class— blazed a path for the spirit. After 1889 (a hiatus in such reading having intervened) I found myself driven into that old world again, to review these my original impressions. The new light had made my voyage easier and more richly endowed its fruits. Once I felt that religions were all of them religions of despair: now I saw that no religion despairs—that all religion before it becomes and as soon as it ceases to be an affair of institutions resolves itself essentially into light and immortality.

I should perhaps say that it has invariably happened that someone—and sometimes many persons—have commented to me, and felicitated me, upon my appearance, upon the occasions of my direct contact with what I have grown to call my subliminal self. This may mean much or nothing. But no one could live through what I do at such periods and not in some way outwardly give it witness.

You have said to me: "State this thing in plain prose." But how can I? I could never state it in the prose that would be understood by one who has not shared my sensations. I could never state it in words which would not make it, if you please, prose to those who can enter collaterally into the channels of its august revelation. After asking you: How can I? I have shown you how I could.

Some things I have said may seem to savor of egotism. But they are simply candid. I am not measuring myself as a genius or an idiot, but as a simple third person whose word and career must be to himself absolute law. I have written you this memorandum impulsively, with no attempt to dress it up, if, indeed, until now it is done, and now I have read it, with any actual understanding of what my pen would commit me to or confess.

The following poem was written by Horace Traubel shortly after his illumination and of course strictly belongs here:

The nights, the days, hold me in thrall,
Toils of men and women drag my faith to the earth—
Furrowed with pain, the casual cares,
I long—I look—I reach forth to life.

Release! Escape!
Shall I speak of the door swung wide, of the unbarred gates?

After the vigil I step across the border-line,
I take my place with the pioneers.

Have I met the hour patiently, without fear, at the portal?
Now is my name called, now the lip of my love has spoken:
Do I mistake you, O divine Signaler? is it after all some other soul that is hailed?
My self is my answer:
There's that in my heart responds, meeting the call with equal voice, establishing forever the unspeakable bond!

Bond that does not bind—bond that frees—bond that discovers and bestows.

Look! I am flushed with inexhaustible possessions!
The old measures vanish, I am expanded to infinite sweep.

O world! Not dead to you—only seeing you, knowing you, at last,
Mixed with countless worlds, knowing with you your companions also:

O year! Not dead to you—only seeing you, knowing you, at last,
Mixed with all time, untangling the knotted thread:

O world! O year!—
Before birth seeing birth, after life seeing life!

The infinite blue, heaven's fond eye, opens upon me.

O voice, mastering me, making me too master—
My ear is close, I hear the syllables fall,
Waves on shores of the farther worlds, waves on shores of the day.

The clouds part: O face—O face—O face!—
Face smiling upon me—smiling me wings, buoyant beyond the discarded cheap-
    ened present.

(You, too, O present, still remaining,
Duly visiting my heart, not forbidden,
Yet yielding the place supreme).

I am all eye—O God! you are all speech:
Melody celestial—sight and voice, color and tone, warring no more,
In the boundless blue uplifted.

Whose hand touches me?—my brow—my breast—my own unasking hand—
Leading me out of self to self?

Divine form—mother, father—sex only now standing revealed, the union irre-
    versible:
Divine form, I made whole in you,
The elements diverse here blended.

This minute grown infinite, the far worlds spread before me,
The endless drift of soul, the long stretch of faces, all lit by the divine sun—
Or swift or slow or early or late the line not anywhere broken,
All—all—equally sustained, swept in the same destiny, on sea and land of life,
The peak lit for all, the triumph inevitable.

O my soul! look yet again:
There too are you, a figure in the panorama,
On your brow the dawn has set its beauteous beam,
Here with me—there not with me.

Death fills me with its abundance.
What is this flood, overcoming body and sense?
I feel the walls of my skull crack, the barriers part, the sun-flood enter—
Love, lore, not lost, only magnified, floating eternal seas of essence—
Before and behind births and deaths, spiritual gravitation, the emergence ever-
    more expanding.

O soul, have I lost you or found you?
Found! the faultless circle born at last to you,
After the waiting years.

Far eras behind, far eras ahead, the simple few years I finger,
Shafts from the central sun,
Speeding for fuller fruition the orbs of space.

Back to the first word of speech,
On to the last utterance of seers,
My soul, knowing its own, wrapt in its protean habit, catches the perfect song.

God! I am circled—I am drunk with the influx of life—
Wheeled in your orbit—given the word I would speak yet must withhold—
Leaving you, O my brother, each one, to say it for yourself.

Brothers, worlds, I greet you!
The wheel turns, the boundless prospect opens:
All, all complicate—the light bearing limitlessly the burdens of all.
Do you think that you are missed, that the large heart beats not for you?
That somewhere on the road you must faint and die?
Strength will be given for all your need,
And the weakest, when the night comes which is the day,
Will greet the king, a giant in stature and grace.

Now the immortal years, the ceaseless round realized—
The doubts shorn of wing and foot,
The farthest league nearest, and the multiplied infinities choking here in my
    breast.

O my questioner! you do not suspect me—you suspect yourself:
To-morrow, seeing yourself, you will see me,
And the illumined spirit, passing the portal,
God-grown, will hail me proudly [60a: 40].

Had we no other writings by this man, these lines alone to all who can understand them—and they are as clear as day from the point of view of this volume—would be proof of illumination. But we have much else. A series of writings in prose and verse extending over the last ten years gives us more evidence than is needed.

Then there is something else to say. Horace Traubel (as he intimates himself in his own words, above) belongs with Blake, Yepes, Behmen, Swedenborg and others, in the class of what may be called automatic writers. These men give their inspiration free way—they drop the reins on his neck and let the horse go. What they write under the divine impulse, for those who can follow their thought, is divine, but to those who can not, is, as Paul says, just in this connection, "foolishness."

Perhaps all these men write automatically, but, in the case of some of them, the expression as it flows from the Cosmic Sense, or as afterwards modified by the self conscious intellect, is more intelligible to the "natural man" than in the case of others. In not one of them does the meaning lie on the surface—they all call for and demand long continued and thoughtful reading. Whitman and Paul are just as unintelligible as Behmen or Swedenborg, until the right point of view is reached, although Whitman (for his part) wrought his whole life, "returning upon (his) poems, lingering long," in order to render them absorbable by the race.

Horace Traubel has not escaped the curse of his tribe—unintelligibility. But in spite of it he has produced his effect. And this is the strangest thing of all—that it should be possible for a man to speak or write what cannot be understood, but to do it in such a divine way that his words shall be revered and remembered through the ages. The "Shakespeare" Sonnets have never been understood, and are yet accepted for what they really are—a revelation.

Horace Traubel has many readers who understand him, and even those who do not comprehend him fully are impressed by his personality, through which streams unmistakably the divine light.

CHAPTER 34.

The Case of Paul Tyner, in His Own Words.

I WAS born March 7, 1860, about midnight, in the city of Cork, Ireland. My mother being Irish, of an old family, the Sarfields, one of whom is celebrated by Macaulay in his account of the conflict in Ireland between the Stuart forces and those under William of Orange. My father was the representative in Ireland of an important London publishing house. He used to say that one of his ancestors fought under William of Orange, and I believe came over with him from Holland.

I was brought to America at the age of four, educated in the public schools of Albany, N. Y., afterwards taking the law course in Columbia College, New York City, but exchanging law for journalism at the age of twenty, when I joined the staff of the New York "World," in which service I remained about eight years, uninterruptedly. In 1887 I went to Central America, to engage in silver mining, exploration and travel. After a year in Honduras, I went to Costa Rica, where I edited and published a daily paper, called "El Comercio," in English and Spanish, for about six months, when I returned to New York and re-engaged in journalistic work there, as editorial writer on the staff of the New York "Press."

The bent of my mind in the direction of mysticism, which has so largely influenced my later work, probably had its beginnings during a year's retire· ment in the Shaker community, at Mt. Lebanon, N. Y. (1891-2). This experi· ence was followed by a special course of study in social economics and history with Professor Richard T. Ely, of the University of Wisconsin. In the early morning of the 11th of May, 1895, came the crowning experience of my life. On the evening of that day I set down in my diary an exact and full account of the whole episode, as then seen by me. This memorandum I here transcribe:

"With this day's dawn come the great revelation and the great charge. 'Crowned with thorns' was the waking thought; then buffeted and spat upon, mocked, insulted, scourged and in the pillory, 'a man of sorrow and acquainted with grief,' nailed to the cross, pierced in the side, utterly 'despised and re- jected of men,' killed as a malefactor, buried; and then the great thought—the truth which maketh free; the absolute demonstration of man's mastery of fate and command of all conditions—the victory of *man*—all men in this racial man, this elder brother of mankind in his triumph over sin, fear and death!

"But one thing had remained in my mind as necessary to prove to the mass of men to-day man's absolute supremacy over death in all its forms as an at· tribute of his oneness with God, with *Eternal Life, Perfect Love, Perfect Justice, Omniscience* and *Omnipotence*, the visible appearance of a man who living longer than the recorded years of any man who had seen death still lived in the flesh without shadow of change or decay. And I said to myself, this would be worth waiting and watching and working a thousand years for! Yet I wished the greater emancipation were not so far off. And lo! in the dawning of this day *I know*—know absolutely as a fact—a *truth* nothing can destroy, that the man who triumphed ever death on Calvary nearly two thousand years ago *lives*— lives on earth in a body of flesh made perfect, a man among men, sharing our struggles and sorrows, our joys and griefs, working with us heart to heart and shoulder to shoulder—inspiring, guiding, leading, supporting, as may be, in every human advance.

"The glory of this truth, the grandeur of this character, the supreme no- bility, patience, wisdom and love of this life, thrilled me with ecstasy and awe unspeakable—filled me, possessed me. He lives, not in some distant heaven on a great white throne, but here and now; is not coming, but *is here* with us, loving, helping, living, cheering and inspiring the race to which he belongs, as wholly and as truly as the race belongs to him. Now, indeed, it is plain, that being lifted up he shall lift all men with him—has lifted, is lifting and must ever continue to lift out of the very essence of his *transcendent humanity.* Immortality is no longer an hypothesis of the theologian, a figment of the imagination, a dream of the poet. Men shall live forever, because *man,* invincible to all effects of time and change, and even of murderous violence, lives to-day in the fullness of life and power that he enjoyed in his thirty-third year, with only added glory of goodness and greatness and beauty—although the world counts 1895 years since his last birth upon this earth.

"This is the truth given age upon age to all men in all lands, and persistently misunderstood—the truth at last to be seen of all men in its fullness and purity. Man is to know himself, and with full command of his conditions and unlimited time for action, is not only to soar toward, but absolutely attain to heights of being and of beauty hitherto undreamed of, and bringing fairly within his realization a heaven on earth, in true grandeur and happiness as far transcending the heaven of the orthodox Christian as that heaven transcends the heaven of the savage.

"This is the *fact* I am given to know; the proof must come in good time. My mission is to bear witness to it—to be the voice crying in the wilderness, 'Prepare ye the way of the Lord! make straight his paths.'

"And in the light of this truth I live anew; I rise up vitalized and energized in every nerve and fibre. Soul and body, no longer strained apart, are linked and glorified. I will be worthy of the great charge of Truth Bearer to my kind, and will manifest in my body, in my thought and words, my life and actions, the truth that has become part of me—the truth of man's oneness with eternal life. . . .

"With these thoughts filling me and dissolving me in happy tears, I sprang from my bed about five o'clock and walked up and down the room in a fervor of adoration and love, for what love is like unto this man's? All this time the atmosphere of the room was vibrant with an intense white light. The presence which had been revealed in the first waking moments seemed now diffused and continuing through the universe. After bathing and dressing I went out for an early walk. The morning was chilly, cloudy, raw and gusty, but the sweet-scented, light-filled air, full of vivid, tender green of spring and vibrant with life, seemed to share my sensation of joy and uplift."

I may add, that my mind, being naturally analytical, I have been able to trace as distinct factors in the mental evolution here indicated, first (and perhaps most of all), Wagner's "Lohengrin" and "Parsifal"; second, "The Venus of Milo"; third, Munkacsy's "Christ Before Pilate"; all of them, however, blended, expanded and illumined by the grand soul of Walt Whitman.

In reply to your question: I do not know whether any change in my physical appearance followed what may be called my illumination and would rather some one else would speak of that. I have been told, however, that my face was that of one aflame, and that is distinctly my own feeling as to the change physically. There is a consciousness of a steady glow which is light and warmth in all my being. It is certain that ever since that morning I have had a larger and surer hold on life and have been able to work with clearer and more active brain and body.

Being asked to explain more fully the continuous life of Christ on earth in a human body, Paul Tyner answered as follows:

In asserting the continued existence on earth of the man Jesus, in the body of flesh and blood, it is by no means intended to deny the law demonstrated throughout the universe in all forms of life, simple or complex, of the passage from birth to maturity, and maturity to decay, so far as outer form is concerned. What this continued existence of Jesus in a body of flesh and blood means is dominion and control over the law of construction, destruction and reconstruction going on in all forms, its deliberate and conscious direction at all times. As a matter of fact, flexibility is the very essence of form, and this is especially true in regard to the human form. The spirit, which is the man himself, formless and unsubstantial, is continually building and rebuilding, calling to himself out of the universal ocean of matter and force all the elements he needs, and rejecting and expelling that which he has used, when it no longer serves his purpose, or when he has taken from it all that he requires.

In the true sense, there is no such thing as disembodied spirit. Spirit must embody itself for manifestation and expression. Jesus, having attained to spiritual self consciousness, deliberately and consciously chose and chooses his embodiment, molding it from day to day, into greater and greater responsiveness to his will—in his case the Cosmic will, the will of the Father. He is able to pass through closed doors and stone walls in this body, because of his power to change its vibrations. That is to say, he passes through stone walls, as ethers or gases pass through substances of lower vibrations or greater density. The component elements of his body, while governed to some extent by normal human anatomical structure and organization, is in what might be called a state of flux. The old Greeks considered the universe in a state of flux, as indeed it is.

Fully aware, as I am, of the difficulties in the way of describing a phenomenon, not merely unfamiliar, but unthinkable by most men, I can only ask the reader who desires a keener comprehension of what is meant by this "immortalization of the flesh," to imagine by way of analogy, and yet an analogy conveying a very close approximate to the actuality—to imagine an architect who has planned a very beautiful and perfect dwelling, whose mind holds the plan very distinctly and completely, and who is himself a master builder, with unlimited command of the materials needed to embody his plan, and unerring knowledge of the best method of building. Imagine, further, that this architect, standing in the midst of the dwelling he has planned and built, should find that the materials he used, by some chance, or rather law, burned up every night without, however, burning him, or in the least injuring his powers. Remember that the plan remains intact. Remember that the builder's skill is not consumed; that his command of material, sufficient to his needs and instantaneous in supply, remains with him. What would happen? He would reproduce this dwelling as quickly as it was destroyed; in fact, there would be no apparent break in the continuity of the dwelling. The only possible changes would be that, with experience and growth, the material part of the building would become ever finer and finer, the adjustments of its various parts one to another more and more exact. This in a rough way, conveys an idea of what is meant by the immortal man in an immortal embodiment.

No difficulty appears to be found in conceiving of the immortal principle in man embodying itself in a succession of bodies, on an ascending or descending scale, any more than we find it difficult to conceive of the universal principle of life embodying itself in a variety of forms in an ascending or descending scale. And yet, any such process must be considered complex and uncertain, compared to the simple and definite processes of the cosmically conscious man consciously and deliberately rebuilding, from day to day, that embodiment which best expresses his thought and answers to his requirements. In this, as in other things, evolution of forms and of processes are all in the direction of increased simplicity—of economy and efficiency in the doing of our work. It is not the personal Jesus that is immortalized, or that has the power of immortalizing the flesh, but the Christ principle clothed in that personality, embodied in it and using it simply as one of its modes of motion, so to speak. The Christ in Jesus, however, came into such fullness and plainness of manifestation that his personality is indeed made the Light of the world that lighteth every man that cometh into the world.

As regards the appearance of Paul Tyner at the time of illumination, I am informed by H. C. as follows: "I am in a position to give a positive statement as to the appearance of Mr. Paul Tyner on the morning of the 11th of May, 1895. His color was unaltered, his flesh warm and natural, his expression peculiarly sweet and bright. His face had at the time and retained for days afterwards, the illuminated look we see at times on the face of the dying, a look of ecstasy, bright, uplifted—it was as if lit up with a glow from some unseen source. No lapse of the ordinary faculties, no failure of full health, both mental and bodily, but on the contrary apparently superabundant health. His day's work (a very large one) was done that day as usual."

It only remains to quote two short passages from a book written and published before Paul Tyner had ever heard of the present editor or his theories:

At daybreak of Friday, the 11th of May, 1895, I woke into full and ab-solute knowledge of the great fact which to me proves man's immortality here and now, and in the body of flesh we know. I know that a man had lived nearly nineteen hundred years, and, knowing only fuller and fuller life with the passing of the years, had lived and still lives in the same body in which, in the beginning of that period, he walked the earth a man of flesh and blood. This man, in whom humanity came to full flower with the conscious manifesta-tion of his oneness with eternal life in the thirty-third year of his present in-carnation, has really destroyed the last enemy, which is death.

To-day, in Europe and America, Australia and Africa, India and the isles of the sea, wherever the Father is worshiped in spirit and in truth—as in the Judea of Herod the Great—Jesus the Christ, Son of God and Son of Man, lives in the midst of us! For this cause came he into the world; that he might be a witness to the truth; a living, unimpeachable witness of the truth that shall make us free—the truth of man's *religion* (reunion) with God, through ab-solute spiritual self consciousness—with God—with the Eternal, Omnipotent and Omniscient Source and Fountain of Life, "in whom we live and move and have our being," without whom we are not!

I have said I knew this greatest fact in the history of humanity in a mo-ment; that what before was as unknown to me as was the Western continent to Columbus before he sighted land, became in an instant a known reality, as much a part of my consciousness as was the air I breathed; a truth as yet faintly comprehended in its fullness, but a truth firmly grasped, irrevocable and indestructible; an eternal verity written in the letters of fire on my brain and in my heart—and so on the mind and in the heart of this age, and of all future ages.

Opening my eyes on the first rays of morning light illuminating my room, I thought of the oneness of Eternal Light and Life in a vague way, when my attention was seemingly diverted by the image of a monk's tonsured head; and I thought of the crown of thorns it symbolized. Then the whole sublime tragedy of the passion moved vividly and rapidly before my eyes; the scourging, the pillory, the cuffs and blows, the jibes and jeers, the mockery and derision of that crowning with thorns; the painful progress of Golgotha, hooted by the blind and cruel mob; the torture and ignominy of the nailing to the cross, the cry of agony telling that the last dregs of the cup had been drained; the shout of victory that proclaimed "It is finished!" I saw then the spear thrust; I saw the burial, the sublime temple of the Divine thus laid low, and I saw—the resurrection on the third day.

At this point my mind opened to the great fact, as to a flood of life. He rose from the dead. He never died again! He lives! The air in my room seemed to vibrate with a more intense light than was ever seen on land or sea. My brain and nerves, my blood and muscles, all my being vibrated in sym-pathetic unison with this light, and in the midst of its shining glory I beheld the Divine Man, the Undying Man—beheld him face to face, and knew that it was he in very flesh and bones, as in flesh-transcending soul; knew that it was he and not another [187:4].

"Verily, verily, I say unto you that he that believeth on me hath ever-lasting life" [John vi, 47]. In these words Jesus announced a scientific prin-ciple of the utmost importance. Belief is essential to the attainment of im-mortality (in or out of the body). Belief in what? Belief in immortality—a state of consciousness of the fact of immortality. Belief in Jesus, in any real sense, is belief in the immortality of man. It is a belief in him who is "the way, the truth and the life"—in body and soul together; and with belief, a realization of oneness with him [187: 97-8].

I offer no criticism of the specific belief of Paul Tyner as to "The Living Christ." It is simply a question as to how the words are understood. Christ (as Paul named the Cosmic Sense) is of course living and will always live.

From the point of view of this present book Paul Tyner is al-most a typical case of Cosmic Consciousness.

a. The subjective light was well marked.

b. There was the characteristic moral elevation.

c. Also the usual intellectual illumination.

d. The sense of immortality.

e. The suddenness of the onset, the instantaneousness of the awakening.

f. The previous mental life of the man was such as is likely to lead to illumination.

g. His age of illumination, thirty-five years and two months.

h. He attained Cosmic Consciousness in the spring, 11th of May.

i. There was the characteristic change in appearance upon illumination.

Chapter 35.

The Case of C. Y. E., in Her Own Words.

I was born April 21, 1864. I was brought up a member of the Church of England, accepted its teaching and loved its services and liturgy. I be-lieved in Christ as God Incarnate—the word made flesh. The doctrine of the atonement, taken in the sense of a sacrifice necessary to appease the anger of an avenging God, had long been rejected by me. I was married on January 1, 1891. My husband possessed an intense and earnest desire for truth. He was an agnostic. Our common ground was a firm conviction that God is Love, that He is also Light and that in Him is no darkness at all. Two years after our marriage my husband became an enthusiastic and ardent admirer of the writings of Walt Whitman, and here, to my sorrow, I was left behind. I tried to read "Leaves of Grass," but could not understand a word of it. I could hear the music of the verse, but the language in which it was written was to me an unknown tongue. I recognized that there was something, and perhaps something beyond the common, in this man's writing, but I was simply unable to see what it was.

In the autumn of 1893 we moved into the country and settled in a little village in Yorkshire. Soon afterwards my husband went to Bolton to meet the "Eagle College" men there. He returned home delighted with the new comrades he had found, with the hearty love and good fellowship with which he had been received, at the indisputable evidence of the powerful magnetism of the man Walt Whitman, who could draw together men of all sorts, diverse in country, calling, habits, station, indeed in everything but this wonderful sense of comradeship. I became still more mystified. Then in September, 1894, a remarkable young Philadelphian, named P. D., who was deeply imbued with Whitman's philosophy, visited us. On Monday and again on Tuesday evening P. D., my husband and myself had long talks about Whitman and his teaching. On the afternoon of Wednesday I went to see a friend, a farmer's wife, and we drove over the harvest fields to take some refreshment to her husband who was working with his men. When I was going away she gave me two very beautiful Maréchal Niel roses. I had always had a passionate love of flowers, but the scent of these and their exquisite form and color appealed to me with quite exceptional force and vividness. I left my friend and was walking slowly homeward, enjoying the calm beauty of the evening, when I became conscious of an unutterable stillness, and simultaneously every object about me became bathed in a soft light, clearer and more ethereal than I had ever before seen. Then a voice whispered in my soul: "God is all. He is not far away in the heaven; He is here. This grass under your feet is He; this bountiful harvest, that blue sky, those roses in your hand—you yourself are all one with Him. All is well for ever and ever, for there is no place or time where God is not." Then the earth and air and sky thrilled and vibrated to one song, and the burden of it was "Glory to God in the highest and on earth, peace, good will toward men."

On my return home both my husband and his sister remarked a change in my face. An infinite peace and joy filled my heart, worldly ambitions and cares died in the light of the glorious truth that was revealed to me—all anxiety and trouble about the future had utterly left me, and my life is one long song of love and peace. When I wake in the night or rise from my bed in the morning—nay, at all hours of the day and night—the song is ever with me, "Glory to God in the highest, on earth, peace, good will toward men."

Now I could read Walt Whitman. Read him! Indeed, it seemed more than reading, for my soul, eagerly drinking in his words, was thereby refreshed and invigorated.

The effects of this experience on my daily life have been many, chiefly, I think, after the deep underlying joy and peace came a faith in the eternal rightness of all things; a ceasing to fret and worry over the problem of evil; a desire to live in the open air as much as possible and an ever-growing delight in the beauties of nature at all times and seasons of the year; a strong tendency towards simplicity of life and deepening sense of the equality and brotherhood of all men.

a. It will be noticed that the subjective light was well, though not strongly marked in the case.

b. That moral elevation was a prominent feature.

c. Intellectual illumination seems to have been present, though we have no conclusive evidence of it.

d. The sense of immortality was pronounced.

e. Fear of death was lost.

f. We are not told in so many words, but it seems plain that there could be no sense of sin in the mental condition which accompanied and followed the experience.

g. The change was sudden, instantaneous.

h. The previous character of the person's mind would mark her as a likely person to have such an experience as this.

i. She was of the right age—in her thirty-first year.

j. The present writer cannot speak of any added charm to the personality of Mrs. E., but it seems to him we must gather from what we are told that such occurred upon her illumination.

k. The phenomenon which in the great cases has been called transfiguration was present in moderate degree in this. It was noticed by both her husband and her sister.

Only one thing more remains to say. What may be called the mental suspension which seems to be a necessary preliminary to illumination was noticed and reported by Mrs. E. "I became conscious of an unutterable stillness," and "simultaneously" she was wrapped in the subjective light. It seems remarkable that this fact should have been noted by the old Hindoo seers, and it is not surprising that it was somewhat misinterpreted by them. It seems that they thought that this mental suspension was not only an inevitable accompaniment of illumination but an efficient cause of it. They therefore laid down the strictest rules for inducing the mental condition in question in the hope and expectation that, that being secured, illumination would follow. So we have such directions as these: "A devotee should constantly devote himself to abstraction, remaining in a secret place, alone, with his mind and self restrained, without expectation and without belongings" [154:68]. And again: "That mental condition, in which the mind restrained by practice of abstraction, ceases to work" [154: 69]. This was supposed to be the mental state out of which Nirvâna must arise. It is the state out of which it arises, but it does not follow and does not appear that the state of mental suspension has any casual relation to the state of illumination or Nirvâna.

This is perhaps as good a place as any for a quotation from Gibbon, which will shed some light on the history of opinion on the above point, and will also show how a great student and great man may utterly fail to see facts, which, though brought immediately to his notice, are out of accord with his preconceptions. He says of the Emperor Cantacuzene [93:193] that he "defended the divine light of Mount Tabor, a memorable question which consummates the religious follies of the Greeks. The fakirs of India, and the monks of the Oriental church were alike persuaded that in total abstraction of the faculties of the mind and body the purer spirit may ascend to the enjoyment and vision of the Deity. The opinion and practice of the monasteries of Mount Athos will be best represented in the words of an abbot who flourished in the eleventh century. 'When thou art alone in thy cell,' says the ascetic teacher, 'shut thy door, and seat thyself in a corner; raise thy mind above all things vain and transitory; recline thy beard and chin on thy breast; turn thy eyes and thy thoughts towards the middle of thy belly, the region of the navel, and search the place of the heart, the seat of the soul. At first all will be dark and comfortless, but if you persevere day and night you will feel an ineffable joy, and no sooner has the soul discovered the place of the heart than it is involved in a mystic and ethereal light.' This light, the production of a distempered fancy, the creature of an empty stomach and an empty brain, was adored by the Quietists as the pure and perfect essence of God himself."

Gibbon has correctly reported the recommendations of the Indian sages. The truth of the matter seems to be as follows: When, without forethought, knowledge or endeavor (as in all the Western cases as far as the writer knows) illumination comes spontaneously, it is preceded (for an instant at least) by what we may call mental suspension. That fact having been noted by the Eastern adepts, who sought to reduce Nirvâna to an art, it was supposed that, mental suspension being secured, illumination would follow—that the first was, in fact, in some way, the cause of the second. Now it seems to the writer certain that where you have a subject on the verge (as it were) of the Cosmic Sense it may be possible to induce this by following the directions given in, for instance, the Bhagavad Gita, when, nothing being done, illumination would not spontaneously supervene. But the Cosmic Sense (though in any case more valuable than all the riches of the earth) when self induced, as by such methods as referred to, is less valuable, probably much less valuable—less potent and masterful— less creative—than it is in cases in which it bursts forth (as it were) of its own strength—self delivered—triumphant.

It seems certain that the monks of Mount Athos really knew of the state here called "Cosmic Consciousness," otherwise how could they have specified, as they did, the subjective light? From whence would they have derived the knowledge of it and of the "ineffable joy" which accompanies it? Concerning the adoration of the Cosmic Sense as God, perhaps it is so.

CHAPTER 36.

Case of A. J. S.

I was born on the 24th of January, 1871, in a country village, the seventh of a family of nine. I was the youngest of six girls. My father, mother, and all of us children were very musical—the girls having fine voices. When I was three or four years old I was taken about to different places to sing, and at that age could sing a song through if it were sung to me. When a little older I would make believe I was a great singer and would spend hours thumping on an old desk of my father's rather than play on the organ, because I would hear the sound I made on the latter, which did not always please me, while from the other there came no sound to interfere with that created in my own imagination. To this day I sometimes wonder whether I did not really hear coming from the old desk the music which my fancy created in myself. I was always very frail. Much of the time I did not care to play with other children, but liked better to listen to this spiritual music which fascinated me. In the end this dream was dissipated by the tragic death of my father, and by an accident which happened to myself. Or did I, perhaps, simply grow out of it?

The thought of becoming a public singer was constantly held before me by my family and friends, and I was sent to a musical school in Boston. It appeared that my voice had all the quality supposed, but my frail physique and some results of the accident alluded to stood in my way; yet I would not give up.

I was married early and afterwards worked at my music harder than ever, and my husband felt that my heart was so much in singing that it would probably kill me to give it up. Soon, however, I broke down entirely as the result of overwork. Everything possible was done for me, but to no avail. I failed steadily and was in constant pain from the effect of a fall in childhood by which my spine was injured. I took various remedies to make me sleep, but they only brought on excitement and delirium. I was sent at last to a sanatorium, took to my bed in a darkened room and refused to see any of my friends. For a time my life was despaired of, and I only rallied to plan to take my life when I should have an opportunity.

At last a time came when I had given up all hope and felt there was nothing more for me to live for or to look forward to. One day while in this state I was lying quietly in my bed when a great calmness seemed to come over me. I fell asleep only to wake a few hours after to find myself in a flood of light. I was alarmed. Then I seemed to hear the words, "𝔓𝔢𝔞𝔠𝔢, 𝔟𝔢 𝔰𝔱𝔦𝔩𝔩," over and over again. I cannot say it was a voice, but I heard the words plainly and distinctly just as I had heard the music coming out of the old desk in my childhood. I put my head under the pillow to shut out the sound, but heard it just the same. I lay for what seemed to me then a long time in that condition, when gradually I was again in the dark. I sat up in my bed. I would not call the nurse, as I felt she would not understand. I did not, of course, understand myself, but I felt it meant something. This same calmness came to me often, and it always came before the light.

After that night my recovery was steady without the aid in any way of a physician or medicine. When the light came to me again later I asked my husband if he did not see it, but he did not. I have not tried to cultivate it, as I do not understand it. I only know that whereas formerly I was a wreck I am to-day well and strong physically and mentally, and whereas I loved the excitement of a public life I now love the quiet of home life and a few friends.

With this calmness has come a power (as I call it) to heal others. With a touch or in some cases by catching the eye I can in many cases induce sleep.

In other cases the person will say to me: "Why is it I feel so restful when I am near you?" When friends have asked me to tell them of my experience I have declined except in one or two cases. It is all so real to me, and I fear that to others it will seem foolish; but some day these things will all be explained, and I hope they may be soon.

At the time I first saw the light I was twenty-four years old. I have seen it three times altogether. Now as to the intellectual and moral experiences that immediately follow the light: It is about impossible to set these forth, for words are very poor as a medium to express either the feeling or the vision that came to me at that time. I think the intellect could never give to me in worlds of study what is revealed to me during this experience and immediately following the presence of the light. To me it is beyond intellectual expression. It is *seeing inwardly,* and the word *harmony* would perhaps express part of what is seen.

Humanity goes on and on almost in despair, hoping some time to find rest and peace and fullness of life in the undefined future, when, in fact, all these and more are here now if we would (could?) only reach out our hand and take them.

My supreme desire is to be of help to humanity, but when I have had this light come to me I have been so filled with the desire to reveal what I see to mankind that it seems as though I were not doing anything at all.

The mental experiences following the light are always essentially the same— namely, an intense desire to reveal man to himself and to aid those who are trying to find something worth living for in what they call "this life."

I do not feel that I have made myself intelligible, but I repeat that, in this subject, at least, words offer a most inadequate medium of expression.

PART VI.

LAST WORDS.

I.

MANY readers, before they have reached this page, will have been struck by the fact that the name of no woman is included in the list of so-called "great cases," and the names of only three in that of "Lesser, Imperfect and Doubtful Instances." Besides these three the editor knows another woman, still living, who is undoubtedly if not a great, still a genuine, case. She would not, however, permit the editor to use her experience even without her name, and the case is therefore reluctantly entirely omitted. The only other woman known to the present writer, either in the past or in the present, who is or was, either certainly or almost certainly, a case of Cosmic Consciousness is Madame Guyon, who was, it seems to him, a genuine and great instance, though unfortunately the evidence in her case is not as definite as could be wished.

II.

Jeanne Marie Bouvieres de la Mothe was born April 13th, 1648, was a sickly and precocious child, with strong religious tendencies, great earnestness of purpose, a leaning towards self renunciation and a passion for spiritual books, especially the Bible, which as a child of ten she used to read from morning till night. At the age of sixteen she was married to M. Guyon, who was then thirty-eight. What with an elderly and stern husband and a most disagreeable mother-in-law her objective life was unhappy, even miserable. For all outward ills she found consolation in religion, and her life was really a happy one, except when this inward joy suffered eclipse, as from time to time it did. At last, however, on the 22d of July, 1680 (that is, in the *summer* of her *thirty-third* year), came final deliverance. The writer does not know of any record of her subjective experience upon that day, but it seems certain that the rest of her life was filled with peace and happiness, which is characteristic of the lives of those who have passed into Cosmic Consciousness.

She describes herself as having ceased from all self-originated action and choice. To her amazement and unspeakable happiness, it appeared as though all such natural movement existed no longer—a higher power had displaced and occupied its room. "I even perceived no more [she writes in her autobiography] the soul which He had formerly conducted by His rod and His staff, because now He alone appeared to me, my soul having given up its place to Him; even as a little drop of water cast into the sea receives the qualities of the sea." She speaks of herself as now practicing the virtues no longer as virtues—that is, not by separate and constrained efforts. It would have required effort not to practice them [180 : 227].

These few words, though not perhaps of themselves proving anything are very characteristic. "I give nothing as duties," says Whitman. "What others give as duties I give as living impulses (shall I give the heart's action as a duty?)" [193 : 190].

III.

Some years ago, when the design of this volume was forming in the mind of the writer, it was his intention to include several chapters treating of other departures from the norm in the mental life of man more or less analogous to that which he has named Cosmic Consciousness, for the special purpose of examining into the relation (if any) between these and the latter. Had he persisted in his plan he would have included (1) a review of hypnotism; (2) of so-called miracles, supra-normal physical, as distinguished from supra-normal mental powers; (3) so-called spiritualism—the notion of the sensible communion of man with other and perhaps higher spirits considered in relation to this other notion of the communion of man with a higher self within himself, and (4) cases in which man seems to be the centre and in some sense the director of forces presumably existing entirely outside of himself, and the relation of such cases (if any) to the preterhuman psychic manifestations of those endowed with the

Cosmic Sense. Time, and probably the necessary ability, failed him for the larger attempt, and he will only allude to one case (belonging to category 4) for the sake of indicating what seems to him the strong probability that all these different classes of cases (wherever genuine, as many of them* undoubtedly are), if they do not always lie side by side, at least touch one another by their angles.

IV.

William Stainton Moses [131: 245 et seq.] was born in Lincolnshire, England, November 5th, 1839. His father was headmaster of a grammar school. William Stainton Moses was educated at Oxford. Took his degree. Was ordained, and was for the rest of his life, as long as health permitted, an active and popular parish clergyman. Up to the age of thirty-three he differed in no special respect from the ordinary university educated English Church clergyman. At that period (about the usual time of life, it will be noted, for the oncoming of Cosmic Consciousness), in the course of 1872, the physical phenomena, which give him interest to us here, began. They continued for some ten years and then, with failing health, passed away. William Stainton Moses died in September, 1892. He never married, and went little into society. "His personal appearance offered no indication of his peculiar gift. He was of middle stature, strongly made, with somewhat heavy features and thick dark hair and beard"

---

* Those who are interested in the matter would do well to turn up the "Atlantic Monthly" for August, 1868, and read "A Remarkable Case of Physical Phenomena." Mary Carrick, an Irish servant girl, just come to America, was working for a family in a town of Massachusetts. For months (from time to time) the bells would ring, articles of furniture move from place to place, tables would rise of themselves from the floor, tubs full of clothes and water move from their benches, always in the room in which Mary was, or in the next room to it, but without being touched by Mary or by any one else. The articles moved were never so large and heavy but that Mary was strong enough to have moved them in the usual way. The extraordinary movements did not take place while Mary was asleep. There was no question of trickery. Mary was more distressed than any other person at the occurrences; besides, others were often in the room with her and saw the chairs, dishes, etc., move without being touched. There seems no possible reason to connect "spirits" with the phenomena in question. The movements seem to have been entirely objectless. That there was something peculiar (on the other hand) about the girl herself is shown by the fact that ultimately she became insane and was sent to an asylum.

[131:250].   It must be understood that the facts as given in this case, as well as the trustworthiness of those who have reported them, including, of course, William Stainton Moses himself, have been very thoroughly inquired into by such competent men as T. W. H. Myers, and it is firmly believed that no deception of any kind has been attempted or thought of.

Whatever explanation of them may ultimately be given and accepted, the facts as set down to-day will almost certainly stand. It would be impossible in this place to give the data upon which the truth of the account rests.   These can be found elsewhere by those who wish to see them.   All that is necessary here and all that can be done is to cite as samples a very few instances of the supra-normal occurrences which, with extraordinary frequency, and in great variety, surrounded the man for at least ten years.

Motion without contact, directed by evident intelligence, is seen markedly in the following instance: I was calling on a friend, and the conversation fell on the phenomena of spiritualism. A sitting was proposed, and nothing, or almost nothing, occurred. We were quite alone in the room, which was well lighted. We drew back from the table, intending to give up the attempt. My friend asked why nothing occurred. The table, untouched by us, rose and gently touched my throat and chest three times. I was suffering from severe bronchial symptoms, and was altogether below par. After this no rap or movement could be elicited, and we were fain to accept the explanation of our want of success.

My first personal experience of levitation was about five months after my introduction to spiritualism. Physical phenomena of a very powerful description had been developed with great rapidity. We were new to the subject, and the phenomena were most interesting. After much movement of objects, and lifting and tilting of the table, a small hand organ, a child's plaything, was floated about the room, making a most inharmonious din. It was a favorite amusement with the little, Puck-like invisible who then manifested. One day (August 30, 1872) the little organ was violently thrown down in a distant corner of the room, and I felt my chair drawn back from the table and turned into the corner near which I sat. It was so placed that my face was turned away from the circle to the angle made by the two walls. In this position the chair was raised from the floor to a distance of, I should judge, twelve or fourteen inches. My feet touched the top of the skirting board, which would be about twelve inches in height. The chair remained suspended for a few moments, and I then felt myself going from it, higher and higher, with a very slow and easy movement. I had no sense of discomfort nor of apprehension. I was perfectly conscious of what was being done, and described the process to those who were sitting at the table. The movement was very steady and occupied what seemed a long time before it was completed. I was close to the wall, so close that I was able to put a pencil firmly against my chest and to mark the spot opposite to me on the wall paper. That mark, when measured afterwards, was found to be rather more than six feet from the floor, and, from its position, it was clear that my head must have been in the very corner of the room, close to the ceiling. I do not think that I was in any way entranced. I was perfectly clear in my mind; quite alive to what was being done, and fully conscious of the curious phenomenon. I felt no pressure on any part of my body, only a sensation of being in a lift, whilst objects seemed to be passing away from below me. I remember a slight difficulty in breathing and a sensation of fullness in the chest, with a general feeling of being lighter than the atmosphere. I was lowered down quite gently and placed in the chair, which had settled in its old position. The measurements and observation were taken immediately and the marks which I had made with my pencil were noted. My voice was said at the time to sound as if from the corner of the room, close to the ceiling.

This experiment was more or less successfully repeated on nine other occasions. On the 2d of September, 1872, I see from my records that I was three times raised on to the table and twice levitated in the corner of the room. The first movement on to the table was very sudden—a sort of instantaneous jerk. I was conscious of nothing until I found myself on the table—my chair being unmoved. This, under ordinary circumstances, is what we call impossible. I was so placed that it would have been out of my power to quit my place at the table without moving my chair. In the second attempt I was placed on the table in a standing posture. In this case I was conscious of the withdrawal of my chair and of being raised to the level of the table and then of being impelled forward so as to stand upon it. I was not entranced, nor was I conscious of any external pressure. In the third case I was thrown on to the table, and from that position on to an adjacent sofa. The movement was instantaneous, as in the first recorded case; and though I was thrown to a considerable distance, and with considerable force, I was in no way hurt. At the time I lay on the sofa I felt the chair in which I had been sitting and which would be four feet from where I lay, come and press my back several times. I was finally placed on the table.

For an enormous number of similar and diverse phenomena occurring in this case, see 131.

V.

As already stated, the above are only quoted as samples of unusual supra-normal incidents said to have taken place—which undoubtedly did take place over and over again for ten years in the experience of this man. Now what (if any) relation exists between this case and one of Cosmic Consciousness?

We have seen that in the case of William Stainton Moses the phenomena with which we are dealing began at about the typical age—thirty-three years—and it is stated that on at least one occasion "the drain on the vital strength of William Stainton Moses was so great" that the manifestations had to be discontinued. It seems clear from the matter-of-course way the above is stated that the "medium" habitually felt fatigue or exhaustion in proportion to the frequency and magnitude of the manifestations. We have also seen that sickness on the part of the "medium" in like manner interfered with the production of the phenomena. These facts point to the "medium" himself as the source of the force exhibited in so many different ways.

If this inference is correct it is at the same time undoubtedly true that he was not aware that the power which caused the phenomena proceeded from himself. Neither should we expect, reasoning from analogy, that he would be, since even in Cosmic Consciousness—where all the phenomena are mental and where consequently we should look that the real actor would be still less liable to be deceived as to the person acting—we see that he is so, not occasionally, but almost or quite constantly. Paul, Mohammed, Yepes, Behmen, Blake, tell us over and over again that the great thoughts, divine emotions, which they express, are not their own but communicated from without. The protestations made by Blake—a hundred times repeated—and the last time to his wife a few minutes before his death, in reference to the songs which he sang as he lay slowly dying: "My beloved! they are *not* mine. No, they are *not* mine," have been, in one shape or another, made by them all. Still we believe to-day that that other self which wrote the Epistles, dictated the Koran, composed the Aurora, was really none other than a part (the more divine part) of Paul, Mohammed and Behmen respectively. The man acts and does not know that it is he who is acting—is sure, in fact, that it is not; scouts (as does Mohammed) indignantly the imputation that the thoughts, the words, proceed from him, and

offers proof that such imputation neither is nor can be founded
on fact: "And if ye are in doubt of what we have revealed unto
our servant" [Gabriel speaks, and "our servant" is, of course,
Mohammed] "then bring a chapter like it . . . but if ye do not,
and ye shall surely do it not," etc. [151:13]. In many cases the
denial has been accepted and the world has agreed with the an-
nunciator that directly, or indirectly, God has revealed to him
the exalted sentiments and sublime truths that have passed his
lips that God, or a messenger from God, lives in him and speaks
through him.

Why not suppose that we have involved in the personality of
William Stainton Moses a parallel fact—a parallel duplex or
multiplex personality—that in some way, so far, perhaps, utterly
inconceivable to us (as to some of their contemporaries and followers it was inconceivable that Jesus and Mohammed merely as
men said and did the words and deeds which proceeded from
them) as well as to himself, William Stainton Moses did himself
evolve the force, did himself furnish the intelligence, which were
operative in the phenomena? It seems corroborative of this view
that bodies, as hundred ton rocks or houses, such as no man could
move, are not lifted or displaced; that the lights are not greater
than could be supplied by the force resident in ordinary man,
supposing that force or some of it to take the form of light; that
the intelligence manifested, though often considerable and sometimes extraordinary, is not above human possibilities, taking into
account the intelligence possessed by persons having Cosmic Consciousness. For if supra-mortal beings were operative in the production of these so-called spiritualistic phenomena, why should
these remain so constantly upon or (taking into account only
the ordinary human faculties) immediately above the plane of
human powers? Then again we have seen in the course of this
study that the whole history of man, as well as that of the organic
world, is simply the history of the evolution of new faculties one
after the other—any one of which (before it was evolved) would
have seemed an impossibility and an absurdity to any member
of the race about to take it on. Have we not in, for instance,

spiritualism and telepathy, with all their almost infinitely varied
phenomena, the germ or germs of some new faculty or faculties,
so far as little understood as was Cosmic Consciousness a thousand years ago, and *not,* as sometimes thought, in any sense, the
action or interference in human affairs, either of disembodied
spirits or of supra-, infra-, or extra-human minds?—such faculties not necessarily destined to expand and become universal (for,
in evolution "Many are called but few chosen"), but almost certainly, in modern times, and down to date, expanding and becoming more common.

And, indeed, may it not well be that in the self conscious human being, as we know him to-day, we have the psychic germ of
not one higher race only, but of several? As in the nebula of a
solar system we have the potentiality not of one sphere only or
one kind of sphere, but of a sun, planets, moons, comets and many
lesser bodies; as in the first, unicellular, living creature we had
the parent not of one only but of many races of multicellular
descendants; as in the alalus homo we had the progenitor, not
merely of one race, but of many races of variously charactered
self conscious men—so it may be (may it not?) that in the foremost race or races of self conscious man to-day we have the eligibility, the germ, of not one superior race only, but of several.
As for example: a cosmic conscious race; another race that shall
possess seemingly miraculous powers of acting upon what we
call objective nature; another with clairvoyant powers far surpassing those possessed by the best specimens so far; another with
miraculous healing powers; and so on.

That so-called miraculous powers are closely allied to what is
here called Cosmic Consciousness, that they appear in relation
with the latter, that they are no more supernatural than it is,
and that these powers, in their natures, cover a large range of operation—all this is clearly recognized and plainly taught by the
men who, of all others, know most on the subject. Gautama's
dicta thereon may be read (supra) in the chapter devoted to him.
Paul is no less explicit, but sets forth in very plain terms "that
there are diversities of gifts, but the same spirit" [20:12:1]—

that "to one is given through the spirit the word of wisdom, to another the word of knowledge, to another faith, to another gifts of healing, to another miraculous powers, to another discernings of spirits, and to another interpretation of tongues" [20: 12: 8-10].

VI.

A main object which the writer of this volume has had before him has been to point out that there have lived in this world certain men who in consequence, not of an extraordinary development of any or all of the ordinary mental faculties, but by the possession of a new one peculiar to themselves and non-existent (or at least undeclared) in ordinary people, see, know and feel spiritual facts and experience psychical phenomena, which being veiled from, are still of most vital import to, the world at large; that if one or two of these men are studied to the exclusion of the rest—as has been the practice with not Christians only but with Buddhists and Mohammedans as well—the result must be inadequate and unsatisfactory as compared with the study of all, for the reason that none of them have been able to tell much of what they have seen, known and felt, and one or two only of them being read, what little they do tell is certain—just because of its incomplete, fragmentary character—to be misunderstood; while if they are all read and compared the testimony of each is found to throw light upon, supplement and strengthen that of all the others; that it is of the greatest importance—as has indeed always been felt—that these men should be as profoundly as possible studied and absorbed by every one who has aspirations for the higher spiritual life because the contact of the mind of the student with the minds of these men has the effect of producing in the mind of the former all the spiritual expansion and growth of which it is by its congenital constitution capable. Through the aid of these men even Cosmic Consciousness itself is often possible of achievement where without them it would certainly not occur; as one of them says: "I bestow upon any man or woman the entrance to all the gifts of the universe" [193: 216].

Or as says another great man, who, though not, it is believed, in the class here treated of, had at least their earnestness if not their vision and their joy: "At least it is with heroes and God-inspired men that I, for my part, would far rather converse, in what dialect soever they speak! Great, ever-fruitful, profitable for reproof, for encouragement, for building up in manful purposes and works, are the words of those that in their day were *MEN*" [64: 75].

And not only is it better to study a number of these men rather than only one or two, but should the student, from idiosyncrasy or any cause, confine his attention to one or two of them, it is immensely important that he should have an opportunity of choosing the master whom he is to follow, since a man born in Europe or America may be more certainly wrought upon, and more deeply influenced for good, by the Upanishads and Suttas than by (for instance) the New Testament. This was true, at least, of Schopenhauer and Thoreau. Of the former, it is told: "In a corner of his room was placed a gilt statuette of Buddha, and on a table not far off lay Duperron's Latin translation of the Upanishads, called the Oupnekhat, which served as the prayer book from which Schopenhauer read his devotions" [87: 456]. Of the Oupnekhat Schopenhauer said: "It has been my comfort in life, it will be the solace of my death" [147: 61]. And as there are many men in the West who are, or would be if they read them, more benefited by Buddhistic and Mohammedan scriptures than they are by Jewish or Christian, so, doubtless, there are thousands of men in southern Asia who, born Buddhists, Brahmans or Mohammedans, would be, from some peculiarity of mental constitution, more readily and profoundly stirred by the Gospels and Pauline epistles, or "Leaves of Grass," than by the Vedas or by any of the books that owe their inspiration to the teachings of Gautama or Mohammed.

VII.

If there is such a vast interval between the man with Cosmic Consciousness and him with self consciousness only, how is it that the former does not stand out before the world as belonging to a separate class from the latter? How is it that there are a hundred painters and poets who, in the estimation of nearly the whole world, over-rank William Blake, though he had Cosmic Consciousness and they had it not? How is it that men, standing on almost the loftiest peaks of fame—Aristotle, Plato, Newton, Cæsar—have self consciousness only, while John Yepes, Las Casas, Edward Carpenter and others, who are said to have this supreme, all-sufficient faculty, are not generally known to have been very extraordinary men?

The answer seems to be: In the first place the literary instinct (or expression of any kind) is not necessarily highly developed in the Cosmic Conscious mind, but is a faculty apart. Balzac worked himself to death endeavoring to acquire an adequate style, and Whitman lived and died vividly conscious of his defects of expression. Again: the average self conscious man can appreciate the faculties of the self conscious mind, even when unusually developed, very much easier, very much more certainly, than he can those of the Cosmic Conscious mind. In spite of these obvious facts, it remains true that self conscious man, even in his blindness, has placed the highest crowns of all upon the heads of men—Gautama, Jesus, Mohammed, Dante, "Shakespeare"—who have had the divine faculty of Cosmic Consciousness.

The intellect of these Cosmic Conscious men has often, if not always, a range and incisiveness—witness especially Dante and "Shakespeare"—which place them clearly above almost any merely self conscious person. It is also clear that their purely moral qualities—witness especially Gautama, Jesus and Whitman—give them a rank apart from their self conscious fellows, but this is not by any means the whole story. The central point, the kernel of the matter, consists in the fact that they possess qualities for which we at present have no names or concepts. Jesus alluded to one of these when he said: "Whoever drinketh of the water that I shall give him shall never thirst; but the water that I shall give him shall become in him a well of water springing up unto eternal life" [17:4:14]. And Whitman points in the same direction when he declares that his book is not linked with the rest nor felt by the intellect, "but has to do with untold latencies" [193:17] in writer and reader, and also when he states that he does not give lectures and charity—that is, either intellectual or moral gifts—but that when he gives he gives himself [193:66]. The ordinary self conscious mind cannot clearly realize the faculty alluded to in these words, and consequently it cannot give it a name. Perhaps the best that can be done is to consider it as analogous to an influx of vitality, admitted into humanity through certain men. permeating and vivifying each and all who permit it to pass into them. To the most the quality in question will seem indefinite and elusive to the last degree. As a matter of fact, it is the most important and the most solid entity that exists to-day in the world.

VIII.

What is it that determines that a given man shall enter into Cosmic Consciousness (for this volume is physiological as well as psychological, and its psychology must tally physiological facts)? In other words: What are the factors that enter into and finally decide for illumination?

a. The first seems to be full maturity, the age of thirty to forty years, according as the man is endowed at birth with greater or less longevity—that is, according to the number of years the man needs to reach full maturity—an average age of, say, thirty-five years. This element could have been predicated a priori, since, if mankind is growing up to Cosmic Consciousness, the individuals who reach the high water mark of mental evolution on the next plain below (that of self consciousness) must be those who will first enter it, and the earliest individuals to enter it must do so when they are at their highest point of spiritual efficiency.

b. Education (so called) seems to have nothing to do with it. Some of the greatest cases (Jesus, Mohammed, Yepes, Behmen and Whitman) have been, from the point of view of the schools, some of them entirely, others almost totally, ignorant. On the other hand, scholastic training does not seem necessarily to have any prejudicial influence, since some cases (as Dante, Bacon and Carpenter) were distinguished students at good colleges. But if "education," in the ordinary sense of that word, has little to do with the matter, there is another sense in which it has a great deal to do with it. We are told, for instance, by a high authority, that those who desire the companionship of the Cosmic Sense, "need the best blood, thews, endurance"; that "none may come to the trial till he or she brings courage and health"; that "only those may come who come in sweet and determined bodies"; that "no diseased person, no rum drinker or venereal taint is permitted to enter" [193:125].

c. It is probably imperative that the man should have a great mother—a woman strong, athletic, spiritual, of good physique, of superior mental and especially moral, powers. Unfortunately we know little or nothing of the mothers of most of our Cosmic Conscious cases. Bacon's, however, and certainly Whitman's, were exceptional women. Probably we should be safe in believing the traditions to the same effect of the mothers of Gautama and Jesus.

d. It is most likely also necessary that the father should be a superior man physically and spiritually, though it is certainly not that he should be intellectually.

e. Perhaps the most important point of all—granted a good average, or above the average, man and woman for father and mother—is that these should have opposite, or at least diverse, temperaments (the secret of success or failure in all marriages is perhaps involved in the fulfillment or violation of this unwritten law). That if the father's, for instance, should be choleric-melancholic, the mother's should be sanguine-phlegmatic, and so on.

f. Then comes the final and supreme physiological necessity—namely, that the union of father and mother from which is to proceed the Cosmic Conscious man shall occur under perfect conditions, so that each parent shall be fully represented in the offspring—each blended with the other—the result being a perfect man with the qualities and temperaments of both father and mother [103 : 65].   It is perhaps not imperative that a man should have all four temperaments as a condition of illumination, but it is probable that all the great cases have had all four, or at least three.

g. The right physical and mental organization granted and full maturity having been reached, the next pre-condition of illumination is the time of year.   Of the total of forty-three cases given in this volume, in every case but three where the season is known, that is in seventeen cases, it took place in the first seven months of the year.   The explanation of the fact that illumination occurs generally in spring and early summer is no doubt the same as that of the age at which it happens—full maturity.   As at present even the foremost members of the race cannot reach the vantage ground—the status—from which Cosmic Consciousness can be entered before full or nearly full maturity, so the further advantage of the time of year of fullest vitality is an element of great importance.   The season of the ascending sun, of increasing temperature, of rising sap and bursting bud, of the pairing of birds, at which the heart of all nature, including human nature, is at flood tide, is the season in which we might (if ever) expect, and is the season in which we find, the blossoming forth of this divine event—an event supreme in the life of the individual and to be supreme in the life of the race.

h. Last of all, the man fitted by heredity, personal growth and the rest to receive the exalted endowment of which there is here question, must himself do something, must place himself (perhaps not intentionally or consciously) in the right mental attitude.   What this is has been pointed out already many times, both indirectly and directly, and may be once again indicated in the words of an undoubtedly inspired writer.   (It is the Deity or Cosmic Sense that speaks) [154: 129]: "Once more listen to my excellent words—most mysterious of all.   Strongly I like you, therefore I will declare what is for your welfare.   On me place your mind, devote yourself to me, reverence me.   I declare to you truly you are dear to me. Forsaking all else, come to me as your sole refuge. I will release you from all sin, from all doubt.''

IX.

If this volume did not threaten to become unduly large, a section or chapter of some length might very properly be devoted to the various artificial means adopted (especially in India) to induce the faculty or condition here treated of. Some of these have been alluded to, and those curious on the subject may consult especially 56 and 154. It does not seem, so far as known to the writer, that any great work has ever been done by persons in whom the faculty was artificially excited, though doubtless the lives of such persons have been made immensely happier and better. The object of the present paragraph, however, is to refer very briefly to a mental condition occasionally induced by anesthetics, which is undoubtedly closely allied to the faculty under consideration. Just as the drinking of alcohol induces a kind of artificial and bastard joy, so the inhalation of ether and chloroform induces (sometimes) a kind of artificial and bastard cosmic consciousness. The following brief cases will make this clear [121:586]: Dr. George Wyld says (upon taking chloroform): "I suddenly experienced the extraordinary impression that my spiritual being stood visibly outside my body, regarding that deserted body lying on the bed. Shortly afterward I called on three different professional chloroformists and asked them if any of their subjects had ever experienced sensations like my own. In reply one gentleman said: 'I have often heard patients express similar ideas.' Another said: 'I myself have experienced on three occasions when under chloroform, exactly similar sensations.' And the third gentleman said: 'My patients have often said that they experienced no pain, but felt as if they saw with their inner eye all I was doing during the operations.' I was told of a patient who said, after anesthesis: *'I thought I had got at the bottom of the secrets of nature.'* And a dentist told me that many of his patients had experienced similar sensations to those I described."

The late John Addington Symonds described his sensations (while under the influence of chloroform) thus: "I seemed at first in a state of utter blankness; then came flashes of intense light, alternating with blankness and with a keen vision of what was going on in the room round me, but no sensation of touch. I thought that I was near death, when suddenly my soul became aware of God, who was manifestly dealing with me, handling me, so to speak, in an intense personal present reality. I felt Him streaming in like light upon me and heard Him saying in no language, but as hands touch hands and communicate sensations: 'I led thee; I guided thee; *you will never sin and weep and wail in madness any more;* for now you have seen Me.' My whole consciousness seemed brought into one point of absolute conviction; the independence of my mind from my body was proved by the phenomena of this acute sensibility to spiritual facts, this utter deadness of the senses. *Life and death seemed mere names.*" . . . Symonds adds: *"I cannot describe the ecstasy I felt,"* and, referring to his experience and its psychological evidence, says: "If this had happened to a man in an uncritical age would it not have carried conviction, like that of Saul of Tarsus, to his soul?"

It is curious that Symonds, who seems to have really passed into a sort of actual Cosmic Consciousness for the moment, should have instinctively selected a genuine case to which to compare his own temporary mental state.

All conditions allowed and the fact of Cosmic Consciousness being granted, what is its place as a psychical entity? And from where does it come? The clue to the answers (the writer thinks) may be picked up in chapters 3 and 4 of 134. It is ably shown there how the simple conscious—circumstances being favorable—passes by slow growth into the self conscious mind. By experience, by inheritance, by accumulation and by a process of psychical masonry, percepts are collected, stored up, and of them are built recepts. Then percepts and recepts are used, as are stones and mortar in a wall, and of them are at last formed concepts. And, as the last touch is given, the completed edifice suddenly flashes into sight as a new entity and the self conscious man has appeared upon the earth. So (it seems) are concepts, emotions, sense perceptions, all the spiritual elements of the thinking, feeling, knowing man, individually and collectively builded up until the walls, buttresses, pinnacles and towers of a still higher consciousness are finished. The moment of completion comes, the signal is given, the scaffolding falls and instantly the new structure stands revealed.

X.

The explanation of what may be called the mystery of religion as it exists among us to-day may be stated simply as follows: All men, so far, with the exception of at most a few hundreds, have lived in the world of self consciousness without the power to leave it. The great religious seers, revealers, teachers, have also lived in that world, but at the same time in another— the world of Cosmic Consciousness—the latter being by far the larger, the most important and the most interesting. Whether either of these worlds has an objective existence is a matter of no consequence. They are equally real and momentous to us on either hypothesis. The men who have lived in the Cosmic Conscious world, that is, in the world made visible by the Cosmic Sense, as the forests and the sky are made visible by the sense of sight, have desired, for the comfort and good of their fellows, to tell mankind at large what they saw there; but as they were obliged (for want of a better) to use the language of self consciousness their accounts have been exceedingly incomplete and the words and phrases used have been so inadequate as to have been to the last degree misleading. Not only so, but, supposing a clear report (an impossibility), it would be beyond the power of the self conscious mind to conceive the Cosmic Conscious world. This being so, the reports made by these spiritual travelers have been not only not understood but misunderstood in an infinite variety of senses, and the essentially similar account given by, for example, Paul, Mohammed, Dante, Jesus, Gautama, Whitman and others, has been looked upon as a variety of accounts, not of the same, but of diverse things. And these accounts, all but one, that one under the influence of which the hearer is born, have been supposed to rest solely upon the imagination of the narrator. A critical study of all these (seeming) diverse accounts will show that they are all more or less unsuccessful attempts to describe the same thing; but because it was out of the power of the original reporter, the seer, to give anything like a full and clear account of what he saw, largely because of the inadequacy of the language belonging to the self conscious mind; because his reporters again (as in the cases of Jesus and Gautama, who did not write), possessing only self consciousness, blurred still further the picture; because translators, possessing only self consciousness and understanding very imperfectly what the teacher wished to convey, still further distorted the record; for all these reasons the important fact of the unity of the teachings of these men has been very generally overlooked; hence the confusion and the so-called mystery; a misunderstanding unavoidable, no doubt, under the circumstances, but which will one day, assuredly, be cleared up.

Already many others besides the present writer have noticed the essential unity of the seeming diverse teachings in question—as, for instance, Hartmann [100: 6], who tells us: "I have carefully compared the doctrines of Behmen with those of the Eastern sages as laid down in the 'Secret Doctrine' and in the religious literature of the East, and I find the most remarkable harmony between them in their esoteric meaning; in fact, the religion of Buddha, Krishna and the Christ seem to me to be one and identical." It is worth nothing that Hartmann's specimen teachers are all cases of Cosmic Consciousness, although of course he knew nothing of that as a specific mental status.

XI.

One word in conclusion. The writer of this book, since it was first conceived some few years ago, has sought diligently for cases of Cosmic Consciousness, and his whole list, so far, including some imperfect and doubtful cases, totals up nearly fifty. Several of these are contemporary, minor cases, such as may have occurred in considerable numbers in any of the recent centuries and no records of them remain. He has, however, as more than once stated, found thirteen, all of them so great that they must, almost inevitably, live. As has been already shown, five of these men lived during the eighteen centuries which elapsed between the birth of Gautama and that of Dante, and the other eight in the six hundred years between the birth of Dante and to-day. This would mean that cases of Cosmic Consciousness are nearly five times as frequent now as they were, say, a thousand years ago. It is not, of course, pretended that they are becoming more frequent in exactly this ratio. There must have occurred a large number of cases in the last twenty-five hundred years all memory of which is lost. No man could say positively how many lived in any given epoch. But it seems tolerably certain that these men are more numerous in the modern than they were in the ancient world, and this fact, taken in connection with the general theory of psychic evolution, fully considered on previous pages, goes far to confirm the conclusion that just as, long ago, self consciousness appeared in the best specimens of our ancestral race in the prime of life, and gradually became more and more universal and appeared in the individual at an earlier and earlier age, until, as we see now, it has become almost universal and appears at the average of about three years—so will Cosmic Consciousness become more and more universal and appear earlier in the individual life until the race at large will possess this faculty. The same race and not the same; for a Cosmic Conscious race will not be the race which exists to-day, any more than the present race of men is the same race which existed prior to the evolution of self consciousness. The simple truth is, that there has lived on the earth, "appearing at intervals," for thousands of years among ordinary men, the first faint beginnings of another race; walking the earth and breathing the air with us, but at the same time walking another earth and breathing another air of which we know little or nothing, but which is, all the same, our spiritual life, as its absence would be our spiritual death. This new race is in act of being born from us, and in the near future it will occupy and possess the earth.

THE END

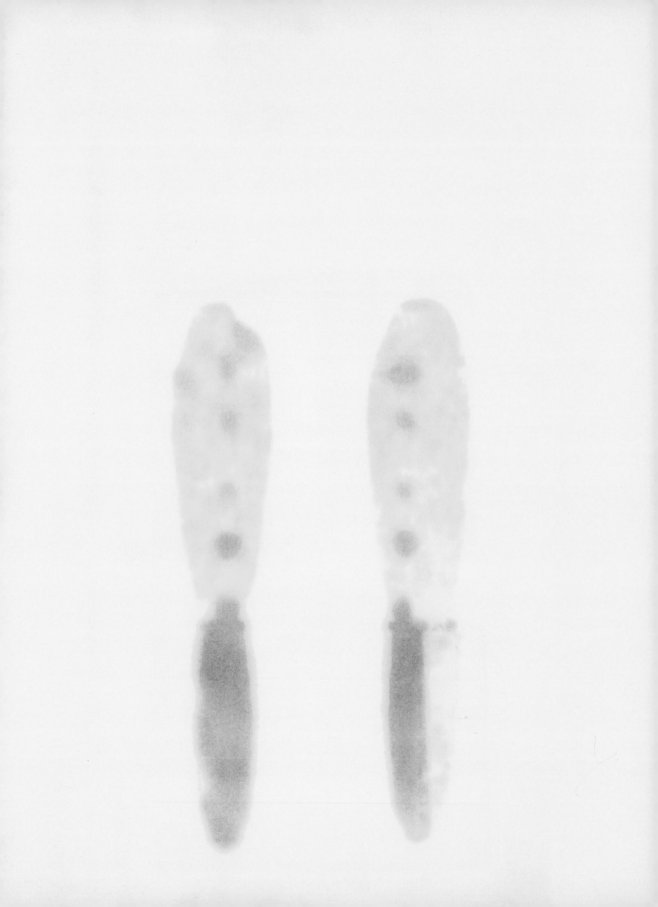